The Environment
A to Z

The Environment AtoZ

David Hosansky

CQ PRESS

A DIVISION OF CONGRESSIONAL QUARTERLY INC.
WASHINGTON, D.C.

CQ Press
A Division of Congressional Quarterly Inc.
1414 22nd Street, N.W.
Washington, D.C. 20037
202-822-1475; 800-638-1710
www.cqpress.com

∞ The paper used in this publication meets the minimum requirements of the American National Standard for Information Sciences—Permanence of Paper for Printed Library Materials, ANSI Z39.48-1992.

The Environment A to Z was designed and typeset by Paul Hotvedt of Blue Heron Typesetters, Inc.

Cover Design: Jill R. Shimabukuro

Printed and bound in the United States of America

04 03 02 01 00   5 4 3 2 1

Library of Congress Cataloging-in-Publication Data

Hosansky, David.
    The environment A-Z / David Hosansky.
            p.   cm.
    Includes bibliographical references and index.
    ISBN 1-56802-583-1 (c)
        1. Environmental sciences—Encyclopedias. 2. Environmental policy—
    Encyclopedias. I. Title.

    GE10.H67 2000
    363.7'003—dc21   00-062163

For my father

Contents

Introduction

When President Theodore Roosevelt visited the southern rim of the Grand Canyon in 1903, he eloquently summed up the conservation ideal in a few sentences: "Leave it as it is . . . . The ages have been at work on it and man can only mar it."

These days, leaving the environment as it is seems a quaint notion. The growing population, surging economy, and development of new chemicals are having inevitable effects on the land, air, and water. Policymakers regularly confront controversial matters such as whether to restrict roads in national forests to protect natural habitat or whether to impose costly air quality standards to protect asthmatics and other vulnerable residents. Their decisions have important ramifications for all of us, even though the issues may be difficult to grasp.

Protecting the environment is an unexpectedly complicated endeavor. When the modern environmental movement gained strength in the 1970s, ecological issues were often portrayed in such basic ways as "Save the Whales" bumper stickers. The reality, however, is that safeguarding the environment is a complex process that demands difficult scientific and political choices. As often as not, environmental debates focus on such technical issues as determining the effects of trace amounts of toxic pesticides in food or the multiple sources of pollution that enter a stream.

When people discuss the environment, they have in mind a broad range of issues. Much environmental policy focuses on natural resource matters—protecting national parks, regulating logging in national forests, setting limits on fishing. In addition, environmental policy encompasses matters that have a direct impact on human society. Some of the most contentious political and legal environmental debates in recent years have centered on regulating contaminants in drinking water, reducing air pollutants that can cause respiratory ailments, and cleaning up toxic waste dumps near residential and business areas.

You will find information about the full range of environmental issues in *The Environment A to Z*. This book contains articles about natural resource topics, such as the management of national parks and the reintroduction of wolves into the wild. Other articles address issues that have health implications for all of us, including water pollution and ozone depletion. The book also summarizes the Clean Air Act and other key laws, and it discusses complex regulatory topics, such as assessing the risks posed by hazardous chemicals.

Much of the book focuses on domestic topics. However, some articles also look at international issues, including population growth and the 1992 Earth Summit in Rio de Janeiro. Global trends are important because environmental problems are not confined to national borders. The destruction of tropical rain forests, for example, has implications for the United States and the rest of the world.

Safeguarding the environment resists easy solution. Heated political battles break out over antipollution measures that can cost many billions of dollars and stifle economic development. All sides agree that a clean environment is important, both to safeguard the public health and to ensure access to outdoor recreational activities. To achieve these goals, conservationists favor strict enforcement of laws that stop pollution and preserve endangered species. But business leaders and property owners rail against government regulations, and they insist that they could do a better job of protecting the environment if bureaucrats left them in peace. Environmental laws such as the Endangered Species Act have infuriated developers, farmers, and loggers who say their livelihood is imperiled by the federal mandate to protect rare types of insects and plants.

Because of the strongly felt opinions on all sides of the debate, it can be difficult to find an evenhanded analysis of environmental issues. *The Environment A to Z* presents objective articles that take into account the views of business leaders and private property rights advocates as well as those of environmentalists. Although it is not a scientific book, it nevertheless summarizes prevailing scientific research into such controversial matters as the influence of industrial activities on global warming and the effects of chemicals on the reproductive systems of people and wildlife. In some cases, the scientific research is too incomplete or contradictory to provide policymakers with a clear direction.

Environmental policy has evolved considerably since the days of Theodore Roosevelt, who established much of the public lands that we still enjoy. Roosevelt, an avid outdoorsman, believed in "utilitarian conservation"—setting aside natural resources for future generations rather than to help wildlife. This philosophy underlay most early environmental laws. The Lacey Act of 1900, for example, sought to restore game birds and other wild animals that were popular with hunters. When Congress established national parks in those days, it wanted primarily to protect beautiful vistas for sightseers (such as the views from Yosemite Valley in California and Mt. Rainier in Washington) rather than to preserve animal and plant habitat.

After World War II environmental sensibilities began to change. The development of pesticides and other toxic chemicals spurred alarms about potentially catastrophic effects on both people and wildlife. Industrial activities, while contributing to the nation's prosperity, drew criticism amid publicity about oil-covered beaches, massive fish kills, and smog-choked skies. In 1962 Rachel Carson's environmental classic, *Silent Spring*, galvanized the public by warning that DDT and other pesticides were depleting populations of birds and other animals and threatening to poison human society. Within ten years, the U.S. government had banned most uses of DDT and enacted sweeping antipollution measures.

When large bipartisan majorities of Congress in the 1970s and early 1980s passed the nation's most important environmental laws—including the Clean Air Act, Clean Water Act, Endangered Species Act, and Superfund hazardous waste law—policymakers predicted that pollution problems would largely be solved by the 1980s. Such a notion now seems naïve. Growing traffic, sprawling development, and increased industrial production are making it more and more challenging to reduce pollution and restore wildlife populations.

The environmental laws are having a mixed impact. The good news is that levels of most air pollutants have dropped significantly since the 1970s. Thanks to billions of dollars in spending on water treatment plants, Americans enjoy one of the world's safest drinking water systems. Formerly polluted waterways such as the Potomac River can now be used for fishing and even swimming. The bald eagle, a national symbol, is flourishing after being nearly wiped out in the continental United States.

Environmentalists, however, caution against complacency. They point out that tens of millions of people live in counties with high levels of air pollution and that many waterways continue to suffer from hazardous wastes. In addition, the United States and other nations are facing the specter of global warming, water scarcity, and the rapid loss of animal and plant species.

As the twenty-first century begins, environmental protection remains a focus of government leaders. We offer *The Environment A to Z* as a reliable source of information about these critical issues.

A

Abandoned Mine Reclamation Fund

The many thousands of MINING operations that were abandoned before 1977 pose a major environmental threat: they can drain highly acidic materials into streams, clog waterways, cause rockslides, and vent hazardous gases. In 1977 Congress established a reclamation fund to address these hazards as part of the SURFACE MINING CONTROL AND RECLAMATION ACT. The fund is supported by production fees of thirty-five cents per ton of surface-mined coal, fifteen cents per ton of coal mined underground, and ten cents per ton of lignite. The U.S. DEPARTMENT OF THE INTERIOR uses the money to acquire both surface and deep mines, sealing off tunnels and shafts while attempting to restore the land to approximately its original contour and planting new vegetation. The U.S. DEPARTMENT OF AGRICULTURE also uses a portion of the money for a rural lands reclamation program. Lands disturbed by surface mining operations, however, are extremely difficult to restore, especially in semiarid western areas.

Acceptable risk

One of the most difficult issues to resolve in environmental policy is determining the acceptable risk of exposure to a hazardous substance. Rather than passing an all-encompassing definition of ac-ceptable risk, Congress has taken an ad hoc approach by inserting approximate standards into various laws. The laws tend to use phrases that are open to interpretation, including "significant risk" and "maximum achievable" technology. As a result, it often falls to regulators to determine allowable exposure to chemicals on food or in the environment that could harm the public health. Complicating the matter, agencies must rely on often conflicting or incomplete research about the dangers of potentially hazardous substances. The resulting regulations, not surprisingly, are routinely challenged in court.

Regulators frequently look to three main criteria to determine acceptable risks:

HEALTH. Several laws direct the ENVIRONMENTAL PROTECTION AGENCY (EPA) to use health-based criteria. The CLEAN AIR ACT, for example, states that the EPA must set air quality standards by "allowing an adequate margin of safety . . . requisite to protect public health," and the FOOD QUALITY PROTECTION ACT states that PESTICIDES in food must pose a "reasonable certainty of no harm." Regulators often aim for a NEGLIGIBLE RISK standard, which is generally defined as ensuring that exposure to a hazardous substance poses no more than a one in one million lifetime risk of cancer.

TECHNOLOGY. Other laws, such as the CLEAN WATER ACT and the SAFE DRINKING WATER ACT, direct regulators to use technology-based standards. The

EPA, for example, may have to ensure that a polluter is using the BEST AVAILABLE CONTROL TECHNOLOGY or the maximum achievable control technology to control discharges. This standard is somewhat easier to enforce, because regulators can focus on the prescribed technology instead of evaluating the public health risks of a pollutant. As long as the correct technology is used, the resulting emissions are assumed to pose acceptable risks to the public health.

COST. A few laws direct regulators to consider the cost or feasibility of a regulation in addition to the threat posed by a substance. The TOXIC SUBSTANCES CONTROL ACT, for example, includes a number of considerations for determining acceptable risk, including the "magnitude of the social and economic costs and benefits of possible control actions." Many conservatives say the government must place a stronger emphasis on the costs of regulations.

Although it might seem simpler if Congress simply imposed a clear standard, such an approach could spark even more controversy. The 1958 DELANEY CLAUSE, for example, prohibited processed food from containing cancer-causing chemicals. But scientists eventually developed new techniques to detect minute traces of such chemicals, spurring lawmakers to amend the law so that farmers could continue to use common pesticides. Similarly, lawmakers attempted to be precise by amending the Clean Air Act in 1990 to direct the EPA to make sure that the risk of cancer from exposure to an air toxic must not exceed one in one million. However, critics charged that EPA risk assessors could easily manipulate their analyses to produce findings on either side of that standard.

Conservative lawmakers have tried repeatedly, without success, to produce a definition for accept-able risk in order to make it more difficult for regulators to impose costly restrictions. In 1995 both the House and the Senate considered controversial regulatory relief legislation that would have directed agencies to conduct detailed risk assessments before imposing major regulations. But the measure failed in the face of vehement opposition by the Clinton administration. (See also RISK ASSESSMENT.)

Acid rain

Acid rain, more accurately called "acid deposition," occurs when emissions of sulfur dioxide and nitrogen oxides react with elements in the atmosphere and return to the earth as acid compounds such as rain, fog, or dry particles. It is a major environmental threat throughout much of the world, even in remote TROPICAL RAIN FORESTS in Africa and elsewhere. But researchers disagree over the source of the pollution as well as the danger it poses to the environment and human health. Although scientists have speculated about acid precipitation for more than a century, they did not begin to investigate its environmental effects until the discovery in the early 1970s that hundreds of previously normal lakes in Sweden had become too acidic to maintain most plant and animal life.

Environmentalists blame acid rain principally for damaging lakes and streams, making the water so acidic that many species of plants and animals cannot survive. Some researchers believe it may severely damage forests by stripping away nutrients in the soil. Acid rain also has been implicated for damaging buildings and monuments, and it may contribute to human respiratory ailments such as asthma. But acid rain is a particularly challenging political issue because the acid-forming pollutants are carried for hundreds of miles by high-altitude winds, affecting areas far from industrial activity. (The Swedish lakes, for example, were largely affected by emissions in Britain, West Germany, and other countries.) This makes it difficult to pinpoint the source of the pollution—or to persuade those responsible to buy expensive antipollution equipment.

In the United States, acid rain began emerging as a major political issue in the 1970s amid reports that emissions from midwestern power plants were killing lakes in the eastern United States and Canada. Whereas normal precipitation has a slightly acidic pH value of about 5.65, precipitation in the Northeast since 1965 has had a pH of a little more than 4. In 1989 the New York State environmental agency reported that one-quarter of surveyed lakes in the Adirondacks were so acidic that they had lost most of their fish. Subsequent surveys by the ENVIRONMENTAL PROTECTION AGENCY (EPA) have blamed acid rain for degrading surface waters in eastern mountains, the upper Midwest, and high-elevation areas of the West. Like many other types of pollution, however, acid rain has sparked debates over the extent of the environmental damage. A landmark ten-year federal government study, released by the federally funded National Acid Precipitation Assessment Program in 1991, concluded that damage from acid rain, while significant, was limited to less than 5 percent of the nation's lakes and about 10 percent of the nation's streams. The controversial government study also stated that the nation's forests remained mostly healthy, despite the contention of other researchers that a massive dying of spruce and fir trees at high elevations in the Appalachian Mountains was caused by pollution.

In Congress, the acid rain problem sparked heated debate throughout much of the 1980s. Lawmakers found themselves divided along regional, rather than ideological, lines. Northeastern legisla-

tors led the charge for tighter emissions regulations, but Midwesterners contended that their constituents should not be saddled with higher utility bills to pay for the installation of expensive antipollution devices in local power plants. The issue also caused friction with Canada, which blamed emissions from the United States for damaging its lakes and forests. After refusing for years to do more than study the problem, President RONALD REAGAN in 1988 committed the United States to reducing its nitrogen oxide emissions.

Congress officially recognized acid rain as a serious environmental problem in 1990, when it substantially amended the CLEAN AIR ACT. Breaking the regional stalemate, President GEORGE BUSH and his administration helped broker a compromise over the costs of antipollution equipment by setting up an innovative system of EMISSIONS TRADING between power plants across the country. The legislation was designed to allow individual plants to pollute at different rates while imposing a cap on total emissions. Overall, the law aimed to cut sulfur dioxide emissions almost in half from 1980 levels and annual nitrogen oxide emissions by about 25 percent.

The new standards appear to be contributing to a significant decline in acid rain–causing pollutants. In a 1997 report the Environmental Protection Agency concluded that sulfur dioxide concentrations had dropped by 39 percent since 1988, and nitrogen oxide concentrations had dropped by 14 percent (see U.S. maps showing acidity of precipitation before and after the Clean Air Act). Furthermore, the emissions-trading approach is so cost effective that the dirtiest power plants emitted just 5.3 million tons of sulfur dioxide in 1995, far less than the 8.7 million ton cap. However, lakes and streams in large parts of North America have failed to return to lower acid levels, possibly because of

Average Sulfate Deposits Before Clean Air Act, 1985–1989

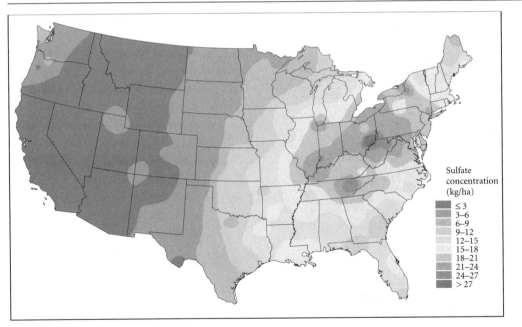

Average Sulfate Deposits After Clean Air Act, 1995–1999

Source: National Atmospheric Deposition Program (NRSP-3)/National Trends Network (2000). NADP Program Office, Illinois State Water Survey, 2204 Griffith Dr., Champaign, Ill. 61820.

Notes: Maps show that sulfate deposits decreased since 1990, when Congress passed the Clean Air Act. Sulfate is a major ingredient of acid rain.

drought or the depletion of naturally occurring acid-neutralizing compounds. Scientists are uncertain about the long-term outlook for the surface waters.

Agricultural runoff

Agricultural runoff refers to PESTICIDES, MANURE, fertilizers, and other farm byproducts that leach into the soil or get washed into streams and other waterways. Environmentalists regard this type of runoff as one of the biggest threats to the nation's water quality, and they want the government to impose strict regulations on farmers. In a 1998 report on water quality, the ENVIRONMENTAL PROTECTION AGENCY (EPA) estimated that close to 60 percent of all water quality problems in rivers and streams were caused by agriculture. The problem appears to be getting worse as farms become concentrated into large, industrial-type operations that are sometimes known as "factory farms."

Agricultural byproducts are rich in phosphorus and nitrogen. These elements promote the growth of algae, which compete for oxygen, choke off fish life, and cause EUTROPHICATION. Scientists believe that agricultural runoff flowing down the Mississippi River has created a 7,000-square-mile dead zone in the Gulf of Mexico near Louisiana—an area the size of New Jersey. In the Florida Everglades, fertilizers used by sugarcane growers are blamed for altering the ecosystem and killing off many plants needed by birds and small mammals.

In 1996 Congress created the ENVIRONMENTAL QUALITY INCENTIVES PROGRAM to help farmers contain manure and take other steps to preserve the environment. Throughout the 1990s, however,

lawmakers deadlocked over proposals to take additional steps by reauthorizing the CLEAN WATER ACT to impose restrictions on agricultural runoff and other types of NONPOINT SOURCE POLLUTION. EPA officials in 1998 unveiled a plan to treat large livestock operations as industries, requiring them to obtain pollution permits. Some lawmakers would like to go further and impose strict national standards for handling animal waste. However, such an approach would be politically difficult because of the powerful agricultural lobby. Influential groups such as the AMERICAN FARM BUREAU FEDERATION want the government instead to provide farmers with technical assistance and incentive payments to reduce runoff. (See also ALGAL BLOOMS.)

Air pollution

Air pollution is a devastating health problem throughout much of the world. Even in the United States, where the CLEAN AIR ACT of 1970 has spurred great improvements in air quality, polluted outdoor air is blamed for causing severe health problems, such as bronchitis and lung cancer, and increasing the mortality rate in heavily polluted cities by as much as 25 percent. In many Asian, Latin American, and eastern European cities, the pollution is even more severe because of weak air quality standards. Mexico City is frequently shrouded in SMOG, and residents are advised to spend as little time as possible outside. Estimates of the worldwide death toll caused by outdoor air pollution have ranged from about 200,000 to 570,000 annually, according to the World Resources Institute. The World Health Organization has estimated that some 1.4 billion people breathe

A factory near Houston burns discarded automobile batteries. The World Resources Institute estimates that outdoor air pollution causes 200,000 to 570,000 deaths per year. Source: Marc St. Gil, EPA-Documerica

unhealthy outdoor air. (INDOOR AIR POLLUTION may pose even greater health threats, but scientists generally treat it as a separate problem.)

Air pollution also has a severe impact on the environment. It is linked to ACID RAIN, GLOBAL WARMING, OZONE DEPLETION, and contamination of surface waters. Because the pollutants are carried by high-altitude winds and scattered across the globe, polluted air affects pristine areas, damaging forests in Scandinavia and impairing visibility in the Grand Canyon. Its reach is so great that it threatens sensitive ecosystems in remote arctic areas and TROPICAL RAIN FORESTS. The economic costs of this environmental damage can be staggering. American farmers lose $2 billion or so yearly in crops because of ground-level ozone. In Europe, dying forests may be setting back the economy by $30 billion a year, according to a 1990 study cited by the UNITED NATIONS ENVIRONMENT PROGRAMME.

Air becomes polluted when harmful chemical compounds are not quickly dissipated by wind or precipitation or broken down by solar energy. The pollutants affect people in various ways. Sulfur dioxide, nitrogen oxides, and ozone are strong oxidizing agents that damage delicate tissues. Fine suspended particles, known as PARTICULATE MATTER or soot, are breathed deep into the lungs, where they can cause serious inflammatory reactions. Carbon monoxide and LEAD make it harder for red blood cells to carry oxygen. Polluted air is especially dangerous when it becomes trapped over a city by a "temperature inversion"—a blanket of cold air that impedes air movement. In 1948 air fouled by coal burning became trapped over Donora, Pennsylvania, killing twenty residents. Four years later, a smog crisis in London claimed the lives of about four thousand people.

The pollutants have complex effects on the environment. For example, researchers believe that various types of airborne chemicals can damage plants by irritating sensitive cell membranes, injuring roots, reducing resistance to disease, and even disrupting plant hormones. GREENHOUSE GASES

Air Quality Trends in Selected U.S. Cities, 1989–1998

MSA	Trend sites	Number of days with AQI values greater than 100									
		1989	1990	1991	1992	1993	1994	1995	1996	1997	1998
Atlanta	7	14	42	23	18	30	12	33	21	26	43
Bakersfield	7	113	97	109	100	97	98	104	109	55	75
Baltimore	15	28	29	50	23	48	41	36	28	30	51
Boston	25	12	7	13	9	6	10	8	2	8	7
Chicago	46	16	4	22	4	3	8	21	6	9	7
Cincinnati	20	19	19	22	3	13	19	23	11	11	14
Cleveland-Lorain-Elyria	24	18	10	23	11	13	23	24	17	11	20
Dallas	8	18	24	2	11	12	15	36	12	15	18
Dayton-Springfield	10	10	13	12	2	11	14	11	18	9	19
Denver	20	14	9	6	8	3	1	2	0	0	5
Detroit	30	18	11	28	8	5	13	14	13	12	17
El Paso	17	25	19	7	10	7	11	5	7	3	5
Houston	26	43	54	37	32	28	45	66	28	47	38
Indianapolis	29	15	9	12	7	9	22	19	13	12	19
Kansas City	21	4	2	11	1	4	10	22	10	18	15
Los Angeles–Long Beach	38	215	173	169	175	134	139	113	94	60	56
Memphis	13	8	24	9	14	15	10	21	19	17	27
Miami	10	5	1	1	3	6	1	2	1	3	8
Minneapolis–St. Paul	24	8	4	2	3	0	4	7	1	0	0
New York	29	29	36	49	10	19	21	19	15	23	17
Orange County	11	56	45	35	35	25	15	9	9	3	6
Philadelphia	36	44	39	49	24	51	26	30	22	32	37
Phoenix-Mesa	23	30	12	11	13	16	10	22	17	12	17
Pittsburgh	41	21	19	21	9	13	19	25	11	20	39
Riverside–San Bernardino	35	187	158	154	174	168	149	124	119	106	94
Sacramento	13	63	36	54	44	14	30	32	30	5	17
St. Louis	54	25	23	32	15	9	32	34	20	15	23
San Diego	23	127	96	67	66	58	46	48	31	14	33
San Francisco	9	0	0	0	0	0	0	2	0	0	0
Seattle-Bellevue-Everett	16	6	9	4	3	0	3	0	6	1	3
Ventura	12	87	70	87	54	37	63	65	62	44	29
Washington, D.C.	32	24	25	48	14	48	20	29	18	29	45
Youngstown-Warren	9	8	3	14	5	2	0	11	5	3	15

Source: U.S. Environmental Protection Agency, Office of Air Quality Planning and Standards, *National Air Quality and Emissions Trends Report, 1998* (Research Triangle Park, N.C.: EPA, OAQPS, 2000).

Notes: MSA = Metropolitan Statistical Area. The Air Quality Index (AQI) provides information on pollutant concentrations for ground-level ozone, particulate matter, carbon monoxide, sulfur dioxide, and nitrogen dioxide. The AQI is "normalized" across pollutants so that an AQI value of 100 represents the level of health protection associated with the national health-based standard for each pollutant and an AQI value of 500 represents the level at which the pollutant causes significant harm.

such as carbon dioxide trap heat and cause global warming, while chlorofluorocarbons (CFCS) release chlorine into the atmosphere and destroy ozone. Many of these processes are related. The reduction of stratospheric ozone, for example, reduces global warming—but it also exposes the planet to deadly ultraviolet radiation. The complex reactions, and the numerous sources that produce air pollution (including motor vehicles, factories, power plants, farming activities, wood burning, and even consumer products) make it difficult to link a particular activity to an environmental effect, complicating regulatory efforts.

Although volcanic eruptions, rotting vegetation, and other natural processes temporarily release harmful gases such as methane and ammonia, air pollution is primarily the byproduct of human activity. Severe instances of pollution can be traced back to coal burning and other industrial activities in the nineteenth century. Antipollution laws in the United States have their origins in the 1880s, when cities blanketed in soot started to pass local ordinances in an attempt to curb coal burning. Researchers in the 1940s began linking air pollution to sickness and death. In 1955 the U.S. Public Health Service launched the first federal efforts to study and remedy the problem, and Congress passed a modest clean air bill in 1963. But the government did not take decisive action until 1970, with the passage of the Clean Air Act, which set strict limits on emissions. Lawmakers amended the law in 1990 to reduce acid rain and impose more comprehensive standards on motor vehicle emissions and hazardous air pollutants such as benzene and MERCURY.

The results have been dramatic. Air quality is far better than in 1970, thanks to a significant decline in five out of six criteria pollutants regulated by the ENVIRONMENTAL PROTECTION AGENCY (EPA). (Levels of carbon monoxide, LEAD, ozone, particulate matter, and sulfur dioxide have all dropped, in some cases dramatically. Nitrogen oxide levels have increased.) However, more than 100 million people live in counties that still have unhealthy levels of at least one of the CRITERIA AIR POLLUTANTS, according to the EPA. (For data on air quality trends in U.S. cities, see table.)

Although virtually everyone agrees that clean air is a worthy goal, efforts to tighten air pollution regulations in the United States continually spawn legislative and judicial battles because of concerns that the costs may be excessive. A 1997 EPA initiative to tighten regulations for ozone and create a standard for certain particles of soot faced scorching criticism from business groups and many in Congress before getting bogged down in court challenges. Similarly, President BILL CLINTON ran into overwhelming Senate opposition in the late 1990s to the KYOTO PROTOCOL on global warming because of reports that the steep emission reductions that would be required would cost tens of billions of dollars. Compounding the political difficulties, air pollution issues typically divide political leaders by region, pitting midwestern states that produce some of the most harmful utility emissions against northeastern states that suffer the fallout. (See also KYOTO PROTOCOL.)

Air quality control regions

Under the CLEAN AIR ACT of 1970 the U.S. government divides the nation into hundreds of air quality control regions. The regions are classified as "attainment" or "nonattainment" for various pollutants, depending on whether they meet national clean air standards. (See also NONATTAINMENT AREAS.)

Air quality index

Called the pollution standards index until 1999, when its name was changed, the air quality index is a system developed by the ENVIRONMENTAL PROTECTION AGENCY (EPA) to measure levels of ozone and other common air pollutants in metropolitan areas with populations greater than two hundred thousand. The five index values are good, moderate, unhealthy, very unhealthy, and hazardous. State and local officials may issue health advisories on days when pollution levels are high. (See also AIR POLLUTION; AIR QUALITY CONTROL REGIONS; CLEAN AIR ACT.)

Alar

Alar is the trade name of daminozide, a chemical that makes apples redder and firmer than they would be without application of the chemical. In 1989 the ENVIRONMENTAL PROTECTION AGENCY (EPA) announced that Alar posed "a significant risk of cancer to humans" but declined to take the chemical off the market immediately.

During the resulting uproar, environmentalists highlighted the potential dangers of all PESTICIDES. The Natural Resources Defense Council claimed that thousands of preschoolers would eventually get cancer because of pesticide residues on fruits and vegetables. Armed with environmental data, the CBS television program *60 Minutes* warned in 1989 that Alar is "the most potent cancer causing agent in the food supply today." On the other side, apple growers and Uniroyal Corp., a pesticide manufacturer, cited laboratory tests to demonstrate that Alar posed no threat to human health. Many health experts also questioned whether the chemical, eventually restricted by the EPA, posed any danger.

The Alar episode, which temporarily sent apple sales plummeting, highlighted the difficulties of RISK ASSESSMENT in environmental regulations. Although Congress passed the FOOD QUALITY PROTECTION ACT in 1996 to try to improve pesticide evaluation, environmentalists and farmers continue to clash over pesticide restrictions. Both sides still cite the Alar example to bolster their case.

Alaska National Interest Lands Conservation Act

Often referred to as the "Alaska lands act," this 1980 legislation (PL 96-487) was one of the crowning achievements of American conservationists. In a single action, Congress set aside more than one hundred million acres of land, more than doubling the size of the country's system of NATIONAL PARKS and wildlife refuges and almost tripling the amount of territory designated as wilderness. Environmentalists wanted to protect additional land and impose greater restrictions on commercial development, but they generally celebrated the new law. President JIMMY CARTER, an avid fisherman who had declared the Alaska measure his chief environmental priority, called the legislation a "truly historic event."

The measure capped a nine-year, often vitriolic battle over development in the nation's largest and wildest state. Environmentalists were determined to save America's last untouched wilderness, home to healthy populations of BALD EAGLES, GRIZZLY BEARS, and other animals that had become rare in the lower forty-eight states. On the other side, MINING, timber, and oil companies—backed by most Alaskans—charged that the bill would needlessly lock up huge energy and timber resources that they said could be developed in an environmentally safe manner.

The battle was touched off by the 1971 Alaska Native Claims Settlement Act (PL 92-203), which ordered the interior secretary to withdraw from

After a bitter nine-year battle between developers and environmentalists, Congress in 1980 passed the Alaska National Interest Lands Conservation Act, which designated more than one hundred million acres of Alaska land as wilderness, national parks, or wildlife refuges. Alaska's Mount McKinley National Park includes the Yentna Glacier (top) *and the Mt. Russell icefall* (left).

Source: Norman Herkenham, National Park Service

development some of the 223 million acres in Alaska that the federal government owned and make recommendations to Congress on protecting that land as national parks and monuments, national wildlife refuges, wild and scenic rivers, and NATIONAL FORESTS. President RICHARD NIXON's administration in 1973 proposed protecting 83 million acres. Carter, who took office in 1977, proposed expanding those areas. Congress appeared split over the plans, with Sen. Mike Gravel, D-Alaska, threatening to filibuster virtually any bill that

would block commercial development of the state's natural resources. Amid concerns that development could render the issue moot, Carter in 1978 used his executive authority under the ANTIQUITIES ACT of 1906 to create seventeen national monuments, protecting some 56 million acres—an area the size of Minnesota.

For much of 1980 the deadlock continued. House environmentalists passed legislation that would have set aside some 127.5 million acres, but Senate conservatives insisted on setting aside fewer acres and allowing oil and gas exploration in an area now encompassed by the ARCTIC NATIONAL WILDLIFE REFUGE. Only after RONALD REAGAN won the 1980 presidential election did House members give in, because they did not want to face the prospect of trying to pass a major conservation bill during Reagan's administration. The final version set aside 104.3 million acres in various conservation units, including 43.6 million acres of national parks and 53.8 million acres of national wildlife refuges. Within the protected land, 56.7 million acres were designated as wilderness.

Even though Congress passed the legislation overwhelmingly, lawmakers remain divided over the level of protection for Alaska's wildlands. In recent years, commercial developers and environmentalists have squared off repeatedly over issues that remain unsettled, including exploratory drilling in the Arctic National Wildlife Refuge, logging in TONGASS NATIONAL FOREST, and building roads and other facilities in Alaska's national parks and national wildlife refuges.

Algal blooms

An algal bloom is a sudden increase in the amount of algae (tiny single-cell or multiple-cell organisms) in a lake or river. It is often caused when excessive numbers of nutrients, such as fertilizers, flow into the water. Algal blooms can cover the surface with an unsightly green. By blocking sunlight and causing shifts in water chemistry, such blooms may kill off many aquatic species and cause EUTROPHICATION. (See also AGRICULTURAL RUNOFF.)

Alliance of Small Island States

The Alliance of Small Island States is an informal organization of low-lying island nations that could be largely submerged if GLOBAL WARMING causes worldwide flooding. The group of about forty nations and observers lobbies for emission limits on GREENHOUSE GASES, but it has limited influence and no budget. It was founded by officials from Maldives, a nation of three hundred thousand people who live on a chain of coral islands in the Indian Ocean that rise only a few feet above sea level.

Alternative Motor Fuels Act

Congress passed the 1988 Alternative Motor Fuels Act (PL 100-494) to try to reduce both AIR POLLUTION and the United States' dependency on foreign oil. The legislation attempted to solve a Catch 22–type dilemma: automakers refused to build alternative-fuel vehicles if the fuel was not available to power the cars, but gas stations refused to supply the fuels if there were no cars operating with them.

The legislation was designed to motivate automakers by giving them a break on their fleetwide CORPORATE AVERAGE FUEL ECONOMY (CAFE) standards. Essentially, only the gasoline burned by their fleets—rather than other fuels—would be counted against CAFE standards. For example, methanol-burning cars would be docked for only 15 percent of the fuel they actually burned because methanol fuel is about 15 percent gasoline.

The measure also required the U.S. DEPARTMENT OF ENERGY to ensure that the maximum practical number of passenger automobiles and light-duty trucks acquired by the federal government would be powered by alternative fuels. The Energy Department set up a federal program to help state and local governments test the use of alternative fuels in passenger buses.

American Farm Bureau Federation

Founded in 1919, the American Farm Bureau Federation, based in Park Ridge, Illinois, is the nation's largest farm organization and a major lobbying force for REGULATORY RELIEF and PRIVATE PROPERTY RIGHTS. It clashes with environmentalists over a broad range of issues encompassing water quality, endangered species protection, and the use of PESTICIDES. Instead of imposing environmental regulations that can drive up farmers' costs, the farm bureau contends that the government should give incentives to farmers for pursuing conservation actions voluntarily.

The nonpartisan group, often allied with lobbies that represent individual grower groups and pesticide manufacturers, strengthens its political hand by maintaining close ties to rural members on both sides of the aisle. Because of its orientation, the farm bureau complements the political reach of industrial and business-oriented anti-regulatory groups, such as the NATIONAL ASSOCIATION OF MANUFACTURERS.

Along with other influential agricultural groups, the farm bureau has joined in lawsuits against the federal government over AGRICULTURAL RUNOFF and the reintroduction of WOLVES in the West. It sued the ENVIRONMENTAL PROTECTION AGENCY (EPA) in 1999 for allegedly basing pesticide decisions on questionable assumptions and incomplete science. "EPA needs to make clear that it is operating under established rules, not whim," Dean Kleckner, the farm bureau's president, said in 1999.

Obtaining regulatory relief for farmers and protecting their private property rights are high on the agenda of the American Farm Bureau Federation, the nation's largest farm organization. Source: Tim McCabe, USDA-SCS

American Heritage Rivers Initative

President BILL CLINTON unveiled the American Heritage Rivers Initiative in his 1997 State of the Union address, saying he wanted to help local communities restore ten rivers of major significance. The Clinton administration intended the voluntary program as something of a beauty pageant for rivers and stressed that it would not cost the federal government any money. But it ran into a maelstrom of opposition. Western Republicans, such as Rep. Helen Chenoweth, R-Idaho, blasted the administration for trying to undercut state sovereignty and usurp PRIVATE PROPERTY RIGHTS and water rights. Major waterways, including parts of the Rio Grande and Missouri River, were removed from consideration at the insistence of area lawmakers. The HOUSE RESOURCES COMMITTEE voted in 1997 to bar the use of federal funds for the initiative, but the legislation eventually died.

Despite the opposition, the Clinton administration received 126 nominations and in 1998 designated fourteen rivers (officials concluded that ten would not be enough). The designated rivers included the Connecticut, Detroit, Hudson, Potomac, Willamette, and parts of the Mississippi. Each river was assigned a "river navigator"—a federal employee whose role was to help riverside communities identify federal programs and grants.

Animal damage control

See PREDATOR AND PEST CONTROL.

Antarctica treaty

To protect Antarctica's pristine environment, the United States and twenty-five other nations that conducted research on the continent signed a 1991 treaty banning exploration for oil and other minerals for fifty years. President GEORGE BUSH originally opposed the treaty because of a provision that would have required unanimous approval by the signatory nations to lift the ban after fifty years. But the Bush administration agreed to a compromise requiring a two-thirds majority to lift the ban.

The treaty expanded upon a landmark 1959 agreement, which declared that Antarctica "shall continue forever to be used exclusively for peaceful purposes and shall not become the scene or object of international discord." The full name of the 1991 agreement is the Protocol on Environmental Protection to the Antarctic Treaty, but it is sometimes called the Madrid Protocol after the city in which it was negotiated. Despite such international protection, the Antarctic environment has been affected by OZONE DEPLETION and other problems caused by air pollutants emitted from thousands of miles away. (See also AIR POLLUTION.)

Antiquities Act

The Antiquities Act of 1906, created during the administration of President THEODORE ROOSEVELT, is a powerful environmental tool that gives the president authority to designate a national monument on federal land. It has been invoked by thirteen presidents to designate more than one hundred national monuments (many of which later became NATIONAL PARKS or historic sites), including Grand Canyon in Arizona, Muir Woods in California, Death Valley in Nevada and California, and Bryce Canyon in Utah. When lawmakers in 1978 failed to take action to protect ecologically sensitive land in Alaska, President JIMMY CARTER used the Antiquities Act to create seventeen new national monuments to forestall MINING, logging, and other commercial development. The combined land area of these new monuments is the size of Minnesota.

The venerable law came under fire in 1996, when President BILL CLINTON dusted it off during his 1996 reelection campaign to set aside 1.7 million acres in Utah as the GRAND STAIRCASE–ESCALANTE NATIONAL MONUMENT. Clinton's act, although praised by environmentalists, drew heavy fire from the Utah delegation and other western conservatives, who denounced it as a federal land grab. The following year, the House of Representatives passed legislation to pare back the law. Under the proposed legislation, both chambers of Congress would have to approve the designation of any national monument larger than 50,000 acres, or the designation would expire within two years. However, the legislation failed because of opposition by environmentalists and the Clinton administration, which called the Antiquities Act one of the most successful environmental laws of the century.

In the final year of his administration, Clinton used the Antiquities Act to create a number of national monuments to protect such environmental priorities as California sequoia trees and ecologically sensitive land near the Grand Canyon.

Aquaculture

Aquaculture, or fish farming, is a fast-growing industry that offers great potential to provide people with seafood without further depleting ocean stocks. Worldwide production doubled from 1984 to 1994, reaching about twenty-five million tons and accounting for an estimated 20 percent of seafood products, according to the United Nations Food and Agriculture Organization.

The farms typically consist either of freshwater ponds or of coastal areas that are enclosed with nets. Although such operations are not intrinsically bad for the environment, some farmers, especially in Asia, have caused severe ecological damage by clearing coastal marshes and mangrove forests to build ponds and by flushing heavy concentrations of fish feces and other debris into nearby waterways. Some farms, paradoxically, have also put more pressure on ocean stocks by using large numbers of wild fish to provide food for shrimp, salmon, and other lucrative captive species.

Aquaculture in the United States has sparked relatively few national environmental battles. State, not federal, officials are generally responsible for issuing required permits. Congress has shown little interest in the industry, other than to pass the 1980 National Aquaculture Act (PL 96-362), administered largely by the U.S. DEPARTMENT OF AGRICULTURE, to promote the commercial cultivation of fish, oysters, and other aquatic species. Environmentalists, however, have suggested tightening regulations or creating economic incentives to ensure that fish farms do not pollute surface water or GROUNDWATER with chemicals and other byproducts.

Arctic National Wildlife Refuge

One of the nation's most pristine ecosystems, the Arctic National Wildlife Refuge (often abbreviated as ANWR) encompasses 19.5 million acres in northeastern Alaska. The preserve, originally set aside in 1960 and greatly expanded as part of the Alaska Public Lands Act in 1980, has been the subject of a bitter tug of war in Congress for many years. Energy companies seek to open it to oil exploration, and environmentalists press just as urgently to keep it off limits to development.

At the heart of the dispute is the future of the refuge's 1.5-million-acre coastal plain, a spectacular landscape that is habitat for millions of migrating birds, elk, WOLVES, and bears—and also covers vast reserves of oil. Oil companies say they can extract the valuable crude without damaging the environment, creating hundreds of thousands of jobs and making the United States less dependent on foreign oil. Environmentalists contend that the continued viability of many arctic species is dependent on the protection of the coastal plain, especially because much of the rest of Alaska's North Slope has been badly scarred by oil development.

Lawmakers fiercely debated the fate of the coastal plain in 1980. Some contended that it should be opened to development, while others argued that it should be permanently protected as wilderness. They reached a compromise of sorts, barring any development without future congressional authorization and requiring surveys of both the plain's wildlife resources and its oil potential. In the late 1980s the U.S. DEPARTMENT OF THE INTERIOR recommended that Congress open the refuge to oil and gas exploration. However, the controversial plan died after the EXXON VALDEZ oil spill in 1989 stirred up antidevelopment sentiment. The Repub-

North to Alaska

Proponents of tapping the Arctic National Wildlife Refuge's petroleum reserves would allow drilling in a 1.5 million-acre section of the park called Area 1002, which is near the Prudhoe Bay oil field.

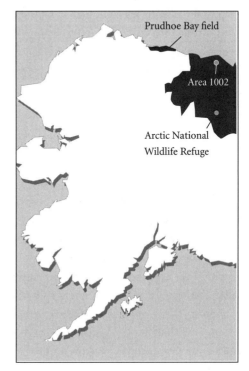

Source: U.S. Fish and Wildlife Service

lican-led Congress revived the issue in 1995, adding a provision to an omnibus budget bill to allow limited oil and gas leasing in a portion of the coastal plain. President BILL CLINTON, who objected to a number of provisions, including the proposed development, vetoed the bill. Three years later, the U.S. Geological Survey estimated that a staggering 11 billion to 31 billion barrels of oil lay beneath the refuge's coastal plain—an assessment that stirred renewed demands to open the refuge to drilling.

Influential Alaska Republican lawmakers such as Rep. DON YOUNG and Sen. FRANK H. MURKOWSKI repeatedly sponsored bills in the late 1990s similar to the 1995 plan that would permit leasing in a portion of the refuge's coastal plain. Environmentalists countered with legislation that would permanently protect the coastal plain by designating it as a federal wilderness area. The two sides, however, remained deadlocked. (See also ALASKA NATIONAL INTEREST LANDS CONSERVATION ACT.)

Asbestos

A natural fibrous mineral material, asbestos formerly was used widely for insulating pipes, furnaces, and buildings. In the 1960s research established a link between lung disease and asbestos because airborne fibers can become permanently lodged in the lungs. The ENVIRONMENTAL PROTECTION AGENCY (EPA) classified asbestos as a hazardous air pollutant in 1972, marking the beginning of an ongoing dispute over how best to handle the material. A year later, the EPA issued rules under the CLEAN AIR ACT that generally required anyone renovating or tearing down a building to remove all asbestos that was "friable"—capable of being crumbled by hand. Later in the decade, the EPA imposed a ban on sprayed-on asbestos, which was used in a dry, foamlike state as insulation in ceilings.

Amid mounting concerns about the material—many asbestos workers from the 1940s and 1950s had developed lung cancer or other health problems—the EPA in 1982 announced a controversial regulation requiring all primary and secondary schools to inspect for asbestos and to notify parents and employees of the result. EPA officials recommended that decisions about asbestos disposal be made at the local level. Critics worried that the agency's rules did not require schools to take remedial action, nor did they set standards for determining when the presence of asbestos posed a health problem. Much of the cleanup work was conducted improperly and may have made the problem worse, studies indicated.

Accordingly, Congress in 1986 passed the Asbestos Hazard Emergency Response Act (PL 99-372). This law directed the EPA to issue rules spelling out procedures for mandatory school inspections and reinspections and to set standards for the safe disposal of asbestos. It also directed states to adopt stringent asbestos programs and to require schools to use accredited contractors for asbestos removal. Over the next few years, the EPA formulated a far-ranging ban on domestic uses of the product.

Asbestos removal remains controversial. By the late 1990s, schools had spent as much as $100 billion on asbestos abatement. But scientists question whether low levels of asbestos is as dangerous as originally thought, and some critics contend that removing asbestos is far more dangerous than sealing it in place. Conservatives often point to the asbestos regulations as an example of the government overreacting to an environmental threat. (See also REGULATORY RELIEF.)

B

Babbitt, Bruce

As President BILL CLINTON's interior secretary, Bruce Babbitt frequently found himself embroiled in land management controversies. Environmentalists initially cheered the 1993 appointment of the former Arizona governor, who had advocated protecting natural resources as the chairman of the League of Conservation Voters. But in his first two years in office, Babbitt failed to win support in the Democratic-controlled Congress for such initiatives as increasing GRAZING FEES and imposing tough MINING restrictions. Instead, he found himself criticized by environmentalists for allowing widespread logging and cutting deals with western conservatives.

Babbitt stiffened his policies after Republicans took control of Congress in 1995. He used his administrative powers to regulate grazing practices and restrict traffic in NATIONAL PARKS, and he nominated ecologically sensitive areas for the administration to protect as national monuments. He oversaw such innovative ecological practices as opening the gates of the Glen Canyon Dam and allowing the Colorado River to flood the floor of the Grand Canyon for a week, thereby replenishing shoreline vegetation. But environmentalists continued to clash with Babbitt over what they viewed as his lax enforcement of the ENDANGERED SPECIES ACT. For example, Babbitt agreed to HABITAT CONSERVATION PLANS that permitted the destruction of some habitat for rare species.

Natural resource issues aside, Babbitt faced an independent counsel investigation in 1998 for allegedly lying to Congress about his department's rejection of a proposed Indian gambling casino in Hudson, Wisconsin. He was ultimately cleared of wrongdoing.

Bald eagle

The recovery of the bald eagle is one of the signal success stories of the U.S. conservation movement. The regal bird has symbolized the nation since the Continental Congress in 1782 selected it for the Great Seal of the United States, but its numbers plummeted from a one-time high of about a half-million birds in the lower forty-eight states to just an estimated 417 nesting pairs in 1963 because of habitat destruction, hunting, and pollution. (In Alaska, however, the bird continued to thrive.) The government began trying to protect the species in 1940 by banning hunting under the Bald Eagle Protection Act, one of the early wildlife protection laws. But widespread use of the pesticide DDT after World War II appeared to devastate the populations of bald eagles and other birds high up on the food chain by thinning the shells of their eggs, causing them to break easily.

The banning of DDT in 1972 and the enactment of the ENDANGERED SPECIES ACT one year later enabled the bird to recover dramatically. In 1999,

Once driven to the brink of extinction by hunting, DDT, pollution, and habitat destruction, the bald eagle has recovered dramatically due to the banning of DDT and the safeguards of the Endangered Species Act. Source: Lee Emery, U.S. Fish and Wildlife Service

with more than 5,000 nesting pairs in the continental United States, President BILL CLINTON launched an administrative process to consider taking the bald eagle off the list of endangered species. "The American bald eagle is now back from the brink of extinction," he said.

However, the administration subsequently delayed removing the bird from the endangered species list because of ongoing concerns about habitat loss.

Barrier islands

Barrier islands are long, narrow, and typically sandy islands that sit off mainland coasts. They are important ecologically because they buffer lagoons, WETLANDS, and salt marshes from pounding waves, especially during storms. Although they regularly shift with storms and currents, beautiful island beaches such as Miami Beach and Atlantic City have beckoned developers for many decades. Unfortunately, dense development tends to make the islands more unstable and prone to erosion, especially at a time of worldwide rising sea levels.

For many decades, the federal government has directly and indirectly aided the development of many of the barrier islands that are located just off the Atlantic and Gulf Coasts. Federal flood insurance and disaster relief policies are particularly important because they enable homeowners and businesses on the islands to recover their losses after a storm. But such policies are controversial because they cost the government billions of dollars and encourage development in ecologically sensitive places. The government also provides housing subsidies and mortgage insurance, supplies grants for community development and wastewater treatment, and engages in massive beach restoration projects—which sometimes deprive undeveloped islands of needed sand.

In 1982 Congress passed the COASTAL BARRIER RESOURCES ACT to discourage building on undeveloped barrier islands. It barred most kinds of federal assistance for such development, as well as spending to stabilize barrier landforms or prevent erosion along inlets. However, developers in the 1990s successfully sued states that tried to prohibit building in erosion areas. (See also PRIVATE PROPERTY RIGHTS.)

Batteries

Batteries are a significant source of MERCURY, which is a toxic metal linked to severe neurological and other health problems. In LANDFILLS batteries can pollute GROUNDWATER; in INCINERATORS, they can produce toxic emissions. U.S. battery manufacturers virtually eliminated mercury from alkaline batteries in the 1980s, and several states passed laws requiring batteries to be mercury-free during the 1990s. In 1996 Congress passed a measure (PL 104-142) to phase out the use of mercury in most batteries and establish new labeling requirements for rechargeable batteries.

Baucus, Max

As the senior Democrat on the SENATE ENVIRONMENT AND PUBLIC WORKS COMMITTEE, Max Baucus, R-Mont., has struggled to advance environmental goals without offending farming and other homestate interests. When he chaired the

committee in the early 1990s, Baucus tried unsuccessfully to reauthorize both the CLEAN WATER ACT and the SUPERFUND hazardous waste program to make them more effective, but found himself unable to bridge the gap between environmentalists and industry. He drew some criticism from environmentalists for opposing the Clinton administration's attempts to raise GRAZING FEES and impose tougher environmental standards on ranchers who use federal land for grazing.

After Republicans gained a Senate majority in the 1994 elections, Baucus battled conservative ENVIRONMENTAL RIDERS on appropriations bills that would have scaled back the ENVIRONMENTAL PROTECTION AGENCY's regulatory authority. He played a role in the successful reauthorization of the SAFE DRINKING WATER ACT in 1996, but had less success trying to designate a large wilderness area in Montana. Terse in person, the son of a wealthy ranching family, Baucus barely won reelection in 1996 because of Montana's increasingly conservative bent.

Below-cost timber sales

Timber sales in the NATIONAL FORESTS are sometimes operated on a "below cost" basis. This means that the U.S. FOREST SERVICE spends more on building roads and engaging in other activities to extract trees than it receives for the resulting lumber. Critics since the early 1980s have charged that this practice amounts to a multimillion-dollar annual subsidy for the timber industry, thereby encouraging the destruction of trees and wildlife habitat. Timber companies and many in the Forest Service, however, say the timber program has benefits that are not easily quantified.

The controversy can be traced back to 1920,

when Forest Service chief William Greeley argued that timber management is profitable when one factors in nonmonetary benefits, such as opening areas for recreation and reducing the risk of fire. In the 1960 Multiple-Use Sustained-Yield Act, lawmakers considered—but ultimately rejected—language that would have established profitability as a Forest Service goal. Nevertheless, the timber program was widely believed to be profitable until a 1980 report by the Natural Resources Defense Council found that about half of the national forests were losing money. When the Forest Service revamped its bookkeeping system at the insistence of lawmakers in the 1980s, it reported that logging was conducted on a below-cost basis in areas where timber value is low or operating costs are high, including Alaska and many forests in the Rocky and Appalachian mountains. Analyzing these reports, the Congressional Research Service (CRS) concluded in 1994 that 77 of the 120 national forests appeared to be losing money, with six of them having each lost more than $10 million over the five-year period. (CRS, however, warned that it was difficult to make conclusions about the profitability of the program because the Forest Service sells timber for many different reasons, including generating revenue, expanding motor vehicle access, and altering vegetation patterns.)

Both the Bush and Clinton administrations proposed phasing out the below-cost timber sales as part of their deficit-cutting efforts. However, the administrations retreated in the face of resistance by lawmakers, especially those on the House and Senate agriculture committees. Instead, the Clinton administration in the late 1990s pursued a moratorium on building roads as part of a strategy to reduce logging and put a greater emphasis on conservation.

Best available control technology

Major environmental laws, such as the CLEAN AIR ACT, CLEAN WATER ACT, and SAFE DRINKING WATER ACT, require polluters to use advanced methods to treat hazardous emissions. By mandating the use of best available control technology (or, in other cases, best available technology or maximum achievable technology), the government is essentially steering a middle course between facilities that want to continue uncontrolled emissions and environmental groups that would prefer the pollution to be eliminated entirely. However, requiring antipollution equipment is controversial because it can be very expensive.

Best available control technology is known as a technology-based standard. Instead of regulating pollution with a health-based standard—such as ensuring that emissions pose a NEGLIGIBLE RISK of causing cancer—the ENVIRONMENTAL PROTECTION AGENCY has the somewhat easier task of prescribing the proper technology and making sure that facilities are using it. As long as the technology is used, the resulting emissions are assumed to pose an ACCEPTABLE RISK to the public health.

Bhopal

In one of the world's worst environmental disasters, an explosion at a Union Carbide chemical manufacturing plant in Bhopal, India, on December 2, 1984, released forty tons of chemicals over the city, including a highly toxic volatile liquid, methyl isocyanate (MIC). The chemical release killed an estimated six thousand people and injured about two hundred thousand others. Compounding the problems, many people lived in crowded conditions near the factory, and neither the company nor the Indian government was prepared for such an emergency. The disaster spawned years of litigation. It also prompted Congress to pass the 1986 EMERGENCY PLANNING AND COMMUNITY RIGHT-TO-KNOW ACT, which mandated emergency plans in the event of toxic releases in the United States.

Biodiversity

Scientists began using the term *biodiversity* in recent years to describe the complexity and vulnerability of life on the planet. Although the term may be applied in different ways, researchers often refer to three types of biodiversity that are needed to sustain ecological systems: (1) *genetic diversity* is the variety of genetic versions of a single species; (2) *species diversity* is the variety of organisms within a community or ecosystem; and (3) *ecological diversity* is the variety of ecosystems on earth.

The evolving view of biodiversity has greatly affected U.S. environmental policy in four ways. First, biologists are discovering more and more types of animals and plants. (As of 2000, biologists had listed more than 200,000 species in the United States and more than 1.7 million worldwide. Estimates of the total number of species on earth range anywhere from 3.6 million to more than 100 million.) The discovery of additional species increases the possibility of more environmental regulations because the government is bound to protect the habitat of rare plants and animals under the ENDANGERED SPECIES ACT.

Second, increased knowledge about the complex interactions of species and habitats is forcing policymakers to make increasingly complex—and often controversial—environmental choices. Whereas in the early 1970s officials focused on preserving individual species, waterways, and habitats, they now contend with sustaining the health of entire ecosystems. This change has led the U.S. FOREST SERVICE to impose logging restrictions to protect watersheds and the U.S. Fish and Wildlife Service to reintroduce WOLVES to keep grazing animal populations in check.

Third, environmentalists are increasingly concerned about preserving the biological diversity of small populations of species that are essentially trapped in NATIONAL PARKS (a potential problem for GRIZZLY BEARS in YELLOWSTONE NATIONAL PARK). As a result, officials are beginning to weigh proposals to create wildlife corridors that would allow isolated animals to interact and breed.

Finally, biodiversity has put a greater focus on international environmental problems, such as the effects of GLOBAL WARMING on ecologically sensitive TROPICAL RAINFORESTS and CORAL REEFS. Nations at the 1992 Conference on Environment and Development, better known as the EARTH SUMMIT, agreed to the CONVENTION ON BIOLOGICAL DIVERSITY to protect endangered species. The United States, however, refused to sign it.

Bliley, Thomas J., Jr.

The chairman of the HOUSE COMMERCE COMMITTEE from 1995 to 2000, Rep. Thomas J. Bliley Jr., R-Va., was a leading player in GOP attempts to scale back government regulations. He drew sharp criticism from environmentalists for proposals to require federal agencies to conduct detailed risk assessments, and to relax regulations in such major environmental laws as SUPERFUND and the CLEAN WATER ACT. Congressional Democrats and the Clinton administration blocked his more far-reaching initiatives. However, Bliley teamed up with the committee's senior Democrat, JOHN DINGELL of Michigan, to pass the 1996 FOOD QUALITY PROTECTION ACT, which established a single health standard for PESTICIDES residues on both raw and processed foods. He also drew praise for 1996 legislation making the SAFE DRINKING WATER ACT more flexible.

A small businessman who ran a Richmond funeral home, Bliley tended to side with conservatives on business issues. But he was also a pragmatist who was willing to compromise with Democrats to pass legislation, even if that meant giving up some goals. Summing up his legislative philosophy, he told his committee: "You only get perfection in the next world, not this one."

During her long tenure at EPA, administrator Carol Browner frequently drew fire—and praise—from many diverse constituencies, including farmers, industry advocates, environmentalists, and Congress. Notable among Browner's achievements were promoting greater efficiency at the agency and reforming the Superfund program. Source: Scott J. Ferrell, Congressional Quarterly

Browner, Carol

The longest-serving administrator of the ENVIRONMENTAL PROTECTION AGENCY (EPA), Carol M. Browner took a significantly more pro-environmental stance than did her Republican predecessors. With President BILL CLINTON regularly failing to win congressional support for environmental proposals, Browner found herself in the difficult position of trying to advance clean water and clean air goals through the rulemaking process. She earned a reputation as one of the most stalwart environmentalists in an administration that otherwise drew mixed environmental reviews.

Browner repeatedly was at the center of contentious policy disputes. In 1997 she approved much stricter air quality standards for ozone and PARTICULATE MATTER. The plan drew kudos from environmentalists and many health advocates, but it spurred industry lawsuits and sharp criticism from many in Congress who felt she had overstepped her authority. Similarly, Browner found herself in a crossfire over PESTICIDES regulations, with environmentalists denouncing her for failing to restrict toxic chemical use and farmers accusing her of ruining their business by barring the use of several common pesticides.

A Florida native and former aide to Vice President AL GORE, Browner became administrator in 1993. She failed to persuade the Democratic-controlled Congress to pass such environmental priorities as reforming the SUPERFUND hazardous waste program, expanding the CLEAN WATER ACT, and elevating the EPA to a cabinet agency. After Republicans won a congressional majority in the 1994 elections, the administrator helped turn back GOP attempts to relax environmental protections and require the agency to conduct more elaborate scientific analyses before promulgating regulations. In 1996 she urged congressional passage of laws overhauling the SAFE DRINKING WATER ACT and pesticide regulations.

Policy disputes aside, Browner focused on trying to improve the EPA's efficiency, initiating more than forty management changes in 1995 alone to improve cooperation with state and local officials, speed the regulatory process, and ensure better coordination between agency offices. She put particular effort into reforming Superfund and reducing the lengthy legal battles that slowed the program's hazardous waste cleanups. Announcing a plan in 1996 to foster legal settlements, she said: "With these reforms, we are following through on our efforts to fundamentally improve the Superfund program by limiting the costly role of lawyers and increasing community participation." However, the long-troubled agency continued to face criticism from all sides over both its policies and its effectiveness.

Brownfields

To lure new businesses to industrial areas, the Clinton administration in 1994 launched a program to clean up abandoned, idled, or underused industrial and commercial facilities. Such facilities, known as brownfields, had been in something of an environmental limbo—too contaminated to attract developers wary of liability, but not contaminated enough to qualify for funding under the SU-

PERFUND hazardous waste program. The Brownfields Economic Redevelopment Initiative, developed by the ENVIRONMENTAL PROTECTION AGENCY under the aegis of Superfund, has won kudos from environmentalists and developers alike for helping to revitalize inner-city areas and ensuring that moderately contaminated levels of waste are cleaned up. This initiative has the additional environmental benefit of reducing sprawl by spurring development within city limits. The oil and chemical industries, however, object to using Superfund taxes to redevelop brownfields instead of cleaning up Superfund sites.

Officials estimate that there are anywhere from several tens of thousands to nearly one-half million brownfields nationwide, most of which are in economically distressed areas. For several years, Congress has debated boosting funding for the brownfields program and codifying it into law. Lawmakers, who finance the program through the annual appropriations process, increased funding from $36.8 million in fiscal 1997 to $91.7 million in fiscal 2000. They also passed a provision in a 1997 budget bill allowing developers to fully deduct their costs in the same year as the cleanup.

Many lawmakers would like to authorize the program and provide guaranteed funding. For example, Sen. Lincoln Chafee, D-R.I. (the son of JOHN CHAFEE) introduced legislation in 2000 that would authorize $150 million annually through fiscal year 2005. Such proposals, however, are complicated by political divisions over Superfund.

Btu tax

As part of his 1993 efforts to reduce the federal deficit, President BILL CLINTON proposed an innovative tax on energy consumption. The plan, dubbed a Btu tax for the method of calculating the levy on the heat content of fuels as measured in British thermal units, would have raised $72 billion over five years. Environmentalists hailed it as a step toward discouraging energy consumption (although they preferred an earlier version that would have taxed carbon use). The House narrowly passed the deficit-reduction package that contained the Btu tax. But when energy state senators refused to go along, Clinton agreed to a substitute plan that instead imposed a 4.3-cent tax on gasoline. This change of plan marked the first of several times that the new president disappointed his environmental allies. His vacillation also angered House Democrats.

Bureau of Land Management

See U.S. DEPARTMENT OF THE INTERIOR.

Bureau of Reclamation

See U.S. DEPARTMENT OF THE INTERIOR.

Bush, George

George Bush campaigned for the White House in 1988 by pledging to be the "environmental president." But once in office, he compiled a mixed record that drew considerable criticism from environmentalists. On the positive side of the ledger (from an environmental viewpoint), his proposal of the innovative concept of EMISSIONS TRADING broke the legislative logjam over ACID RAIN and power plant regulation, thereby enabling passage of the landmark 1990 amendments to the CLEAN AIR ACT. Bush also pressed for energy conservation programs and the development of RENEWABLE ENERGY sources in the 1992 ENERGY POLICY ACT. Other notable administration policies included increasing funding for the ENVIRONMENTAL PROTECTION AGENCY (although not as much as environmentalists wanted) and acknowledging past federal wrongdoing that had led to disastrous environmental contamination at nuclear weapons facilities.

But Bush opposed new regulatory measures and seemed unwilling to address international environmental problems. He tried to resolve the NORTHERN SPOTTED OWL controversy by proposing to exempt timber sales in the Pacific Northwest from environmental laws and amend the ENDANGERED SPECIES ACT to put a greater focus on economic factors. He also wanted to spur development by scaling back protections for WETLANDS. In the last year of his one-term presidency, Bush infuriated environmentalists by hesitating for months over attending the EARTH SUMMIT in Rio de Janeiro. The House and Senate passed nonbinding resolutions calling on him to show "leadership" on international environmental issues. Finally, Bush announced he would go—but only after U.S. negotiators won concessions scaling back the scope of the conference. He was a conservative presence at the conference, balking over proposed environmental restrictions and refusing to sign the CONVENTION ON BIOLOGICAL DIVERSITY, which seeks to protect rare plants and animals.

Perhaps Bush's greatest environmental shortcoming was his reluctance to come to grips with the issue of GLOBAL WARMING. He refused to concur with other industrialized countries that wanted to place caps on the emissions of CARBON DIOXIDE and other GREENHOUSE GASES. Rather, he initiated a "NO REGRETS" policy that focused on conserving energy and reducing AIR POLLUTION instead of taking specific actions to curtail global warming. Nevertheless, Bush was far more amenable to environmental protection than his predecessor, RONALD REAGAN. Toward the end of his term, he acknowledged the importance of international efforts to protect the environment. When he announced that he would attend the Earth Summit, Bush said: "Environmental problems are global and every nation must help in solving them."

Bycatch

Also known as "incidental catch," this term refers to unwanted fish and other sea creatures that are inadvertently killed by fishing fleets and discarded. Such marine mammals, turtles, seabirds, and fish account for an estimated 20 percent of the fish harvest, both in the United States and worldwide. Biologists warn that bycatch is depleting the world's fisheries, already severely strained by OVERFISHING. Congress in 1996 revised the MAGNUSON FISHERY CONSERVATION AND MANAGEMENT ACT to require regional fishing councils to draft plans to try to minimize bycatch. Lawmakers have also taken steps to protect individual marine species from being accidentally drowned in nets by requiring the use of TURTLE EXCLUDER DEVICES and setting standards for DOLPHIN-SAFE TUNA. However, fishing fleets tend to resist such measures because they can be costly and reduce their overall catch. U.S. efforts to boycott fish from countries that do not practice such conservation techniques have spurred international legal challenges. (See also GLOBAL ECONOMY.)

C

Carbon dioxide

A colorless and odorless gas, carbon dioxide is believed to play a primary role in GLOBAL WARMING. People emit more than 6 billion tons of the gas into the atmosphere each year, mostly through activities such as burning coal, oil, and natural gas, and by chopping down trees that store carbon. As a result, atmospheric levels of carbon dioxide have increased from 280 parts per million in the pre-industrial era to an estimated 367 parts per million in 2000 (see table).

Scientists estimate that carbon dioxide is responsible for 50 to 60 percent of the effect that human activities may be having on the climate. However, the earth's carbon cycle is highly complex. Scientists are struggling to understand the effects of the gas on world climate and the dynamics that cause the earth's soils and oceans to absorb perhaps half of the carbon dioxide emitted by human activities. Another area of debate is the effect that higher carbon dioxide levels have on plants. Some conservatives, contending that concerns about global warming are overstated, point to research indicating that higher carbon dioxide levels may stimulate plants and boost crop yields. But scientists warn that the gas could have detrimental effects.

Policymakers in the United States and other nations, alarmed at the prospect of severe weather changes and rising sea levels, moved tentatively in the 1990s to reduce carbon dioxide emissions. Some 167 nations signed the 1997 KYOTO PROTO-

Concentration of Carbon Dioxide Emissions in the Atmosphere (parts per million)

Pre-industrial	280.0
1960	316.8
1965	319.9
1970	325.5
1975	331.0
1980	338.5
1985	345.7
1990	354.0
1995	360.9
1999	368.4
2000	367.0 (est.)

Source: C. D. Keeling and T. P. Whorf, "Atmospheric CO_2 Concentrations (ppmv) Derived from In Situ Air Samples Collected at Mauna Loa Observatory, Hawaii" (La Jolla, Calif.: Scripps Institution of Oceanography, University of California, August 16, 2000); and the Carbon Dioxide Information Analysis Center.

COL, which established goals to reduce emissions of six GREENHOUSE GASES, including carbon dioxide. But with the U.S. Senate refusing to ratify the treaty, other nations have balked at imposing expensive restrictions on industry or significantly curbing DEFORESTATION. The United States has drawn much international criticism over the issue because it emits about 20 percent of the world's carbon dioxide—far more than any other country.

The Clinton administration took modest steps in the 1990s to try to curb carbon dioxide emissions, such as promoting the use of RENEWABLE ENERGY. U.S. carbon dioxide emissions increased more slowly in the late 1990s, but the U.S. DEPARTMENT OF ENERGY has predicted that carbon emissions in 2010 could exceed 1990 levels by about one-third.

Carbon sequestration

Carbon sequestration is a natural process by which carbon is cycled out of the atmosphere and stored in CARBON SINKS, such as oceans, vegetation, soil, and rocks. Many policymakers favor a greater focus on sequestration to reduce atmospheric concentrations of CARBON DIOXIDE and thereby limit GLOBAL WARMING. Environmentalists look to such straightforward tactics as planting trees and curbing DEFORESTATION. But scientists also are exploring more radical strategies, including the possibility of injecting carbon deep underground or into the oceans.

Storing carbon may be a politically easier way to combat global warming than paring back carbon dioxide emissions and risking economic harm. Accordingly, the KYOTO PROTOCOL on global warming allows nations to engage in a type of EMISSIONS TRADING, in which industrialized countries can avoid having to reduce their emissions by buying credits from developing countries with vast forests that absorb carbon. However, it is unclear whether sequestration could offset the more than 6 billion tons of carbon dioxide that people emit yearly into the atmosphere.

Skeptics warn that using new technology to try to store carbon could be unreasonably expensive and pose new threats to the environment. Nevertheless, the U.S. DEPARTMENT OF ENERGY spent about $30 million in 2000 to study carbon sequestration.

Carbon sinks

Carbon sinks, such as oceans and forests, are natural storage deposits for carbon. By removing carbon from the atmosphere for long periods of time, they help prevent a buildup of CARBON DIOXIDE. Environmentalists hope that fostering carbon sinks can help offset carbon dioxide emissions and thereby stop GLOBAL WARMING.

Carter, Jimmy

In the first two years of his 1977–1981 administration, Jimmy Carter built a reputation as one of the most stalwart environmentalists ever to occupy the White House. He quickly moved to strengthen clean air and clean water laws and helped win passage of bills to restrict strip mining and control oil drilling on the outer continental shelf. Perhaps his most lasting environmental achievement was the protection of millions of acres of Alaskan wilderness. When Congress failed to pass an Alaskan lands bill in 1978, Carter used his authority to designate 56 million acres as national monuments, thereby forestalling development and earning praise from environmentalists as "the greatest conservation president of all time." Eventually, Carter won passage of the ALASKA NATIONAL INTEREST LANDS CONSERVATION ACT, a landmark bill that preserved more than 100 million acres. He also spurred Congress to consider proposals to safely dispose of NUCLEAR WASTE and pressed lawmakers in 1980 to pass far-reaching SUPERFUND legislation to clean up HAZARDOUS WASTE.

Carter was less successful when he tried to eliminate funding for Western water projects, which drew criticism for being environmentally destructive and overly costly. The president succeeded in ending or modifying some of the proposed projects, but he disappointed environmentalists by allowing other projects to go forward. In 1979, he re-

Initially praised by environmentalists for strengthening clean air and clean water laws and fighting to preserve more than one hundred million acres of Alaskan wilderness, Jimmy Carter drew criticism in his last two years of office for backing environmentally harmful energy measures. Source: The White House

luctantly signed legislation exempting construction of the Tellico Dam in Tennessee from the EN-DANGERED SPECIES ACT.

Despite his concern about the environment—the president was an avid fisherman with a strong appreciation of nature—Carter repeatedly clashed with environmentalists during his last two years of office. The rupture began in 1979, when Carter pushed for greater use of coal to wean the nation away from its dependence on foreign oil. Environmentalists warned that coal-burning power plants would emit tons of sulfur dioxide and exacerbate problems with ACID RAIN. Carter also supported a massive government investment to develop synthetic fuels, even though environmentalists feared that the plan would impose impossible demands on water supplies in the arid West and lead to more strip mining and AIR POLLUTION.

CFCs

Chlorofluorocarbons, often abbreviated as CFCs, are well-known chemicals such as freon that are used as coolants for refrigeration and air conditioning, as well as for insulation, solvents, and aerosol propellants. When these chemicals drift into the upper atmosphere, their chlorine components destroy ozone, a natural gas. This is a potentially catastrophic problem, since the ozone layer filters out most of the sun's harmful ultraviolet rays and protects life on Earth from being irradiated. CFCs also are believed to trap heat and contribute to GLOBAL WARMING. (CFCs, it should be noted, were developed in the 1920s as environmentally benign chemicals that could replace toxic refrigerants such as ammonia and sulfur dioxide.)

Research in the mid-1970s that linked CFCs to ozone destruction provoked an unusually quick government response. In 1977, Congress authorized the ENVIRONMENTAL PROTECTION AGENCY to regulate the chemicals, which led to a ban on CFCs from domestic aerosol products one year later. Alarmed at the discovery of an ozone hole over antarctica, the United States and more than 160 other nations agreed to gradually phase out CFCs under the 1987 MONTREAL PROTOCOL ON SUBSTANCES THAT DEPLETE THE OZONE LAYER, one of the most successful environmental agreements ever negotiated. Subsequent treaties imposed more stringent timelines for the phase-out of CFCs and other ozone-destroying chemicals.

At the time the Montreal Protocol was negotiated, annual world production of CFCs was close to 2 billion tons, of which the United States produced about 30 percent. Since the late 1980s, global consumption of CFCs and other ozone-destroying substances has dropped by more than 70 percent.

Most industrialized countries met the protocol's requirement of ceasing production at the end of 1995. However, a booming black market in CFCs and halons, which are firefighting chemicals that also contribute to ozone depletion, has emerged in many countries. As a result, it is uncertain whether developing countries, which remain heavily dependent on the chemicals, will meet the Montreal Protocol's requirement to phase out all production by 2010.

Because CFCs persist in the environment for some time, scientists warn that atmospheric levels will continue to rise for a number of years before leveling off and declining. The ozone layer is expected to recover, at least partially, by about 2050. (See OZONE DEPLETION.)

Chafee, John H.

John H. Chafee, a four-term Republican senator from Rhode Island, was an influential voice for the environment at a time when many of his GOP colleagues tended to side with industry in attempts to scale back regulations. He chaired the SENATE ENVIRONMENT AND PUBLIC WORKS COMMITTEE from 1995 until his death from heart failure in 1999. His son, Lincoln, replaced him in the Senate (but not as committee chairman).

First elected in 1976, Chafee belonged to a dwindling number of moderates in an era of increasing partisanship. A former marine and descendent of one of five families who originally settled Rhode Island, the patrician Chafee earned a lifetime 70 percent score from the League of Conservation Voters for his steadfast support of conservation issues. He played a key role in strengthening the SAFE DRINKING WATER ACT and supported precedent-setting provisions in the 1991 INTER-MODAL SURFACE TRANSPORTATION EFFICIENCY ACT to protect the environment and promote alternatives to highway building. After Republicans took control of Congress in 1995, Chafee warded off conservative attempts to pare back water-quality and other environmental regulations.

Chafee's views provoked well-publicized conflicts with other Republicans. He was ousted from the chairmanship of the Senate Republican Conference in 1990, the number three position in the GOP leadership, and faced rumblings in the late 1990s that he could lose his chairmanship of the Environment and Public Works Committee as well. But the unassuming Chafee kept steering an independent course. A moderate who occasionally drew criticism from environmentalists as well as industry, Chafee sided with conservatives on some major environmental issues, such as collaborating on a proposed GOP rewrite of the Endangered Species Act and opposing stringent clean air regulations that the Clinton administration proposed in 1997. But he also backed the controversial 1997 KYOTO PROTOCOL, warning that "the consequences are mammoth if we do nothing."

Just one month before his death, Chafee was presented with the League of Conservation Voters' 1999 Lifetime Achievement Award.

Chernobyl

See THREE-MILE ISLAND.

Citizen lawsuits

Citizen lawsuits are a driving force in environmental protection. Major environmental laws, including the CLEAN AIR ACT, CLEAN WATER ACT, ENDANGERED SPECIES ACT, RESOURCE CONSERVATION AND RECOVERY ACT, and the SUPERFUND hazardous waste law grant citizens standing to sue federal agencies that fail to impose required regulations. Many laws also allow citizens to file suits against polluters and require federal and state agencies to solicit public input when drafting regulations.

However, businesses may file countersuits, often called strategic lawsuits against political participation (SLAPPs). Although SLAPPs often are thrown out by courts, they can discourage citizen lawsuits because of the amount of time and money needed for legal defense.

Lawsuits by environmental groups and other organizations have played an integral role in the promulgation of landmark regulations, from the 1972 federal ban on DDT to the 1997 clean air standards for ozone and PARTICULATE MATTER. Conservationists scored their first big legal victory in 1965, when a federal appellate court blocked construction of a power plant on New York's Storm King Mountain in *Hudson Preservation Conference v. Federal Power.* Subsequent court decisions mandated clean air standards for pristine areas, restricted CLEARCUTTING, blocked development that could destroy endangered species habitat, broadened WETLANDS and clean water protections, tightened restrictions on the use of PESTICIDES, and prevented new road construction in heavily polluted cities. However, environmentalists cannot count on consistent court support. Polluters have sued the ENVIRONMENTAL PROTECTION AGENCY repeatedly for exceeding its authority, and developers have scored legal victories against the U.S. ARMY CORPS OF ENGINEERS and state regulators over restrictions on new building.

Many of the environmental court battles center on the legal issue of standing—that is, the degree to which the citizens filing the lawsuit must show personal injury as well as harm to the environment. In the 1970s, when the ENVIRONMENTAL MOVEMENT enjoyed considerable political support, federal judges generally used broad criteria for standing. But the tide gradually turned because of increasingly sophisticated industry legal tactics (businesses in the 1970s began to create nonprofit groups patterned after successful environmental and consumer legal foundations) and a more conservative judiciary. In the 1980s, the administration of RONALD REAGAN was reluctant to enforce regulations, so environmental groups turned to filing lawsuits directly against polluters. However, the environmentalists suffered a major setback when the Chesapeake Bay Foundation and the Natural Resources Defense Council tried to sue Gwaltney of Smithfield, Ltd. for violating the Clean Water Act by repeatedly discharging more pollutants than allowed under the company's permit. Gwaltney contended that the suit should be dismissed because the last recorded violation had occurred weeks before the suit was filed. The Supreme Court agreed, ruling that citizens could sue only if a violation was ongoing.

Environmentalists lost another major case in 1992, when the Supreme Court ruled in *Manuel Lujan v. Defenders of Wildlife* that citizens cannot sue the government solely on behalf of flora or fauna, but rather must demonstrate harm to themselves. But environmentalists scored a stunning victory in 2000. In *Friends of the Earth v. Laidlaw Environmental Services,* the Supreme Court ruled that an environmental group could file a lawsuit

based on the sworn testimony of individuals who said they could no longer enjoy South Carolina's North Tyger River because of pollution. Furthermore, the court declined to dismiss the case even though Laidlaw began complying with environmental regulations (and even closed the offending HAZARDOUS WASTE facility) after the suit was filed. Industry lawyers warned that the ruling could open the floodgates to numerous citizen suits.

Clean Air Act

One of the nation's landmark environmental laws, the Clean Air Act (PL 91-604) forms the basis for federal and state regulations to reduce AIR POLLUTION. The act is designed to improve air quality in areas with high levels of pollutants and prevent significant deterioration in other areas. Far-reaching and complex, the 1970 law has generated controversy almost continuously for three decades. Although the Clean Air Act has succeeded in improving the nation's air quality, the ENVIRONMENTAL PROTECTION AGENCY (EPA) reported in 1998 that more than 130 million Americans lived in counties that still failed to comply with at least one air pollution standard.

The sweeping act, extensively revised in 1990, governs emissions from thousands of area, STATIONARY, and MOBILE SOURCES ranging from factories to consumer products. It requires the EPA to set NATIONAL AMBIENT AIR QUALITY STANDARDS for common pollutants such as carbon monoxide, sulfur dioxide, and LEAD. It imposes two types of standards: Primary standards protect human health (with an added margin of safety for infants, the elderly, and other vulnerable people), and secondary standards protect buildings, crops, visibility, wildlife, and anything else that may affect public welfare. The EPA also regulates nearly 200 HAZ-ARDOUS AIR POLLUTANTS. It oversees the permitting of stationary sources (such as industrial plants) and sets emission standards for automobiles and light trucks. States are responsible for their own air quality, and they must develop STATE IMPLEMENTATION PLANS to implement the federal standards.

From its inception, the Clean Air Act has sparked numerous legal and judicial battles. Few people argue against the value of clean air, but policymakers repeatedly have pushed back the law's deadlines because of concerns over the possibility of lost jobs and increased costs to consumers and industry. Affected industries criticize the COM-MAND-AND-CONTROL approach of the law, which sets fixed requirements regardless of costs. They say the regulations are saddling them with considerable costs, which averaged about $25 billion to $35 billion yearly during the 1970s and 1980s. Conservative critics question whether regulators are basing their decisions on SOUND SCIENCE and promulgating rules that will result in appreciable air quality gains. Environmentalists contend that the act needs to address underlying social and eco-

nomic issues that lead to air pollution, such as the distance that most Americans drive to work.

Such criticism aside, the Clean Air Act in many respects has been a signal success. Concentrations of five CRITERIA AIR POLLUTANTS regulated under the act—carbon monoxide, ground-level ozone, lead, PARTICULATE MATTER, and sulfur dioxide—have declined significantly. Only nitrogen oxide has increased. (For emissions data on major air pollutants, see table.) Clear blue skies have returned to industrial cities in the Midwest and elsewhere. One of the most striking illustrations of the law's success is that, in the 27 years following its enactment, the nation's population increased 31 percent and vehicle miles more than doubled, yet total emissions of the six criteria pollutants decreased by about one-third. Although environmentalists acknowledge the costs of the regulation, they say the benefits are more significant. The EPA released a report in 1997 claiming that the law produced health and environmental benefits from 1970 to 1990 that were worth somewhere in the range of $6 trillion to $50 trillion. By comparison, the costs of the regulations during that period were just $523 billion. Without the law, 205,000 Americans would have died prematurely and millions of others would

Emissions of Major Air Pollutants, 1940–1998 (thousand short tons)[a]

	1940	1950	1960	1970	1980	1990	1996	1998
Lead	NA	NA	NA	220,869	74,153	4,975	3,899	3,973
Sulfur dioxide	19,952	22,357	22,227	31,161	25,905	23,660	19,121	19,647
Nitrogen oxides	7,374	10,093	14,140	20,928	24,384	24,049	24,676	24,454
Carbon monoxide	93,616	102,609	109,745	129,444	117,434	98,523	95,480	89,455
Volatile organic compounds	17,161	20,936	24,459	30,982	26,336	20,936	18,736	17,917
Directly emitted particulate matter	15,957	17,133	15,558	13,042	7,119	29,962	33,041	34,741

Source: U.S. Environmental Protection Agency, *National Air Pollutant Emission Trends, 1900–1998*, Tables 3-1 through 3-5 and Table 3-7 (Washington, D.C.: EPA, 1999), 3-9–3-13, 3-15.

Notes: NA = not available.

[a]Figures are in thousands of short tons for all pollutants except lead, for which figures are in short tons.

have suffered from such diseases as asthma, bronchitis, and heart disease, the agency contended.

The other side of the picture is that dozens of counties across the country, especially in California and industrialized sections of the Northeast and Midwest, exceed allowable levels of ground-level ozone, more commonly known as SMOG. HAZE is so pervasive that it obscures views in NATIONAL PARKS. Pollution takes a significant toll on both human health and the economy. Studies in the 1990s indicated that mortality rates increase in the most polluted cities, with residents more likely to suffer from heart attacks, lung cancer, and respiratory problems. By weakening plants, excessive amounts of ground-level ozone cause up to $2 billion in crop losses yearly, and other pollutants erode buildings and monuments.

Congress substantially amended the Clean Air Act in 1990, tightening motor vehicle and industrial emission requirements and imposing new restrictions on coal-burning utilities to address the problem of ACID RAIN. At the same time, Congress tried to assuage industry concerns by creating an innovative EMISSIONS TRADING plan that allows companies to buy and sell pollution allowances. The amendments succeeded in dramatically cutting sulfur dioxide emissions at a comparatively low cost. In addition, more than half of the metropolitan areas that were out of compliance with ozone standards in 1990 were able to meet the standards by 2000.

Nevertheless, conflicts over the law remain intense. The fundamental issue is how the government can bring heavily polluted urban areas into compliance to safeguard the public welfare without endangering economic growth or treading on the needs of motorists. In addition to revising standards on motor vehicles and industrial facilities, regulators face disputes over clean-burning oxygenated gasoline and local highway plans that may not conform to clean air goals. Regional disputes complicate the matter. Officials in some NONATTAINMENT AREAS blame their poor air quality on polluters beyond their jurisdictional boundaries. Much of the air pollution in the Northeast, for example, is caused by coal-burning power plant emissions that are blown east from the Ohio River Valley.

In the early and mid-1990s, cost concerns and other considerations led the EPA to back off from strict auto emissions testing requirements and a controversial program aimed at reducing commuting in areas with exceptionally high ozone levels. But in 1997, EPA administrator CAROL BROWNER set off a political firestorm by imposing stringent new regulations. Her plan, endorsed somewhat hesitantly by President BILL CLINTON, sought to tighten existing environmental regulations for ozone, a main component of smog, and create an additional standard for particulate matter, tiny airborne particles of soot produced by sources such as coal-fired power plants and diesel engines. Browner defended the new standards, which were spurred in part by a lawsuit by the American Lung Association, as necessary to protect asthmatics, children, and the elderly.

But the new rules sparked a furor in Congress. Midwestern and oil-state Democrats joined the Republican opposition because their home-state power plants and refineries stood to lose billions of dollars. In contrast, many northeastern Republicans who lived downwind from polluting facilities joined Democrats in hailing the rules. With lawmakers split, congressional opponents of new regulations failed to block them from taking effect. Industry won at least a temporary victory in the courts, however, when a federal appeals court in 1999 blocked the implementation of the new standards and cited the EPA for "an unconstitutional delegation of legislative power." The EPA appealed the landmark case, *American Trucking Associations v. EPA,* to the Supreme Court, which may issue a ruling in 2001.

Despite such criticism, the Clinton administration in its final years continued to press for improved air quality. It filed lawsuits against seven large electric companies in the Midwest and South, accusing them of modernizing their generating plants without modernizing their pollution controls as required by the Clean Air Act. The administration also announced TIER 2 STANDARDS in 1999 that require oil companies to produce cleaning gasoline and impose stringent emission standards for SPORT UTILITY VEHICLES.

History

Congressional air quality measures date back to 1955, when lawmakers passed a bill (PL 84-159) authorizing $5 million for the Public Health Service to conduct air pollution research. Faced with studies linking air pollution to sickness and even death, Congress passed the Clean Air Act of 1963 (PL 88-206), boosting funding for research and enabling state and local officials, as well as the federal government, to curb emissions of air pollutants. Lawmakers authorized emissions standards two years later. The 1967 Air Quality Act (PL 90-148) added additional antipollution measures, including the establishment of metropolitan AIR QUALITY REGIONS. By 1970, however, no state had issued standards for any pollutant, and only a few air quality regions had been created.

Concerned that these laws would lead to a patchwork system in which regulated industries would relocate to the most lenient jurisdictions, President RICHARD NIXON called for amendments to the Air Quality Act to establish national air quality standards. Driven by a rising tide of support for environmental action—1970 was the year of the first EARTH DAY rallies—Congress overcame objections from automakers and other businesses to pass a sweeping new version of the Clean Air Act.

One of the first in a series of landmark environmental laws, the measure set an ambitious deadline of five years to bring all areas of the country into compliance with national ambient air quality standards. It put the newly created EPA in charge of promulgating primary standards to specify the minimum air quality necessary to protect public health. States were given the responsibility of devising plans for secondary standards, which promote public welfare. The EPA administrator had the authority to specify and set emission standards for hazardous air pollutants—those having a proven relationship to increased human death rates or serious illness. Factories, power plants, and other stationary sources of air pollution had to comply with the state plans by 1975 and were allowed a two-year extension if needed.

The law mandated a 90 percent reduction in motor vehicle emissions of CARBON DIOXIDE and hydrocarbons over the five-year period, with a similar cut in nitrogen oxides by 1976. However, the EPA administrator could grant automakers a one-year extension. The law authorized the inspection of cars, trucks, and other modes of transportation to ensure compliance with the emission standards. Anyone who removed automobile pollution-control devices could face a $10,000 fine.

To give the law teeth, Congress authorized the EPA to seek injunctions to curtail emissions deemed harmful to human health. It also allowed citizens to sue the agency for failure to enforce the law and to sue polluters for violating the standards. Each willful violation of the law was punishable by a fine of up to $25,000 a day and up to a year in prison. The EPA also had considerable power to impose sanctions on states, such as banning the construction of large new pollution sources or cutting off federal highway funds.

Despite the law's deadlines and enforcement provisions, both stationary and mobile pollution sources failed to comply with the new standards. As early as 1973, EPA administrator WILLIAM D. RUCKELSHAUS granted the auto industry an extension to meet the law's strict emission standards. Ruckelshaus's action set a pattern that persists to the present: Government officials in both the White House and Congress often scale back air-quality requirements in the face of industry protests, state official objections, and such distractions as gas shortages.

In 1977, Congress passed a significant rewrite of the Clean Air Act that delayed emission standards for automobiles and extended the deadline for cities to meet national air quality standards. At the same time, lawmakers tightened the law by creating the PREVENTION OF SIGNIFICANT DETERIORA-TION program, which was intended to protect relatively clean areas from becoming polluted. The program imposed particularly stringent standards on pristine areas, such as national parks and wilderness areas.

During the administration of RONALD REAGAN, affected industries won a dilution of air-quality regulations. The government relaxed some pollution standards, such as doubling allowable tailpipe emissions. By 1990, the nation was making uneven progress in the battle against air pollution. Some pollutants, such as particulates and sulfur dioxide, had declined because of the installation of scrubbers in factory smokestacks. (Scrubbers are devices that use sprays or dry processes to trap pollutants.) But most urban areas remained in violation of air-quality standards for ozone, largely because of

emissions from industrial facilities, chemical plants, and motor vehicles, and for carbon monoxide, emitted primarily by automobiles. The EPA drew criticism for its reluctance to sanction states. Furthermore, the agency was moving so slowly to limit industrial emissions of air toxics such as benzene that, by 1990, it had brought just 7 of some 275 industrial air toxics under federal regulation.

Deeply divided along ideological and regional lines, lawmakers appeared nearly incapable of strengthening the Clean Air Act. House Energy and Commerce Committee Chairman JOHN DINGELL (D-Mich.) used his position to stall any bills that would impose tough new standards on Detroit automakers, and Sen. Robert C. Byrd (D-W.Va.), who served as Democratic leader until taking over the Appropriations Committee in 1989, blocked actions that could have thrown coal miners out of work. While northeastern lawmakers demanded action on sulfur dioxide and nitrogen oxide emissions to reduce the acid rain that was damaging their lakes and streams, midwesterners balked because of concerns that their constituents would have to pay for the cost of refitting aging power plants with expensive antipollution equipment.

1990 Amendments

President GEORGE BUSH broke the logjam by proposing an innovative solution in 1989. Rather than impose the costs of new regulations on any region of the country, he suggested an emissions trading program that would allow power plants to trade pollution allowances across the nation. That way, utilities that found it too costly to retrofit aging coal-fired plants could instead buy pollution allowances from utilities that were able to meet pollution guidelines.

The resulting 1990 amendments to the Clean Air Act left the basic law intact but created new programs to combat acid rain, OZONE DEPLETION, and hazardous air pollutants. Congress also imposed more elaborate standards to reduce levels of the major pollutants regulated under the original act. Lawmakers were spurred in part by air pollution research in the 1980s indicating that acid rain was destroying life in many lakes and streams and that chlorofluorocarbons (CFCS) were depleting the ozone level high in the atmosphere.

Under the 1990 amendments, cities and towns face a series of staggered deadlines to meet the federal ozone standard. Marginal areas had until 1993 to achieve the standard, whereas the most extreme area (Los Angeles) has until 2010. The law required the nation's smoggiest cities to begin selling reformulated gasoline in 1995. Utilities had to limit their overall sulfur dioxide emissions to 10 million tons by 2000. The amendments gradually phased in the regulation of toxic pollutants, with such major sources as chemical plants and oil refineries having until 2003 to apply BEST AVAILABLE CONTROL TECHNOLOGY to reduce emissions. Other highlights of the bill included provisions dealing with acid rain, ozone depletion, and air toxics.

ACID RAIN. Proposals to reduce acid rain had foundered for years because of divisions between midwestern lawmakers, who represented areas where acid-causing pollutants rose from towering smokestacks, and northeastern lawmakers, who represented areas where acid rain fell on trees, mountains, and streams. However, Bush was able to break the logjam by proposing an innovative market-based system of pollution allowances that could be granted to utilities that limited sulfur dioxide emissions. The legislation mandates plants to gradually phase in antipollution controls to reduce sulfur dioxide and nitrogen oxide emissions. It allows affected industries to earn emission credits for reducing their sulfur dioxide emissions below the minimum allowable levels, usually by installing smokestack scrubbers. The plants can later sell these credits to other businesses that have failed to curb their emissions, which helps to defray the cost of the scrubbers.

OZONE DEPLETION. The amendments targeted CFCs and other compounds used as refrigerants and solvents, which had been found to deplete stratospheric ozone. The legislation required industries to find alternative chemicals, enabling the United States to comply with the 1987 MONTREAL PROTOCOL ON SUBSTANCES THAT DEPLETE THE OZONE LAYER.

AIR TOXICS. Plants that emit any of 189 substances and compounds considered to be hazardous air pollutants have to cut those emissions to the average level of the cleanest 12 percent of similar facilities. The amendments require plants to shut down if they still pose more than a one-in-ten-thousand risk of cancer to nearby residents in 2003, after the best available technology is installed. Steel industry coke ovens have until 2020 to meet the standards, as long as they fulfill certain interim conditions.

MOBILE SOURCES. The amendments established more than 90 new emission standards for cars and trucks. The standards included significant reductions in tailpipe emissions of hydrocarbons and nitrogen oxides in all new cars by 1996 and pollution control devices with a 10-year, 100,000-mile warranty in all new cars beginning in 1998. Car manufacturers had to produce a fleet of experimental cars in Southern California in 1996 that met especially strict emission standards. In addition, petroleum companies had to produce cleaner-burning fuel beginning in 1992. (See also WINDBLOWN POLLUTION.)

Clean coal

Under a program that Congress launched in 1985 to reduce ACID RAIN and other forms of AIR POLLUTION, the U.S. DEPARTMENT OF ENERGY has engaged in demonstration projects on a cost-share basis with industry to develop clean coal technologies. The projects, which cost the government about $2 billion from the mid-1980s to the late 1990s, seek to develop cost-effective ways to burn coal without harming the environment. Clean coal technologies include using scrubbers to reduce sulfur dioxide and other emissions, as well as applying biological or chemical agents to clean coal before burning. Without the use of such technologies, coal may emit more pollutants than other FOSSIL FUELS and contribute significantly to GLOBAL WARMING. The issue of clean coal is important because the United States has enough coal to last for 200 years or more, meaning that it could greatly reduce its dependence on imported oil if it can burn coal without severely harming air quality. Clean coal technology also could relieve air pollution problems in developing countries such as China that rely heavily on coal-burning electric plants.

Clean Water Act

The Clean Water Act is the primary federal law that governs the discharge of pollutants into the nation's waterways, including lakes, rivers, aquifers, and coastal areas. The law, consisting of the 1972 FEDERAL WATER POLLUTION CONTROL ACT and subsequent amendments, is credited with reducing the amount of polluted waterways by close to half, slowing the destruction of WETLANDS, and funding the construction of sewage treatment plants. However, it is highly controversial because it imposes enormous costs on affected industries and taxpayers while falling well short of the goals outlined in the 1972 legislation. In recent years, Congress has been at odds over whether to impose more stringent—and expensive—controls on NONPOINT SOURCE POLLUTION, such as pollutants on streets and fields that wash off into waterways.

The Clean Water Act consists of two general parts. The more complex part regulates pollution discharges into waterways with the goal of making surface waters "fishable and swimmable." To that end, the ENVIRONMENTAL PROTECTION AGENCY (EPA) sets water-quality standards for all contaminants in surface waters, including organic substances such as phosphorus and bacteria as well as such toxins as cyanide and heavy metals. Industries must treat discharges, and municipal waste treatment plants must provide SECONDARY TREATMENT to remove most pollutants. In addition, anyone who discharges pollutants directly into surface water must obtain a permit. Not all Clean Water Act programs are administered by the EPA. The U.S. ARMY CORPS OF ENGINEERS issues permits for wetlands development, the U.S. DEPARTMENT OF AGRICULTURE tries to minimize runoff from farms, and the NATIONAL OCEANIC AND ATMOSPHERIC ADMINISTRATION helps protect coastal waters.

The other part of the law is the federal government's program of grants to help cities build wastewater treatment plants. From 1972 to 2000, the government provided $69 billion for such plants, and state and local governments spent an additional $25 billion or more, according to a Congressional Research Service analysis. Officials warn, however, that far more money is needed. In 1996, the EPA released a report projecting demands for an additional $139.5 billion in projects over the next twenty years, largely because of the need to overhaul aging sewage systems.

More than most environmental laws, the Clean Water Act from its inception has provoked furious debate over how much the nation should spend to reduce pollution problems. Even many political moderates who supported other environmental laws initially opposed the Clean Water Act because of the billions of dollars in private and public funds needed to implement it. To enact the law in 1972, congressional Democrats had to override a veto by President RICHARD NIXON, who normally favored environmental regulations. In 1987, Congress again overrode a presidential veto, this time by RONALD REAGAN, to authorize grants to help pay for sewage systems and require the EPA to impose stringent standards. New battles erupted when Republicans took control of Congress in 1995 and immediately focused much of their energies on a politically risky attempt to scale back the bill. They suffered a stinging defeat, with Democrats deriding their legislation as a "dirty water" bill and President BILL CLINTON accusing them of waging a "war on the environment."

Mixed Results

Reflecting these political divisions, the Clean Water Act has been a success in some ways and a failure in others. In general, the act has done a better job reducing conventional pollutants, such as suspended solids, bacteria, and nutrients, than in controlling discharges of toxic substances such as MERCURY, LEAD, and PESTICIDES. Even critics concede that the Clean Water Act notably reduced contamination in the nation's waterways at a time of surging population and development. Largely be-

cause of upgraded sewage treatment and requirements that industries remove billions of pounds of pollutants yearly, federal and state estimates in the late 1990s indicated that 60 to 70 percent of monitored water was safe for such activities as fishing and swimming. This percentage compared favorably with 30 to 40 percent in 1972. Whereas the Potomac River once carried raw sewage through Washington, D.C., residents now use the waterway for fishing, boating, and even swimming. Similarly, formerly contaminated bodies of water such as Cleveland's Cuyahoga River, the GREAT LAKES, and Oregon's Willamette River now support a multibillion-dollar recreational industry. The law also is credited with reducing annual wetland loss by about 75 percent and with slowing the amount of sediment and nutrients from soil that is swept into waterways.

On the other hand, the Clean Water Act has fallen so far short of its original goal—to make U.S. waters safe for both people and aquatic life by 1983 and eliminate all pollutant discharges into the waters by 1985—that environmentalists have filed a number of lawsuits against the EPA to require more stringent enforcement. Federal and state officials consistently have failed to meet deadlines for imposing new standards. Even though surface waters are significantly cleaner, up to 40 percent of rivers and lakes in the late 1990s remained so polluted that wildlife was affected or activities such as swimming and fishing were banned, and many more were threatened by growing development. Environmentalists warn that the pollution problem may be even worse than indicated by such statistics, because government estimates are based on state surveys that examine only a portion of the water bodies and test for a limited number of pollutants. Environmentalists also are concerned by highly publicized outbreaks of dangerous microorganisms, such as CRYPTOSPORIDIUM and PFIESTERIA.

Signs began emerging in the late 1990s that, despite the progress of the past quarter-century, some problems could be getting worse. The number of water-related health advisories began rising each year, and coastal states regularly reported dangerous levels of pollution-related bacteria. With officials concerned about the effects of eating fish contaminated by mercury, DDT, DIOXIN, and other toxins, the Congressional Research Service reported in 2000 that forty-seven states had imposed some type of fish consumption advisory and one-third of shellfishing beds were closed or restricted. Catastrophic environmental problems included a seven-thousand-square-mile dead zone in the Gulf of Mexico near Louisiana that scientists believe was caused by runoff from farming activities inland along the Mississippi River. In addition, municipal sewers across the country overflowed thousands of times yearly, releasing pathogens into waterways and beach areas.

Critics blame a number of factors for the uneven results: The EPA is slow in issuing the guidance and assistance needed to reduce pollution; states fail to undertake innovative antipollution initiatives; environmentalists refuse to sanction a more flexible approach; and Congress balks over providing adequate funding for antipollution programs. Many critics fault the Clean Water Act as a highly prescriptive COMMAND-AND-CONTROL law that imposes costly and unrealistic mandates. Furthermore, the law's traditional focus on cleaning up easily monitored POINT SOURCES, such as factories and wastewater treatment plants, does limited good when some of the worst water-quality problems have been caused by nonpoint source pollution, such as runoff from agricultural, industrial, and residential activities. Congress has been unable

to reform the law. Democrats in the early 1990s failed to win passage of amendments to crack down on nonpoint source pollution, and Republicans who tried to make the law more flexible in the mid-1990s found themselves stalemated by environmentalists.

On the law's twenty-fifth anniversary in 1997, the Clinton administration announced a far-ranging clean-water initiative designed to boost protection for watersheds and wetlands and to place a greater emphasis on controlling nonpoint source pollution. Spurred by numerous environmental lawsuits, the EPA in 1998 unveiled a plan to require permits and inspections of large farms in an effort to keep MANURE out of waterways. The following year, President Clinton announced that his administration would begin enforcing Clean Water Act provisions known as TOTAL MAXIMUM DAILY LOADS. Under this highly controversial proposal, states would have to inventory their rivers and lakes, identify the worst cases, and reduce the amount of pollution flowing into them by allocating pollution reductions among various classes of polluters, such as farms, industrial plants, and cities. "This is the last chapter in how we get to fishable, swimmable waters for the people of this country," said EPA administrator CAROL BROWNER. However, the ambitious plan provoked sharp criticism from conservative lawmakers, industry representatives, and even state officials. They warned that it would be highly expensive and difficult to administer, and it could provoke a desperate fight for survival between factories, farmers, and others vying for the right to continue to discharge pollutants within the same watershed.

History

The United States took the first step toward protecting surface water from pollution with the

Rivers and Harbors Act in 1899. Passed amid growing recognition of the link between contaminated water and diseases such as cholera, the pioneering law prohibited the discharge of refuse into navigable waters. In 1948, Congress passed the Federal Water Pollution Control Act, which set up a system to regulate polluters such as factories and sewage treatment plants, requiring them to pretreat their effluents to reduce pollution.

The law proved inadequate to protect water quality at a time of increased industrialization and growing population. Even though the government spent billions of dollars on treatment facilities in the two decades following the Federal Water Pollution Control Act, some fourteen hundred U.S. communities and hundreds of industrial plants were continuing to dump untreated waste into waters in the early 1970s. Water quality throughout the nation deteriorated so severely that the Cuyahoga River in Cleveland caught fire in 1969, officials found arsenic in the Kansas River, Ohio banned commercial fishing in Lake Erie, and environmentalists warned that industrial pollutants in Lake Superior were killing millions of fish. A series of offshore oil spills spurred passage of the Water Quality Improvement Act in 1970 to authorize cleanups of major spills. But President Nixon and congressional Democrats disagreed over more-comprehensive clean water legislation because of the high price tag—an estimated $10 billion for sewage treatment plants and more than triple that amount for industrial plant facilities.

With polls showing a majority of Americans willing to pay more in taxes to finance federal pollution control programs, Congress in 1972 passed comprehensive amendments to the Federal Water Pollution Control Act (PL 92-500). The legislation, now known as the Clean Water Act, authorized $24.7 billion over three years—the most expensive price tag for any environmental law up to that time. Nixon, who had proposed a $6 billion cleanup program, called the bill "staggering, budget-wrecking." He vetoed it, but Congress overrode the veto. In a historic constitutional showdown, Nixon then claimed the authority to impound most of the money in the law in order to cut government spending. But he was overruled in federal court, and the EPA began distributing state grants in 1973.

The new law directed the EPA to set national water quality standards and to restrict toxic discharges to ensure "an ample margin of safety." Publicly owned treatment works were to use secondary treatment to remove 85 percent of pollutants by 1977 and use the best practicable technology by 1983. To that end, Congress authorized more than $18 billion in state grants for the construction of waste treatment plants. In addition, industrial polluters had to treat effluent with the "best-available technology economically achievable" by 1983, after meeting an interim standard of using "the best practicable control technology" by 1977. Anyone discharging pollution into a waterway had to obtain a discharge permit. SECTION 404 of the law required the U.S. Army Corps of Engineers to issue permits for dredge and fill operations in waters and wetlands.

Overall, the law set the goal of entirely eliminating pollutant discharges into U.S. waters by 1985. Its interim goal was to make water quality safe for fish, shellfish, wildlife, and recreation by July 1, 1983.

Continuing Battles

Congress addressed the law again in 1977. An estimated 80 to 90 percent of the nation's industries had successfully met the deadline for best practicable control technology. Businesses argued forcefully for a postponement of the 1983 dead-line, contending that the equipment needed to meet the best available technology standard would cost $60 billion and result in little improvement in water quality. Lawmakers agreed to ease the re-quirement for conventional pollutants. But they ratified a court-approved settlement agreement that had been reached by environmentalists and the EPA in 1976 to impose strict standards on six-ty-five toxic chemicals and classes of chemicals re-ferred to as priority pollutants.

Congress returned to the fray in 1987, overrid-ing a veto by Reagan to reauthorize the law and provide $20 billion in grants for sewage treatment facilities and other pollution control programs. The legislation expanded programs to control nonpoint source pollution, requiring every state to submit a plan to the EPA on reducing such pollu-tion. It strengthened efforts to clean up the Great Lakes and the Chesapeake Bay, and it established a National Estuary Program for environmental man-agement of the nation's estuaries. Congress also gave Native American tribes equal standing with states on water-quality issues, which spurred tribal attempts to force cities to clean up discharges in rivers that flow through reservations.

In addition, Congress eliminated the law's grant program in 1987, replacing it with a state revolving loan fund. Under the new system, the federal gov-ernment provided seed money to states, which in turn made low-interest loans to local communities to help build or refurbish sewage treatment plants. Lawmakers failed to reauthorize the revolving loan fund after it expired in 1994, but appropriators continued to provide money for it.

Leaders in the Democratic-controlled Congress of the early 1990s unsuccessfully tried to reautho-rize the law to emphasize nonpoint source pollu-tion and wetlands protection while giving more flexibility to landowners and state officials. Their efforts ended in stalemate, with farmers and PRI-VATE PROPERTY RIGHTS advocates increasingly crit-ical of the law's permitting requirements.

For Republicans, who gained control of Con-gress in 1995, rewriting the Clean Water Act be-came a top environmental priority. The House passed a bill to allow officials to waive a number of regulatory requirements for point source pollution and to allow states to use a voluntary incentive sys-tem to ease nonpoint source pollution. The legisla-tion also would have required RISK ASSESSMENT and COST-BENEFIT ANALYSIS for many water pollu-tion regulations, relaxed wetlands regulations, and repealed the requirement that industrial facilities and municipalities obtain federal permits to dis-charge polluted stormwater into waterways.

Advocates said that the bill would achieve the goals of the Clean Water Act at a lower cost while providing REGULATORY RELIEF. But opponents dubbed the bill "the dirty water act" and used im-passioned rhetoric to club conservative Republi-cans for opening the door to more pollution. Sen. JOHN H. CHAFEE, R-R.I., refused to take up the measure. The stinging legislative defeat represent-ed a major political turning point. Fearing retribu-tion at the polls, conservatives subsequently backed away from attempts to significantly scale back the nation's environmental laws, while Demo-crats scored points with the voters by casting them-selves as defenders of the environment.

Clearcutting

Clearcutting is a controversial logging practice in which all trees in a stand are cut at the same time. The practice has been widely used since the

1960s, when loggers turned to more powerful equipment to clear away all trees regardless of their value as timber. Previously, loggers had relied on selection cutting, targeting only those trees destined for the sawmill. Environmentalists warn that clearcutting can significantly damage the environment by causing soil erosion and RUNOFF, potentially contaminating WATERSHEDS. The practice also destroys wildlife habitat and leaves ugly scars on the landscape. Logging companies, however, defend clearcutting as an economical way of removing trees that, if practiced correctly, does not damage the environment. Research has indicated that the ecological impact of clearcutting is complex. The practice is most destructive on steep slopes and in areas of heavy rainfall. However, in places where the ground is generally level, the rainfall is moderate, and desirable tree species need open areas to grow, clearcutting can help regenerate economically valuable species.

Clearcutting became a significant political issue in the 1970s. The Natural Resources Defense Council, trying to stop widespread clearcutting in the Monongahela National Forest, filed a lawsuit alleging that the U.S. FOREST SERVICE was failing to protect NATIONAL FORESTS as required by law. The council won a 1975 appellate court decision that led to the temporary halt of clearcutting in the southern Appalachian Mountains. But Congress in 1976 passed the NATIONAL FOREST MANAGEMENT ACT, which sanctioned clearcutting within certain limits. In recent years, the Forest Service has scaled back clearcutting and other types of logging in many national forests.

Logging companies sometimes face additional criticism for clearcutting on private lands. Widespread logging in Maine led to a 1996 statewide referendum that would have barred clearcutting, but voters rejected the measure. Overseas, clearcutting in TROPICAL RAIN FORESTS and other ecologically diverse ecosystems has stirred considerable controversy, especially because cut trees release carbon into the atmosphere, potentially contributing to GLOBAL WARMING. Under pressure from environmentalists, some major Canadian logging companies have replaced clearcutting with a system known as variable retention, which leaves trees standing within a cut block.

Clinton, Bill

Environmentalists had high hopes when Governor Bill Clinton of Arkansas won the 1992 presidential election. The Democrat promised a more environmentally friendly agenda than the previous Republican administrations, and his vice president, AL GORE, had been widely praised for his environmental manifesto, *Earth in the Balance*. At a time of considerable unease about the negative impact of environmental laws on the economy, the new president insisted it was possible to help both businesses and the environment by introducing more flexibility into government regulations.

But Clinton's plans quickly ran into a hailstorm of opposition. The administration's much-watched plan to balance the demands of environmentalists and loggers in a dispute over the rare NORTHERN SPOTTED OWL in the Pacific Northwest drew fire from all sides even though it survived court challenges. On Capitol Hill, the Democratic-controlled Congress of the administration's first two years deadlocked over proposals to overhaul the SUPERFUND hazardous waste program and the CLEAN WATER ACT, and to elevate the ENVIRONMENTAL PROTECTION AGENCY (EPA) to the cabinet. A strong tide of antienvironmental sentiment, fueled by concerns over the rights of property owners and the effects of costly government regulations on job creation, doomed many environmental proposals. But Clinton was partly to blame for supporting a long list of environmental initiatives while failing to focus on any one of them long enough to ensure congressional approval. The president particularly disappointed environmentalists by retreating from legislative proposals to raise GRAZING FEES and impose an energy or BTU TAX.

Clinton appeared to gain his footing, rather paradoxically, when Republicans swept to control of Congress in the 1994 elections. Better at playing defense than offense, the president accused the GOP of waging a "war on the environment" by trying to scale back the Clean Water Act and other environmental regulations. Making adroit use of his position by holding press conferences in such natural settings as Rock Creek Park in Washington, D.C., Clinton insisted that he would never swerve from a commitment to clean water and clean air. He successfully picked off antienvironmental provisions in appropriations bills, scoring political points by blocking most (but not all) attempts to allow increased logging and weaken clean air rules.

But Clinton could do little better with Congress than fight lawmakers to a draw. To be sure, the White House and Republican lawmakers occasionally worked together to pass legislation, most notably in 1996, when bipartisan majorities in Congress reauthorized the SAFE DRINKING WATER ACT and imposed new regulations on PESTICIDE residue in food. But such cooperation was rare at a time when deteriorating relations between the Democratic administration and the GOP-led Congress culminated in the 1998 House vote to impeach the president. Although Clinton proposed legislation to slow URBAN SPRAWL, grant tax credits

for ENERGY EFFICIENCY, and reduce GLOBAL WARMING, lawmakers generally declared such plans dead on arrival. Frustrated by the impasse, some environmentalists questioned whether Clinton was really committed to their agenda or just trying to shore up political support. In many respects, the president's most important legislative victories had to do with modest funding increases for regulatory programs and land purchases.

On the regulatory front, Clinton faced equally daunting challenges. Balancing the demands of business leaders and environmentalists often proved impossible, especially because lawmakers stalled over reauthorizing major environmental laws to make them more flexible. In the late 1990s, the administration unveiled rules to significantly tighten air-quality standards and reduce the amount of polluted RUNOFF in waterways. But the regulatory effort ran into industry lawsuits and congressional criticism. From the other side, environmentalists objected to attempts to add flexibility to the ENDANGERED SPECIES ACT, warning that the resulting HABITAT CONSERVATION PLANS could spur the extinction of rare plants and animals. And administration efforts to steer a middle course on pesticide regulations drew fire from all parties. Farmers went to court to stop the EPA from barring popular PESTICIDES, and environmental and consumer organizations denounced the administration for continuing to allow the use of many dangerous chemicals on crops.

Toward the end of Clinton's tenure, however, the resourceful president found a way to make his environmental mark without relying on Congress or the regulatory process. He first signaled a more aggressive approach in his 1996 reelection campaign. Despite furious protests by western conservatives, Clinton dusted off the 1906 ANTIQUITIES ACT to

In his second term, President Bill Clinton prohibited road-building in national forests and designated several wilderness areas as national monuments. Clinton in September 1996 set aside millions of acres in Arizona and Utah to create the Grand Staircase–Escalante National Monument, at the southern rim of the Grand Canyon.
Source: Sam Mircovich, Reuters

create the GRAND STAIRCASE–ESCALANTE NATIONAL MONUMENT in Utah by presidential proclamation, preserving fragile desert land from valuable MINING operations. Two years later, the administration used its authority to impose a moratorium on building roads in NATIONAL FORESTS. Despite criticism from conservatives, Clinton went a step further in 2000 by initiating a process to ban all roads in more than 40 million acres of national forest land. Environmentalists generally applauded the move, although they faulted Clinton for allowing logging in the roadless areas. Conservatives, especially in the west,

accused the president of overstepping his authority and creating de facto wilderness areas.

In the last two years of his presidency, Clinton appeared to be linking his environmental legacy to that of THEODORE ROOSEVELT, who aggressively used his power to set aside more than 150 million acres of public lands. When Clinton used his authority to create a series of national monuments without first seeking support from Congress, conservative critics—and even some environmentalists—worried about the precedent that the White House was setting by circumventing Congress. "The president's action says more about the arrogant use of power than preservation," said Utah Republican governor Mike Leavitt. Rejecting such objections, Clinton said that the paramount issue was protecting the land for future generations. "This is an act of humility for all of us . . . 10,000 or 20,000 years from now, if the good Lord lets us all survive as a human race, no one will remember who set aside this land on this day," he said at the announcement of the Grand Canyon–Parashant National Monument. "But the children will still enjoy it."

Coastal Barrier Resources Act

Congress in 1982 passed the Coastal Barrier Resources Act (PL 97-348) to discourage development on fragile coastal barrier islands. The law designated a Coastal Barrier Resources System, and it bars most federal spending for building roads, airports, boat landings, or other structures that would spur development on the islands in that system. The law also prohibits federal spending to stabilize barrier landforms or prevent erosion along inlets, shorelines, or inshore lands, except to protect adjacent areas.

Environmentalists in 1982 backed the legislation to protect the ecology of the sensitive BARRIER ISLANDS, and the administration of president RONALD REAGAN supported the legislation for budgetary reasons. After some clashes over specifying which land would be included in the system, lawmakers agreed to designate about 450,000 acres on islands that stretched from Maine to Texas. In 1990, Congress added about 700,000 acres to the system, including islands along the GREAT LAKES, Florida Keys, Puerto Rico, and U.S. Virgin Islands.

Coastal Zone Management Act

The Coastal Zone Management Act (PL 92-583) is a cornerstone of the nation's efforts to protect sensitive coastal waters and adjacent shorelines. Passed by Congress during a burst of environmental activity in 1972, the law provides for federal grants to help states develop coastal management programs to preserve or restore coastal waters as well as tidal areas, salt marshes, WETLANDS, and beaches. The act also requires that federal coastline activities be consistent with federally approved state plans. Lawmakers were jolted into action because rapidly spreading development threatened U.S. coasts with "deterioration and irreparable damage." Some 75 percent of the population lived in coastal states in 1972, and the population density has since increased.

In 1982, the Supreme Court watered down the provision requiring that federal actions be consistent with state preservation plans. In the case of *Secretary of the Interior v. California,* the Court held that the law did not cover federal oil and gas drilling lease sales on the outer continental shelf. Environmentalists feared this would lead to more OFFSHORE DRILLING. Congress largely overturned the ruling in 1990, when it amended the law to stipulate that federal activities, whether in or outside the coastal zone, were subject to the consistency requirement. The revised law authorized the president to grant a waiver, but only if he found that a specific activity was "in the paramount interest of the United States."

President GEORGE BUSH initially objected to this requirement, even threatening to veto the bill. White House officials worried about the law's effects on offshore drilling for oil and gas and onshore-area military exercises. But voters in California and Florida strongly opposed offshore drilling because of the potential for environmental damage, and lawmakers passed the measure overwhelmingly.

Command and control

Command and control refers to a regulatory approach in which the government establishes environmental targets and specifies the pollution controls that must be used to meet those targets. Also known as the standards-and-enforcement approach, command and control is typified by landmark 1970s laws, such as the CLEAN AIR ACT and CLEAN WATER ACT, that called for pollution levels to be reduced by specific percentages in a short period of time. Lawmakers took this strict approach because more flexible legislation in the 1950s and 1960s had failed to appreciably change industry practices. The command-and-control laws are credited with significantly improving the nation's air and water quality. But they fell short of their targets and cost industries billions of dollars.

Not surprisingly, command and control has spurred an antiregulatory backlash. That is partly because the ENVIRONMENTAL PROTECTION AGENCY (EPA) lacks the resources to follow up on specific antipollution goals and stay abreast of new environmental technologies, and partly because polluters contend that they can do a better job cleaning up the environment if the government gives them more leeway. Accordingly, policymakers began taking a somewhat more flexible approach with the 1990 amendments to the Clean Air Act, setting up a much-touted EMISSIONS TRADING program in which coal-fired power plants trade pollution allowances with each other as long as they stay

within an overall pollution cap. The 1996 reauthorization of the SAFE DRINKING WATER ACT and changes in the administration of the ENDANGERED SPECIES ACT also have given more flexibility to local governments and private landowners. However, command and control remains a major component of environmental protection.

Conformity

Federal activities generally have to conform to antipollution laws. Conformity is particularly important for minimizing traffic and motor vehicle AIR POLLUTION.

When Congress amended the CLEAN AIR ACT in 1990, it included a provision requiring states to conduct comprehensive analyses of planned transportation systems to make sure that they conformed to clean-air goals. To help states meet the goals, lawmakers increased funding for public transit and other, less-polluting transportation modes the following year as part of the INTERMODAL SURFACE TRANSPORTATION EFFICIENCY ACT.

Environmental groups have used the conformity requirements to stop URBAN SPRAWL, which can destroy WILDLIFE HABITAT as well as increase air pollution. In 1999, environmental organizations won an appellate court decision halting the construction of dozens of new highway projects in Atlanta because they failed to conform to the city's clean-air plans.

Conservation Reserve Program

One of the nation's more significant land protection programs, the Conservation Reserve Program sets aside more than thirty million acres of privately owned agricultural land. Under the $1.3 billion program, farmers who voluntarily sign ten- to fifteen-year contracts to leave land idle for conservation purposes receive payments from the government. Congress created the program in the 1985 farm bill and most recently reauthorized it in omnibus farm legislation in 1996. U.S. DEPARTMENT OF AGRICULTURE officials credit the initiative with helping to reverse wildlife HABITAT LOSS, restore WETLANDS, and reduce soil erosion.

Because the Conservation Reserve Program is voluntary, farmers and PRIVATE PROPERTY RIGHTS advocates generally support it. However, some fiscal conservatives criticize the program's price tag, and environmentalists have raised concerns that the program emphasizes renting land from large (and politically influential) midwestern grain farmers instead of from smaller farmers in ecologically sensitive watersheds such as the Chesapeake Bay area. In the 1996 farm bill, lawmakers capped the program at 36.4 million acres and directed the U.S. Department of Agriculture to enroll more lands in watershed areas.

Consumption

The consumption of materials, energy, and food is a significant environmental concern. As the world population increases and people use more goods, consumption threatens to deplete many of the world's

Developed Nations Use the Most Resources

The United States accounts for only 5 percent of the world's population but uses a third of its paper and dumps three-quarters of the hazardous waste. Similarly, other developed countries account for a small fraction of Earth's population but use the largest percentage of its metals and paper.

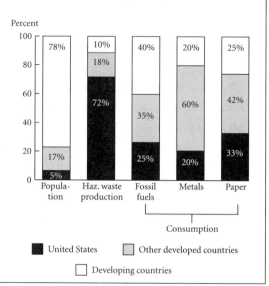

Share of Population, Waste Production, and Resource Consumption

Sources: *CQ Researcher,* "Population and the Environment," July 17, 1998, 618; "New Perspectives on Population: Lessons from Cairo," *Population Bulletin,* March 1995; Natural Resources Defense Council.

resources. Growing demand for cars, seafood, and paper goods, for example, contributes to AIR POLLUTION, OVERFISHING, and DEFORESTATION.

Because they consume so much, U.S. residents strain the environment far more on a per capita basis than do the residents of any other country (see box). Studies have indicated that, on average, an American consumes more than fifty times the goods and services of a person in China, and causes as much as thirty-five times more damage to the environment as a person in India. Exacerbating the problem, people in much of the world are consuming more—partly to follow the American example.

Because the U.S. economy relies heavily on consumerism, policymakers rarely try to discourage consumption. Instead, they have focused on improving efficiency. For example, lawmakers in 1975 passed CORPORATE AVERAGE FUEL ECONOMY standards to require automakers to design more gas-efficient cars, and they inserted numerous provisions in the 1992 ENERGY POLICY ACT to reduce energy use. Another strategy is to recycle goods—a primary goal of the 1976 RESOURCE CONSERVATION AND RECOVERY ACT. Environmental groups urge consumers to avoid using disposable items, keep packaging to a minimum, and buy "green" products, such as lumber that is produced using sustainable forestry operations. Some analysts believe that technology will ultimately reduce consumption, contending, for example, that computers could lessen paper use.

Convention on Biological Diversity

Negotiated in 1992 and signed shortly thereafter by more than 150 nations, the Convention on Biological Diversity is an international agreement that aims to protect the world's plants and animals. The treaty is notable for proclaiming that conserving biological resources is a common concern of all people. It directs signatory nations to develop national plans to conserve plant and animal species. The plans may include setting aside protected preserves, promoting environmentally sound development, minimizing risks that could result from developing GENETICALLY MODIFIED ORGANISMS, and preventing the introduction of destructive EXOTIC SPECIES. The agreement, which was opened for signatures at the 1992 EARTH SUMMIT, helped focus international attention on the risks of HABITAT LOSS and widespread EXTINCTION.

To the dismay of environmentalists, the United States was the only Earth Summit participant that refused to sign the treaty. The administration of President GEORGE BUSH cited concerns about treaty provisions that could limit U.S. biotechnology firms conducting genetic research from gaining access to plants and animals in developing countries. White House officials also criticized provisions to transfer technology to developing countries to help spur development without harming the environment.

President BILL CLINTON signed the treaty in 1993. He sent it to the Senate for ratification without any implementing legislation. (The administration believed that existing laws, such as the ENDANGERED SPECIES ACT, were sufficient to meet the treaty's obligations.) However, the Senate failed to ratify the treaty before the Democrats lost their majority in the 1994 elections. Senator Jesse Helms (R-NC), a staunch conservative who assumed the chairmanship of the Senate Foreign Relations Committee in 1995, has declined to take up the treaty.

Convention on International Trade in Endangered Species of Wild Fauna and Flora (CITES)

The Convention on International Trade in Endangered Species of Wild Fauna and Flora (CITES) is an international agreement, signed by more than 120 countries, that seeks to protect

Concerned about the depletion of plant and animal species caused by wildlife trading, the international community in 1973 passed the Convention on International Trade in Endangered Species of Fauna and Flora. Among other protections, the convention restricted ivory trading and created African elephant conservation programs. Source: Antony Njuguna, Reuters

both well-known endangered animals, such as tigers and rhinoceroses, and more obscure animals and plants. The convention, which was negotiated in 1973 and took effect in 1975, was spurred by concerns that the multibillion-dollar international wildlife trade had caused massive declines in the numbers of many species. The agreement divides species into three categories. The first category consists of animals and plants that are threatened with extinction and therefore generally cannot be commercially traded. The second category consists of species that could become threat-

ened with extinction if trade is not controlled. Species in this category may be traded, but both the importing and exporting countries must issue permits. The third category consists of species that are locally depleted. The exporting country must issue a permit to trade them.

In the United States, the ENDANGERED SPECIES ACT of 1973 implemented U.S. membership in CITES. Congress subsequently has passed bills to conform to CITES restrictions. The African Elephant Conservation Act of 1988, for example, authorized funding for elephant conservation programs and imposed penalties for illegal ivory trading. The 1994 Rhinoceros and Tiger Conservation Act also authorized funding for conservation programs.

Environmentalists give CITES mixed reviews. Because the treaty focuses on wildlife trade, it does little to mitigate HABITAT LOSS, which is a more substantial conservation issue. Furthermore, some analysts believe that the law drives the trade underground, potentially complicating regulatory efforts. Nevertheless, the law is credited with helping to restore the populations of certain animals, such as sea turtles and African elephants.

Conventional pollutants

Under the CLEAN WATER ACT, the ENVIRONMENTAL PROTECTION AGENCY (EPA) determines water quality by measuring the presence of six types of conventional pollutants. These pollutants are:

BIOCHEMICAL OXYGEN DEMAND (BOD). BOD consists of oxygen-consuming microbes that can deplete oxygen in a body of water and kill fish. Sources of BOD pollution include wastewater treatment plants; food processing, pulp, and chemical plants; and slaughterhouses.

NUTRIENTS. When fertilizers that contain NUTRIENTS such as phosphorus and nitrogen enter a body of water, they stimulate the growth of algae. Excessive amounts of algae block sunlight from reaching underwater plants, consume oxygen, and wipe out much of the natural ecosystem. Nutrients in marine coastal waters can stimulate a toxic group of organisms known as dinoflagellates, which cause red tides and made shellfish toxic.

PH. Acidic compounds such as sulfur dioxide (a major component of ACID RAIN) can destroy most life in a body of water. The pH is a measure of the acidity or alkalinity of water.

SUSPENDED SOLIDS. These are physical pollutants, such as particles from soil runoff or construction activities, that cloud bodies of water. In high concentrations, suspended solids prevent underwater plants from receiving sufficient sunlight and clog the gills of fish and other animals.

OIL AND GREASE. Massive oil spills have caused environmental disasters by fouling pristine beaches and marshes and killing massive numbers of shorebirds and other animals. More damage takes place when oil leaks from recreational boats or is washed off roads into waterways.

PATHOGENIC ORGANISMS. AGRICULTURAL RUNOFF and sewage overflows can spur infectious outbreaks of microorganisms such as bacteria, viruses, and protozoa. These organisms cause myriad problems, including contaminating drinking water systems and forcing the closure of shellfish beds.

Coral reefs

Coral reefs, which lure snorklers and divers with complex formations of corals and schools of brightly colored tropical fish, are among the richest ecosystems on Earth. Scientists believe they contain as much as 25 percent of marine life even though they cover just 0.2 percent of the ocean floor. Coral reefs also protect fragile shoreline ecosystems by absorbing the force of ocean waves, slowing them as they approach island and coastal shorelines. However, the corals—which thrive in clear, tropical waters—are severely threatened by OVERFISHING, pollution, shoreline development, and GLOBAL WARMING. Reefs worldwide are suffering from bleaching, a process in which coral polyps lose symbiotic algae inside them and eventually stop growing or even die. Scientists estimate that about 10 percent of the world's coral reefs already have been lost and an additional 60 percent are threatened. Environmentalists warn that, unless protective steps are taken, the world may lose most of its coral reefs by the end of the twenty-first century—an event that could severely affect such industries as commercial fishing and tourism, and that would leave many coastal areas exposed to destructive ocean waves.

In the United States, coral reefs are concentrated off the coasts of south Florida and Hawaii. Some reefs are protected in preserves such as Biscayne National Park. The NATIONAL OCEANIC AND ATMOSPHERIC ADMINISTRATION (NOAA) spearheads efforts to research the biology of reefs and the effects that human activities have on them. In 2000, amid growing concerns about coral bleaching, a U.S. task force on coral reefs proposed mapping reefs worldwide, restoring damaged reefs, and restricting trade in hard corals and aquarium species. It also called for protecting 20 percent of reef areas as wilderness. "Coral reefs are deteriorating globally at alarming rates," said NOAA administrator James Baker. "Without a strong understanding of these complicated ecosystems and the challenges that face them, the health of our marine environment and our economy will be jeopardized."

Corporate Average Fuel Economy

To reduce U.S. dependence on imported oil, Congress in 1975 approved Corporate Average Fuel Economy (CAFE) standards for cars and light trucks as part of the Energy Policy and Conservation Act. The law required manufacturers by 1985 to produce cars averaging at least 27.5 miles per gallon, and light trucks averaging 20.6 miles per gallon.

Ever since those goals were met, officials have debated increasing the standards. President BILL CLINTON supported increasing the standard to 45 miles per gallon but failed to win support on Capitol Hill. When Republicans took control of Congress in 1995, they successfully inserted language in annual transportation appropriations bills to freeze the standards for one year at a time. However, they could not produce the votes to permanently cap the standards.

Environmentalists favor tighter standards to reduce dependence on FOSSIL FUELS, which can be highly polluting. However, automobile manufacturers and some safety advocates warn that the only way to increase fuel efficiency would be to make cars lighter and less safe. Complicating the debate, consumers have been turning away from small, fuel-efficient cars. Light trucks and SPORT UTILITY VEHICLES—which did not have to meet the same stringent standards as passenger cars—made up the fastest growing segment of the motor vehicle market in the late 1990s.

Cost-benefit analysis

Also known as benefit-cost analysis, this term refers to a process by which a federal agency weighs the various costs and benefits of a proposed regulation before deciding whether the regulation would be worthwhile. Industry groups generally want to require agencies to conduct such analyses because this could discourage the promulgation of highly expensive requirements that have comparatively little effect on pollution. Environmentalists, however, tend to regard cost-benefit analyses with suspicion. They contend that it is easier to capture the cost of, say, a new piece of antipollution equipment than it is to quantify the benefit of reduced AIR POLLUTION. As a result, they fear the analyses tend to present environmental regulations as undesirable.

Early environmental laws often forbid cost-benefit considerations as regulatory criteria. But as one environmental regulation after another took a toll on industry, policymakers began putting a greater emphasis on studying the costs of government requirements. President RONALD REAGAN infuriated environmentalists by issuing an executive order in 1981 directing federal agencies to demonstrate that the benefits of their proposed regulations would outweigh the costs. Although his successors backed away from that directive, BILL CLINTON required cost-benefit analyses for some regulations.

When Republicans took over Congress in 1995, they put emphasis on cost-benefit analyses. They failed to win passage of a sweeping 1995 regulatory initiative that would have required agencies to conduct detailed analyses of proposed regulations and explore alternative approaches. However, they successfully pressed for an UNFUNDED MANDATES bill that directed agencies to conduct cost-benefit analyses of many new regulations. The following year, Congress passed a rewrite of the SAFE DRINKING WATER ACT requiring the ENVIRONMENTAL PROTECTION AGENCY to publish an analysis of the costs and benefits for most of the regulations it proposed under the act. With Republicans and Democrats more interested in evaluating the costs of regulations, both environmental groups and their industry adversaries now regularly issue estimates (sometimes wildly suspect) of the costs and benefits of regulations. (See also CLEAN AIR ACT; REGULATORY RELIEF.)

Council on Environmental Quality

The Council on Environmental Quality is a presidential advisory commission intended to raise the profile of environmental issues in White House decisionmaking. Established in 1971 under the NATIONAL ENVIRONMENTAL POLICY ACT, the council enjoyed influence in the 1970s as an important source of annual reports and periodic appraisals of environmental trends. Early in the Reagan administration, however, its staff was cut from 49 to 15 people, and its budget was cut by 50 percent. The office has never completely recovered. When BILL CLINTON took office as president in 1993, he briefly weighed a plan to abolish the council and transfer its functions to another agency, but he changed his mind when environmentalists objected. For many environmentalists, the council has symbolic importance as an indicator of an administration's interest in environmental issues. The council's general report on environmental quality, although no longer published annually, remains a helpful resource for those looking for a quick overview of government efforts to improve the environment.

Criteria air pollutants

The ENVIRONMENTAL PROTECTION AGENCY monitors common types of pollutants, known as criteria air pollutants, to meet the air quality standards of the 1970 CLEAN AIR ACT. These pollutants, which are a major cause of AIR POLLUTION globally, can cause eye irritation, painful breathing, headaches, and other health effects in humans, and also affect plants and animals. Since 1970, the concentration of each pollutant except nitrogen dioxide has dropped. The six criteria

To enforce national air quality standards, the Environmental Protection Agency monitors criteria air pollutants. Two of the pollutants—lead and sulfur dioxide—are routinely discharged by metal refineries like this steel factory in Gary, Indiana. Source: Paul Sequeira, EPA-Documerica

air pollutants are ozone, PARTICULATE MATTER, nitrogen dioxide, LEAD, carbon monoxide, and sulfur dioxide.

OZONE. Ground-level ozone (O_2), the main component of SMOG, is the most pervasive and hardest to control of the six criteria air pollutants. Unlike the others, ozone is not emitted directly into the air. Instead, it results from a chemical reaction when sunlight acts on nitrogen oxides and volatile organic compounds. Thousands of sources contribute to ozone, including gasoline vapors, chemical solvents, fuel combustion, and consumer prod-

ucts. Health effects include breathing problems and reduced resistance to colds and other diseases. High amounts of ground-level ozone also damages plants, reducing crop yields and affecting forests. The EPA in 1997 proposed tightening ozone regulations. But industry groups went to court to block the new rule. The case, *American Trucking Associations v. EPA,* may be decided by the Supreme Court in 2001.

PARTICULATE MATTER. These suspended liquid or solid particles can be visible as dust, smoke, and soot, depending on their size and chemical composition. Particulate matter can be emitted directly into the air or formed when gaseous pollutants react in the air. Sources of particulate matter include the burning of diesel, wood, and other fuels, as well as industrial and agricultural activities. Health effects include lung damage and bronchitis, which may lead to early death for highly vulnerable people. Particulate matter is the main source of regional HAZE, which reduces visibility. Particulates also dirty and discolor buildings, clothing, and other objects. As with ozone, the EPA proposed tougher standards for fine particulate matter in 1997 but faced a court challenge.

NITROGEN DIOXIDE. One of a number of highly reactive gases called nitrogen oxides, nitrogen dioxide is a suffocating, brownish gas that reacts in the air to form corrosive nitric acid and toxic organic nitrates. Nitrogen dioxide plays a major role in the formation of smog. Sources of nitrogen dioxide include burning fuels, vehicle emissions, and electric utilities. The gas irritates the lungs and can lower resistance to respiratory diseases. Nitrogen dioxide is a major ingredient in ACID RAIN.

LEAD. A heavy, soft metal used in a variety of industrial applications, lead—when inhaled or ingested—can cause devastating health problems, such as kidney disease, neurological defects, and reproductive system disorders. Metal refineries and lead battery plants are now the major sources of airborne lead. Thanks to the introduction of unleaded gasoline, lead concentrations have fallen by more than 90 percent.

CARBON MONOXIDE. A colorless and odorless gas, carbon monoxide is formed when carbon in fuels is not burned completely. The gas is produced primarily by vehicle exhaust, industrial boilers, and

incinerators. Exposure at high levels can cause visual impairment, reduced work capacity, reduced manual dexterity, decreased learning ability, and even death. The gas also poses a grave threat to people with cardiovascular disease because it reduces oxygen supply to organs and tissues.

SULFUR DIOXIDE. This gas is formed by the burning of fuel, such as coal or oil, that contains sulfur, and by such industrial processes as metal smelting. It produces sulfates, which cause acid rain and reduce visibility. In humans, the gas causes respiratory illnesses and aggravates cardiovascular conditions.

Critical habitat

Critical habitat is a controversial, though infrequently used, provision of the ENDANGERED SPECIES ACT. When the U.S. Fish and Wildlife Service declares a species endangered or threatened, it generally is supposed to identify the critical habitat the species needs to survive. The habitat may include land occupied by the species and additional land that is essential to restore viable populations of the species. The Fish and Wildlife Service then restricts projects that could damage the habitat. Environmental groups disagree over the importance of critical habitat. Some contend that the provision is needed to ensure habitat protection, as well as to spur the government to set aside land that, even if not currently occupied by the species, could be used for reintroduced populations or to connect isolated populations. Others, however, believe that the requirement largely duplicates other provisions of the Endangered Species Act that prohibit any actions that could harm a rare species. Many landowners view the critical habitat provision as an infringement on their ability to use their property, although other provisions of the law actually are more restrictive.

Because of the expense and controversy, the Fish and Wildlife Service rarely identifies critical habitat. During the administration of President BILL CLINTON, officials contended that the exercise diverted its resources from more cost-effective ways or protecting endangered species. Environmental groups responded with a series of successful lawsuits that forced the Fish and Wildlife Service to designate critical habitat when listing a species. In the late 1990s, the Clinton administration backed congressional efforts in appropriations bills to limit funding for critical habitat designation—a switch for an administration that generally fought for increased environmental spending. Lawmakers also have discussed scaling back the deadlines for identifying a species' critical habitat.

Cryptosporidium

Cryptosporidium parvum is the full name of a protozoan that can occur in drinking water and cause serious illness. Although healthy people who develop cryptosporidiosis usually recover within two weeks, those with weakened immune systems may develop chronic diarrhea or even die. Since the 1980s, several outbreaks of cryptosporidium have occurred in the United States. The largest was in 1993 in Milwaukee, when an estimated four hundred thousand people became sick and as many as one hundred died from the microorganism. The outbreak helped spur Congress to reauthorize the SAFE DRINKING WATER ACT in 1996 and assist local water systems to handle such contaminations.

Cryptosporidium is resistant to traditional water-disinfection techniques, such as chlorination. Some environmentalists and health experts want water systems to use FILTRATION to ensure that water is safe to drink. However, public officials worry that the costs of such systems would be prohibitive, contending that it would be more efficient for people with impaired immune systems to filter or boil the water they use.

Evidence exists that most of the surface waters in this country contain low concentrations of cryptosporidium. Experts are unsure of the concentration at which the microorganism becomes dangerous to human health. In 1998, the ENVIRONMENTAL PROTECTION AGENCY began monitoring cryptosporidium levels.

Cumulative impact

Cumulative impact refers to the environmental effects of multiple industrial activities or chemical exposures over time. A single activity (such as discharging some waste into a waterway) may be harmless, but a number of such activities over time can threaten the environment or public health. Government regulators often must take cumulative impact into account when setting limits on activities that damage the environment. For example, federal agencies have to consider cumulative impact when drawing up ENVIRONMENTAL IMPACT STATEMENTS under the NATIONAL ENVIRONMENTAL POLICY ACT. Similarly, the ENVIRONMENTAL PROTECTION AGENCY weighs the cumulative exposure of PESTICIDES when it sets allowable chemical residue levels in food under the FOOD QUALITY PROTECTION ACT.

D

Dams

Few issues have sparked as many generations of environmental battles as the construction of dams and other water projects. In the early 1900s conservationists led by John Muir passionately denounced plans to provide San Francisco with water by damming Tuolumne River in Yosemite National Park and flooding the spectacular Hetch-Hetchy Valley. The project—still regarded as the most environmentally destructive in any U.S. national park—won federal approval anyway. It set the tone for decades of failed conservation efforts to block a seemingly irresistible tide of dam construction. Only in recent years has Congress begun to take a more skeptical stance toward the projects, driven both by fiscal concerns and the legal requirement to protect endangered species.

The United States has approximately seventy-five thousand dams. Dam-building projects are credited with taming rivers in every state, generating vast amounts of electricity, controlling flooding, and turning millions of otherwise unusable acres into bountiful farmland. Across the country, and especially in arid western states, lawmakers for much of the twentieth century gave almost unquestioning support for dam construction and other projects that create channels or otherwise divert waterways. "To a degree that is impossible for most people to fathom, water projects are the grease gun that lubricates the nation's legislative machinery," Mark Reisner wrote in his book about water development in the West, *Cadillac Desert.* "Congress without water projects would be like an engine without oil; it would simply seize up."

In the 1970s the momentum behind the projects began to slow—in part because there were a limited number of remaining sites for them. The newly powerful environmental movement raised alarms by warning that dams can kill off whole populations of fish, damage shorelines, dry up wetlands, and divert water needed by downstream plants and animals. Supporting their cause, fiscal conservatives contended that dams are often a waste of money. The first major assault on water projects took place in 1978, when President JIMMY CARTER tried to delete funding for eighteen dams that he considered unnecessary. Carter lost that battle and got a lesson in "water pork" politics as Congress insisted on funding seventeen of the projects. At the same time, dam advocates faced powerful opposition in Tennessee, where antidevelopment groups tried to stop construction of the Tellico Dam by contending it would harm an endangered fish called the SNAIL DARTER. Congress amended the ENDANGERED SPECIES ACT to allow the project to proceed.

The Reagan administration evinced little enthusiasm for large water projects because of the expense. By the 1990s the same agencies that had constructed dams and diverted water systems— the Defense Department's Army Corps of Engineers and the Interior Department's Bureau of

Because of fiscal concerns and environmental laws, Congress in recent years has been reluctant to authorize new dam-building projects. That situation could soon change, as lawmakers grapple with rising electricity costs and dwindling water supplies in the West.

Reclamation—were focusing on undoing past environmental damage. Federal officials in 1996 opened the gates of the Glen Canyon Dam and allowed the Colorado River to flood the floor of the Grand Canyon for a week to replenish the shoreline and allow more vegetation to take root. The following year, the Federal Energy Regulatory Commission set a precedent by ordering the removal of the aging Edwards Dam on Maine's Kennebec River—the first time a private dam was destroyed over the owners' objections. Nevertheless, WATER SCARCITY in the West is driving proposals for new projects, such as the Animas–La Plata water supply project in Colorado and the Garrison Diversion Unit in North Dakota.

The backlash against dams is spurring concerns in the West about the possible loss of navigable rivers and inexpensive power. Western lawmakers have floated plans to restrict the Federal Energy Regulatory Commission from stressing environmental issues when considering licensing nonfederal hydroelectric dams. On the other side, some eastern lawmakers want to create a fund to either rehabilitate aging dams or tear them down. In the late 1990s policymakers began squaring off over proposals to breach four relatively new dams on the Snake River at a cost of about $1 billion. The government warned that the dams were blocking the spawning runs of SALMON and steelhead trout, which were listed as threatened species under the Endangered Species Act. But Washington and Idaho lawmakers said destroying the dams would devastate local communities by raising the price of power and transportation and lowering the value of farmland.

Outside the United States, the construction of dams and other water projects is a significant environmental issue because it can have catastrophic consequences for wildlife habitat. The number of large dams worldwide has increased by sevenfold since 1950, and they are blamed for virtually wiping out fish populations in many rivers. Despite the environmental costs, economic officials in developing countries say the dams are necessary for shipping, agriculture, and energy production. Perhaps the most controversial of all dam projects is the Three Gorges Dam on China's Yangtze River. The world's largest hydroelectric project, it will create a reservoir several hundred miles long, potentially forcing the relocation of more than one million people.

DDT

DDT (dichloro-diphenyl-trichloroethane) is a highly toxic synthetic PESTICIDE that was widely used after World War II to protect crops from insect infestations and wipe out mosquito-borne diseases such as malaria. Officials believed the chemical was harmless. However, scientists discovered it accumulated in the tissues of animals, moving up the food chain from wildlife to people throughout the world. In high concentrations, DDT can cause severe health side effects in humans, including nerve damage and reproductive disorders. Biologists believe it can act as an ENDOCRINE DISRUPTOR, affecting the hormone systems of both people and animals.

A movement to ban DDT sprang up in the early 1960s, fueled by Rachel Carson's 1962 bestseller, SILENT SPRING. Carson blamed DDT for causing a global environmental catastrophe, leaving many animals sterile, and thinning the shells of birds' eggs. Environmental groups won a landmark federal court decision in 1971 to force the ENVIRONMENTAL PROTECTION AGENCY (EPA) to take steps to end use of the pesticide. One year later, EPA administrator WILLIAM D. RUCKELSHAUS announced a ban on almost all remaining uses of

Greenpeace activists in Buenos Aires, Argentina, cover a waste pipe emitting DDT and other toxic substances into the Matanza River. The message on the cover reads, "Enough Polluting." Source: Rickey Rogers, Reuters

DDT over the protests by chemical manufacturers that the pesticide was safe.

Despite the environmental risks, DDT continues to be used in many developing countries, mostly to control disease-carrying insects. Traces of the chemical can still be detected throughout the world.

Debt-for-nature swaps

Debt-for-nature swaps are agreements engineered by government officials or private environmental groups to forgive the debt of a developing nation in exchange for that nation's taking steps to protect rain forests or other biologically diverse habitat. The environmental group Conservation International helped pioneer the concept in 1987 by paying off $650,000 of Bolivian debt at a discount. The Bolivian government promised to use the money to protect several million acres of forests. The Bush administration expanded on this strategy by developing a program to forgive outstanding debts by several Latin American nations in return for the creation of forested preserves. Congress in 1998 passed the Tropical Forest Conservation Act (PL 105-214) to forgive $400 million of debts by developing countries and use the money to protect ecologically important forests. Conservatives tend to prefer debt-for-nature swaps to other environmental programs because they view them as a cost-effective and market-oriented approach to protecting nature.

Deep-well injection

See UNDERGROUND INJECTION WELLS.

Deforestation

The destruction of forests throughout much of the world for farming, pastures, lumber, or development has severe environmental consequences, especially in developing countries. Biologists believe that nearly one-half of the forests that once covered the earth have been converted to other uses. Much of what remains has been greatly altered because of repeated logging. Although the United States and many other industrialized

Forest Loss by Continent, 1990 and 1995

| | Forest cover (thousands of hectares) | |
	1990	1995
World	3,510,728	3,454,382
Africa	538,978	520,237
Asia	490,812	474,172
Central America	84,628	79,443
Europe	144,044	145,988
North America	453,270	457,086
Oceania	91,149	90,695
South America	894,466	870,594

Source: Adapted from World Resources Institute data.

countries are maintaining or even increasing the size of their forests, developing countries lost more than thirty million acres yearly from 1990 to 1995, according to the United National Food and Agriculture Organization. The destruction intensified in the late 1990s because of catastrophic fires in TROPICAL RAIN FORESTS in Indonesia and other countries.

The forces behind deforestation are difficult or impossible to stop. They include POPULATION GROWTH, global demand for timber products, and government-backed schemes to convert forests to other, more profitable uses, such as large-scale ranching. In impoverished countries millions of landless peasants clear forests for subsistence farming. Although forest preservation has become a high priority for international organizations such as the U.N. ENVIRONMENT PROGRAMME and the WORLD BANK, environmentalists fear that the need for more farmland and timber to support the growing population is likely to spur additional destruction in coming decades.

Deforestation has wide-ranging and often catastrophic effects on the environment. It eliminates habitat and devastates local plant and animal species, contributing to the high rate of EX-

A government official inspects deforestation caused by subsistence farming in Mexico's Lacandon rain forest, which is on the brink of extinction. Two-thirds of the forest's nearly five million acres are now pastureland or farmland. Source: *Daniel Aguilar, Reuters*

TINCTION. Since forests absorb carbon, cutting down trees also increases the amount of carbon dioxide in the atmosphere and contributes significantly to GLOBAL WARMING. In addition, forests help prevent soil erosion and landslides, stabilize the flow of streams and other waterways, and play a vital—and imperfectly understood—role in regulating local weather patterns. Stripped of trees, the land is dangerously exposed to the elements. Thousands of Nicaraguans perished during Hurricane Mitch in 1998 when an entire side of a denuded volcano collapsed. In Haiti the destruction of lush forests has led to the loss of topsoil, and the island is slowly turning into a desert.

In the United States deforestation is a comparatively minor environmental issue. The country has about six hundred million acres of forests, and its forested areas have actually increased slightly in recent years. However, much of the forests are regularly logged. This activity disrupts habitat and results in a younger mix of trees that typically provide less soil and watershed protection than do OLD-GROWTH forests. CLEARCUTTING and other logging practices in NATIONAL FORESTS are regulated by the government, spurring political clashes over whether to build more roads through the forests and permit expanded logging. Although the Reagan and Bush administrations took steps to increase logging in old-growth areas, environmentalists in the late 1980s went to court to force restrictions on loggers in the Pacific Northwest in order to preserve habitat for the rare NORTHERN SPOTTED OWL. In the late 1990s the Clinton administration imposed restrictions on building roads in national forests.

In addition to the issue of protecting large forests, environmentalists have also raised concerns about clearing trees on private land for new houses, offices, and roads. In metropolitan Atlanta, one of the nation's fastest-growing urban areas, geographers have estimated that an average of more than fifty acres of trees are cut down every day, contributing to higher local temperatures.

Delaney clause

Until it was amended in 1996, the Delaney clause was one of the most controversial and stringent regulations governing PESTICIDES. Rep. James J. Delaney, D-N.Y., added the provision in 1958 to the FOOD, DRUG, AND COSMETIC ACT to prohibit the use of all cancer-causing chemicals on commodities used in processed foods—a much tougher standard than the one applied to fresh produce. Over the years, technological advances enabled regulators to detect increasingly minute traces of carcinogens in foods. Instead of strictly enforcing the Delaney clause and imposing extraordinarily tight restrictions on pesticides, the government began permitting pesticide residues on both processed and fresh food that posed no more than a "negligible risk" of causing cancer.

Congress deadlocked throughout the 1980s and early 1990s over proposals to amend the Delaney clause. But a federal appeals court jolted

lawmakers into action when it ruled that the ENVIRONMENTAL PROTECTION AGENCY (EPA) would have to apply the stricter standard contained in the Delaney clause to both raw and processed foods, potentially forcing the government to ban farmers from using common pesticides. Reacting with uncommon speed, members in both chambers unanimously passed the FOOD QUALITY PROTECTION ACT in July 1996. The new law replaced the Delaney clause with a single health standard requiring the EPA to make sure that the chemicals in both raw and processed food pose a "reasonable certainty" of no harm from all combined sources of exposure.

Dingell, John D.

One of the most powerful lawmakers of the late twentieth century, Rep. John D. Dingell, D-Mich., chaired the House Energy and Commerce Committee (later renamed the HOUSE COMMERCE COMMITTEE). He had a substantial role in crafting most of the major antipollution and waste disposal laws of the 1970s and 1980s, as well as the 1992 ENERGY POLICY ACT. The burly legislator exasperated environmentalists by blocking efforts in the 1980s to impose tough clean air standards on Detroit automakers. But he finally agreed to a compromise on tailpipe emissions that cleared the way to a substantial 1990 expansion of the CLEAN AIR ACT.

After Republicans won the 1994 congressional elections, Dingell gave up the perquisites of his chairmanship with surprising grace. As the ranking Democrat on the Commerce Committee, he was a key voice against GOP efforts to scale back environmental regulations. He gradually forged a

As chairman of the House Energy and Commerce Committee from 1981 to 1995, Rep. John D. Dingell, D-Mich., spearheaded major antipollution, waste disposal, and energy conservation laws, including 1992's Energy Policy Act. Source: R. Michael Jenkins, Congressional Quarterly

close working relationship with the chairman, THOMAS J. BLILEY JR. of Virginia, and helped work out compromises to overhaul the SAFE DRINKING WATER ACT and restrict pesticides under the FOOD QUALITY PROTECTION ACT.

Dioxin

Dioxin is a group of about seventy-five toxic chlorinated chemicals, related to PCBs, that have been linked to cancer and reproductive disorders. Scientists are sharply at odds over the risks posed by dioxin. The chemicals are the unwanted byproducts of herbicide production, wood pulp

bleaching, the incineration of medical and other waste, and other combustion activities (including wood burning). Dioxin particulates can drift far in the atmosphere before settling onto land and water, where they eventually enter the food chain.

In the 1970s the ENVIRONMENTAL PROTECTION AGENCY (EPA) imposed stringent standards for dioxin after animal experiments indicated that some of the chemicals could be dangerous at concentrations of one-in-one-billion. When tests showed that soil in the town of Times Beach, Missouri, had become contaminated with dioxin, the government ordered the evacuation of all 2,247 residents, spending $37 million to reimburse the residents and about $100 million more to clean up nearby sites. During the 1980s Vietnam veterans filed hundreds of lawsuits against the government seeking compensation for health problems that they blamed on exposure to dioxin in the defoliant Agent Orange. The chemicals became known as "Toxic Enemy Number One." To meet government standards, the paper and pulp industry spent an estimated $2 billion for pollution control.

By the 1990s, however, many scientists questioned whether the EPA standards, which had been largely extrapolated from animal experiments, were overly stringent. In 1991 the federal scientist who had ordered the Times Beach evacuation told a congressional committee that he had made a mistake. "Given what we know now about this chemical's toxicity," said assistant surgeon general Vernon N. Houk, "it looks as if the evacuation was unnecessary." Also in 1991, the World Health Organization supported standards increasing the permissible human exposure to seventeen times greater than EPA limits.

Other studies, however, have indicated that minute doses can pose health risks. In 2000 the

EPA concluded for the first time that dioxin is a human carcinogen. Environmentalists have resisted proposals to relax dioxin standards, especially as concerns mount about ENDOCRINE DISRUPTORS that can wreak havoc on hormonal systems. (See RISK ASSESSMENT.)

Dolphin-safe tuna

Concerns over dolphins becoming entangled in tuna fishing nets and drowning date back to the late 1950s. That was when commercial fishermen, who located schools of large yellowfin tuna by looking for the dolphins that tended to swim above them, began using large purse seine nets around the dolphins. After the fish and dolphins were encircled, the nets were drawn shut, like a purse. Although the fishing boats' target was tuna, not dolphins, the nets killed more than six million dolphins through the early 1990s.

Congress first waded into the controversy in 1972. The MARINE MAMMAL PROTECTION ACT authorized a comprehensive research and development program to reduce dolphin deaths while eventually restricting commercial fishing techniques to protect the mammals. This rather tepid action helped reform U.S. fishing practices but failed to satisfy a generation raised on the television series *Flipper*. Lawmakers took a tougher stance in the 1980s, prohibiting the import of yellowfin tuna and tuna products from nations that failed to attain an average rate of dolphin mortality comparable to the U.S. rate. The government accordingly banned tuna imports of Mexico, Venezuela, and the island of Vanuatu (formerly New Hebrides). Amid consumer boycotts of canned tuna, seafood companies in 1990 agreed

to quit distributing tuna caught in association with dolphins. That same year, Congress specified that dolphin-safe labels could not be used on eastern tropical Pacific tuna that were caught during fishing trips in which purse seine nets were used to encircle dolphins.

The U.S. actions set off vigorous international protests and the threat of trade sanctions because they were seen as an illegal barrier to trade. But when Congress in 1992 called for a five-year global moratorium on the practice of intentionally encircling dolphins with purse seines, foreign nations that fished the eastern tropical Pacific agreed to modify their fishing practices. In 1995 the United States and eleven other nations at a Panama meeting signed off on various dolphin protection fishing practices, including making it easier for dolphins to swim over the back edge of the net and using rafts and divers to herd dolphins out of the nets. This Declaration of Panama also established an initial annual limit of five thousand dolphins that could be killed during such fishing. In return, the United States agreed to lift its embargoes on tuna products and modify the definition of dolphin-safe tuna to include tuna caught in purse seine nets in which no dolphin mortalities were observed.

Congress made some changes to the agreement before implementing it in 1997. The two-year debate exposed an unusually deep division among environmental groups. Some environmentalists hailed the Declaration of Panama as a breakthrough because it brought many countries into a compact to protect dolphins and the ecosystem as a whole. Others, however, viewed it as weakening the dolphin-safe standard in the United States and caving in to the demands of the U.S. trading partners and the WORLD TRADE ORGANIZATION. Lawmakers struck a compromise to delay the label change for eighteen months and require the Department of Commerce to study the effects of the nets, and whether the repeated chasing and capturing of dolphins caused permanent harm.

Dombeck, Michael P.

From the time he took over the U.S. FOREST SERVICE for the Clinton administration in 1997, Michael P. Dombeck cheered environmentalists and angered timber companies by steering the agency sharply away from its traditional emphasis on logging. Dombeck, a fisheries biologist, unveiled a "Natural Resources Agenda" that emphasized protecting watersheds and ecosystems and promoting recreation. In 1998 he announced an eighteen-month moratorium on building new roads in the NATIONAL FORESTS, drawing fire from many western conservatives who said the moratorium would hurt logging, depress rural economies, and even set back the health of the forests. Undeterred, Dombeck wrote a letter to the Forest Service's thirty thousand employees stating: "In fifty years, we will not be remembered for the resources we developed; we will be thanked for those we maintained and restored for future generations." Within two years, the Clinton administration took steps to ban roadbuilding in more than forty million acres of forest.

Drift-net fishing

Drift nets are highly efficient fishing tools that may be as large as forty miles across and dangle thirty to one hundred feet below the surface of the water. Environmentalists refer to them as "walls of death" because they kill nearly every animal that swims into them, including such noncommercial species as seabirds, dolphins, and turtles. Critics of drift-net techniques in the early 1990s warned that as much as 70 percent of the harvest was BYCATCH—unwanted species that were dumped over the side, usually dead or dying. As a result, widespread use of the nets devastated ocean populations.

With OVERFISHING becoming a major concern, the United Nations in 1989 adopted the first of a number of resolutions calling for an end to the controversial fishing technique. One year later, Congress amended the 1976 MAGNUSON FISHERY CONSERVATION AND MANAGEMENT ACT to impose a ban on the use of large-scale drift nets in U.S. waters and direct the administration to pursue a worldwide ban. Amid international pressure, many nations banned the nets in the 1990s, and European Union member countries agreed to end their use in 2001. However, policing such bans is difficult. Illegal use of drift nets remains a significant environmental concern.

E

Earth Day

Earth Day, which takes place on April 22 every year, consists of rallies, lectures, and other events worldwide that are designed to promote environmental awareness. The first Earth Day was in 1970, and it is generally cited as the beginning of the nation's powerful ENVIRONMENTAL MOVEMENT. Sen. Gaylord Nelson, D-Wis., organized the event after years of trying to garner support for clean water and other ecological causes. He conceived of it as a 1960s type of teach-in. The public responded in overwhelming numbers: more than two hundred thousand people gathered on the national Mall in Washington, D.C., and millions more convened in cities and on campuses around the country. "The objective was to get a nationwide demonstration of concern for the environment so large that it would shake the political arena," Nelson recalled in a speech twenty years later. "It was a gamble, but it worked."

The outpouring of support for environmental protection helped spur a cascade of landmark laws in the early 1970s, including the CLEAN AIR ACT, the CLEAN WATER ACT, and the ENDANGERED SPECIES ACT. Over the years Earth Day has grown into a major international event, with many tens of millions of people participating in more than one hundred countries.

First organized in 1970 by Sen. Gaylord Nelson, D-Wis., Earth Day marked the beginning of the environmental movement. On Earth Day 1999, Secretary of State Madeleine K. Albright urged developing countries to sign an international global warming treaty. Source: Larry Downing, Reuters

67

Earth Summit

Officially called the United Nations Conference on Environment and Development, the 1992 Earth Summit, in Rio de Janeiro, was in many ways an important milestone in the international commitment to protect the environment. More than one hundred heads of state attended the conference, in addition to representatives from dozens of other nations and thousands of nongovernmental organizations. The conference theme, "Our Last Chance to Save the Earth," underscored the increasingly urgent concerns about global environmental problems, especially DEFORESTATION, GLOBAL WARMING, pollution, and widespread HABITAT LOSS.

In many ways the conference failed to meet the high expectations of environmentalists. Negotiators produced two treaties, the Convention on Climate Change to combat global warming and the CONVENTION ON BIOLOGICAL DIVERSITY to protect ecosystems and habitat. However, the treaties consisted largely of general goals instead of specific targets, and they lacked enforcement mechanisms. The conference also resulted in three nonbinding statements of principles. Perhaps the best known was the Rio Declaration on Environment and Development, which proclaimed twenty-seven principles to govern the protection of natural resources. Another statement, Agenda 21, outlined a catalog of steps nations could take to achieve sustainable development in the twenty-first century. But negotiators failed to come up with the means to finance their goals. The conference exposed a deep split between developing countries that wanted financial and technological assistance to help them conserve their natural resources and indus-

trialized countries (especially the United States) that were reluctant to commit to any actions that could cost them their technological edge.

Environmentalists were particularly disappointed in the failure to take on emissions of GREENHOUSE GASES. Whereas Japan and the entire European Union were willing to cut their CARBON DIOXIDE emissions to 1990 levels by 2000, the United States opposed any caps. However, the Earth Summit set the stage for the 1997 KYOTO PROTOCOL on global warming, in which negotiators did agree to specific emission limits. The much-publicized gathering in Rio also drew attention to the need to coordinate global conservation strategies.

Much of the blame for the Earth Summit's shortcomings fell on President GEORGE BUSH. Environmentalists believed that the United States, as the world's wealthiest country and greatest source of industrial pollution, needed to show leadership at the conference. But in the months leading up to the conference, Bush was uncertain about whether he would even attend it. Both the House and Senate passed nonbinding resolutions urging him to go to Rio and show "leadership." Bush agreed to attend only after U.S. negotiators succeeded in scaling back the scope of the conference and removing treaty language containing specific requirements on cutting greenhouse gas emissions.

Emergency Planning and Community Right-to-Know Act

When Congress reauthorized the SUPERFUND HAZARDOUS WASTE program in 1986, it also created a freestanding law in Title III of the legislation to help guard communities from deadly releases of toxic substances. The law, known as the Emergency Planning and Community Right-to-Know Act (PL 99-499), was largely inspired by the 1984 BHOPAL tragedy in India that killed thousands of people, as well as a subsequent accident at a Union Carbide plant in South Charleston, West Virginia. It requires industries and communities to prepare emergency plans in the event that a toxic substance is released into the environment. A facility must immediately notify the appropriate state and local emergency coordinators of any accidental release that exceeds certain standards. The ENVIRONMENTAL PROTECTION AGENCY (EPA) is responsible for publishing a list of extremely hazardous substances regulated in the bill.

One of the most law's most important provisions requires businesses to report yearly on the emissions (including legal emissions) of hundreds of hazardous chemicals. The resulting TOXICS RELEASE INVENTORY, compiled annually by the EPA, is an important indicator of trends in toxic air emissions.

Emissions trading

When Congress amended the CLEAN AIR ACT in 1990, it created an innovative program to reduce sulfur dioxide emissions. Rather than relying solely on caps on allowable emissions levels—which was the COMMAND-AND-CONTROL approach used in many 1970s environmental laws—lawmakers also set up a free-market system giving polluters the option of reducing their emissions or buying reductions from another polluter that was successful in cutting emissions. The way this program works is that the ENVIRONMENTAL PROTECTION AGENCY (EPA) allocates an allowance to coal-fired electric utilities for every ton of sulfur dioxide they emit

annually. The power plants also face an overall emissions cap of 8.9 million tons of sulfur dioxide nationally, beginning in 2000. The utilities can buy, sell, and trade the allowances. The allowances can also be purchased by outsiders, such as environmentalists wishing to retire them (and thereby reduce ACID RAIN).

Proposed by the Bush administration, the emissions trading program served two important political purposes. It minimized the resistance of industry lobbyists, who opposed government mandates. It also broke a regional deadlock between "clean" states, whose utilities had either installed antipollution devices or relied on less polluting, low-sulfur coal, and "dirty" states in the Midwest that mined and burned high-sulfur coal. The regional differences had stalled action for years in part because the states battled over who should fund the costs of emissions reductions.

The emissions trading program, which became fully implemented in 1995, is credited with contributing to a 39 percent decrease in sulfur dioxide concentrations from 1988 to 1997. It is also highly economical, costing the utilities only about $100 per ton or less (the EPA had initially predicted the costs would be in the range of $500 per ton).

However, environmentalists worry that power plants will find ways to exceed their allowable allowances, and some northeastern officials warn that the emissions trading program is not doing enough to protect forests and lakes. In addition, some facilities that have bought the right to continue polluting have drawn criticism from civil rights groups because they are located in low-income areas (see ENVIRONMENTAL JUSTICE).

Emissions trading may become a global phenomenon. In 1997 negotiators seeking to control GLOBAL WARMING agreed to add emissions trading language to the KYOTO PROTOCOL on global warming. This language stipulates that industrialized countries that fail to cut GREENHOUSE GAS emissions significantly can buy credits from those countries that emit fewer pollutants. Some environmentalists see this provision as a loophole that would allow the United States to continue polluting. But it can also curb DEFORESTATION. That is because industrialized countries could meet their obligations by paying developing countries to preserve their forests, which lower global warming by keeping carbon out of the atmosphere. (See also CARBON SEQUESTRATION.)

Endangered Species Act

Passed in 1973 with scant opposition, this act (PL 93-205) has grown into one of the nation's most powerful and controversial laws. Unlike most other environmental actions that seek to protect human health or enhance outdoor recreation, the Endangered Species Act exists to protect rare animals and plants. For that reason, it has been called the most noble of environmental laws. But developers and property rights advocates deliver scathing verdicts on the act, saying it puts the interests of obscure plants and animals above the rights of people.

The Endangered Species Act, which is administered primarily by the U.S. FISH AND WILDLIFE SERVICE, provides for the conservation of threatened and endangered plants and animals, as well as that of their habitat. It requires the government to list certain species of plants and animals as either endangered or threatened, depending on their risk of becoming extinct. A listed species cannot be hunted or traded, nor can its habitat be disturbed. The law is so powerful that major federal projects,

Endangered and Threatened Species in the United States, 2000

Group	Endangered	Threatened
Animals		
Mammals	63	9
Birds	78	15
Reptiles	14	22
Amphibians	10	8
Fishes	69	44
Clams	61	8
Snails	20	11
Insects	30	9
Arachnids	6	0
Crustaceans	18	3
Subtotal	369	129
Plants		
Flowering plants	565	139
Conifers and cycads	2	1
Ferns and allies	24	2
Lichens	2	0
Subtotal	593	142
Total	962	271

Source: U.S. Department of the Interior, Fish and Wildlife Service.
Notes: Table is current as of August 31, 2000. Total U.S. endangered and threatened species = 1,233 (498 animals, 735 plants). "Endangered" species have the potential to become extinct; "threatened" species are those with the potential to become endangered.

such as highways and DAMS, have been halted because of the threats they pose to listed species. Similarly, property owners whose land is habitat to a listed species may face severe restrictions on developing the land. As of August 31, 2000, the government listed 1,233 species of animals and plants in the United States as threatened or endangered (see table). High-profile species such as the BALD EAGLE and GRIZZLY BEAR owe their recovery to the law and other environmental efforts. The law has won praise from conservationists worldwide as a pioneering effort to protect the earth's BIODIVERSITY. The Endangered Species Act also has an international component. It implemented the CONVENTION ON INTERNATIONAL TRADE IN ENDANGERED

SPECIES OF WILD FAUNA AND FLORA, a worldwide agreement to protect rare species.

Despite its far-reaching provisions, the act has had limited success. As of 1999 only eleven species had been taken off the list due to recovery. Seven species had become extinct since their listing, and nine others that had been on the list were taken off due to improved data. Pointing to such statistics, critics say the act has largely been a failure. On the other hand, proponents of the law say it has successfully stabilized the populations of about 40 percent of listed species. Furthermore, although species such as the California condor and the red wolf remain very rare, they likely would be extinct were it not for the law's protection.

Judging the success of the law is difficult because of the challenges in monitoring rare species. Due to limited funding, environmentalists believe that many obscure types of animals and plants are disappearing without anyone taking notice. They also contend that it takes years to list a species and then additional years to reach agreement on specific recovery plans. Even though scientists warn that worldwide rates of EXTINCTION are a major environmental problem, the U.S. government fails to track domestic extinctions on a comprehensive basis. A 1996 study by the Nature Conservancy on more than twenty thousand American plant and animal species concluded that one-third were rare or threatened—far more than were being protected by the government. On the other hand, developers say bad data can lead to the listing of relatively common animals that may not need protection or are in decline for reasons that have little to do with human activities.

Constant Battles

The Endangered Species Act has sparked numerous lawsuits by environmentalists seeking stronger enforcement and by businesses and property owners contending that the government is overstepping its bounds. The two sides are particularly at odds over provisions in the law that bar the "taking" of a species. Environmentalists claim these provisions forbid the destruction of an endangered species' habitat. They won a key victory in the 1995 case of *Babbitt v. Sweet Home Chapter of Communities for a Greater Oregon* when the Supreme Court, 6-3, backed the Fish and Wildlife Service's contention that it could restrict habitat modification that might harm a species. Other battles have centered on whether the government must designate critical habitat for an endangered species, leading to certain increased protections; whether the government must compensate private landowners who own endangered species habitat; and whether government officials and landowners can enter into flexible arrangements that permit the destruction of habitat used by rare species in exchange for protecting similar habitat nearby.

The Endangered Species Act has spurred controversy for two reasons that were unforeseen in 1973. First, although it originally was conceived to protect species such as the bald eagle, it lists mostly obscure species of plants and animals, including rodents and insects like the kangaroo rat and the Delhi fly. Environmentalists say such species are vital to maintain ecosystems, but conservative critics say they are not worth slowing economic growth. Critics point to such efforts as stopping a Pennsylvania highway because of the Indiana bat and restricting California development to preserve the Smith Blue butterfly as examples of the law overreaching. Second, activists have used the law as a tactic to stop development even when their primary interest is not saving a rare species. This approach dates back to the late 1970s, when residents along the Little Tennessee River went to court over

Interior Secretary Bruce Babbitt called the Endangered Species Act "the most visionary environmental law that has ever been passed." Not without its critics, some of whom say it hinders economic growth, the law has aided the recovery of species on the brink of extinction, including the bald eagle, grizzly bear, and gray whale (shown breaching off California Sur, Mexico). Source: Heriberto Rodriguez, Reuters

the endangered SNAIL DARTER to try to stop a $31 million dam that threatened their homes. Environmentalists sparked years of legislative and court battles in the late 1980s; in the early 1990s they used the rare NORTHERN SPOTTED OWL to block logging in Northwest OLD-GROWTH forests.

Perhaps more than any other environmental law, the Endangered Species Act has created a backlash from the PRIVATE PROPERTY RIGHTS movement, especially in the West. Ranchers and other property owners say they live in fear that government agents will find an obscure endangered bug or weed on their land, which could lower their property values by restricting uses of the land and expose them to heavy fines for damaging habitat.

As a result, they say the law has the perverse effect of encouraging them to destroy habitat to prevent the discovery of rare species on their lands. Critics even contend that the law places a greater value on obscure species than on human safety. In the late 1990s some conservatives blamed the law for causing the destruction of dozens of houses in a southern California wildfire, charging that residents could not cut down brush near their houses because it would threaten the habitat of the kangaroo rat. They were not appeased when investigators said the fires, driven by eighty-mile-per-hour winds, would have destroyed the homes even if the brush had been removed. "The law punishes private property owners for having endangered species on their property which, in turn, has caused people to fear the Endangered Species Act, not embrace it," said Rep. Richard W. Pombo, R-Calif., who chaired a House endangered species task force in the mid-1990s.

More Flexibility

To ease conflict with landowners, the Clinton administration in the 1990s took several steps intended to make the law more flexible. One of its most important initiatives was to negotiate hundreds of agreements known as habitat conservation plans with landowners. These agreements permitted landowners to develop portions of their property even if that meant the destruction of habitat used by an endangered species, so long as the landowner took other actions to ensure that the species overall would benefit. Such actions could include creating habitat in other areas, removing predators, or funding conservation research.

The habitat conservation plans often contained controversial "SAFE HARBOR" and "NO SURPRISES" provisions, which generally shielded a landowner from facing further restrictions on the property regardless of subsequent information about the species. Property owners tended to welcome the agreements. But conservationists blasted them, contending that they failed to take into account needed steps to ensure a species' recovery. Following an environmental lawsuit over the matter, the administration in 1999 modified the policy to try to ensure that the destruction or "incidental taking" of a member of an endangered species would not reduce the likelihood of recovery for the entire species.

Despite the many criticisms, the Endangered Species Act continues to enjoy considerable support in Washington. Environmentalists view the law as critical to preserving ecologically valuable species at a time of relentless HABITAT LOSS. They credit it with helping to restore natural balance by providing for the resurgence of traditional predators such as WOLVES. In addition, environmentalists point to examples of rare species yielding priceless medical benefits for humans—the bark of the Pacific yew tree, for example, has been used to produce potent anticancer drugs. At a time when the world is facing a nearly unprecedented wave of species extinction, supporters say the law must not be discarded, although it can be made more flexible. "It's the most visionary environmental law that has ever been passed," said BRUCE BABBITT, secretary of the U.S. DEPARTMENT OF THE INTERIOR.

Lawmakers failed to reauthorize the law in 1992, opting instead to fund it each year through the appropriations process. Estimates vary on how much the government is spending to protect endangered species, partly because the Fish and Wildlife Service does not distinguish between its activities under the Endangered Species Act and the MARINE MAMMAL PROTECTION ACT. One much-cited Fish and Wildlife Service report estimated that federal and state agencies spent $233 million in fiscal year 1993 on activities to protect endangered species, but some conservative lawmakers say the hidden costs may be far greater.

Since 1992, Congress has deadlocked repeatedly over proposals to amend the law by giving incentives to landowners to leave at least part of their property undisturbed. The issue is particularly difficult to resolve because it divides lawmakers by region as well as ideology, with many northeastern and midwestern Republicans siding with Democrats to block efforts to scale back the act.

History

Comprehensive federal efforts to save endangered species date back to 1966, when Congress passed the Endangered Species Preservation Act (PL 89-669). It directed the Interior Department's Fish and Wildlife Service to compile a list of fish and wildlife that were in immediate danger of extinction and to purchase lands for a NATIONAL WILDLIFE REFUGE SYSTEM to protect them. In March 1967 the government published its first endangered species list, which included seventy-two native species. Three years later, that law was strengthened by the Endangered Species Conservation Act of 1969 (PL 91-135), which restricted importation of endangered species, protected more native species and certain species in other countries, and established penalties for violation of the act.

Amid continuing concerns about the fate of such familiar animals as the American alligator and the bald eagle, Congress in 1973 passed the Endangered Species Act by an overwhelming margin: 92-0 in the Senate and 355-4 in the House. The law authorized the Fish and Wildlife Service to begin keeping a list of species threatened with extinction, in addition to its list of species in immediate danger of becoming extinct. It established penalties against hunting or capturing a threatened or endangered species, and against importing or exporting such species or any products made from them. Under the new law, citizens could petition the government to add or remove a species from the endangered and threatened lists. The law largely exempted Native American subsistence hunting—a provision that has since caused some conflicts because environmentalists fear that such hunting could make it much harder for rare animals to recover.

The measure continued the Interior Department's program of land acquisition for wildlife refuges, financed by the LAND AND WATER CONSERVATION FUND. It authorized $10 million in grants to states that set up their own wildlife conservation programs under cooperative agreements with the Interior Department. It also implemented the Convention on International Trade in Endangered Species of Wild Fauna and Flora, which sought to protect endangered species overseas.

Although little noticed at the time, another provision of the bill required federal agencies to ensure that their projects did not jeopardize a listed species or adversely affect its habitat. This provision became an important tool for environmentalists seeking to block federal projects such as DAMS and highways, and it caused an uproar when the Supreme Court ruled in 1978 that construction of Tellico Dam must be halted to save the habitat of the snail darter. Similarly, efforts to build the Dickey-Lincoln Dam in northern Maine were blocked by efforts to save a variety of snapdragon known as the furbish lousewort. Rep. Morris K. Udall, D-Ariz., then chairman of the House Interior Committee, warned in 1978 that such conflicts "get the whole act into trouble, into disrepute."

To give the act more flexibility, Congress in 1978 set up a seven-member, Cabinet-level ENDANGERED SPECIES COMMITTEE to allow construction of federal projects even if they might kill off endangered species. However, lawmakers broadened the law at the same time by extending protection to endangered plants as well as animals.

Recent Deadlock

Conflicts over the act deepened throughout the 1980s. When the Reagan administration moved slowly in listing new species, Congress in 1982 set a one-year deadline for decisions on petitions to list species for preservation. It also ordered the Interior Department to make decisions solely on biological grounds, ruling out the consideration of economic consequences. By the mid-1980s lawmakers were at odds over plans to reintroduce WOLVES and grizzly bears in the West and to require shrimp fishermen to use TURTLE EXCLUDER DEVICES. After a three-year delay, Congress reauthorized the law in 1988, increasing the amount of funding and setting up an African elephant conservation fund to help African nations trying to protect elephant populations.

As divisive as the Endangered Species Act was in the 1980s, it resisted all efforts at compromise throughout the 1990s. When the authorization for funding expired in 1992, an antienvironmental backlash, fueled by unemployment concerns, made the act a highly charged issue in the West. California builders worried about losing up to 200,000 jobs because of plans to list the California gnatcatcher—a small bird that nested in prime development coastal areas—as a threatened species. Environmentalists and loggers in the Pacific Northwest fought bitterly over plans to set aside as much as nine million acres of forest for the threatened northern spotted owl. When the Clinton administration took over in 1993 and proposed a compromise on Northwest forests that officials hoped would serve as a model for endangered species protection, it was assailed on all sides.

Critics demanding major revisions to the act stepped up their rhetoric in 1995, when the Supreme Court ruled against them on a key provision of the law. In the case of *Babbitt v. Sweet Home,* the Court sided with the government that the law's provisions against the taking of a species barred any land modification that destroyed the actual or potential habitat of an endangered species. Republican leaders who had just won a congressional majority sought to overturn the ruling, narrowing the law's definition of "harm" to only those direct actions that killed or injured a member of an endangered or threatened species—not actions that destroyed habitat. Their plan also would have provided compensation to property owners under certain circumstances and provided financial incentives to encourage people to assist with species protection. But it foundered in the face of a veto threat by President BILL CLINTON and strong environmental opposition. In the end, conservative critics won only a six-month freeze on new species listing.

Two years later, Sen. Dirk Kempthorne, R-Idaho, won the support of the SENATE ENVIRONMENT AND PUBLIC WORKS COMMITTEE with a painstakingly crafted compromise that offered greater flexibility for landowners, but the bill died because of opposition on all sides. That same year, conservatives also attempted to waive provisions of the act as they pertained to flood-control projects. In a sign of the law's enduring strength, they had to settle for a compromise that temporarily waived the reviews required under the Endangered Species Act only for repairs that were necessary to respond to an imminent threat to human lives and property.

Since then, conservatives have continued to press for legislation making it more difficult to list new species and requiring the government to compensate landowners. In addition, lawmakers have debated relatively minor changes to the law, such as changing the procedures used to designate a species' critical habitat.

Endangered Species Committee

Sometimes called the "God Squad" because of its power, the Endangered Species Committee has the authority to exempt projects from the ENDAN-

GERED SPECIES ACT even if that could result in the elimination of a species. The seven-member committee is composed of the secretaries of agriculture, the army, and the interior; the chair of the Council of Economic Advisors; the administrators of the ENVIRONMENTAL PROTECTION AGENCY and the NATIONAL OCEANIC AND ATMOSPHERIC ADMINISTRATION; and a presidential appointee from the affected state. At least five votes are required to grant an exemption, which can be granted only if there is no "reasonable and prudent alternative" to the project, the project's benefits outweigh the continued existence of a species, and the project is of national and regional significance. Even then, the committee must establish methods to try to save a species, such as breeding it in captivity or transplanting it.

Congress created the committee in 1978 during debate over whether to construct the $31 million Tallico Dam and wipe out the habitat of the endangered SNAIL DARTER. In 1992 the committee generated controversy by voting to allow limited logging in Northwest forests that were home to the threatened NORTHERN SPOTTED OWL. Court injunctions prevented such logging from taking place.

Endocrine disruptors

Environmentalists and many policymakers have grown increasingly concerned in recent years about certain chemicals that can act as endocrine disruptors, potentially causing significant harm to the health of both humans and wildlife. These chemicals, which include natural plant estrogens, common plastics found in household items, and PESTICIDES and industrial contaminants such as DDT and polychlorinated biphenyls (PCBS), mimic the effects of estrogen or other hormones in the endocrine system. (The endocrine system, including female ovaries and male testes, as well as such glands as the pituitary, thyroid, and adrenal, guides development, behavior, and reproduction.) Scientific research has linked endocrine disruptors with major health problems in wildlife and laboratory animals, such as certain types of tumors, nervous system disorders, and reproductive problems. It is not clear whether low levels of the chemicals affect human health. Under the direction of Congress, the ENVIRONMENTAL PROTECTION AGENCY (EPA) in 1998 began screening thousands of chemicals for their possible hormone-like effects.

Scientists are in disagreement over how the chemicals affect humans and animals, and whether the effects are due to endocrine disruption or some other cause. Although health advocates claim that endocrine disruptors may cause numerous problems—including reduced sperm counts in men, intelligence deficits in children, genital defects, and changes in the ratio of male births to female births—other researchers caution against drawing conclusions too quickly. A much-cited 1999 study by a National Research Council committee concluded that the research to date did not show a link between the chemicals and an increased cancer risk. On the other hand, the committee did warn that PCBs appear to pose a significant health risk, citing studies that children of women who had eaten PCB-contaminated freshwater fish while pregnant suffered from intelligence deficits and other problems.

Concerns over endocrine disruptors date back to the 1960s. Biologists at the time began speculating that chemicals with hormone-like actions were causing reproductive disorders in animals, including thinner eggshells and abnormal sexual activity. In the early 1970s several women whose mothers had taken a synthetic estrogen, DES, during pregnancy were found to be suffering from a rare cancer of the vagina. This finding spurred a series of animal studies that confirmed that estrogenic exposure before birth could cause cancer and reduced fertility in later life, raising alarms that widespread synthetic chemicals were causing long-term health disorders.

A 1996 book by World Wildlife Fund biologist Theo Colborn and two co-authors popularized the term "endocrine disruptor" and warned of a dramatic threat to the health of living creatures around the planet. The book, which included a foreword by Vice President AL GORE and detailed information about reproductive failures and sexual abnormalities, sparked a major public debate that reverberated in Congress. Lawmakers added a provision to a 1996 pesticide law, the FOOD QUALITY AND PROTECTION ACT, directing the EPA to study the possible estrogenic effects of pesticides and other environmental contaminants. The EPA responded in 1998, announcing a massive—and controversial—initiative to screen tens of thousands of chemicals for their hormone-like effects. Lynn Goldman, the EPA's assistant administrator for toxic substances at the time, acknowledged that the program would be difficult but said it would represent "a major step forward in public health protection." Chemical manufacturers, which faced costs of $100 million for the tests, warned that the program could lead to false positive findings. But many scientists applauded the move as necessary to address the worrisome questions about estrogenic effects.

Energy efficiency

Since the 1970s, the government has funded programs to develop more efficient uses of energy. Its initial goal was to reduce the nation's dependence on foreign oil, but policymakers increasingly are concerned about the effects of energy consumption on such environmental problems as GLOBAL WARMING. That is because power plants, factories, and motor vehicles that use energy derived from FOSSIL FUELS emit tons of pollutants daily into the air, affecting both the environment and human health.

There are many ways of increasing energy efficiency. Buildings can be better insulated, communities can be planned in a way that minimizes driving, and machines can be engineered to run on less energy without sacrificing performance. Scientists are also exploring less-polluting RENEWABLE ENERGY sources, including sunlight and wind.

After the 1973 oil embargo, Congress took a number of steps to promote energy efficiency. It funded research into improved use of existing fuels and the development of new sources of energy, passed the 1975 automobile fuel efficiency act (PL 96-426) to impose fuel efficiency standards on new cars, set up a program to apply energy-efficiency ratings to appliances, and ultimately established the U.S. DEPARTMENT OF ENERGY.

Interest in energy conservation waned in the 1980s, when oil prices dropped. In recent years, however, officials have looked to energy efficiency to reduce emissions of GREENHOUSE GASES. The Clinton administration worked with automakers to produce experimental cars that get eighty miles per gallon, and Congress in the 1990s appropriated hundreds of millions of dollars yearly for Energy Department energy-efficiency programs. But such

Energy Consumption per Person, 1949–1999

Year	Total energy consumption (quadrillion Btu)	Energy consumption per person (quadrillion Btu)	Year	Total energy consumption (quadrillion Btu)	Energy consumption per person (quadrillion Btu)
1949	32.00	215	1976	76.07	350
1950	34.63	229	1977	78.12	355
			1978	80.12	361
1951	37.00	240	1979	81.04	361
1952	36.77	235	1980	R78.43	346
1953	37.68	237			
1954	36.66	226	1981	76.57	334
1955	40.24	244	1982	73.44	317
			1983	73.32	314
1956	41.79	249	1984	76.97	326
1957	41.82	244	1985	R76.78	323
1958	41.67	239			
1959	43.49	246	1986	R77.06	321
1960	45.12	252	1987	R79.63	329
			1988	R83.07	340
1961	45.76	250	1989	R,*84.59	R,*343
1962	47.83	258	1990	R84.19	338
1963	49.65	263			
1964	51.83	271	1991	R84.06	333
1965	54.02	279	1992	R85.51	335
			1993	87.31	339
1966	57.02	292	1994	R89.23	343
1967	58.91	298	1995	R90.94	346
1968	62.41	313			
1969	65.63	326	1996	R93.91	354
1970	67.86	334	1997	R94.32	352
			1998	R94.57	R350
1971	69.31	335	1999	P96.60	354
1972	72.76	348			
1973	75.81	359			
1974	74.08	347			
1975	72.04	334			

Source: U.S. Department of Energy, Energy Information Administration, http://www.eia.doe.gov/pub/energy.overview/aer1999/txt/aer0105.txt.
Notes: R = revised. P = preliminary.
* There is a discontinuity in this time series between 1988 and 1989 due to the expanded coverage of renewable energy beginning in 1989.

programs have had mixed results. Per-capita energy consumption in the United States, which increased sharply after World War II, dipped for about a decade following the energy crises. By 1995, however, consumption had returned to roughly the same level as the early 1970s, or about 350 million Btus yearly (see table). The United States continues to use far more energy than any other country.

Energy Policy Act

The 1992 Energy Policy Act (PL 102-486) represented the first effort by Congress since the late 1970s to reduce dependence on foreign oil. The massive bill sought to boost alternative energy use and increase ENERGY EFFICIENCY—two major goals of environmentalists. However, lawmakers deadlocked over other environmental priorities, including barring oil drilling in the ARCTIC NATIONAL WILDLIFE REFUGE, making cars and trucks more fuel-efficient, and imposing energy taxes to reduce consumption. As a result, the law has restrained the growth in energy consumption somewhat, not stopped it.

The Energy Policy Act made a number of changes across the spectrum of energy industries and issues. Perhaps the most dramatic provisions amended the 1935 Public Utility Holding Company Act to allow established utilities and independent producers to compete freely in the wholesale power market, which lawmakers said would increase efficiency. Congress also authorized billions of dollars for research and development projects sponsored by the U.S. DEPARTMENT OF ENERGY, as well as tax incentives to encourage conservation and the use of renewable fuels. It set national goals of attaining a 30 percent increase in efficiency by 2010 and a 75 percent increase in the use of RENEWABLE ENERGY by 2005, both based on 1988 levels. To help meet those goals, it set benchmarks for federal and state agencies to buy alternative-fuel vehicles and to design government buildings to energy efficient standards. It also required the Energy Department to develop both alternative fuels and so-called replacement fuels (motor fuels that can be mixed with conventional gasoline or diesel fuel).

Taking aim at GLOBAL WARMING, the law required an administration study on the methods and costs of curbing GREENHOUSE GAS emissions. In an attempt to encourage water conservation, lawmakers agreed to a little-noticed provision mandating LOW-FLOW TOILETS.

Environmental impact statements

Under the 1970 NATIONAL ENVIRONMENTAL POLICY ACT, federal agencies must draw up environmental impact statements when undertaking any major action that may have a significant impact on the environment. The statements, which vary somewhat from agency to agency, typically specify the estimated impact on wildlife, air and water quality, and other environmental factors, as well as detail alternative actions that may be less environmentally destructive. They are reviewed by the ENVIRONMENTAL PROTECTION AGENCY. Many states have similar requirements for their own agencies.

The environmental impact statements do not necessarily commit an agency to reducing environmental damage. Their larger significance is enabling opponents of the proposed action to identify severe environmental consequences, such as the destruction of WETLANDS or the habitat of an endangered species, that could trigger a court decision against the action. Environmental and antidevelopment groups have used the statements to win court decisions against highway construction, HAZARDOUS WASTE disposal, and other government actions. Many conservatives worry that environmental impact statement requirements are overly cumbersome, costing taxpayer dollars and slowing down vital government projects, but advocates say they are necessary to ensure environmental protection.

Environmental justice

Environmental justice, which combines civil rights with environmental protection, is the principle that all people have the right to a safe and healthy environment. It has sparked considerable debate since studies in the 1980s showed that minority communities were far more likely than white communities to be exposed to toxic waste and other environmental threats. The issue has also put an uncomfortable spotlight on the "GROUP OF TEN" environmental organizations, which were dominated by white, upper-income people.

Concerns over environmental racism crystallized in 1982, when residents of Warren County, N.C., a predominantly African-American community, demonstrated against a state plan to dump six thousand truckloads of soil contaminated with PCBS. Although the landfill was completed, the protests sparked national attention and North Carolina agreed to put no more LANDFILLS in Warren.

The following year, the General Accounting Office found that three of four HAZARDOUS WASTE facilities in the Southeast were in African-American communities. In 1987 the United Church of Christ Commission for Racial Justice released an explosive report, *Toxic Waste and Race in the United States*, revealing that minority communities were disproportionately targeted for hazardous waste facilities. It warned that three of every five black and Hispanic residents lived in communities with uncontrolled waste sites.

With civil rights and environmental organizations alike calling for greater protection of minority communities, the Bush administration in 1990 established the Environmental Equity Workgroup to study the issue. Two years later, the environmental justice movement gained permanent status when President GEORGE BUSH created the Office of Environmental Equity. The Clinton administration subsequently renamed it the Office of Environmental Justice and pledged to focus on increased environmental protection for minorities.

Studies show that minority communities are more likely than white communities to be exposed to hazardous toxic waste. Riverbank State Park was built on top of the North River Sewage Treatment Plant in West Harlem, New York. Source: Environmental Justice Resource Center

In Executive Order 12898, President BILL CLINTON in 1994 required every federal agency involved in public health or environmental matters to "make achieving environmental justice part of its mission." The ENVIRONMENTAL PROTECTION AGENCY's Office of Civil Rights helps enforce environmental justice requirements by investigating complaints based on Title VI of the Civil Rights Act, which prohibits discrimination based on race, color, or national origin in programs or activities that receive federal funds.

Siting a hazardous waste dump in a minority neighborhood may have more to do with economics than deliberate discrimination. Minority areas tend to attract waste dumps because of low land costs and weak political clout. The pollution, in turn, keeps land values depressed, thereby luring additional low-income people who cannot afford to live elsewhere.

The recent emphasis on environmental justice has helped minority communities stave off some potentially harmful industrial proposals. In 1997 a citizens' group in northwest Louisiana blocked plans by a German-owned firm to build the first private uranium-enrichment plant in the United States. After a seven-year battle, the group persuaded the NUCLEAR REGULATORY COMMISSION to deny the company the required license based on evidence that race had played a part in the site selection.

Minority communities have also lost some high-profile battles. In 1998 Congress voted to proceed with plans for a low-level NUCLEAR WASTE facility outside Sierra Blanca, Texas, despite concerns that it amounted to racism against the area's predominantly low-income Hispanic population.

In addition to the problem of waste dumps, minorities are more likely to be exposed to environmental toxins because of poor housing conditions. For example, black and Hispanic children in the United States are two to three times more likely than whites to suffer from LEAD poisoning. Moreover, minority workers are more likely to work in jobs where they are exposed to toxic chemicals. This is a particularly serious problem for migrant workers in fields that have been treated with PESTICIDES, and for workers in plants along the U.S.-Mexico border where wages are low and pollution controls are weak.

Environmental justice is a complex issue that may be difficult to settle by simply halting the practice of building waste dumps and other types of hazardous waste facilities in minority communities. Low-income residents are sometimes willing to accept health risks and noxious odors for the prospect that a new industrial plant will bring jobs. This is a major issue on Native American reservations, which are not covered by state environmental laws and badly need the type of income that a waste disposal operation can produce.

Like many other environmental concerns, environmental justice has international ramifications. Just as states tend to direct hazardous waste to minority communities in the United States, wealthy countries sometimes send poorer countries their hazardous wastes, and they often build high-risk industrial plants overseas. The 1989 Basel Convention imposed international toxic waste shipping restrictions, which were tightened in 1995.

Environmental movement

The modern environmental movement emerged as a powerful, although sometimes uncoordinated, political force in the 1970s, born of mounting concerns about oil spills, PESTICIDE poisonings, and other disasters. It is generally said to have begun on

U.S. Government Spending on Natural Resources and the Environment, Selected Years (in billions of current dollars)

Year	Water resources	Conservation and land management	Recreational resources	Pollution control and abatement	Other natural resources	Total
1965	1.546	0.341	0.218	0.134	0.292	2.531
1970	1.514	0.376	0.363	0.384	0.428	3.065
1975	2.608	0.655	0.803	2.523	0.757	7.346
1980	4.223	1.043	1.677	5.510	1.405	13.858
1985	4.122	1.481	1.621	4.465	1.668	13.357
1990	4.401	3.553	1.876	5.170	2.080	17.080
1995	4.628	5.318	2.801	6.513	2.655	21.915
1999	4.728	5.679	3.498	6.898	3.165	23.968

Source: U.S. Office of Management and Budget. *The Budget of the United States, Fiscal Year 2001*, Table 3.2, "Outlays by Function and Superfunction: 1962–2005" (Washington, D.C.: OMB, 2000).

Notes: These outlays constitute the U.S. budget subfunction "300 Natural Resources and Environment" by fiscal year. The federal fiscal year begins on October 1 and ends on the subsequent September 30. It is designated by the year in which it ends; for example, fiscal year 1999 began on October 1, 1998, and ended on September 30, 1999. Before fiscal year 1977, the federal fiscal years began on July 1 and ended on June 30.

the first EARTH DAY—April 22, 1970—although conservationists had already influenced U.S. policy for more than a century. In its 1970s heyday, the modern movement appeared unstoppable as it whipped up overwhelming bipartisan support for landmark clean air, clean water, and endangered species laws. Although environmentalists have since run into stiff resistance from businesses and PRIVATE PROPERTY RIGHTS advocates, they can take credit for significant improvements in the nation's air and water quality.

Environmental policy in the United States is often traced to 1864, when geographer George Perkins Marsh published the influential book, *Man and Nature*, about the ecological consequences of overgrazing, DEFORESTATION, and other environmentally destructive practices. The book helped spur early conservation policies, including the establishment of YELLOWSTONE NATIONAL PARK, in 1872, and the creation of national forest reserves. But environmental protection remained a minority view. Americans in the late nineteenth century were so focused on subduing nature, rather than

preserving it, that hunters engaged in a highly publicized competition to wipe out the last wild bison herd in the 1880s. (Conservationists saved the species from extinction by protecting a small herd in captivity and establishing a breeding program.)

Conservation emerged as a potent political issue at the beginning of the twentieth century. In 1900 President William McKinley signed the LACEY ACT, barring interstate sales of any animals killed in violation of state laws. Subsequently, President THEODORE ROOSEVELT set aside tens of millions of acres of land in NATIONAL FORESTS, NATIONAL PARKS, and other preserves. Although Roosevelt emphasized "utilitarian conservation"—the protection of land for jobs and the harvesting of resources, rather than for wilderness—his administration ensured the indefinite protection of such spectacular areas as the Grand Canyon and Yosemite Valley. Other early government actions included local ordinances at the end of the nineteenth century to curtail AIR POLLUTION from coalburning and other sources; the 1899 Rivers and Harbors Act, which prohibited the dumping of most nonsewage waste into navigable waters; and various federal funding initiatives to set aside or restore habitat for migrating birds and other wildlife, such as the 1937 PITTMAN-ROBERTSON Act.

After World War II the booming population and development of new, highly toxic PESTICIDES and other chemicals overwhelmed existing environmental laws. Rachel Carson's 1962 bestseller, *Silent Spring,* crystallized public anxiety about environmental degradation by documenting the effects of chemical pollution on all life on earth. During the 1960s the nation faced signs everywhere of severe environmental degradation: the Cuyahoga River outside Cleveland caught fire, oil spills fouled numerous beaches, and the national symbol, the BALD EAGLE, faced EXTINCTION. Amid demands for increased environmental protection, Congress passed a few major laws, most notably the 1964 WILDERNESS ACT, which set up a system to preserve large tracts of untamed land, and the 1970 NATIONAL ENVIRONMENTAL POLICY ACT, which required federal agencies to consider the environmental impacts of all their major activities. Generally, however, Congress took an incremental approach to environmental protection. It focused on funding research and authorizing states to improve air and water quality (for data on U.S. government spending on the environment, see table). This proved ineffectual because state officials hesitated to crack down on polluters.

Frustrated by the slow pace of environmental legislation, Sen. Gaylord Nelson, D-Wis., conceived of designating a day for teach-ins across the country to focus attention on the environment. The resulting Earth Day far surpassed expectations: millions of people dramatically illustrated their concerns about the environment by convening in cities and campuses across the country. Just three

months later, President RICHARD NIXON sent legislation to Congress to establish the ENVIRONMENTAL PROTECTION AGENCY and consolidate federal antipollution efforts. Responding to the public clamor, Nixon vowed in his 1971 State of the Union address "to restore and enhance our natural environment."

In the early 1970s the environmental movement crested. Despite warnings that pollution restrictions could cost the economy billions of dollars yearly, lawmakers of both parties came together to pass the laws that today comprise the backbone of environmental protection: the CLEAN AIR ACT of 1970, the CLEAN WATER ACT of 1972, the ENDANGERED SPECIES ACT of 1973, the SAFE DRINKING WATER ACT of 1974, and the RESOURCE CONSERVATION AND RECOVERY ACT of 1976. In those optimistic days, many policymakers foresaw the end of most air and WATER POLLUTION by the 1980s. Even later in the decade, when concerns about energy shortages and double-digit inflation distracted policymakers, lawmakers set aside tens of millions of acres of wilderness in Alaska and passed the landmark HAZARDOUS WASTE law known as SUPERFUND.

Business opposition to proliferating regulations and a sense among many in the general public that the environment did not need further protection set the stage for a major backlash in the 1980s. President RONALD REAGAN came to office pledging to cut the costs that federal environmental regulations imposed on businesses and communities. JAMES G. WATT, Reagan's controversial interior secretary, stressed economic growth over environmental protection. Forced on the defensive, environmentalists showed impressive strength in blocking proposals to pare back the laws of the 1970s, and they repeatedly went to court to force the government to enforce endangered species and antipollution laws. Despite their rising membership numbers and legal acumen, however, environmental groups such as the SIERRA CLUB and Environmental Defense Fund generally lacked the lobbying power to force Congress to expand environmental protections.

After Reagan left office, the environmental movement could not regain the momentum of the early 1970s. Setting environmental goals, once a seemingly straightforward matter of stopping pollution and protecting rare animals, had evolved into a dizzyingly complex task of testing tens of thousands of chemicals, mapping entire watersheds and ecosystems, and assigning liability for past legal dumping of hazardous waste. The solutions were also becoming less certain: housing the growing population without causing URBAN SPRAWL, feeding people without OVERFISHING, and stopping GLOBAL WARMING at a time of economic growth.

Acknowledging the resistance to costly regulations, some environmentalists began adjusting their tactics in the 1990s to emphasize negotiated settlements instead of the 1970s "COMMAND-AND-CONTROL" approach that imposed strict mandates. They scored a few signature victories in Congress, such as amending the Clean Air Act to curb ACID RAIN, and fended off most Republican attempts to scale back regulations. But throughout the 1990s, lawmakers deadlocked over reauthorizing major environmental laws such as the Endangered Species Act and the Clean Water Act despite warnings that the aging laws needed to have more flexibility and a broader focus. The environmental movement itself showed signs of splintering. Environmentalists publicly disagreed over ratification of the NORTH AMERICAN FREE TRADE AGREEMENT and DOLPHIN-SAFE TUNA policies. Established environmental groups such as the Environmental

Defense Fund (now called Environmental Defense!), the Audubon Society, and others came under criticism from more radical environmentalists for their bureaucratic structures and willingness to compromise. Businesses, however, complained that the groups stubbornly defended outmoded and inflexible regulations.

Paradoxically, the environmental movement has gained strength internationally even as it seems stalemated at home. In 1987 environmentalists won an extraordinary victory with the MONTREAL PROTOCOL ON SUBSTANCES THAT DEPLETE THE OZONE LAYER, eventually signed by more than 160 countries. The precedent-setting agreement committed both industrialized and developing countries to gradually phase out chlorofluorocarbons (CFCS) and other chemicals blamed for depleting stratospheric ozone and potentially exposing the earth to fatal ultraviolet radiation. The following decade saw a series of international agreements on preventing deforestation and promoting BIODIVERSITY. The 1997 KYOTO PROTOCOL on global warming sought to reduce emissions of GREENHOUSE GASES, although the U.S. Senate showed little interest in ratifying it.

At the beginning of the new century, the environmental movement can be credited with significantly reducing air and water pollution, nurturing high-profile species such as the bald eagle and gray whale back from the brink of extinction in the continental United States, and cleaning up hazardous waste. However, the successes are threatened by a new generation of domestic and global problems that divide policymakers and resist easy solutions. Even though most Americans identify environmental protection as an important priority, they disagree over how to go about it.

Environmental Protection Agency

The U.S. Environmental Protection Agency (EPA) is the leading federal agency on pollution issues. It administers several of the nation's most important environmental laws, including the CLEAN AIR ACT, CLEAN WATER ACT, SAFE DRINKING WATER ACT, and SUPERFUND hazardous waste law, and it regulates HAZARDOUS WASTE disposal and the use of hazardous chemicals such as PESTICIDES. Primary responsibilities include such controversial matters as establishing AIR POLLUTION limits, controlling the discharge of water pollutants, setting standards for hazardous waste transportation, regulating radiation levels in the environment, and determining acceptable noise levels for equipment. It also maintains a website, www.epa.gov, that is a major source of information about environmental programs and issues. With a budget of about $8 billion and eighteen thousand employees, the EPA is Washington's largest regulatory agency. Despite its broad mandate, it does not oversee public lands such as national parks—that responsibility falls to the interior and agriculture departments.

Created in 1970 during the Nixon administration to consolidate antipollution efforts, the EPA faces a Herculean task in enforcing the growing mass of environmental regulations. Environmentalists warn that the agency suffers from a chronically inadequate budget, as well as relentless congressional oversight and detailed management instructions. Congress has frequently cut its budget while piling on more and more responsibilities. As early as the mid-1980s, the COUNCIL ON ENVIRONMENTAL QUALITY reported that "the Environmental Protection Agency cannot possibly do all the things its various mandates tell it to do." Even with increased funding in the 1990s, the agency regularly failed to meet statutory deadlines for such tasks as cleaning up Superfund sites. Critics say the EPA remains a poorly organized agency that lacks the flexibility to respond to changing environmental conditions.

Complicating matters, the agency is constantly buffeted by environmental and health advocates who contend it does not vigorously enforce environmental laws and by business and industry groups that accuse it of overstepping its authority and promulgating overly broad regulations without conducting COST-BENEFIT ANALYSES. As a result, many of EPA's actions are driven by lawsuits from all sides. In 1997, for example, EPA director CAROL BROWNER responded to an American Lung Association lawsuit by unveiling tougher clean air regulations—only to have business groups block the new policy in court.

The agency began operations under the leadership of WILLIAM D. RUCKELSHAUS with a budget of $455 million in the early 1970s (for names of EPA administrators, see table). At the time, government

EPA Administrators, 1970–2000

	Dates of service
William D. Ruckelshaus	Dec. 4, 1970–April 30, 1973
Robert Fri (acting)	April 30, 1973–Sept. 12, 1973
Russell E. Train	Sept. 13, 1973–Jan. 20, 1977
John Quarles Jr. (acting)	Jan. 21, 1977–March 6, 1977
Douglas M. Costle	March 7, 1977–Jan. 20, 1981
Steve Jellinek (acting)	Jan. 21, 1981–Jan. 25, 1981
Walter Barber Jr. (acting)	Jan. 26, 1981–May 19, 1981
Anne M. Gorsuch [Burford]	May 20, 1981–March 9, 1983
Lee Verstandig (acting)	March 10, 1983–May 17, 1983
William D. Ruckelshaus	May 18, 1983–Jan. 4, 1985
Lee M. Thomas (acting)	Jan. 4, 1985–Feb. 7, 1985
Lee M. Thomas	Feb. 8, 1985–Jan. 20, 1989
John Moore (acting)	Jan. 21, 1989–Feb. 5, 1989
William K. Reilly	Feb. 6, 1989–Jan. 20, 1993
Carol M. Browner	Jan. 21, 1993–

Source: U.S. Environmental Protection Agency, http://www.epa.gov/history/admin/agency/index.htm.

officials anticipated a quick end to most pollution. Proliferating regulations and increasingly complex environmental laws spurred a backlash from business leaders, who blamed overzealous regulators for costing them billions of dollars every year. In the early 1980s the Reagan administration tried to pare back the EPA's reach, sparking angry protests on Capitol Hill. The ensuing confrontation culminated in congressional investigations into the EPA's management of the Superfund program and the 1983 resignation of EPA director Anne M. Burford. Even though President RONALD REAGAN brought back Ruckelshaus to restore the agency's effectiveness, morale was slow to recover. By 1988 the beleaguered agency had met just 20 percent of its 800 statutory deadlines.

Beginning in 1989 environmental-minded lawmakers proposed elevating the EPA to cabinet level. They said this higher status would give the agency additional lobbying clout during the budget season, provide its secretary with more management flexibility, and strengthen EPA's hand in international negotiations. President BILL CLINTON pressed for the cabinet proposal in 1993 but failed to win support from House members who insisted on imposing COST-BENEFIT ANALYSIS and RISK ASSESSMENT requirements on the new department.

Environmental Quality Incentives Program

As part of the 1996 farm bill (PL 104-127), Congress created the Environmental Quality Incentives Program to help farmers conserve water, soil, and ecologically sensitive habitats such as WETLANDS. The program provides technical assistance, cost-share payments (in which the government pays part of a project's cost), and incentive payments for such projects as MANURE management, irrigation, tillage methods, filter strips, and other conservation initiatives. Lawmakers created the program at a time of growing concern about the environmental impact of agriculture, especially large, industrial-type farming operations that were fouling waterways.

Congress authorized the program for $130 million in fiscal year 1996 and $200 million in each subsequent year through 2002. Half the funds were earmarked for assistance to livestock producers (see also AGRICULTURAL RUNOFF).

Environmental riders

Environmental riders are narrowly tailored provisions that lawmakers add to larger measures, such as annual appropriations bills, to scale back environmental regulations. This is a venerable legislative tactic—Congress used it in 1907 to stop THEODORE ROOSEVELT from creating new NATIONAL FORESTS—but it gained new life in the mid-1990s when Republicans won control of Congress. Unable to muster enough votes to pass sweeping overhauls of environmental bills, conservatives instead tried to scale back unpopular regulations with narrowly crafted appropriations provisions. As a result, President BILL CLINTON frequently was put in the awkward position of deciding whether to veto a sweeping and popular spending bill over a handful of antienvironmental provisions.

Conservative Republicans scored their first big victory in 1995 when Clinton signed a fiscal rescissions bill (PL 104-19) that contained a provision allowing companies to expedite SALVAGE LOGGING in OLD-GROWTH FORESTS. House conservatives in

1995 also tried to add seventeen riders to a spending bill that would have limited the EPA's ability to regulate such things as emissions from industrial facilities and oil refineries, raw sewage overflows, arsenic and RADON in drinking water, and traces of cancer-causing substances in processed food. Lawmakers ultimately dropped most of the riders in the face of fierce environmental protests, but the legislation was vetoed because of political battles over spending levels.

After suffering the political fallout over spending battles in 1995 and 1996, Republicans grew more cautious about adding riders. But environmental provisions continued to provoke some of the most stubborn appropriations battles of the late 1990s. One of the most spectacular fights erupted in 1998 when Alaska's two Republican senators, Ted Stevens and FRANK H. MURKOWSKI, pressed for money to build a road through the Izembek National Wildlife Refuge to Cold Bay in Alaska. They relented only after winning $37.5 million for an all-weather airport and other projects in Cold Bay. The following year, Sen. Robert C. Byrd, D-W.Va., unsuccessfully pressed for a provision scaling back regulations of the controversial mining technique known as MOUNTAINTOP REMOVAL.

Other efforts to retain riders have been more successful. Western conservatives, for example, used riders in the late 1990s to expand logging on national forests in California and allow automatic renewal of grazing leases on some public lands.

Estuaries

An estuary is a type of inlet or bay where a river empties into the ocean. Estuaries tend to be especially biologically productive because of the mix of salt and fresh water ecosystems. In 1987 Congress passed legislation (PL 100-4) amending the CLEAN WATER ACT and creating a National Estuary Program within the ENVIRONMENTAL PROTECTION AGENCY. The program coordinates federal, state, and local antipollution efforts, seeking to protect the ecological health of more than two dozen estuaries while maintaining the economies of nearby communities.

A separate 1983 program seeks to preserve the nation's largest estuary, the Chesapeake Bay, by coordinating the environmental protection programs of the neighboring states. Despite such efforts, the Chesapeake is severely threatened by local development and agricultural activities. The bay's oyster population, which helped reduce the impact of pollutants, was nearly wiped out by the early 1990s. It is recovering slowly.

Eutrophication

Eutrophication is the process by which a lake or other body of water becomes choked with aquatic plants, eventually resulting in deoxygenated water and, potentially, the death of all fish. This process occurs naturally and also as a result of increased levels of compounds such as nitrogen and phosphorus in the water due to various types of RUNOFF from agriculture or other human activities.

To address this problem, Congress has debated amending the CLEAN WATER ACT to reduce runoff from farms, city streets, and other places. The ENVIRONMENTAL PROTECTION AGENCY in the late 1990s announced a series of initiatives designed to tighten regulations of such runoff, known as NONPOINT SOURCE POLLUTION, and impose tougher requirements on large farm operations.

Everglades

The Florida Everglades are the nation's largest WETLAND and a major focus of environmental policymakers. The vast subtropical marshes are home to dozens of endangered species, including the Florida panther and the American crocodile, as well as to large flocks of herons, egrets, and other spectacular wading birds. Known as the "river of grass," the Everglades once covered the southern half of Florida from Lake Okeechobee to Florida Bay. During the twentieth century, however, the U.S. ARMY CORPS OF ENGINEERS built a vast network of canals and dikes to divert the natural water flow, clearing the way for the construction of housing developments and sugar plantations. About half of the Everglades has been destroyed, and the rest is threatened by AGRICULTURAL RUNOFF, the spread of EXOTIC SPECIES, and changes in water flow. Some scientists believe that the marshes are dying.

Conservationists have tried to protect the Everglades since the early twentieth century. They persuaded the federal government to establish Everglades National Park in 1947 and to set aside additional land subsequently in Biscayne National Park and Big Cypress National Preserve. In 1994 Florida agreed to a landmark plan to try to restore the Everglades by creating filtering marshes to absorb phosphorus and other runoff from sugar fields. The plan ended a six-year lawsuit that the federal government brought against the state for failing to protect the Everglades, but it drew heated criticism from environmentalists for deferring cleanup standards and for placing the bulk of the costs on taxpayers rather than the sugar industry. Congress has subsequently considered a multibillion-dollar proposal to redistribute the water in order to revive the marshes. But some scientists question whether such a plan is feasible. (See also SUGAR PRICE SUPPORTS.)

Exotic species

The term *exotic species* is often used to describe animals and plants that are transported into regions where they do not appear naturally. Also described as "invasive," "nonindigenous," or "nonnative," such species are viewed as a major economic and ecological threat in the United States and elsewhere. They often flourish in the new habitat because of the absence of natural predators, sometimes crowding out indigenous species and causing environmental havoc. Biologists believe that at least five thousand exotic plant and animal species have established themselves in the United States, including such familiar species as kudzu, starlings, and the house mouse. Harmful invaders, such as ZEBRA MUSSELS, gypsy moths, and fire ants, may cause economic losses of $100 billion annually by damaging crops, clogging underwater pipes, eating away at the foundations of buildings, and even endangering human health.

The economic toll aside, exotic species can cause catastrophic damage to sensitive ecosystems. Some scientists believe that exotic species pose as grave a threat to the environment as HABITAT LOSS, greatly accelerating the rate of worldwide EXTINCTION of plant and animal species. In Guam, for example, the brown tree snake has wiped out much of the native bird population since being introduced inadvertently after World War II. Parasitic invaders, although less visible, also take a toll: an Asian fungus disease of elm trees, known as Dutch elm disease because it was found in Europe, has wiped out the American elm over much of its range. Other countries also are contending with exotic species. Many of the native cichlids in Africa's Lake Victoria, for example, have been driven to extinction by newly introduced species of perch and tilapia.

The problem of exotic species dates back many centuries. Wandering tribes used to introduce their favorite crops and domestic animals into sensitive habitats, particularly on islands. The ill-fated dodo bird was wiped out partly because its ground-laid eggs were easy prey for dogs. In recent years the

Some scientists estimate that one-half of the world's species will be extinct by the end of the twenty-first century. Poaching and habitat loss have reduced the population of the giant panda, China's most prized endangered animal, to about one thousand worldwide. Source: Natalie Behring, Reuters

boom in global transportation and trade has greatly accelerated the spread of exotic species, which may be transported inadvertently in the ballast water of ships, wooden crates and other packing material, the mud on a traveler's shoes, or virtually any other conveyance.

The United States has no comprehensive law addressing the problem of exotic species. For most of the past century, Congress instead adopted an ad hoc approach to stop particular types of species invasions, such as regulating impure seed stocks. Jolted into action by the introduction of the destructive zebra mussel, lawmakers in 1990 passed the NON-INDIGENOUS AQUATIC NUISANCE PREVENTION AND CONTROL ACT to stop the introduction of harmful aquatic species. In 1999 President BILL CLINTON signed an executive order establishing an interagency Invasive Species Council and directing all federal agencies to address exotic species concerns. Experts warn that halting the introduction of exotic species will be difficult because so many species can cause severe damage, but they urge more research into identifying the pathways that allow species to move from one continent to another.

Extinction

Many biologists believe that a mass extinction of animal and plant species worldwide is taking place, largely because of human activities that cause HABITAT LOSS, introduce EXOTIC SPECIES into fragile ecosystems, and create pollution. Some scientists worry that as many as one-fifth of the world's animal and plant species may be lost within the next thirty years and half of all species by the end of the twenty-first century. Such an eventuality

could have severe economic impacts, making it hard to develop cures from natural sources, minimize soil erosion, or even feed a growing population. A 1998 survey by New York's American Museum of Natural History indicated that scientists regard this apparent mass extinction as one of the planet's gravest environmental problems. The issue has yet to raise wide public concerns because the extinctions, unlike polluted air or sprawling development, do not affect everyday life. Most of the disappearing species are relatively obscure, such as insects, plants, and marine invertebrates.

The full extent of the current episode of extinction is a matter of debate. Extinction is a natural event because of changing environmental conditions, but under normal circumstances it claims no more than one to ten species per ten million every year, according to various scientific analyses of geologic records. In contrast, thousands of the world's species (estimated at anywhere from 3.6 million to more than one hundred million) appear to be disappearing every year, an extinction rate that may be one hundred to ten thousand times the normal rate. Estimates of species loss are controversial because it is almost impossible to prove that a species no longer exists—and many of the species that may be disappearing have never even been discovered by scientists. Instead, scientists estimate the rate of extinction through statistical models that look at the destruction of such rich habitats as tropical rain forests and coral reefs. Critics say the estimates are overblown and there is little evidence that the current extinction rate surpasses normal levels or is threatening ecological harm. But many scientists compare the current situation with massive extinctions that have happened just five times in the world's history, most recently when dinosaurs disappeared about sixty-five million years ago. The past mass extinctions may have been spurred by cataclysmic volcanic eruptions or collisions between the earth and asteroids.

In the United States, the main law seeking to prevent extinctions is the ENDANGERED SPECIES ACT, which generally bars hunting rare species or destroying their habitat. Internationally, some government agencies are trying to slow the destruction of fragile habitats, especially rain forests; protect well-known endangered species, such as the giant panda and black rhinoceros; and crack down on the international trading of products made from endangered species. The 1992 CONVENTION ON BIOLOGICAL DIVERSITY encourages such conservation efforts.

Industrialization and POPULATION GROWTH are frustrating efforts to protect rare species. Air and WATER POLLUTION is a mounting problem in developing countries, and the world's six billion people need ever-increasing amounts of land cleared for agriculture and housing. Whereas wealthier countries like the United States can afford to set aside land for rare species, starving populations in developing countries are forced to focus on their own survival, even if that means trespassing into protected natural preserves to hunt, fish, or grow crops. Exacerbating the situation, industrialized nations are consuming ever-increasing quantities of natural resources such as lumber, which leads to more habitat loss.

Exxon Valdez

The *Exxon Valdez* oil spill in Alaska's Prince William Sound remains a vivid symbol of the intense damage that a human accident can inflict on a pristine environment. When the tanker ran aground March 24, 1989, it spilled an estimated eleven million gallons of crude oil, fouling more than one thousand miles of coastline and three national parks, and killing thousands of birds and sea otters, as well as large numbers of BALD EAGLES, harbor seals, and killer whales.

Many species in the area have yet to recover. Exxon was widely criticized for failing to mount a more comprehensive cleanup response to the nation's worst oil spill. The oil company reached an out-of-court settlement with the government of Alaska but faced years of litigation over a $5 billion lawsuit by affected Alaska communities. In Congress the disaster spurred 1990 legislation (PL 101-380) intended to prevent oil spills and punish those responsible for spills.

F

Federal Insecticide, Fungicide, and Rodenticide Act

The Federal Insecticide, Fungicide, and Rodenticide Act (FIFRA), first passed in 1947 and then substantially amended, regulates the sale and use of PESTICIDES. It requires chemical manufacturers to register their products with the ENVIRONMENTAL PROTECTION AGENCY (EPA) for every intended use. Manufacturers are responsible for providing the government with adequate data from safety tests on every product, including the product's potential effects on the environment and human health. Before the product can be sold, the EPA must approve label instructions for use and safety warnings. The law also requires users to take tests to become certified as pesticide applicators.

Congress passed the law at a time of comparatively little concern about the environmental effects of pesticides. To meet environmental concerns, lawmakers in 1947 agreed that a pesticide must not cause "unreasonable adverse effects on the environment" when applied as the manufacturer intended. But lawmakers also gave chemical manufacturers a boost by requiring regulators to take into account "the economic, social and environmental costs as well as the potential benefits of the use of any pesticide."

As concerns mounted about the public health and environmental effects of pesticides, Congress in 1972 amended FIFRA to require the EPA to review the use of all pesticides, including those that had been on the market for years. In 1988 lawmakers set up a nine-year timetable to complete registration of previously approved products. But the agency, coping with inadequate funding and incomplete scientific data, moved so slowly that Rep. Mike Synar, D-Okla., predicted it would take until the year 15,520 A.D. to complete the registration process.

The 1996 FOOD QUALITY PROTECTION ACT amended FIFRA to require the EPA to review all registrations on a fifteen-year timetable. It also empowered the agency to issue an emergency order immediately suspending or changing the use of a pesticide.

Federal Land Policy and Management Act

Congress gave the Interior Department's Bureau of Land Management guidance for managing about 450 million acres of federal lands by passing the 1976 Federal Land Policy and Management Act (PL 94-579). The legislation, based on laws governing the national forests, stated that the lands should be administered according to the principles of MULTIPLE USE and sustained yield. The principles, although not precisely defined, mean that the Interior Department should keep the lands open for such uses as grazing, MINING, and recreation, while also taking steps to ensure sustainability by preventing the resources from being depleted. This policy has placed the Bureau of Land Management in the difficult position of trying to satisfy both environmentalists and developers.

The 1976 act also called for a study on the contentious issue of GRAZING FEES. (See also U.S. DEPARTMENT OF THE INTERIOR.)

Federal Water Pollution Control Act

The Federal Water Pollution Control Act is the official name of the landmark 1972 law commonly referred to as the CLEAN WATER ACT (PL 92-500). Accordingly, bills to reauthorize the Clean Water Act are actually drafted as amendments to the Federal Water Pollution Control Act.

The 1972 version is an amendment of an earlier law. The Federal Water Pollution Control Act of 1948 was one of the nation's first major efforts to combat WATER POLLUTION. It authorized the surgeon general of the Public Health Service, in conjunction with other federal, state, and local entities, to prepare strategies to reduce pollution in interstate waters and improve the sanitary condition of surface and underground waters.

Filtration

Filtration is a highly effective but potentially costly method of removing harmful particles from drinking water. Pathogenic organisms such as CRYPTOSPORIDIUM, which are resistant to conventional treatments like chlorination, can be removed from water with manufactured filters that separate out any substance larger than one micron (one millionth of a meter) in diameter. However, the SAFE DRINKING WATER ACT does not require public water systems to use such fine filters because they are very expensive to operate. Instead, most water systems use somewhat coarser filtering materials such as sand, gravel, or charcoal, in combination with other treatments. The coarser filtering removes most, but not all, contaminants.

Some environmentalists and public health experts would like to upgrade filtering and other purification methods to make drinking water so safe that even people with impaired immune systems can drink tap water. But local officials contend that it would be more cost-effective for people at risk to use filters at home. The ENVIRONMENTAL PROTECTION AGENCY began monitoring cryptosporidium levels in 1998 in an effort to determine the extent that public water systems may be contaminated.

Finding of no significant impact

Federal agencies may report a "finding of no significant impact" (commonly known as "FONSI") when they assess the possible environmental effects of their proposed actions. This finding means their activities will essentially leave the environment undisturbed. In such cases, an agency is exempt from filing an ENVIRONMENTAL IMPACT STATEMENT under the NATIONAL ENVIRONMENTAL POLICY ACT.

Fish and Wildlife Foundation

Congress established the Fish and Wildlife Foundation in 1984 to research fish, wildlife, and plant conservation issues, as well as to conduct environmental education programs. The foundation helps create public-private partnerships to restore and preserve habitat, investing in conservation projects through challenge grants. It works with state and local governments, universities, conservation groups, and businesses. A nonprofit, nonpartisan organization, the Fish and Wildlife Foundation relies on private contributions for its operating expenses.

Fish and Wildlife Service

See U.S. DEPARTMENT OF THE INTERIOR.

Flood insurance

Many environmentalists criticize the federal flood insurance program as being a subsidy to property owners that encourages development in ecologically sensitive floodplains and coastal areas. The program, created by the National Flood Insurance Act of 1968 (PL 90-448), pays property owners to rebuild damaged houses and businesses on BARRIER ISLANDS and other highly exposed areas, regardless of the risks of flooding. Premiums, which average about $300 nationwide for about $80,000 worth of coverage, fail to offset claims. In 2000 the General Accounting Office concluded that the pro-

The controversial federal flood insurance program, which pays property owners to rebuild flood-damaged houses and businesses, has been criticized as a financial liability and a threat to the environment. Four businesses in Bound Brook, New Jersey, were destroyed in September 1999 when Hurricane Floyd caused the nearby Raritan River to overflow its banks. Source: Tom Mihalek, AFP

gram paid $7 billion of claims from 1986 to 1998, borrowing more than $500 million from the U.S. Treasury. As a result, fiscal conservatives tend to join forces with environmentalists in trying to scale back the program.

But officials with the Federal Emergency Management Agency, which administers the program, say that it actually discourages risky development because flood insurance is a condition for any federally insured mortgage or construction loan in a flood-hazard area. Moreover, they point out that the policies since the late 1970s have required coastal property owners who rebuild after a flood to adhere to tougher standards.

In the 1982 COASTAL BARRIER RESOURCES ACT, Congress prohibited federal support, including flood insurance, for development on many sensitive barrier islands.

Flow control

Flow control refers to attempts by state and local governments to direct waste to specific LANDFILLS or INCINERATORS, sometimes over the protests of waste haulers who want to use less expensive facilities. Until the mid-1990s thirty-nine states and the District of Columbia had some form of flow control. However, a 1994 U.S. Supreme Court decision, *C&A Carbone v. Town of Clarkstown,* held that flow control ordinances were an unconstitutional restriction of interstate commerce. The decision was a major setback for municipalities that issued billions of dollars in bonds to build solid waste disposal sites and relied on flow control ordinances to guarantee that the sites would be heavily used.

After the *Carbone* decision, at least eighteen bond issues valued at $2 billion were downgraded by rating services. New Jersey, which had developed a statewide system of flow control to pay for the construction of new waste management facilities, found itself especially hard-pressed to keep waste haulers from taking their business to other states. Local governments across the country scrambled to cut disposal fees (known as "tipping" fees) to remain competitive, trying to offset the lost revenue by imposing other types of fees or paring back their solid waste programs. They also urged Congress to blunt the *Carbone* decision and restore some type of flow control authority.

Lawmakers could not agree on flow control legislation. Instead, they clashed repeatedly over the issue of INTERSTATE SHIPMENTS OF WASTE. In the same year as the Supreme Court decision, the House of Representatives passed a flow control bill, but Sen. JOHN H. CHAFEE, R-R.I., blocked it. He argued that it disadvantaged states such as Rhode Island that exported waste. Lawmakers in both the House and the Senate also considered measures that would have allowed certain towns and cities with preexisting flow control ordinances to continue the practice for a number of years. A House proposal in 1996, for example, would have granted flow control authority to local governments that had recently issued bonds or entered into contracts guaranteeing a minimum quantity of waste at a given facility. Other plans floated in the late 1990s would have grandfathered in some facilities with RECYCLING provisions. But lawmakers splintered into several competing camps, dooming the proposals. Some members insisted that the free market should dictate waste disposal; others wanted flow control legislation to give states new powers to keep out interstate waste; and a third camp objected because their localities would not be included in the grandfathering provisions. (See also GRANDFATHER CLAUSES; SOLID WASTE DISPOSAL ACT.)

Food Quality Protection Act

The Food Quality Protection Act of 1996 is one of the primary laws in the United States governing the use of PESTICIDES. Its most important provision is a strict health standard requiring that any chemical residue in either fresh or processed food pose a "REASONABLE CERTAINTY OF NO HARM." Lawmakers believed that this provision, which did away with past inconsistencies governing pesticide residues, represented a fair compromise that would ensure the safety of food, while allowing farmers to continue using common pesticides. However, the law has failed to quell the often heated public debate over the use of pesticides.

Prior to 1996, lawmakers had deadlocked for the better part of two decades over the contentious issue of pesticide residues in foods. At the heart of the debate was the inconsistent standard for food safety provided by the federal FOOD, DRUG, AND COSMETIC ACT. The law permitted traces of cancer-causing chemicals in fresh food. But the law's controversial DELANEY CLAUSE barred any trace of cancer-causing chemicals in processed food.

Environmentalists and health advocates throughout the 1980s and early 1990s assailed the administration of the law as outdated and weak. They warned that the government was allowing pesticide residues in food that posed numerous health risks, especially in infants and young children. One of the advocacy organizations, the Environmental Working Group, released a series of reports showing that residues of highly toxic pesticides could be found in baby foods, fruit, and drinking water. On the other side, farmers and chemical manufacturers insisted that the residues were well within safe limits. Complicating the issue, scientific advances enabled regulators to detect increasingly minute—and possibly harmless—traces of cancer-causing chemicals in processed food. Rather than ban all such chemicals under a strict enforcement of the Delaney clause, regulators decided to allow pesticides that posed no more than a "negligible risk" of cancer.

In the early 1990s environmentalists finally forced legislative action by winning federal court battles requiring the ENVIRONMENTAL PROTECTION AGENCY (EPA) to strictly uphold the Delaney clause, even if that meant banning the use of popular pesticides. With farmers facing economically costly regulations, agricultural supporters in Congress agreed to far-reaching pesticide restrictions in the Food Quality Protection Act in exchange for ending the Delaney clause. Both the House and Senate swiftly passed the bill without any opposition—evidence that lawmakers can act expeditiously on complex regulatory issues in a crisis. Environmentalists generally backed the measure, despite concerns that it would permit carcinogens (albeit in minute amounts) in processed food.

The law requires the EPA, when determining whether a pesticide residue may be harmful, to consider the cumulative human health effects of the many pesticides on food, as well as in houses, offices, and other places. The agency also has to take into account the greater vulnerability of infants and children, assuming an additional tenfold safety factor in cases in which the science is incomplete. The EPA has until 2006 to finish reviewing existing pesticide regulations to make sure they meet the new safety standard. Under the law's consumer right-to-know provisions, the agency publishes and distributes information about pesticide residues. It has also begun to study the effects of ENDOCRINE DISRUPTORS—chemicals believed to interfere with the hormonal systems of people and wildlife.

Although the Food Quality Protection Act was intended to end years of debates and lawsuits, it appears to have moved the battle from Congress to the EPA. In 1999 seven environmental, consumer, and health organizations quit an EPA advisory group in protest of what they viewed as government policies that favored the chemical industry. When the EPA announced a few months later that it would restrict the use of two widely used pesticides, the organizations criticized the agency for permitting the continued use of many other dangerous chemicals, including classes of pesticides known as organophosphates and carbamates. On the other hand, farmers and chemical manufacturers denounced the ban of the two pesticides, saying it could throw many growers out of business. Rural lawmakers proposed amending the law to make it more difficult for the EPA to ban pesticides.

Fossil fuels

The three fossil fuels—oil, coal, and natural gas—are a driving force behind the U.S. economy. Despite environmental concerns and government funding of RENEWABLE ENERGY programs, these fuels supply about 85 percent of the nation's energy needs, providing electricity, heat, and motor vehicle fuel. The rest of the energy comes from nuclear power plants and various types of RENEWABLE ENERGY.

The oil, coal, and natural gas industries can rightly take credit for fostering technological advances and enabling Americans to live in comfort. As a result, they enjoy tremendous clout in Washington, D.C. However, energy supplies come with an environmental price. MINING or drilling for fossil fuels can rip apart the landscape and spoil pristine areas, and combusting the fuels severely pollutes the air and water. In recent years, concerns about the effect of fossil fuel emissions on GLOBAL WARMING have reinvigorated efforts among environmentalists to conserve energy and develop alternative energy sources. But the government has given lukewarm support to such efforts.

Since highly publicized oil spills fouled California beaches in the 1960s, environmentalists have waged a series of battles to regulate the extraction and transportation of fossil fuels. They have won some key battles in Congress, notably by regulating strip mining with the 1976 SURFACE MINING CONTROL AND RECLAMATION ACT, punishing oil spillers with the 1990 OIL POLLUTION ACT, and restricting OFFSHORE DRILLING with a series of congressional votes. But they failed to stop construction of the Alaska pipeline, and they repeatedly deadlocked with energy companies over allowing oil and gas exploration in the ARCTIC NATIONAL WILDLIFE REFUGE. Despite the power of the environmental lobby, coal mining operations continue to scar the Appalachian mountains, and oil and gas drilling in the Gulf of Mexico raise fears of marine contamination.

When energy prices are low, environmentalists generally can hold the line against opening up ecologically fragile areas to fossil fuel extraction. But when U.S. policymakers worry about oil shortages, environmental concerns are often pushed to the back burner—as happened during the oil embargoes of the 1970s (although lawmakers tend to pass conservation measures at the same time that they open up new areas to exploration).

Extraction aside, the actual combustion of the fuels is hotly controversial. Electric power plants that use fossil fuels emit tons of pollutants that threaten human health, cause ACID RAIN, and contribute to GLOBAL WARMING. The 1970 CLEAN AIR

Fossil Fuel Consumption, 1949–1999 (quadrillion Btu)

Year	Coal	Natural gas[1]	Petroleum[2]	Total fossil fuels	Year	Coal	Natural gas[1]	Petroleum[2]	Total fossil fuels
		Fossil fuels					*Fossil fuels*		
1949	11.981	5.145	11.883	29.002	1976	13.584	20.345	35.175	69.104
1950	12.347	5.968	13.315	31.632	1977	13.922	19.931	37.122	70.989
					1978	13.766	20.000	37.965	71.856
1951	12.553	7.049	14.428	34.008	1979	15.040	20.666	37.123	72.892
1952	11.306	7.550	14.956	33.800	1980	15.423	20.394	34.202	69.984
1953	11.373	7.907	15.556	34.826					
1954	9.715	8.330	15.839	33.877	1981	15.908	19.928	31.931	67.750
1955	11.167	8.998	17.255	37.410	1982	15.322	18.505	30.232	64.037
					1983	15.894	17.357	30.054	63.290
1956	11.350	9.614	17.937	38.888	1984	17.071	18.507	31.051	66.617
1957	10.821	10.191	17.932	38.926	1985	17.478	17.834	30.922	66.221
1958	9.533	10.663	18.527	38.717					
1959	9.518	11.717	19.323	40.550	1986	17.260	16.708	32.196	66.148
1960	9.838	12.385	19.919	42.137	1987	18.008	17.744	32.865	68.626
					1988	18.846	18.552	34.222	71.660
1961	9.623	12.926	20.216	42.758	1989	18.926	19.384	34.211	72.551
1962	9.906	13.731	21.049	44.681	1990	19.101	19.296	33.553	71.955
1963	10.413	14.403	21.701	46.509					
1964	10.964	15.288	22.301	48.543	1991	18.770	19.606	32.845	R71.231
1965	11.581	15.769	23.246	50.577	1992	1219.158	20.131	33.527	R1272.850
					1993		19.776	20.827	33.841	R74.471
1966	12.143	16.995	24.401	53.514	1994	19.960	21.288	R34.670	R75.976
1967	11.914	17.945	25.284	55.127	1995	20.024	22.163	R34.553	R76.802
1968	12.331	19.210	26.979	58.502					
1969	12.382	20.678	28.338	61.362	1996	20.940	R22.559	R35.757	R79.279
1970	12.265	21.795	29.521	63.522	1997	21.444	R22.530	R36.266	R80.286
					1998	R21.593	R21.921	R36.934	R80.515
1971	11.598	22.469	30.561	64.596	1999P	21.698	22.096	37.706	81.557
1972	12.077	22.698	32.947	67.696					
1973	12.971	22.512	34.840	70.316					
1974	12.663	21.732	33.455	67.906					
1975	12.663	19.948	32.731	65.355					

Source: Energy Information Administration, U.S. Department of Energy. Data available on the Web at http://www.eia.doe.gov/pub/energy.overview/aer1999/txt/aer0103.txt. See also http://www.eia.doe.gov/fueloverview.html.

Notes: Totals may not equal sum of components due to independent rounding. R = revised. P = preliminary.

[1]Includes supplemental gaseous fuels.

[2]Petroleum products supplied, including natural gas plant liquids and crude oil burned as fuel.

ACT is the primary law governing discharges by power plants, motor vehicles, and other pollution sources. Using its considerable regulatory authority under the law, the ENVIRONMENTAL PROTECTION AGENCY (EPA) has required oil refineries to produce cleaner-burning gasoline and automakers to reduce tailpipe emissions. But many older coal-burning power plants have taken advantage of grandfather clauses in the Clean Air Act to avoid installing expensive scrubbers and other antipollution devices, complicating efforts to further improve air quality.

Jolted by the oil shocks of the 1970s, President JIMMY CARTER's administration pressed for programs to reduce energy consumption and promote alternatives to fossil fuels. Congress returned to the issue in 1992 with the ENERGY POLICY ACT, which promoted ENERGY EFFICIENCY and the use of alternative energy, and also required a study on global warming. (For data on fossil fuel consumption, see table.) In recent years, Congress has appropriated hundreds of millions of dollars annually for research and development into renewable energy sources such as wind, biomass (vegetative matter such as wood that can release energy), and the warmth of the earth. But such programs have done little to cut the nation's reliance on fossil fuels. Lawmakers balked at a BTU TAX proposed by President BILL CLINTON's administration in 1993 that could have discouraged consumption, and they have often opposed tax credits to promote alternative energy.

The three fossil fuels are:

OIL. Perhaps the most important of the fossil fuels, oil supplies more than a third of the nation's energy needs. It is drilled from subsurface reservoirs and then refined into jet fuel, motor vehicle gasoline, home heating oil, and other products. Petroleum byproducts are widely used by the chemical industry. Oil emits numerous pollutants when it is burned, although it generally is cleaner burning than coal.

NATURAL GAS. Composed primarily of methane, natural gas is also drilled from subsurface reservoirs. Distributed across the country by a vast network of pipes, it is used by industrial plants, private residences, and electricity utility plants. Gas burns more cleanly than other fossil fuels, but malfunctioning natural gas pipelines can explode or leak methane into the atmosphere, potentially contributing to global warming.

COAL. A black solid mineral, coal exists in enormous quantities throughout much of the United States. It is used primarily by power plants and factories. From an environmental viewpoint, coal is perhaps the most problematic of the fossil fuels, both because coal mines can severely pollute water systems and because burning coal emits high quantities of pollutants that are blamed for global warming, acid rain, and other problems. The government is investigating ways to burn coal more cleanly. (See also CLEAN COAL; MOUNTAINTOP REMOVAL; NUCLEAR ENERGY.)

G

Garbage

The United States produces far more garbage than any other country on a per capita basis (household waste levels are about double those of western Europe), and disposing of it is a major environmental concern. According to the ENVIRONMENTAL PROTECTION AGENCY (EPA), Americans generate an estimated twelve to thirteen billion tons of all kinds of waste annually. More than 50 percent is classified as industrial solid waste, which is the byproduct of manufacturing processes. So-called special wastes, such as residue from MINING operations and waters pumped out by oil and gas drilling, account for an additional 40 percent. HAZARDOUS WASTE, which may be toxic, corrosive, ignitable, explosive, or radioactive, accounts for 2 to 4 percent of the nation's total waste. Americans also produce more than 200 million tons of MUNICIPAL SOLID WASTE—the everyday refuse from households, businesses, and institutions. Every type of waste can have an environmental and public health impact if it is disposed of improperly and leaks into the air, soil, or water. In some instances—such as the LOVE CANAL disaster in western New York State in the late 1970s—government officials have permanently relocated residents because of leaking hazardous waste.

State and local officials have primary oversight over most waste disposal issues. However, the federal government sets standards for waste disposal, including the design of LANDFILLS, and encourages efforts to recycle used products and reduce consumption. The primary federal law governing solid waste disposal is the 1976 RESOURCE CONSERVATION AND RECOVERY ACT, which regulates the production and disposal of hazardous wastes as well as solid waste disposal operations. The 1980 SUPERFUND law governs the cleanup of hazardous waste sites. Other laws set standards for discharges into air and water and for cleanups of oil spills.

One of the major environmental issues facing government officials at both the federal and the state level is how to handle agricultural waste. Amid concerns that MANURE produced by industrial-type farm operations poses a major threat to water quality in much of the nation, EPA officials are considering imposing strict conditions for permits. Some lawmakers want to establish national standards for handling animal waste. Another key legislative issue is whether to allow state officials to impose restrictions on INTERSTATE SHIPMENTS OF WASTE. As northeastern states run out of landfill space, they are shipping millions of tons of waste to nearby states with more capacity, such as Virginia and Pennsylvania. These shipments have sparked regional tensions, with officials of the importing states battling to keep out much of the garbage. Even if Congress agreed to give state officials more authority over the issue, the combination of increased amounts of garbage and fewer places to dispose of it means that more and more waste is likely to be transported across state borders and, in some cases, even overseas. (See also SOLID WASTE DISPOSAL ACT.)

General Mining Law

Passed in 1872 to attract settlers to the western frontier, the General Mining Law now is a top target of environmentalists and some fiscal conservatives who assail it as a federal giveaway program that opens the door to environmental degradation. The law allows individuals and businesses to prospect for minerals on public lands. If they make a discovery, they can stake a claim for $2.50 to $5 an acre. The federal government is barred from charging royalties for the ensuing extraction of gold, silver, copper, platinum, zinc, or other hard-rock minerals. Passed in an era of comparatively little concern about the environment, the long-lived law also imposes few requirements for prospectors to restore lands and waterways that can be severely degraded.

Critics for years have lambasted the General Mining Law for allowing MINING companies to extract billions of dollars of minerals annually from federal lands without paying for it. They also point to cases in which developers have bought land for a comparatively low price and then made millions of dollars by selling it to private companies or developing it. Many western lawmakers agree that the law needs to be tightened somewhat, but they also contend that it helps generate thousands of mining jobs. They say that overhauling the law too drastically would force mines to close and encourage U.S. mining companies to set up operations overseas, where environmental regulations are less restrictive than in the United States.

The law has withstood numerous congressional battles. One of the biggest erupted in 1993, when the newly installed administration of President BILL CLINTON proposed charging a royalty on hard-rock mineral extraction, imposing tough reclamation standards to protect water supplies, and giving the government more authority to declare some parcels off-limits to mining. The House of Representatives accordingly passed a sweeping bill that imposed an 8 percent royalty on mineral extraction as well as charging various fees. But the Senate passed a much more modest measure with a 2 percent royalty. Negotiations between the two chambers broke down in a major setback for BRUCE BABBITT, the secretary of the interior.

Since then, lawmakers have debated various plans to impose royalties, charge the fair-market value for claims, and require new reclamation standards. Unable to agree on changes to the law, they instead have passed moratoriums on new patents as part of the annual spending bill for the U.S. DEPARTMENT OF THE INTERIOR.

Genetically modified organisms

Genetic modification refers to crops or animals that are altered with genes from viruses, bacteria, PESTICIDES, or other plants or animals. Using this biotechnology, researchers can develop new varieties of food that are insect- and disease-resistant, have a longer shelf life than unaltered food, or have improved nutritional characteristics. Although much of the focus of biotechnology has been on plants, scientists are "inventing" other new foods, including varieties of fish. Some of the organisms have powerful attributes, producing their own in-secticides or growing unusually quickly.

In the United States, food companies have mar-keted genetically modified foods since 1996. The agricultural industry embraced the new technology so enthusiastically that, in 1999, farmers planted 50 percent of soybean acres, and large amounts of corn and cotton acres, with genetically modified seeds.

However, few technological innovations have provoked such a passionate international backlash. Policymakers and consumers alike in Europe, Japan, and other countries have virulently de-nounced the new strains as potentially destructive "frankenfoods." In the United States, environmen-talists and consumer groups demand that gene-al-tered products undergo rigorous testing before be-ing marketed. They also insist that the government label food made with such products. Although U.S. policymakers denounced trading partners for clos-ing their markets to an apparently safe product, they agreed in 2000 to international restrictions. American farmers, bowing to the global outcry, have begun to curb their use of genetically modi-fied seeds.

Environmentalists are concerned about the widespread adoption of gene-altering techniques because they fear that such organisms could have unforeseen ecological effects. Engineered pest-re-sistant weeds, they warn, could cross-pollinate with their wild relatives to create monster weeds resistant to organic farming techniques. They also point to a 1999 study indicating that the new plants could harm the monarch butterfly, a beneficial in-sect. Although government scientists insist there is no evidence that genetically modified organisms are unsafe, environmental and consumer advocates say the products are being rushed to market with-out adequate testing.

Advocates of genetic modification respond that the new technology is vital to feeding the world's growing population and curing diseases. As an ex-ample, they point to a new strain of "golden rice," which contains transplanted genes to prevent vita-min A deficiencies that cause blindness in millions of children in developing countries. They also con-tend that genetically modified crops are environ-mentally friendly because they can be grown with-out an excessive reliance on pesticides or irrigation.

The Food and Drug Administration, a federal agency that ensures the safety of food under the Food, Drug, and Cosmetic Act, is responsible for approving the use of genetically modified food. With the issue becoming increasingly controver-sial, President BILL CLINTON's administration took steps in 2000 that would require companies to sub-mit to the government research findings affirming the safety of a genetically modified product, as well as to set up a labeling system allowing consumers to differentiate between traditional and genetically modified foods.

The use of genetically modified organisms has provoked intense trade battles. Under the CONVEN-TION ON BIOLOGICAL DIVERSITY, adopted at the 1992 EARTH SUMMIT, more than 170 countries agreed to regulate trade in "living modified organ-isms" to prevent human health or environmental problems. The U.S. Senate never ratified the treaty. But, in 2000, the Clinton administration acceded to an elaboration of the treaty that was drawn up by delegates of 140 countries in Montreal to regu-late genetically modified organisms. The language in the Montreal agreement allows a country to ban the import of a genetically modified food. But U.S. negotiators won a two-year delay in setting up an international system to track bioengineered seeds.

Global Climate Change Prevention Act

Passed in 1990, the Global Climate Change Prevention Act (PL 101-606) was one of the first formal steps by the U.S. Congress to combat GLOBAL WARMING. The law created a national plan to study global warming, which many scientists believed was caused by rising levels of CARBON DIOXIDE and other industrial emissions in the earth's atmosphere. It authorized a series of initiatives in the U.S. DEPARTMENT OF AGRICULTURE, including a global climate change program, an office of international forestry, and a biomass energy demonstration projects. The law also created two institutes of tropical forestry to study the effects of DEFORESTATION on global climate.

Global economy

The term *global economy* (or GLOBALIZATION) refers to the increased levels of coordination among nations in trade and other matters. Globalization can be traced to the post–World War II era, when the United States and other governments established international financial organizations, such as the INTERNATIONAL MONETARY FUND (IMF) and the WORLD BANK, to stabilize the world's economies and reduce the chances of another catastrophic war. Following the end of the cold war in the 1990s, Russia and other former communist countries allowed expanded international commerce, and the WORLD TRADE ORGANIZATION was created. In recent years, the world has experienced a boom in global commerce.

Environmental Concerns

Although the concept of a global economy may appear benign, it has sparked intense protests by labor leaders, environmentalists, and other advocates. These protests culminated in demonstrations in Seattle in 1999 during a World Trade Organization meeting and in Washington, D.C., during meetings of the IMF and World Bank in the spring of 2000. Environmentalists are concerned about globalization for three primary reasons.

First, they warn that it can emphasize economic development at the expense of the environment. As a result, the United States and other industrialized countries must sacrifice their environmental laws to meet their trade obligations. For example, trade organizations have ruled that the United States cannot restrict imports of shrimp that are caught in a way that kills sea turtles, nor can the nation block imports of gasoline that fail to meet clean air standards.

Second, the global economy may give developing countries an incentive to sacrifice their natural resources in order to compete in the world marketplace. With assistance from the World Bank, countries such as Brazil have constructed enormous DAMS and other public works projects that have devastated TROPICAL RAIN FORESTS and other ecologically diverse habitats and wiped out many small-scale farming operations. In addition, Indonesia and other nations trying to meet IMF loan requirements have cut back on environmental protections to make money from lumber and other resources.

Third, environmentalists warn that the increased level of trade has contributed to the spread of EXOTIC SPECIES—nonindigenous plants and animals that compete with local species. This trend contributes to the extinction of many unique

Environmentalists warn that globalization could weaken environmental laws, encourage the growth of exotic species, and force developing countries to sacrifice their natural resources to compete in world markets. Some critics of globalization who sought to block access to the 1999 World Trade Organization conference in Seattle were pelted by police with teargas and pepper spray.
Source: Andy Clark, Reuters

species and, ultimately, to a homogenization of the world's ecosystems.

Background

Since the end of World War II, the United States has generally supported free trade. But after the end of the cold war, protectionist sentiment began to strengthen. Conservatives and liberals alike criticize the global economy, warning that it can set back environmental and labor protections and un-

dermine U.S. sovereignty. However, centrists generally support globalization because it gives U.S. businesses access to worldwide markets. They also say it will ultimately benefit the environment by increasing worldwide prosperity, thereby fostering peace and a greater focus on SUSTAINABLE USE of natural resources.

In 1993 President BILL CLINTON won congressional approval of the NORTH AMERICAN FREE TRADE AGREEMENT after a protracted fight in which he agreed to place a greater emphasis on environmental protection. But lawmakers compiled a mixed record on globalization throughout the 1990s. In 1998 the House of Representatives voted against renewing the president's "fast track" trading authority, thereby making it harder for the White House to win congressional approval of trade agreements.

This coolness toward global engagement is viewed with wariness by environmental organizations. That is because some of the same lawmakers who do not want to surrender U.S. sovereignty on economic issues also resist international environmental treaties, such as the CONVENTION ON BIOLOGICAL DIVERSITY. These reactions are complicating efforts to combat international environmental problems, such as GLOBAL WARMING.

Global Environment Facility

The Global Environment Facility is an international organization that provides developing countries with grants for projects that help prevent GLOBAL WARMING, OZONE DEPLETION, WATER POLLUTION, and loss of BIODIVERSITY. The concept behind the organization is to encourage developing countries to take environmental steps that they could not afford on their own.

Created in 1991, the Global Environment Facility has received several billion dollars in funding from the United States and other wealthy nations. But conservatives in Congress often target it for budget cuts. In 1995 moderates preserved $30 million allocated for the agency after the House majority whip, Tom DeLay, R-Texas, tried to eliminate the full $50 million in funding. Three years later, conservatives tried again to slash funding for the

agency, this time out of concern that its programs could indirectly support the goals of the controversial KYOTO PROTOCOL on global warming.

Global warming

Global warming (also known as global climate change) is the common term for a worldwide increase in temperatures that could, if it continues, have severe environmental effects. The issue of global warming has sparked international negotiations, congressional battles, and a high-profile scientific debate over whether warming temperatures are the result of human activities or natural climate patterns.

Most scientists blame rising temperatures at least in part on human activities that emit CARBON DIOXIDE, methane, and other GREENHOUSE GASES. These gases can create a "greenhouse effect" by trapping solar heat in the atmosphere, much as the glass roof and walls of a greenhouse trap heat. As a result, temperatures rose by about 1 degree Fahrenheit in the twentieth century, and researchers expect the increase to accelerate in the twenty-first century. Compounding the problem, millions of acres of forests that absorb carbon are being chopped down in developing countries, releasing additional carbon into the atmosphere. Although the science is highly complex—involving calculations that factor in solar activities, the degree to which oceans, trees, and soil act as "CARBON SINKS," and the offsetting effects of some air pollutants that cool the earth—mounting evidence throughout the 1990s pointed to human activities having a significant effect on global climate.

Alarmed at the prospect that a warming trend could trigger rising sea levels, widespread disease

Environmentalists at the 2000 New Hampshire primary protest candidate George W. Bush's stance on global warming. Bush and other opponents of global warming initiatives say that science has failed to establish a strong link between industry emissions and ecological harm. Source: Paul J. Richards, AFP

outbreaks, and increasingly severe weather systems, environmentalists want officials in the United States and other nations to curb industrial emissions, such as the burning of coal, oil, and natural gas, and implement the 1997 international climate accord known as the KYOTO PROTOCOL on global warming. Business groups, however, are implacably opposed to such restrictions. Industry leaders worry that the economic costs of reducing emissions from automobiles, coal-burning plants, and other sources of greenhouse gases could undermine the U.S. economy, and many are unconvinced that warming temperatures would cause severe environmental problems. Opponents of the Kyoto agreement also point out that, even if implemented, the restrictions would merely slow down the increase in concentrations of atmospheric greenhouse gases, not reverse it. Instead of spending billions in reducing emissions, some policymakers believe the United States should look to new technologies to reduce carbon dioxide levels—perhaps growing plankton that absorbs carbon dioxide or injecting carbon dioxide under the seabed.

Perhaps no major ecological issue has created such a disconnect between environmentalists and Congress. In the view of environmentalists—and many in the scientific community—global warming is a grave threat to the well-being of humanity. It could bring drought to vital food-producing regions, flood low-lying coastal areas from Bangladesh to Louisiana, cause massive plant and animal extinctions, and extend the range of disease-carrying mosquitoes. Environmentalists believe that American action on global warming is especially important because the United States is responsible for about one-fifth of industrial emissions, even though it contains just 4 percent of the world's population. Acknowledging the threat, President BILL CLINTON in his 2000 State of the Union address said, "The greatest environmental challenge of the new century is global warming." Despite such warnings, lawmakers have repeatedly criticized the Kyoto Protocol and resisted potentially costly plans to reduce greenhouse gas emissions.

History

As long ago as 1896, a Swedish chemist named Svante Arrhenius theorized that industrial activity, by creating a greenhouse effect, would raise the earth's temperatures by several degrees. Scientists began confirming the theory in 1958, when a research team at the Scripps Institute of Oceanography in La Jolla, California, monitored carbon dioxide levels at Hawaii's Mauna Loa volcano (see table). Advanced computers and satellite technology provided more confirmation. In 1988 the threat of global warming was brought to the world's attention when James E. Hansen of the Goddard Institute for Space Studies in New York testified before the Senate. Hansen testified that evidence that global warming was already under way was growing daily. That year the United Nations created a special body of scientists, the Intergovernmental Panel on Climate Change (IPCC), to study the issue.

Rapidly warming temperatures throughout the 1990s lent urgency to the controversy. Surface temperatures in the twentieth century increased between 0.7 and 1.4 degrees Fahrenheit, according to a 2000 report by the National Research Council of the National Academy of Sciences, and temperatures in the late 1990s were the hottest on record. The IPCC predicted in 1999 that mean global surface temperatures will rise from 2.3 to 7.3 degrees in the twenty-first century. Melting polar ice caps will raise sea levels by 7 to 39 inches, the organization concluded—an event that could virtually wipe out island nations such as the Maldives and endanger heavily populated low-lying areas in the United States such as New York City.

Government officials have reacted cautiously because the task of reducing emissions of carbon dioxide and other greenhouse gases appears overwhelming. It could involve curbing the world's oil, coal, and natural gas industries, which were worth more than $1 trillion by the 1990s, as well as reversing the trend of DEFORESTATION in the developing world. Nevertheless, the United States and more than 160 other countries signed a 1992 agreement, the United Nations Framework Convention on Climate Change. Most industrialized countries agreed to try to reduce their greenhouse gas emissions to 1990 levels by 2000, while developing countries were granted more time to meet the target. But few countries moved quickly to meet the goal, and international divisions

Top Ten Producers of Carbon Dioxide, by Nation, 1996 (million metric tons)

United States	1,447
China	918
Russia	431
Japan	319
India	272
Germany	235
United Kingdom	152
Canada	112
South Korea	111
Italy	110
Worldwide total	6,518

Source: Carbon Dioxide Information Analysis Center, http://cdiac.esd.ornl.gov/trends/emis/tre_tp20.htm.
Note: Worldwide total can be calculated from figures at http://cdiac.esd.ornl.gov/trends/emis/annex.htm.

emerged. The European Union called for the adoption of a carbon tax based on the amount of carbon dioxide released by a given energy source. A group of 37 countries, known as the ALLIANCE OF SMALL ISLAND STATES, which were threatened by rising sea levels, urged industrial countries to cut their emissions 20 percent below the 1990 levels by 2005. The United States and other industrialized nations refused, saying such a stringent reduction would ruin their fossil fuel–driven economies.

Despite such differences, officials of 167 nations in 1997 reached an agreement in Kyoto that was brokered in part by Vice President AL GORE. The Kyoto Protocol required industrialized countries to reduce greenhouse gas emissions by an average of about 5 percent below 1990 levels by 2012. The nations could use innovative approaches, including EMISSIONS TRADING with other countries, to reach the target. The agreement also called on developing nations, including China and India, to reduce their emissions. But it did not set such stringent standards for them. Members of the U.S. Congress immediately panned the agreement. "The Kyoto deal is dead on arrival," said FRANK H. MURKOWSKI,

R-Alaska, chairman of the SENATE ENERGY AND NATURAL RESOURCES COMMITTEE.

Arguments Against Action

Even before final negotiations on the Kyoto Protocol, the Senate passed a resolution by a vote of 95-0 requiring the participation of developing nations as a precondition for ratification of the pact—although developing nations were not bound by the treaty. Lawmakers said excluding developing countries (which emit relatively small amounts of greenhouse gases) would put the United States at a competitive disadvantage. Conservatives voted to cut funding for RENEWABLE ENERGY programs and bar the ENVIRONMENTAL PROTECTION AGENCY (EPA) from writing rules that could be connected to goals embodied in the Kyoto agreement. Many lawmakers, arguing that global warming could be part of a natural climate cycle rather than a result of industrial activity, warn that efforts to restrict emissions could cost more than two million jobs and undermine the nation's economy without cooling the planet at all. "Make no mistake: If implemented, the Kyoto Treaty will result in American jobs flowing overseas," said Rep. Joe Knollenberg, R-Mich., at a 1998 hearing.

There are several reasons for congressional opposition to global warming initiatives. First, trying to cut greenhouse gas emissions would be a staggering undertaking, because virtually every sector of the country—transportation, power generation, manufacturing, farming—is associated with the FOSSIL FUELS that emit the gases. Business leaders warn of dire consequences if the nation were to adhere to the Kyoto Protocol's target of cutting emissions to 7 percent below 1990 levels. One estimate by Wharton Econometrics Forecasting Associates, a Pennsylvania economics firm, indicated cutting emissions to the target level would cost every American household $2,700 a year. (Clinton's Council of Economic Advisers, however, produced a much lower estimate: $112 per family per year.)

Second, people in the United States appear less concerned about higher temperatures than about more tangible environmental threats, such as polluted water and NUCLEAR WASTE. In fact, Americans are turning increasingly to large cars and SPORT UTILITY VEHICLES, which emit more greenhouse gases than economy cars.

Finally, business leaders and many in Congress say that science has failed to establish a sound link between industry emissions and ecological harm. They point out that scientists cannot fully explain the impact of natural activities—such as ocean currents and plant activity—on global climate, let alone determine the impact of industrial activities. Some go as far as to suggest that emissions of carbon dioxide may be more beneficial than harmful. "It is plant food," Marlo Thomas, an analyst with the conservative Competitive Enterprise Institute, said in 1998. "The more we put in the atmosphere the better it is for trees." (Scientists warn that such assumptions are overly simplistic. Research has indicated that high levels of carbon dioxide produce variable effects on vegetation—sometimes stimulating growth and sometimes harming plants.) But a few businesses have broken ranks because of mounting evidence of global warming. Major corporations such as British Petroleum, Dow Chemical, and Ford Motor Co. withdrew in the late 1990s from the Global Climate Coalition, a lobbying group opposed to the Kyoto treaty.

Incremental Changes

Conceding that they lacked the votes for Senate ratification of the Kyoto Protocol, environmentalists have focused instead on incremental steps that could build momentum for future restrictions. To this end, lawmakers in the 1990s debated promoting subsidies and tax breaks for ENERGY EFFICIENCY, pressing for more aggressive use of renewable energy sources, and increasing the CORPORATE AVERAGE FUEL ECONOMY standards for cars and light trucks. In most cases, Congress declined to take any action.

President BILL CLINTON's administration announced a series of modest initiatives, including a pledge to cut fossil fuel emissions by the federal government by 30 percent over ten years and tripling national production of nongreenhouse "biomass" fuels, which are derived from agricultural products. The administration also encouraged industries to reduce greenhouse gas emissions voluntarily by taking such steps as installing energy-efficient lighting in plants and stores. It won several billion dollars in funding for climate change initiatives, with most of the money going to research into energy efficiency and renewable energy.

These relatively limited steps on the part of the United States have clouded the international situation. Other nations are balking at reducing their emissions, citing American intransigence. However, international negotiators continue to work out such details as allowable emissions levels. The Clinton administration, conceding that it faced overwhelming opposition in the Senate, declined to submit the treaty for ratification. Even when Clinton signed the Kyoto Protocol in 1998, the White House took pains to play down its significance "Signing does not legally commit the United States to implement the protocol," said White House spokesman Joe Lockhart. "The protocol would become binding only with the advice and consent of the U.S. Senate. President Clinton has made clear that the United State regards the Kyoto Protocol as a work in progress."

Globalization

Although globalization can refer to the GLOBAL ECONOMY, environmentalists often use the term to describe the fact that pollution and environmental degradation are not confined by national borders. Instead, problems such as GLOBAL WARMING and OVERFISHING are global in nature. Many policymakers believe that the environment can be protected only through international agreements. (See also TRANSBOUNDARY POLLUTION.)

Gore, Al

As vice president under BILL CLINTON, Al Gore helped to oversee White House environmental policies. Known as a stalwart environmentalist since his days as a Tennessee senator, he won national attention with his 1992 book, *Earth in the Balance,* which called for policymakers to move decisively to ward off such environmental catastrophes as GLOBAL WARMING. Gore stressed environmental protection as "the central organizing principle for civilization."

Once he became vice president, however, Gore got mixed reviews from environmentalists. In the face of a hostile Republican Congress, he appeared to back away from efforts to curb CARBON DIOXIDE emissions. He also urged the ENVIRONMENTAL PROTECTION AGENCY to consider the interests of farmers before imposing new restrictions on PESTICIDES, and, in 1997, he hesitated before endorsing tougher clean air standards. On the other hand, he helped broker the 1997 KYOTO PROTOCOL, which sought to reduce worldwide emissions of GREENHOUSE GASES. Gore also played a role in

As vice president, Al Gore championed the Clinton administration's environmental priorities, such as improving visibility in national parks, raising water quality standards, and preserving roadless areas in national forests. During the 1992 presidential campaign, Gore and actor Christopher Reeve (right) joined members of Clean Ocean Action in an annual beach cleanup project in Sandy Hook, New Jersey.
Source: Mike Derer, AP

many of the Clinton administration's top environmental initiatives, including taking steps to improve visibility in NATIONAL PARKS, upgrade water quality, and preserve vast stretches in NATIONAL FORESTS as ROADLESS AREAS.

When Gore ran for president in 2000, he had to struggle to win some environmental endorsements. Although he won praise for being exceptionally well informed on natural resource issues, environmentalists questioned his ability to stand up to political pressure. Some of Gore's aides dismissed the criticism, contending that he did the best he could with a Republican majority in Congress that opposed sweeping regulations in the Capitol.

Grand Staircase–Escalante National Monument

President BILL CLINTON set off a political firestorm during the 1996 campaign when he used his executive authority to designate 1.7 million acres in Utah as the Grand Staircase–Escalante National Monument. Environmentalists applauded the move, which protected a vast expanse of labyrinthine canyons and red rock cliffs from potential MINING operations. But conservatives in western states assailed it as a shameless land grab exercised with no regard for local concerns. The House of Representatives passed legislation in 1997 that would have pared back the 1906 ANTIQUITIES ACT—the law that enabled Clinton to designate the national monument. But the administration threatened to veto the bill, and it died in the Senate.

Grandfather clauses

Some environmental statutes, such as the CLEAN AIR ACT, contain so-called grandfather clauses that exempt older industrial facilities from having to meet new standards. The reasoning is that it would be unfair to impose high costs on companies to retrofit aging plants, which are likely to be taken out of service anyway within a few years.

Many plants built before the imposition of clean air requirements in the 1970s continue to be in use, however, and they contribute substantially to AIR POLLUTION. Environmentalists contend that some companies are taking advantage of the law by overhauling the old plants instead of building new ones that would be subject to tougher emissions standards. The issue has provoked tensions between midwestern states, where many aging power plants are based, and eastern states, which suffer from the pollution fallout. It has also led to court battles between the ENVIRONMENTAL PROTECTION AGENCY and polluters.

Grazing fees

The fees and rules governing grazing of cattle on federal RANGELANDS have set off divisive environmental and budgetary battles for years. Western lawmakers generally want to keep the grazing fees low and give ranchers considerable leeway over the use of the land. But environmentalists and many fiscal conservatives say the current fees amount to a giveaway to the approximately 25,000 ranchers who use PUBLIC LANDS for grazing.

Grazing on public lands has been an issue since the first years of the twentieth century, when the Forest Service launched a leasing policy to protect deteriorating rangelands. Subsequently, Congress passed the Taylor Grazing Act of 1934, which set up a grazing fee and permit program. The current fees are based on a formula established by a 1986 executive order issued by President RONALD REAGAN. The fees average about $1.35 per animal month, a unit that measures the amount of acreage needed to feed a cow and her calf for a month. Grazing fees on private land, in comparison, often top $10 per animal month. Ranchers say the reason for the price discrepancy is that they often have to pay for improvements, such as fences and stock ponds, that usually are provided on private lands.

When BILL CLINTON took office as president in 1993, he pledged to overhaul grazing fees as part of a larger budget package. He retreated in the face of stiff resistance by western senators, but his interior secretary, BRUCE BABBITT, took up the fight. Babbitt announced administrative steps to increase grazing fees gradually to $4.28 and impose tougher environmental standards. Western senators fired back by maneuvering to block funding for the proposal. After the collapse of compromise legislation that would have raised the fees to $3.45, a chastened Babbitt agreed to defer to Congress on the issue. This defeat represented one of the Clinton administration's first major environmental setbacks.

In 1995 Babbitt used his administrative authority to impose new regulations on the lands, which are administered by the Bureau of Land Management in the U.S. DEPARTMENT OF THE INTERIOR. The new rules allowed the government to claim title to all land improvements and water developments that ranchers made on public lands, and they laid the groundwork for strong environmental participation in the creation of comprehensive plans to preserve ecosystems in rangelands. Ranchers turned to both Congress and the courts to try to modify the rules, but they lost in both venues.

In Congress, attempts to override the rules in the Senate in 1995 ran into a threatened filibuster. In 1997 western lawmakers in the House of Representatives scored a victory of sorts by winning passage of a measure that would have modified the new rules to give ranchers more say over the management of rangelands. It also would have raised grazing fees to $1.84 per animal month. But the White House criticized the bill for its complexity, and the Senate did not take it up.

Farming and ranching groups had no better success in the courts. They won a district court decision in Wyoming by alleging that the rules violated the Taylor Grazing Act. But the U.S. Supreme Court, in *Public Lands Council vs. Babbitt,* unanimously upheld the government in 2000, ruling that the interior secretary has "broad discretionary powers" to set grazing rules.

Great Lakes

The five Great Lakes—Erie, Huron, Michigan, Ontario, and Superior—are the focus of pitched battles between environmentalists and industries. Decades of cleanup efforts have reopened much of the waters to swimming and other recreation, but major pollution problems persist. This is a top environmental concern, both because about thirty-eight million people in the United States and Canada live in the Great Lakes region and because the lakes collectively hold close to 20 percent of the world's surface freshwater—an increasingly scarce resource.

The lakes are difficult to clean for two primary reasons. One, they are a nearly closed ecological system, meaning that it may take several years, or even decades, for water to cycle through them. In such a system, waste tends to accumulate. Second, the region is heavily populated and industrialized, making it hard to control all the sources of pollution. The many environmental threats to the Great Lakes include the loss of WETLANDS and other habitats, the introduction of EXOTIC SPECIES (including the economically costly ZEBRA MUSSELS), and toxic chemicals such as PESTICIDES and PCBS that move up the food chain and accumulate in the flesh of fish. In the 1990s studies by the ENVIRONMENTAL PROTECTION AGENCY (EPA) and the eight Great Lakes states showed that 97 percent of shoreline waters could not be used completely for designated purposes because of problems with persistent toxic pollutants. Officials regularly post advisories on the safety of fish consumption.

These conditions, however serious, mark an improvement over the 1960s. At that time, pollution in the lakes was so severe that it helped to galvanize the modern ENVIRONMENTAL MOVEMENT. Officials curtailed or even banned fishing and swimming. Lake Erie, choked with algae that fed on municipal wastes, was declared "dead"—a symbol of the nation's environmental problems. Toxins claimed the lives of millions of birds and fish.

International cooperation to manage the Great Lakes began in 1909, when the United States and Canada established the International Joint Commission to resolve disputes over the shared boundary waters. Coordinated cleanup efforts date back to passage of the 1972 CLEAN WATER ACT, which sought to cut discharges of sewage and other types of waste into waterways, and the U.S.–Canadian Great Lakes Water Quality Agreement of the same year. The international agreement focused initially on controlling excessive phosphorus and other substances that cause algae growth. It is credited, along with the Clean Water Act, in cutting the amount of phosphorus that flows into the lakes by about half. This decrease is because of reduced runoff from farming operations, improved municipal sewage treatment, and restrictions on phosphorus in detergents.

Subsequent international agreements and congressional measures that would virtually eliminate the release of persistent toxic pollutants have been less successful. The International Joint Commission, which oversees cleanup efforts but lacks enforcement authority, has identified forty-two "areas of concern" where contaminants have become concentrated in the bottom of lakes or harbors. Removing the contaminants and protecting the lakes from various types of polluted runoff, air toxins, and other pollution is expected to cost tens of billions of dollars in public and private funding.

In 1990 Congress passed the Great Lakes Critical Programs Act (PL 101-596), setting up a process for cutting pollution in the lakes. Five years later, the EPA issued cleanup guidance, known as the Great Lakes Water Quality Initiative, which established water quality criteria for twenty-nine pollutants. The program focused on persistent bioaccumulative toxics, which tend to occur in higher concentration in aquatic life than in open waters. However, the initiative soon faced legal challenges and severe criticism on all fronts. Industries worried that it could set a precedent for new and far more stringent standards; environmentalists criticized it for failing to set zero-discharge standards for bioaccumulative toxics.

Trying to end years of little action on cleaning up the most heavily polluted sites, President BILL CLINTON in 2000 proposed $80 million to begin cleanup of the Great Lakes. Environmentalists applauded the proposal as a good first step but warned that many billions of dollars more were needed. (See also EUTROPHICATION.)

Green parties

Green parties in the United States, Europe, and other places are beginning to play a significant role in public policy. Their platforms stress antipollution measures, the use of RENEWABLE ENERGY, and SUSTAINABLE USE of natural resources. On nonenvironmental matters, the green parties tend to emphasize values that are often associated with the political left, including social justice and nonviolence.

Ecology parties began forming with the birth of the modern ENVIRONMENTAL MOVEMENT in the early 1970s. Although poorly organized at first, they scored a breakthrough in West Germany in 1983, when the Green Party (Die Grunen) won 5.6 percent of the national vote and gained more than two dozen seats in Parliament. The German greens have expanded their influence since then, participating in the Social Democratic coalition government that was formed after the 1998 elections and pressing for more environmentally oriented tax and energy policies. Other European green parties have also gained a toehold on local boards and in national legislative bodies, but they rarely garner more than about 5 percent of the national vote. The European Federation of Green Parties represents politicians in twenty-nine countries.

Green parties have not fared as well in the United States as in some European countries, in part because the U.S. electoral college tends to work to the disadvantage of alternative parties. However, the Association of State Green Parties has built up some influence on the local level, coordinating the efforts of grassroots parties in about two dozen states. As of early 2000, the association claimed that greens held fifty-nine elected offices in twelve states. In 1996 and 2000, the greens nominated consumer activist Ralph Nader for president in a bid to gain more national attention and become a viable third party. An older party, called the Green Party USA, advocates such radical positions as abolishing the U.S. Senate. But it attracts little national attention.

The greens have occasionally played the role of spoiler in political races. In 1998 New Mexico Republican Heather Wilson won election to Congress when her Democratic opponent split the vote with liberal Green Party nominee Robert L. Anderson.

Greenhouse effect

See GLOBAL WARMING.

Greenhouse gases

Greenhouse gases, such as CARBON DIOXIDE and water vapor, trap solar heat in the earth's atmosphere by absorbing infrared radiation, thereby contributing to GLOBAL WARMING. Although these gases occur naturally and warm the earth enough to sustain life, scientists warn that industrial emissions and DEFORESTATION are dramatically increasing the atmospheric concentrations of the gases and potentially changing the world's climate in dangerous ways. Repeated international attempts to reduce greenhouse gas emissions have had limited success, however, and some industry leaders claim the effects of greenhouse gases have been overstated.

Scientists believe that carbon dioxide, the primary greenhouse gas emitted by human activities, accounts for more than half of the warming caused by human activities. Other significant greenhouse gases include methane, nitrous oxide, hydrofluorocarbons, perfluorocarbons, and sulfur hexafluoride. Another gas that greatly contributes to global warming, water vapor, does not appear to be directly associated with human activities, and policymakers generally disregard it.

Altogether, greenhouse gases make up less than 1 percent of the earth's atmosphere. Their levels are determined by "sources," which are natural and industrial activities that release them into the air, and

U.S. Emissions of Greenhouse Gases, 1990–1997 (million metric tons)

	1990	1991	1992	1993	1994	1995	1996	1997
Carbon dioxide	4,971.7	4,916.3	4,988.8	5,109.8	5,183.9	5,236.4	5,422.3	5,503.0
Methane	30.2	30.4	30.4	29.7	29.9	30.0	29.1	29.1
Nitrous oxide	1.0	1.0	1.0	1.0	1.1	1.0	1.0	1.0
HFCs, PFCs, and SF_6	*	*	*	*	*	*	*	*
Methyl chloroform	0.2	0.2	0.1	0.1	0.1	*	*	*
Carbon monoxide	87.4	89.2	86.2	86.3	90.3	81.3	80.4	NA
Nitrogen oxides	21.6	21.5	21.9	22.2	22.5	21.7	21.3	NA

Source: U.S. Department of Energy, Energy Information Administration, *Emissions of Greenhouse Gases in the United States 1997—Executive Summary,* Table ES1 (Washington, D.C.: EIA, 1998).

Notes:
    HFCs = hydrofluorocarbons
    PFCs = perfluorocarbons
    SF_6 = sulfur hexafluoride
    * = less than 50,000 metric tons of gas
    NA = not available

"sinks," which are processes that remove them. Scientists have yet to fully understand the cycle of these gases.

Studies suggest that the concentration of carbon dioxide in the atmosphere has increased by almost one-third, from an estimated 280 parts per million in the early nineteenth century to about 368 parts per million at the end of the twentieth century. (See table on greenhouse gas emissions.) This upward trend is continuing. The increase is blamed on the burning of FOSSIL FUELS, such as coal, oil, and natural gas, and on the logging of trees, which release carbon when cut down. Industrialized nations such as the United States, Japan, and the countries of the European Union are responsible for most of the world's carbon dioxide emissions. However, some developing countries also have significant problems with emissions: Kazakhstan, for example, has a high per capita rate of carbon dioxide emissions because of its considerable production of oil. China and India, the world's two most populous countries, are rapidly industrializing and could account for more than half the developing world's carbon dioxide emissions by 2010.

The international community tried repeatedly in the 1990s to reduce greenhouse gas emissions. Negotiators in 1997 produced the KYOTO PROTO-COL on global warming, which aimed to set strict emission limits. But implementation of the treaty has been uncertain because of disagreements between the United States, which would have to cut its emissions significantly, and developing countries, which would face less stringent restrictions.

The issue has provoked some international tension because of reluctance on the part of the United States to curb its emissions. The United States is responsible for about 20 percent of greenhouse gas emissions. Some environmentalists believe that it must show more leadership in tackling global warming, potentially a major problem.

Congress has resisted efforts to impose emission restrictions or ratify the Kyoto Protocol. But it funds research on global warming and alternative energy programs. U.S. emissions increased during the 1990s because of increased fossil fuel consumption, but the rate of increase appeared to slow toward the end of the decade.

Grizzly bear

One of the most feared predators in North America, the grizzly bear was hunted relentlessly for much of the nineteenth and twentieth centuries. Several subspecies, such as the California grizzly, were driven into EXTINCTION. Although grizzlies in Alaska continue to thrive, the bears in the continental United States are limited to isolated areas of YELLOWSTONE NATIONAL PARK and the northern Rocky Mountains.

The plight of the grizzly and other rare species spurred federal wildlife protection efforts in the 1960s and early 1970s, culminating with the EN-DANGERED SPECIES ACT of 1973. The law is credited with helping to restore some grizzly populations, although biologists differ over whether the bear is truly coming back. In the late 1990s federal officials proposed removing the Yellowstone population from the endangered list. But environmentalists contended that the reclusive bears had failed to recover their numbers. Federal officials also are facing some opposition to a plan that would reintroduce grizzlies to the Bitterroot Mountains in Idaho and Montana as an experimental population without full endangered species protection.

Restoring the grizzly presents daunting policy

Although environmentalists and federal officials agree that the Endangered Species Act of 1973 has helped to restore grizzly populations that once were close to extinction, they differ over whether the bears have recovered completely and whether they should be removed from endangered species lists. Source: William S. Keller, National Park Service

challenges because of the predator's fearsome reputation and need for space. Some environmentalists want to establish wildlife corridors that would enable the bear to roam from Yellowstone to Canada, but they face overwhelming opposition from various interests in the western United States.

Groundwater

Groundwater, which is water that collects in cracks and spaces underground, has generally received less attention from the public than has surface water—perhaps because it is out of sight and cannot be used for recreation. But it is of vital environmental importance because it supplies drinking water to half the U.S. population, including virtu-

Major Sources of Groundwater Contamination

Source	Number of states, tribes, and territories
Storage tanks (underground)	37
Septic systems	31
Landfills	31
Large industrial facilities	25
Spills	24
Fertilizer applications	23
Surface impoundments	21
Pesticide applications	20
Hazardous waste sites	19
Animal feedlots	18
Storage tanks (aboveground)	18
Shallow injection wells	14
Agricultural chemical facilities	13
Saltwater intrusion	13
Pipelines and sewerlines	13
Mining and mine drainage	12
Urban runoff	12
Salt storage and road salting	11
Hazardous waste generators	8
Wastepiles	8
Irrigation practices	6
Deep-injection wells	6

Source: U.S. Environmental Protection Agency, Office of Water, *National Water Quality Inventory: 1998 Report to Congress,* Figure 7-6 (Washington, D.C.: EPA, 1999), 164.

Note: Figures represent the number of states, tribes, and territories that identified each source as a contaminant of groundwater.

ally all rural residents, and it provides most of the water in lakes and wetlands. Farmers and industrial plants rely heavily on it. For these reasons, government officials are taking steps to study and protect groundwater more intensively.

Many of the same pollutants that contaminate surface water leach through the soil and contaminate groundwater (see table). PESTICIDES, fertilizers, motor oil, road salt, and toxic wastes from MINING sites all pose a threat to underground aquifers (subterranean reservoirs of water). Furthermore, overpumping of groundwater can drain aquifers and induce saltwater intrusion. On a global level, environmentalists warn that nations that are running short on water for drinking and irrigation may be extracting too much groundwater. This is a particularly severe problem in China, which is contending with saltwater intrusion and the contamination of as much as half of its groundwater. Many analysts believe that contamination or depletion of groundwater will lead to WATER SCARCITY in much of the world, and they are urging governments to monitor the resources more carefully.

In a 1999 report to Congress, the ENVIRONMENTAL PROTECTION AGENCY (EPA) concluded that groundwater in the United States generally seemed to be less polluted than surface water. However, the agency conceded that it has limited information about the extent and condition of the country's groundwater. Because contamination and overpumping pose a threat to localized groundwater supplies, the EPA recommended a coordinated effort among federal, state, and local officials to protect the resource. It also warned that cleaning up groundwater could become costly. Indeed, the National Academy of Sciences in 1994 estimated that the United States would spend more than $1 trillion on a cleanup of contaminated soil and groundwater.

In 1984 the EPA established a national Ground Water Protection Strategy, which directed states to set standards for groundwater and protect it from degradation. The 1996 reauthorization of the SAFE DRINKING WATER ACT put increased focus on the resource, requiring states to implement source water assessment and protection programs to identify potential threats to drinking water sources. Groundwater is also protected by various federal and state laws that are concerned with HAZARDOUS WASTE and water quality, including SUPERFUND and the RESOURCE CONSERVATION AND RECOVERY ACT.

Group of Ten

The larger and more mainstream environmental organizations make up an informal alliance known as the Group of Ten. These organizations typically are said to include Environmental Defense (formerly Environmental Defense Fund), Friends of the Earth, Izaak Walton League, National Audubon Society, National Parks and Conservation Association, National Wildlife Federation, Natural Resources Defense Council, SIERRA CLUB, Wilderness Society, and World Wildlife Fund. They rank among the most powerful and well organized of Washington's political interest groups, with teams of professional lobbyists, direct-mail campaigns that target hundreds of thousands of members, and attorneys who have won numerous lawsuits against federal agencies and industrial companies. To a large degree, some of these groups laid the foundation for the nation's extensive antipollution laws and land preservation programs.

Such successes aside, the Group of Ten organizations face criticism from environmental activists as well as industry officials. On the one side, confrontational environmental groups such as Greenpeace and Rainforest Action Network (as well as some local grassroots organizations) view the Group of Ten as complacent and overly willing to compromise. Some critics on the left also fault the organizations, which have a predominantly white, highly educated membership, for spending little time on issues that concern minorities—especially ENVIRONMENTAL JUSTICE. On the other side, industry lobbyists and many conservative lawmakers denounce the organizations for insisting on stringent regulations when a flexible approach seems more sensible. In some ways, the Group of Ten organizations are paying the price for their own successes: as they become part of the political establishment and draw some corporate support, they are growing increasingly bureaucratic.

The Group of Ten organizations are not the monolithic lobby they sometimes seem to be. The Senate debate in 1993 over ratifying the NORTH AMERICAN FREE TRADE AGREEMENT exposed differences, with supporters of the treaty, such as the National Audubon Society and the National Wildlife Federation, squaring off against opponents of the treaty, such as the Sierra Club and Friends of the Earth. Four years later, environmental groups clashed over standards for DOLPHIN-SAFE TUNA.

H

Habitat conservation plans

Habitat conservation plans are controversial compromises between the government and individual landowners to protect rare species under the ENDANGERED SPECIES ACT. Federal law generally prohibits the destruction of habitat used by rare plants and animals. But Congress in 1982 amended the Endangered Species Act with a little-noticed provision to allow landowners to develop part of their land if they drafted plans for protecting species through such means as improving habitat in other areas or removing predators. In the 1990s the Clinton administration turned to this provision to negotiate hundreds of plans under which developers could continue work on land that was home to endangered species. This innovative approach helped ease criticism of the law by making it more flexible. The agreements were used to protect the HEADWATERS FOREST in northern California and permit some logging in Northwest forests that are home to the threatened NORTHERN SPOTTED OWL.

Although developers generally are receptive to habitat conservation plans, environmentalists worry that they tend to be shaped by political considerations rather than the needs of rare species. They object in particular to SAFE HARBOR clauses, which allow future actions that could hurt additional members of the species, and to NO SURPRISES clauses, which protect the landowner from facing additional restrictions. In 1999 the Clinton administration proposed tightening the rules for habitat conservation plans by improving monitoring of endangered species and requiring measurable biological goals, such as the amount of acreage needed to sustain a rare plant.

Congress in the late 1990s considered amending the Endangered Species Act to give landowners more input into habitat decisionmaking. But lawmakers, divided over many aspects of the controversial law, failed to reach a consensus.

Habitat loss

Habitat loss refers to the destruction of natural habitat, usually for agriculture or urban development. Environmentalists rate habitat loss as one of the top threats to wildlife in this country (and worldwide). It is perhaps the number one reason for the increasing EXTINCTION rate of animal and plant species. By filling in WETLANDS, clearing forests, converting prairies to farmland, and damming rivers, people have transformed almost half the land on the planet, according to some estimates. Habitat protection is a contentious political issue in the United States, pitting PRIVATE PROPERTY RIGHTS advocates who want to develop their land against environmentalists who want to preserve ecologically sensitive areas.

The United States has set aside natural habitat in NATIONAL PARKS and other preserves for more than a century. These efforts initially were tailored principally for hunters and sightseers. But after years of lobbying, environmentalists won passage of the 1964 WILDERNESS ACT, which put an emphasis on protecting land for ecological reasons. Perhaps the most significant acts of Congress to set aside land in wilderness areas and national parks are the 1980 ALASKA NATIONAL INTEREST LANDS CONSERVATION ACT and the 1994 California Desert Protection Act, which protected more than one hundred million acres of pristine areas. The government also restricts ecologically damaging development on private land. The 1973 ENDANGERED SPECIES ACT is the nation's primary law for protecting the habitat of rare species. Other key U.S. habitat laws include the CLEAN WATER ACT, which protects wetlands, and the CONSERVATION RESERVE PROGRAM, which pays farmers to set aside land for wildlife. The LAND AND WATER CONSERVATION FUND is a principal tool for acquiring ecologically sensitive land.

Government ownership of land is no guarantee that habitat will be entirely protected. Lawmakers have sparred for decades over proposals to build roads in public coastal and inland areas and allow oil, gas, and mineral exploration. Environmentalists blocked efforts in the early 1980s that would have permitted oil and gas exploration in national forest wilderness areas. In the 1990s they turned back attempts to weaken the Endangered Species Act and open up the ARCTIC NATIONAL WILDLIFE REFUGE to exploratory drilling. President BILL CLINTON in 2000 unveiled a plan to bar roadbuilding in more than forty million acres in NATIONAL FORESTS—an initiative backed by environmentalists since roads fragment habitat.

Policymakers are also looking into the feasibility of linking national parks and other isolated tracts of protected habitat with a series of "biological corridors" to prevent small populations of species from becoming inbred. For example, the Northern Rockies Ecosystem Protection Act, proposed by some lawmakers in the 1990s, would protect and restore eighteen million acres of land in the West. But such plans face strong opposition because of concerns about local economic effects.

Habitat loss is a significant concern in virtually every country. Environmentalists are especially worried about the destruction of rain forests, which may harbor as many as 50 percent of the world's animal and plant species. They have proposed setting aside as much as 10 percent of TROPICAL RAIN FORESTS and 20 percent of CORAL REEFS. But the world's growing population and its need for land and natural resources are making such goals difficult to reach. Even placing land in national parks is no guarantee of habitat protection: many national parks and other government-owned preserves in developing countries are used for hunting, farming, and mining and are degraded by pollution. Policymakers in some countries are focusing instead on setting aside land in small private preserves or giving financial incentives to private landowners who leave natural habitat undisturbed.

Hazardous air pollutants

In the 1990 amendments to the CLEAN AIR ACT, Congress required the ENVIRONMENTAL PROTECTION AGENCY to regulate 189 hazardous air pollutants. These pollutants, also known as air toxics or toxic air pollutants, are poisonous substances that can, in significant concentrations, cause severe health problems such as cancer, neurological disorders, and birth defects. Hazardous air pollutants

The 1990 Clean Air Act contained guidelines for reducing the toxic air pollutants discharged by industrial plants, including this steel factory in Baltimore. *Source: R. Michael Jenkins, Congressional Quarterly*

are categorized as volatile organic compounds, PESTICIDES, herbicides, or radionuclides. They include such substances as benzene, chlorine, and MERCURY. Sources include motor vehicles, metal refining operations, manufacturing plants, and common household chemicals such as paints and solvents.

Many factories took steps to begin reducing emissions of hazardous air pollutants in the late 1980s, spurred both by federal requests and by government requirements that they publicly report the emissions of many chemicals. In rewriting the Clean Air Act in 1990, lawmakers went further by requiring industrial plants that emit significant amounts of any of the 189 hazardous air pollutants to cut their emissions to the average level of the cleanest 12 percent of similar facilities. Plants that pose more than a one-in-ten-thousand risk of cancer to nearby residents after installing the BEST AVAILABLE CONTROL TECHNOLOGY are to be shut down after 2003. Steel industry coke ovens have until 2020 to reach the standard, if they meet certain interim conditions.

Hazardous Materials Transportation Act

The Hazardous Materials Transportation Act (PL 93-633) is the primary federal law designed to prevent spills of chemicals and other dangerous substances contained in interstate shipments.

First passed by Congress in 1975, it was substantially overhauled in 1990 due to concerns about the several billion tons of hazardous materials that are transported across the country yearly. Spills of highly toxic gases or liquids can have disastrous environmental consequences, sometimes forcing evacuations of nearby residents, shutting down roads, and wiping out fish in local rivers.

The law, administered by the Transportation Department, requires states to develop emergency response plans and train emergency crews. Shippers who transport extremely dangerous materials, such as explosives, poison gases, and radioactive materials, must get safety permits. The shipping companies have to register and pay fees to help pay for enforcement and clean-up efforts. (See also HAZARDOUS WASTE.)

Hazardous waste

Hazardous waste is material that may be ignitable, explosive, corrosive, toxic, or radioactive. The world's largest producer of hazardous waste, the United States generates an estimated 270 million to 300 million tons a year (about 2 to 4 percent of all waste in the country). Most hazardous materials are produced by large industries, including chemical, petroleum, metal processing, plastics, and textiles plants. Approximately 10 percent is generated by small businesses, such as photo labs, service stations, and dry cleaners, as well as by households. Household hazardous waste includes batteries, used motor oil, paint, certain cosmetics, and cleaning chemicals.

When significant amounts of hazardous waste are released into the environment, they can have severe ecological and public health effects. They may increase the risk of cancer, birth defects, and other health problems in people, as well as sicken or even kill local species of animals and plants.

Prior to the 1970s, hazardous waste was often deposited in lagoons or trenches or injected into deep underground wells. Congress in 1976 passed the RESOURCE CONSERVATION AND RECOVERY ACT to impose "cradle to grave" regulations for the production and disposal of hazardous waste. In 1980 lawmakers passed SUPERFUND, an ambitious effort to clean up abandoned hazardous waste dumps. Some hazardous waste can be recycled; the rest is treated to reduce its toxicity and disposed of in a LANDFILL or special hazardous waste facility.

Haze

Sometimes known as regional haze, this is a white or brown veil of air that obscures the landscape. Although it can occur naturally, it is often caused by tiny particulates of pollution that reduce visibility by absorbing and scattering light, especially under humid conditions. The sulfates, nitrates, and other particles that make up haze come from motor vehicles, electric utility plants, industrial boilers, and other artificial sources. Haze can also contain windblown dust and soot from wildfires. The ENVIRONMENTAL PROTECTION AGENCY (EPA) estimates that such pollution has reduced visibility in the West to sixty to ninety miles, or one-half of natural levels, and to fifteen to thirty miles in the East, or about one-third of natural levels.

Because the particulates are blown hundreds of miles, haze is not confined to metropolitan areas. It frequently obscures views in NATIONAL

Haze covers the Philadelphia cityscape. A controversial plan introduced in 1999 by the EPA sought to reduce haze by cutting emissions from motor vehicles and industrial plants. Source: Dick Swanson, EPA-DOCUMERICA

PARKS. Haze is particularly severe in the Appalachians, where visibility has dropped from fifty to about fifteen miles in just a few years. It also is worsening across the West, obscuring the once clear vistas of the Grand Canyon by as much as 50 percent. Aesthetics aside, severe haze can cause respiratory problems.

Congress, in amendments to the CLEAN AIR ACT in 1977, required the EPA to establish national goals for visibility in national parks and wilderness areas. In 1999 the EPA announced a regional haze rule designed to restore national parks and wilderness areas to pristine air quality conditions in sixty-five years. The complex proposal requires states to draw up plans by 2003 that would cut vehicle emissions and force older industrial plants to use the best available technology to reduce emissions. However, affected industries have filed suit against the plan, and some lawmakers want to overturn it because of concerns that it could cost billions of dollars.

Headwaters Forest

A spectacular redwood forest on the northern California coast, the Headwaters Forest was the subject of a decade of legal battles and emotional demonstrations in the 1990s as environmentalists struggled to save one-thousand-year-old trees from loggers' chainsaws. In 1999 the federal government and the state of California agreed to a controversial deal in which they paid $480 million to Pacific Lumber Co. for a 10,000-acre tract containing the largest stand of privately owned OLD-GROWTH redwood. Officials in the Clinton administration compared the dramatic site to Yosemite Valley. "These redwoods are a natural treasure, as much a part of our legacy as the world's great libraries and cathedrals," President Clinton said.

Although environmentalists generally praised the purchase of the ecologically sensitive area, they criticized provisions of the deal allowing Pacific Lumber to continue logging in nearby areas. Under the fifty-year agreement, or HABITAT CONSERVATION PLAN, the logging company accepted severe restrictions on about 100,000 acres of adjoining company-owned land. In exchange, it received a green light for logging in the other 111,000 acres it owned in the region, despite concerns about the impact on endangered species. Government biologists predicted that as a result the NORTHERN SPOTTED OWL population would decline from 150 to about 100.

High-level nuclear waste

A highly dangerous type of NUCLEAR WASTE, high-level nuclear waste consists of intensely radioactive liquid materials from reprocessing nuclear fuel (separating uranium and plutonium from other elements) and producing materials for nuclear weapons. It may include transuranic waste, which is refuse produced by nuclear weapons plants that are contaminated with certain isotopes of plutonium and manufactured elements with an atomic number greater than uranium (92). Spent fuel from nuclear reactors is also highly radioactive and is sometimes classified as high-level waste.

High-level waste can remain dangerously radioactive for thousands of years, making safe storage problematic. One of the nation's worst spills of high-level waste occurred at Hanford, Washington, where tanks corroded faster than expected and leaked about five hundred thousand gallons into the ground from the 1950s to the 1970s. The government is expected to spend about $150 billion through 2070 on cleaning up

high-level waste at weapons plants, sometimes by relying on a process to turn the liquid waste into radioactive glass before disposing of it.

Storing waste from nuclear power plants also presents policymakers with a difficult challenge. Nuclear plants across the country are running out of storage space for spent fuel. In 1987 Congress amended the Nuclear Waste Policy Act (PL 97-425) to explore the feasibility of storing spent fuel in a single underground repository in Nevada's YUCCA MOUNTAIN. But the plan has sparked repeated political battles and cost the government billions of dollars in feasibility studies. When the Energy Department warned that the repository would not be ready before 2012, lawmakers weighed plans to temporarily store the waste near Yucca Mountain. But the Clinton administration opposed such an approach.

House Commerce Committee

One of the most powerful committees in Congress, the House Commerce Committee has jurisdiction over a number of environmental issues, including energy programs, the disposal of NUCLEAR WASTE, and PESTICIDES regulations. The committee, which debates public health matters, also oversees such keystone environmental laws as the CLEAN AIR ACT and the SUPERFUND hazardous waste program.

In the 1980s and early 1990s, chairman JOHN D. DINGELL, D-Mich., expanded the reach of the committee (then called the House Energy and Commerce Committee) and initiated aggressive investigations of government agencies and private companies. After the Republican takeover of

Congress following the 1994 elections, the committee assumed a lower profile under its new chairman, THOMAS J. BLILEY JR., of Virginia. Despite partisan and ideological differences, the Commerce Committee in 1996 crafted two of the most important environmental bills of the 1990s —a rewrite of the SAFE DRINKING WATER ACT and a revised pesticide law known as the FOOD QUALITY PROTECTION ACT. But committee members, despite repeated efforts, could not hammer out a compromise on reauthorizing Superfund.

House Resources Committee

The House Resources Committee is the primary committee in the U.S. House of Representatives that oversees wildlife and conservation issues. Its members consider bills relating to public lands, such as NATIONAL PARKS and NATIONAL FORESTS. The Resources Committee also works on fisheries, oceans, energy, mineral resources, and hydroelectric issues. For that reason, it has jurisdiction over a wide variety of controversial issues, including the ENDANGERED SPECIES ACT, federal GRAZING FEES, and exploration for oil in the ARCTIC NATIONAL WILDLIFE REFUGE.

Even in the hotly partisan House, Resources stands out as one of the most polarized committees. It has been the forum for heated battles over protecting endangered species and overhauling federal land management agencies. Many of its members are drawn from southern and western states that traditionally oppose government regulations. Throughout much of the 1990s, Republican DON YOUNG of Alaska, a strong advocate of PRIVATE PROPERTY RIGHTS who chaired the committee, clashed repeatedly with GEORGE MILLER of California, the senior Democrat and an outspoken environmental advocate.

I

Incidental catch

See BYCATCH.

Incinerators

As landfills began closing in the 1980s because of space restrictions and new regulations, local officials turned increasingly to waste-burning incinerators, also known as waste-to-energy plants or combustors. In the 1980s and early 1990s, such plants increased their capacity tenfold. By 1996 incinerators were used to dispose 17 percent of the nation's MUNICIPAL SOLID WASTE, according to the ENVIRONMENTAL PROTECTION AGENCY (EPA).

The plants have the advantage of producing energy from waste, but they also emit HAZARDOUS AIR POLLUTANTS such as MERCURY. As a result of environmental concerns, the EPA in the late 1990s imposed stricter regulations on the type of waste that could be incinerated. The growth of waste-to-energy plants has stalled in recent years as officials look to other methods to handle waste, such as RECYCLING.

As concerns have mounted over hazardous emissions from incinerators, officials have turned to other methods of waste disposal, such as recycling. The Wingate Incinerator, in Fort Lauderdale, Florida, is now a Superfund cleanup site. Source: Environmental Justice Resource Center

Indoor air pollution

Although clean air efforts have typically focused on outdoor pollution, most Americans are exposed to indoor air contaminants that can cause significant health problems. The concentrations of air pollutants may be twenty times higher or more indoors than outdoors, especially in warm places with poor ventilation and high humidity. Improved insulation, along with central heating and air conditioning systems, exacerbates the problem by preventing indoor contaminants from being diluted by outdoor air. Because people spend as much as 90 percent of their time inside, the ENVIRONMENTAL PROTECTION AGENCY (EPA) ranks indoor air pollution as one of the five top environmental risks to public health.

Sources of the pollution include combustion activities (such as lighting a gas stove or a cigarette), household cleaning products, damp carpeting, central heating and cooling units, insulation that contains ASBESTOS, and outdoor air pollution that may fail to dissipate indoors. The most serious indoor air pollutants are RADON and environmental tobacco smoke, also known as secondhand smoke.

The EPA warns that indoor air pollutants in high concentrations can cause respiratory ailments, fatigue, headaches, and even cancer. It has estimated that such pollution costs society tens of billions of dollars yearly in direct medical costs, lost earnings due to illness, and reduced productivity. The pollution is sometimes blamed for what the World Health Organization in 1982 called "sick building syndrome." The organization broadly defined sick buildings as those in which a significant percentage of occupants report symptoms such as dizziness and nausea that cannot be attributed to any specific source.

The government's sporadic efforts to combat indoor air pollution have generally run into controversy. Congress passed the INDOOR RADON ABATEMENT ACT in 1988 to temporarily fund state radon abatement programs, but it failed to renew the act in the early 1990s. After a series of sometimes conflicting EPA actions on asbestos, Congress in 1986 passed the Asbestos Hazard Emergency Response Act requiring the agency to set guidelines for inspections and the safe disposal of asbestos. However, the cost of asbestos abatement in schools, estimated at more than $100 billion, has spurred charges of regulatory overkill. In 1989 Congress took on the issue of environmental tobacco smoke by banning smoking on virtually all domestic flights. The EPA released a report in 1993 warning that such smoke is even more dangerous than previously thought, responsible for three thousand lung cancer deaths among nonsmokers every year. But lawmakers have balked at more restrictive smoking laws, and the tobacco industry won a victory of sorts when a federal judge in 1998 ruled that the EPA had failed to follow legally required procedures in linking secondhand smoke to cancer.

Like most types of pollution, indoor air pollution is a problem worldwide. Whereas residents of industrialized countries are susceptible because of airtight rooms, those in developing countries contend with smoke from firewood and other fuel. The World Health Organization has estimated that as many as 2.5 billion people are adversely affected by the carbon monoxide and other pollutants given off by indoor fires and unventilated stoves.

Indoor Radon Abatement Act

With research indicating that RADON can cause cancer, Congress in 1988 passed the Indoor Radon Abatement Act (PL 100-551) to help states establish radon-abatement programs. The $45-million measure authorized federal programs to study and mitigate radon contamination in homes, schools, and federal buildings. It also certified radon measurement devices and authorized the ENVIRONMENTAL PROTECTION AGENCY to develop standards for building construction.

Radon, an invisible radioactive gas that occurs naturally from decaying uranium deposits in soil, can seep into buildings and elevate the risk of lung cancer. However, scientists are sharply divided over whether low exposures are harmful. When the EPA in 1993 proposed voluntary guidelines under the Indoor Radon Abatement Act, advising builders to take protective measures against the gas, critics said the costs of such a program were excessive for the relatively small risk posed by radon. (See also INDOOR AIR POLLUTION.)

Instream flows

The term *instream flows* refers to water that is left in a river or lake for ecological or recreational purposes, rather than being extracted for drinking water, irrigation, or industrial use. Traditional water policies, especially in arid western states, have focused on "out of stream" uses to promote economic development. But policymakers are increasingly concerned about maintaining instream flows, especially because WATER SCARCITY threatens to deplete many rivers and lakes, threatening the habitat of rare species and even wiping out aquatic ecosystems.

Integrated pest management

Integrated pest management (IPM) refers to a set of farming techniques that aim to control parasitic insects, diseases, and weeds through natural strategies rather than the use of PESTICIDES. The U.S. DEPARTMENT OF AGRICULTURE helps to educate farmers about IPM, and much of the money that Congress provides annually to fund agricultural research programs goes toward developing such techniques. Environmentalists, however, say the government can do far more to encourage IPM, both by providing more funding and by developing markets for specialty crops that are used in rotation to reduce insect infestations.

Common IPM techniques include encouraging the proliferation of "friendly" insects that feed on pests, planting a more diverse mix of crops, and growing crops more closely together to block weeds from getting sun. Organic farmers also use such techniques, but they rely strictly on natural pesticides such as sulfur instead of the synthetic pesticides that have been marketed since World War II.

Conventional farmers warn that IPM is of limited value. It enables them at best to reduce synthetic pesticide use, but not eliminate it. Even more worrisome, attempts to control natural pests by importing predatory insects have led to the spread of EXOTIC SPECIES, threatening indigenous ecosystems.

Members of the National Association of Counties rally on Capitol Hill in support of the 1991 Intermodal Surface Transportation Efficiency Act (ISTEA). The act, which sought to reduce air pollution and curtail urban sprawl, provided local governments with funding for addressing traffic congestion and improving air quality. Source: Scott J. Ferrell, Congressional Quarterly

U.S. Vehicle Travel (selected years)

	Year				
	1969	*1977*	*1983*	*1990*	*1995*
Vehicles per household	1.16	1.59	1.68	1.77	1.78
Daily vehicle trips per household	3.83	3.95	4.07	4.66	6.36
Daily vehicle miles per household	34.01	32.97	32.16	41.37	57.25
Average vehicle occupancy rate (persons per vehicle)	NA	1.90	1.75	1.64	1.59
Average vehicle trip length (miles)	8.90	8.35	7.90	8.85	9.06
Average annual travel per driver (miles)	8.69	10.01	10.54	13.13	13.48

Sources: Hu, P. A., and J. R. Young, *Summary of Travel Trends: 1995 Nationwide Personal Transportation Survey* (draft), prepared for the U.S. Department of Transportation, Federal Highway Administration (Oak Ridge, Tenn.: Oak Ridge National Laboratory, Center for Transportation Analysis, 1999); U.S. Department of Transportation, Federal Highway Administration, *1990 NPTS Databook: Nationwide Personal Transportation Study*, vol. 1 (Washington, D.C.: DOT, FHA, 1993); U.S. Department of Transportation, Federal Highway Administration, *1990 NPTS Databook: Nationwide Personal Transportation Study*, vol. 2 (Washington, D.C.: DOT, FHA, 1995).

Notes: NA = not available. Household vehicles include automobiles, station wagons, vanbuses/minibuses, and, except for 1969, light pickups and other light trucks. Household vehicles are those that are owned, leased, rented, or company-owned and left at home to be regularly used by household members. They also include vehicles used solely for business purposes or business-owned vehicles if left at home and used for the home-to-work trip (for example, taxicabs and police cars). Average vehicle trip length for 1969 is for automobiles only.

Intermodal Surface Transportation Efficiency Act

The Intermodal Surface Transportation Efficiency Act, better known by its acronym ISTEA (pronounced "ice tea"), was a landmark 1991 bill that sought to make the nation's transportation network more environmentally friendly. Unlike previous highway bills, the $151-billion measure included funding for pedestrian and bicycle paths, and it put an emphasis on less-polluting modes of transportation, such as trains and buses. One of its key programs, the $6-billion Congestion Mitigation and Air Quality program, provided funding to local governments to reduce congestion and improve air quality in areas that failed to meet CLEAN AIR ACT requirements. The money could be used for such projects as building high-occupancy vehicle lanes to encourage carpooling.

ISTEA marked a major departure from traditional highway bills that focused almost entirely on roads. Two factors spurred the change: the completion of the interstate system and heightened concerns about the effects of AIR POLLUTION and URBAN SPRAWL. The legislation, backed by both environmentalists and the highway industry, helped foster a network of bicycle paths and resulted in more commuter trains and buses. But Americans continue to drive more than people in any other country, and the per capita rate of motor vehicle use is on the rise—a disturbing portent for such environmental problems as GLOBAL WARMING and air pollution.

Despite the law's mixed results, Congress again emphasized alternative forms of transportation when it reauthorized ISTEA in 1998. Lawmakers named the new bill the Transportation Equity Act for the 21st Century—or TEA 21.

International Monetary Fund

An international lending organization created after World War II to help stabilize currency rates, the International Monetary Fund (IMF) provides short-term aid or "bailouts" to countries facing economic crises. Environmentalists have criticized the organization for requiring lender countries to focus on boosting economic activity even if that means cutting back on environmental protections or depleting natural resources. The IMF has also drawn fire from both liberals and conservatives for insisting on harsh austerity measures and interfering in free markets. The criticism has increased in recent years because of resistance to the GLOBAL ECONOMY.

But supporters credit the IMF with heading off economic crises. In 1998 the U.S. Congress approved $17.9 billion in new lending authority to the IMF, but only after a protracted political battle. At the beginning of 2000 the IMF, which is run by the United States and its other member nations, had more than two thousand employees and about $90 billion in outstanding loans.

International Whaling Commission

Formed in 1946 to regulate WHALING, the International Whaling Commission has been embroiled in controversy since it imposed a moratorium in the mid-1980s on the hunting of great whales. The moratorium is often breached, because the commission has limited regulatory powers. Japan has been allowed to hunt minke whales by claiming it is conducting scientific research. Norway has exploited a provision in the commission's bylaws that allows a member nation to disregard a regulation if it promptly files a formal objection to the regulation. As a result, environmentalists regard the commission as largely a toothless body. But officials of the commission contend that maritime nations never would have agreed to form an international body if that had meant facing inflexible regulations.

To resolve bitter international disputes over taking whales, member nations have floated such proposals as banning whaling on the high seas while allowing limited hunting in coastal areas. Such attempts at compromise have failed, partly because governments disagree over whether many of the whale species are endangered or recovering.

The commission, comprising about forty nations, is based in Cambridge, England. Its main goals are to set limits on the number and types of whales that may be hunted, designate specified areas as whale sanctuaries, fund whale research, and establish guidelines for whalewatching. The commission's focus is primarily on twelve great whale species, such as blue, sperm, and humpback whales. Members disagree over the commission's authority to regulate small members of the cetacean family, such as dolphins and porpoises.

Interstate shipments of waste

The issue of interstate shipments of waste has sparked regional tensions and congressional battles in recent years, as states with limited LANDFILLS and other waste disposal facilities are exporting increasing amounts of trash to their neighbors. By the late 1990s, interstate shipments of waste exceeded twenty-five million tons yearly—an amount certain to rise early in the twenty-first century as New York City is making plans to close its last remaining landfill. Officials in Pennsylvania, Virginia, Ohio, and other states want to slow the tide of trash coming from such northeastern states as New York and New Jersey. But their attempts to ban the shipments or impose special fees on the trash have been ruled unconstitutional in a recent series of decisions by federal courts, including three by the U.S. Supreme Court, because states may not constrain interstate commerce.

State officials repeatedly have appealed to Congress for more authority to regulate interstate waste shipments. Testifying before a Senate panel in 1999, Pennsylvania Department of Environmental Protection secretary James M. Seif said: "It is unfair that states like Pennsylvania, who have made the hard choices to build recycling programs and promote waste management programs to take care of the waste we generate, have no choice when it comes to trash imports. . . . We must have federal legislation in order to implement an effective solution."

Lawmakers, however, have deadlocked repeatedly over proposals to impose per-ton charges on interstate shipments, set national limits on interstate waste, or give state officials the authority to cap the shipments. Powerful northeastern lawmakers oppose such bills. Even some lawmakers in recipient states—such as Rep. THOMAS J. BLILEY JR., R-Va., who chaired the HOUSE COMMERCE COMMITTEE in the 1990s—criticized the proposals for interfering with the unrestricted flow of goods. The divisions over interstate shipments have complicated congressional efforts to give FLOW CONTROL authority to municipalities that want to direct locally generated waste to specific facilities. (See also GARBAGE.)

Invasive species

See EXOTIC SPECIES.

IUCN—The World Conservation Union

IUCN—The World Conservation Union is the world's largest conservation agency (IUCN stands for the International Union for the Conservation of Nature and Natural Resources). An international organization with a staff of about a thousand, it coordinates the conservation strategies of hundreds of government agencies and NONGOVERNMENTAL ORGANIZATIONS. It also issues reports on such problems as DEFORESTATION and loss of BIODIVERSITY. Founded in 1948 to promote scientifically based conservation strategies, the IUCN is located in Gland, Switzerland, and has offices in more than forty countries.

J

Jobs vs. the environment

One of the major arguments against environmental regulations is that they allegedly undercut the economy and cost people their jobs, especially in high-polluting industries such as manufacturing. As far back as 1975, President Gerald R. Ford argued that expensive pollution controls contributed to both inflation and unemployment. "Unemployment is as real and sickening a blight as any pollutant that threatens the nation," he said. The "jobs vs. the environment" debate became particularly contentious in the early 1990s.

Government attempts to restrict logging in Pacific Northwest forests to protect the rare NORTHERN SPOTTED OWL infuriated logging companies, which warned that the plan could cost as many as thirty-two thousand jobs. More recent proposals to set aside tens of millions of acres of NATIONAL FORESTS have incited similar protests, with many rural lawmakers warning that such action could lock out logging, mining, and farming activities and set back the rural economy.

Whether environmental regulations actually do spur unemployment is disputed. Regulations are definitely costly: public and private institu-

Timber companies assert that logging restrictions cause unemployment and undercut the rural economy. Proponents of the restrictions, including these Canadian protesters who opposed clearcutting in the Clayoquot Sound forests of British Columbia, counter that the regulations safeguard the economy by protecting the land from overexploitation. Source: Jeff Vinnick, Reuters

tions in the United States spend more than $150 billion a year on pollution abatement and control measures, with petroleum and primary metals industries shouldering a particularly high percentage of the expense. Furthermore, in numerous instances the government has weakened a local economy by restricting development on public lands (TONGASS NATIONAL FOREST logging restrictions, for example, have fueled unemployment in southeastern Alaska). Regulatory costs have been cited as a reason for companies to move operations to developing countries with fewer regulations. However, cheap labor is usually a more important factor since labor costs tend to form a much bigger percentage of a company's expenses than do regulatory costs.

Many environmentalists reject the notion that environmental protection is bad for job growth. On the contrary, they make a strong case that the regulations fuel new types of business ventures, and even entire industries, because of increased demand for antipollution devices and energy-efficient equipment. They also contend that the restrictions on logging, fishing, and other harvesting of natural resources, although dislocating workers, safeguard the economy in the long run by preventing overexploitation. Such arguments impressed President BILL CLINTON, who arrived at the White House in 1993 insisting that there was no inherent conflict between job growth and environmental regulations. However, his attempts to strike a compromise over the spotted owl by opening up limited tracts of forest to logging and spending $1.2 billion for economic retraining ran into opposition from both loggers and environmentalists.

Studies by the Labor Department in the early 1990s suggested that environmental regulations may be contributing to a shift in the economy away from such industries as logging and mining toward more environmentally benign jobs in the service sector. But economists are unsure whether the regulations are a significant factor, especially when technological innovations appear to be having a larger impact.

The issue of "jobs vs. the environment" tends to flare up most during economic downturns when people are most concerned about job creation. It faded as an issue in the 1990s because the unemployment rate dipped to near-record lows.

K

Kyoto Protocol

This 1997 agreement, reached in the Japanese city of Kyoto, is the most sweeping international attempt to curb GLOBAL WARMING. Yet it may never be fully implemented. Negotiated by 167 nations, the Kyoto Protocol would commit industrialized nations to reduce emissions of carbon dioxide and five other GREENHOUSE GASES to an average of about 5 percent below 1990 levels by the period of 2008–2012. Higher-polluting countries would face more ambitious targets. The United States, which is balking at the agreement, would have to reduce emissions to 7 percent below 1990 levels, and the European Union to 8 percent. Developing counties would not face binding emissions limits.

The agreement, which built on the 1992 Framework Convention on Climate Change, marked the first time world leaders negotiated binding limits on greenhouse gas emissions. Negotiators were spurred by concerns that higher worldwide temperatures could trigger catastrophic flooding, droughts, and severe storms. If fully implemented, the protocol would significantly slow—but not halt—the buildup of greenhouse gases in the atmosphere. Environmentalists had pressed for much more stringent restrictions. Nevertheless, they hailed the protocol as an important first step toward ending global warming.

Policymakers in the United States, which is the world's biggest producer of greenhouse gases, are

Kyoto Protocol Targets for Reduction of Greenhouse Gas Emissions by 2012

Country	Kyoto target (percent change from 1990 emissions)
Australia	+8
Bulgaria	–8
Canada	–6
Croatia	–5
Estonia	–8
European Union	–8
Hungary	–6
Iceland	+10
Japan	–6
Latvia	–8
Liechtenstein	–8
Lithuania	–8
Monaco	–8
New Zealand	0
Norway	+1
Poland	–6
Romania	–8
Russian Federation	0
Slovakia	–8
Slovenia	–8
Switzerland	–8
Ukraine	0
United States	–7

Source: United Nations, *Kyoto Protocol to the United Nations Framework Convention on Climate Change,* Article 3, Annex B (New York: United Nations, 1997). Available online at: http://www.unfccc.de (January 18, 1998).

sharply divided over whether to implement the treaty. Even before the Kyoto Protocol was negotiated, senators voted 95-0 for a resolution insisting that developing countries also agree to specific reduction targets so the United States would not be placed at a competitive disadvantage. Faced with overwhelming opposition, the Clinton administration chose not to submit the treaty to the Senate for ratification. Instead, it pursued funding for programs to increase ENERGY EFFICIENCY and otherwise reduce greenhouse gas emissions.

Although a 7 percent reduction may not appear ambitious, the nation's emissions have risen so substantially since 1990 that they may have to be cut by 20 to 25 percent to hit the target. Critics warn that this goal would force the nation to sharply cut its use of coal, oil, and natural gas, undercutting the U.S. economy and costing as many as two million jobs. But environmentalists dispute such estimates as exaggerated. The Clinton administration contended that it could use innovative approaches to reach the target, earning credit for EMISSIONS TRADING with other countries that exceed their targets and investing in projects that reduce emissions in developing countries.

With the United States hesitating, few countries have ratified the treaty. But negotiators are continuing to try to work out such details as how to sell credits for emissions allotments.

L

Lacey Act

The first significant U.S. federal law to protect rare animals, the Lacey Act of 1900 prohibited interstate shipments of birds and other animals killed in violation of state laws. It also marked the beginning of national wildlife management efforts by authorizing the secretary of agriculture to adopt measures needed for the "preservation" and "restoration" of game birds and other wildlife.

The law, signed by President William McKinley, took effect after a number of states passed wildlife-protection laws amid concerns over the depletion of such animals as the PASSENGER PIGEON (which would become extinct in 1914) and the American bison. The House report that accompanied the bill noted that native birds in many states had been "well-nigh exterminated."

Land and Water Conservation Fund

Under 1964 legislation establishing the Land and Water Conservation Fund (PL 88-578), the U.S. government uses revenues from offshore oil and gas receipts to buy land threatened by development. In addition to financing federal land purchases, the fund provides matching grants to state and local governments to obtain outdoor recreation areas. Over the years, the fund has been instrumental in protecting popular recreation areas such as beaches and ecologically sensitive habitats such as WETLANDS. Many states run similar programs with bond revenues to provide more open space for residents.

Unlike some trust funds, Land and Water Conservation Fund spending is determined each year by the congressional appropriations process. As a result, it is vulnerable to fiscal pressures. In the 1970s lawmakers gradually increased annual funding for land purchases to about $800 million. But budget cuts during the 1980s and early 1990s drastically reduced the amount of money available, even though conservationists warned that the government should purchase additional land before it became prohibitively expensive. In fiscal year 2000 the Clinton administration persuaded a divided Congress to appropriate $240 million for the fund.

Lawmakers have considered proposals to provide about $900 million in guaranteed funding for the Land and Water Conservation Fund that would not face cutbacks during the annual appropriations process. However, environmentalists worry that such a proposal could include incentives to increase OFFSHORE DRILLING. The idea of guaranteed funding also faces opposition from PRIVATE PROPERTY RIGHTS advocates, who contend the federal government already owns enough land. (See also PUBLIC LANDS.)

Over half of all municipal solid waste generated in the United States ends up in landfills. Source: PhotoDisc

Landfills

Landfills, defined by the ENVIRONMENTAL PROTECTION AGENCY as engineered areas where waste is placed into the land, are used for the disposal of slightly more than 50 percent of all MUNICIPAL SOLID WASTE. Since the promulgation of tougher federal landfill regulations in the early 1990s, many older landfills have closed. The overall number of landfills dropped during the decade from eight thousand to about twenty-four hundred. However, landfill capacity has remained steady because of the construction of large, regional landfills. Northeastern states that are running out of landfill space are shipping their waste to nearby states such as Pennsylvania, sparking regional battles over whether such shipments can be restricted. (See also INTERSTATE SHIPMENTS OF WASTE.)

Lands Legacy Initiative

First unveiled in 1999, the Lands Legacy Initiative comprised several proposals by President BILL CLINTON to protect land and marine ecosystems, preserve open space for public use, and prevent farms from being swallowed up by development. Clinton asked Congress for $1 billion for the initiative in 1999 and close to $1.5 billion in 2000. Despite considerable resistance among conservative lawmakers, Congress agreed to some of the funding—including $420 million in 1999 for the LAND AND WATER CONSERVATION FUND. Clinton was helped by public demand for recreation areas, as well as by a comparatively flush federal treasury.

Law of the Sea

The United Nations Convention on the Law of the Sea is an international agreement governing many oceanic issues, including marine pollution. First negotiated in 1982, it seeks to regulate the development of seabed resources as a common global heritage. It also directs nations to protect the oceans from all sources of pollution, including air deposition, underwater exploration, and dumping from both land facilities and ships. The agreement is stronger than most other environmental treaties because it calls for compulsory arbitration or adjudication to enforce its antipollution measures. However, the United States and other industrialized countries have refused to ratify it. They oppose provisions that could limit their influence over deep seabed mining activities. When President BILL CLINTON signed an agreement in 1994 amending the Law of the Sea, administration officials said they intended "to apply the agreement provisionally."

Lead

Although lead poisoning persists as a significant health problem in the United States, it is far less common than it was thirty years ago because of strict restrictions on lead use. Lead is a toxic metal that was once widely used in many consumer and household products, including paint, plumbing, gasoline, food cans, and even toys. Long thought to be harmless, lead is now known to be dangerous to the health of humans, especially children, if inhaled or ingested. The metal can cause severe men-

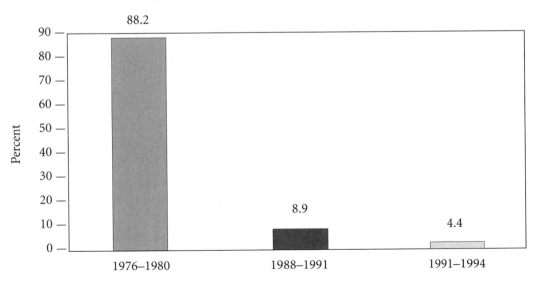

U.S. Children with Elevated Blood Lead Levels

Source: National Health and Nutrition Examination Survey. Data available on the Web at http:www.cdc.gov/nceh/lead/images/leadslide2.jpg.

Note: Percentages are for children ages one through five who have blood lead levels greater than or equal to 10 mg/dl.

tal and physical problems, ranging from insomnia and stunted growth to mental retardation, convulsions, and even death at high levels. Lead poisoning is believed to be the single most preventable disease worldwide associated with an environmental and occupational toxin.

Beginning in the 1970s, the federal government took steps to reduce lead poisoning by sharply limiting lead in paint, gasoline, and other products. Its requirement that carmakers reduce tailpipe emissions by installing catalytic converters, which are incompatible with leaded gasoline, is one of the nation's most dramatic environmental success stories. Since the passage of the 1970 CLEAN AIR ACT, air emissions of lead have dropped by more than 90 percent. Government studies show that the percentage of U.S. children with elevated lead levels plummeted from 88.2 percent in the late 1970s to 4.4 percent in the early 1990s (see figure). However, close to one million children still suffer from dangerously high levels of lead, partly because the metal does not break down in the environment and can persist for many years.

The greatest source of lead poisoning in American children is dust from lead-based paint in older homes, especially in low-income areas. Congress passed 1992 legislation (PL 102-550) to require the disclosure of information about lead-based paint and other hazards during the sale or rental of housing built before 1978, when the government outlawed lead in paint. Other sources of lead include tap water and soil. The metal is still used in many products, such as glassware, furniture finishes, and pesticides, and workers must take steps to avoid dangerous levels of exposure.

Lead levels remain high in developing countries that continue to use lead in gasoline and other products. An estimated fifteen to eighteen million children worldwide have high levels of the metal in their blood, and some studies have suggested that a majority of children under the age of two in urban areas in developing countries may be exposed to unhealthy amounts of lead. Principal sources of the toxin in poorer countries are vehicle emissions, lead-based paint, lead drinking water pipes, and such industrial activities as lead MINING and smelting.

Long-range transport of pollution

See TRANSBOUNDARY POLLUTION.

Love Canal

A national symbol of HAZARDOUS WASTE, *Love Canal* refers to a middle-class subdivision in upstate New York that was built in the 1950s next to a LANDFILL that contained thousands of tons of toxic substances. Beginning with rising river waters in the 1970s, the hazardous waste problem escalated until GROUNDWATER contaminated with such cancer-causing substances as DIOXIN and benzene flooded residents' basements. State and federal officials gradually evacuated all but eighty-six of nine hundred families in a $20 million buyout. President JIMMY CARTER declared Love Canal a federal environmental emergency in 1980. The disaster spurred Congress to pass the SUPERFUND hazardous waste program, which led to cleanups at Love Canal and hundreds of other contaminated sites across the country.

The disaster continues to evoke strong feelings, with some former residents angry that state and federal officials failed to inform them promptly of

Declared a federal environmental emergency in 1980 by President Jimmy Carter, the Love Canal disaster compelled Congress to create the Superfund hazardous waste program. The LaSalle housing project was among the Love Canal developments slated for demolition in 1984 as part of the EPA's cleanup effort. Source: Joe Traver, Reuters

the dangers and others contending that the risks were overstated. Studies of the residents have suggested the possibility of such health problems as high rates of miscarriages, birth defects, and babies born with low birth weights. In 1988 state and federal officials decided to redevelop the area and sell the remaining houses.

Low-flow toilets

Although it is not normally the subject of environmental policy, the common household toilet became embroiled in a spirited 1990s battle over water conservation. Touching off the controversy, Congress in the 1992 ENERGY POLICY ACT mandated that new residential toilets discharge no more than 1.6 gallons per flush. The provision was designed to conserve water (most toilets at the time used 3.5 gallons) and relieve overloaded sewage treatment plants. But many of the new toilets were so ineffectual that people complained about having to flush two or three times. Radio talk show hosts attacked the low-flow requirement as a prime example of government overreaching, and frustrated residents in northern states reportedly smuggled in 3.5-gallon toilets from Canada. Beginning in 1995, Rep. Joe Knollenberg, R-Mich., repeatedly introduced bills to repeal the regulation. He eventually became dubbed "the Prince of Porcelain." But the House refused to take action. Both environmentalists and plumbing manufacturers back the low-flow requirement, contending that newer models of toilets flush effectively with just 1.6 gallons.

Low-level radioactive waste

The disposal of low-level radioactive waste has been a major policy concern since the 1970s. The waste is generated in every state through such commercial activities as nuclear power generation, industrial production, and medical research and treatment. It consists of items that have become contaminated with radioactivity—plastic, clothing, lab equipment, vials, tools, animal carcasses, and internal components from reactors. Unlike HIGH-LEVEL NUCLEAR WASTE, which includes spent nuclear reactor fuel, low-level waste typically has lesser levels of contamination that decay in ten to one hundred years. Nevertheless, the radioactive materials present a significant health hazard, and states are reluctant to develop storage sites within their own borders.

Prior to the 1960s, the United States dumped low-level waste in the ocean. Six commercial disposal sites began accepting waste in the 1960s and 1970s, but they experienced problems with erosion and water accumulation. By the end of the 1970s, three had closed down and required extensive cleanup. The states that contained the remaining sites—Washington, Nevada, and South Carolina—began taking steps to curtail out-of-state shipments. Congress tried to spur states to build new waste sites by passing the 1980 Low-Level Radioactive Waste Policy Act (PL 96-573). The law made states responsible for guaranteeing the disposal of nonfederal wastes generated within their borders, and it encouraged them to take care of the problem by forming regional waste disposal compacts (subject to approval by lawmakers). Despite such incentives, states made little progress for the next few years in building disposal sites. Increasingly concerned, Congress in 1985 imposed deadlines for the new facilities, made states liable for businesses that had to shut down because they could not dispose of their wastes, and approved the plans of thirty-seven states to form seven regional compacts.

Since then, states have formed additional compacts and spent about $600 million in an unsuccessful effort to try to develop new sites, according to a 1999 General Accounting Office report. State officials have been stymied by concerns about safely transporting and storing the waste. For example, Congress in 1998 designated Hudspeth County in Texas to accept low-level radioactive waste from Maine and Vermont. But a Texas commission rejected the site because of geological faults beneath it.

As a result of the impasse, much low-level waste is stored in temporary facilities across the country despite safety concerns. "If you have a hospital or a university in your city, you have low-level waste being stored nearby," SENATE ENERGY AND NATURAL RESOURCES COMMITTEE chairman FRANK H. MURKOWSKI, R-Alaska, said in 1999. "Do we really want this stuff in our neighborhoods when it could be properly buried somewhere?"

In 1999 the General Accounting Office reported that most commercial waste generators had access to disposal sites in South Carolina, Utah, and Washington. But it warned that capacity was decreasing. It proposed three courses of action: retaining the system of compacts, repealing the Low-Level Radioactive Waste Act and allowing private companies to handle waste disposal, or using Energy Department disposal facilities for low-level wastes.

LULU (Locally Unwanted Land Use)

See NIMBY.

M

Magnuson Fishery Conservation and Management Act

Congress in 1976 passed the Magnuson Fishery Conservation and Management Act (PL 94-265) at a time of emerging concern about the marine environment. Lawmakers had two main goals: defending U.S. coastal fisheries against foreign competition and preventing them from becoming depleted. The law (named after Sen. Warren D. Magnuson, D-Wash.) succeeded in the first goal. But it failed so completely in the second that Congress greatly overhauled it in 1996 to try to restore overfished areas.

As passed in 1976, the law extended the exclusive economic zone in waters off U.S. coasts from twelve to two hundred miles, restricted fishing in U.S. waters by foreign fleets, and created eight regional management councils to oversee fisheries. The law kept factory ships from the Soviet Union and other countries out of U.S. waters. But in gaining control over its waters, the United States simply traded OVERFISHING by foreigners for overfishing by its domestic fleets. Helped by more than $500 million of federal loan guarantees, American fishermen soon replaced their aging boats with dozens of state-of-the-art factory vessels.

The law required the establishment of fishery management plans to prevent overfishing while achieving optimum yields. But the regional management councils, made up largely of fishing representatives appointed by the secretary of commerce,

failed to set the harvest quotas and other restrictions needed to sustain the fisheries. Instead, they focused on bolstering struggling fishing communities. In 1981 the New England council yielded to local pressure and removed all catch quotas on cod, haddock, and flounder. This led to the disastrous depletion of the most commercially valuable species, causing an environmental and economic disaster. By the mid-1990s the NATIONAL MARINE FISHERIES SERVICE estimated that 40 percent of the nation's fish species were overfished. Fishing communities acknowledged that their economic interests were inextricably tied to safeguards against overfishing.

In 1996 Congress revised the law (renamed the Magnuson-Stevens Fishery Conservation and Management Act) to require councils in overfished areas to put a management plan in place to restore fish populations to sustainable levels, conserve fish habitat, and minimize the BYCATCH, or incidental kill of unwanted fish and other marine life. The amendments, known as the SUSTAINABLE FISHERIES ACT, also required council members to recuse themselves from voting on decisions that would have a "significant and predictable effect" on their financial interests. Although the rewrite attracted support from both environmental groups and the fishing industry, it nearly foundered because of a dispute between senators from Washington and Alaska over a provision to require crabbers in Washington and elsewhere to set aside 7.5 percent of their catch for economically distressed Alaskan fishing communities. Senators eventually reached a compromise that gradually phased in the requirement.

Manure

Farm animal manure has emerged as a major environmental issue because of concerns that the waste is contaminating waterways and reducing the quality of life in neighboring communities. Large livestock operations, sometimes called "factory farms," build lagoons to contain the waste, but stormy weather, leaks, and accidents allow millions of gallons to leak into waterways every year. The manure is blamed for killing massive numbers of fish, contaminating the drinking water of nearby wells, polluting WETLANDS, and possibly triggering the growth of PFIESTERIA, a microbe that releases a toxin into the water.

The problem is particularly acute in the agricultural Midwest and parts of the East Coast such as Delaware and North Carolina. Cattle, hog, poultry, and dairy cow operations produce an estimated 1.4 billion tons of manure annually, or more than one hundred times the amount of human waste produced in the country. In 1996 the ENVIRONMENTAL PROTECTION AGENCY (EPA) estimated that manure and other types of AGRICULTURAL RUNOFF cause up to 70 percent of the pollution problems in rivers and streams. Regulators are especially concerned about lagoons, many of which have grown from the size of large swimming pools to the size of football fields or bigger, polluting the air by releasing ammonia and other gases while often leaking into GROUNDWATER.

In 1996 Congress created the ENVIRONMENTAL QUALITY INCENTIVES PROGRAM to give farmers assistance with the disposal of manure and help them with other environmentally sensitive matters. Two years later, the EPA, which safeguards water quality under the CLEAN WATER ACT, proposed requiring new pollution permits for the largest livestock operations. Some lawmakers, such as Rep. GEORGE MILLER, D-Calif., and Sen. Tom Harkin, D-Iowa, suggested taking the additional step of setting national standards for animal waste handling. But such a policy would anger rural lawmakers who contend that expensive new government regulations could put farmers out of business without solving the problem of manure. "I am a little concerned with the emphasis on fines and punishment rather than doing something to clean up the problem," Rep. Richard W. Pombo, R-Calif., said during a 1998 hearing of a House Agriculture subcommittee.

With Congress deadlocked, some states have taken action on their own. Maryland began implementing poultry farm regulations in the late 1990s, and Oklahoma imposed restrictions on hog operations.

Marine Mammal Protection Act

Passed by Congress in 1972 and subsequently amended, the Marine Mammal Protection Act is designed to protect the warm-blooded animals that inhabit the oceans. Previously, protection of marine mammals in U.S. waters had been the responsibility of coastal states or international authorities such as the INTERNATIONAL WHALING COMMISSION and the North Pacific Fur Seal Commission. But during the 1960s the public became increasingly concerned about the photogenic and intelligent marine mammals. Commercial whal-

Responding to public concern about the killing of marine mammals, Congress in 1972 passed the Marine Mammal Protection Act. The law, which was amended in 1988, prohibits the killing and importation of the animals, including sea lions. Source: M. Woodbridge Williams, National Park Service

ing, the incidental killing of dolphins by commercial tuna fleets in the tropical Pacific, and the clubbing of harp seals in the North Atlantic drew environmental protests.

In response, Congress acted to protect declining populations of those animals, as well as sea lions, sea otters, manatees, walruses, and polar bears. The Marine Mammal Protection Act imposes a permanent moratorium on the killing and importation of the mammals. But lawmakers in 1972 also granted several exceptions despite environmental objections. They allowed the killing or capture of marine mammals for scientific research or public display, and the hunting of the animals by Native American groups. Perhaps most significantly, they largely exempted the commercial fishing industry from the moratorium while a comprehensive research and development study aimed at reducing porpoise mortality was undertaken.

In 1988 Congress amended the law to impose further restrictions on commercial fishing. It required the commerce secretary to review and mod-

ify the permits under which domestic tuna fishermen operated, authorizing the secretary to add conditions requiring less lethal fishing methods. It also required the Marine Mammal Commission—established under the original act—to come up with guidelines to reduce incidental killing or BYCATCH. The bill sparked international protests by seeking to prohibit foreign nations from selling tuna in American markets if they did not have dolphin protection programs. Lawmakers sought to settle the controversy with DOLPHIN-SAFE TUNA legislation in 1997, which implemented an international pact aimed at protecting dolphins.

The Marine Mammal Protection Act, along with the 1973 ENDANGERED SPECIES ACT, is credited with helping to restore the populations of such mammals as gray whales. However, WATER POLLUTION, coastal development, and heavy boat traffic are continuing to take a toll on such rare species as the northern right whale and the West Indian manatee, and biologists are uncertain about their long-term prospects.

Marine Plastic Pollution Research and Control Act

Congress in 1987 banned the dumping of plastics at sea by passing the Marine Plastic Pollution Research and Control Act (PL 100-220). The legislation put into effect a portion of an international agreement, the International Convention for the Prevention of Pollution from Ships (better known as MARPOL), which was designed to restrict ocean dumping. Like the MARINE PROTECTION, RESEARCH, AND SANCTUARIES ACT, the U.S. law is designed to curb the longtime practice of using oceans as waste areas. Seven years earlier, Congress had implemented another portion of MARPOL by passing the 1980 Act to Prevent Pollution From Ships, which placed restrictions on dumping by U.S. vessels.

The 1987 legislation prohibits the dumping of plastics by any vessel within two hundred miles of the U.S. coast and by U.S.-flag vessels anywhere in the world. It also bans the dumping of other types of garbage closer to the coast.

Plastics that neither sink nor decompose represent a major environmental threat and can entangle, choke, or poison marine life. Garbage has become so ubiquitous in oceans that many remote beaches are littered with plastics and other trash that float ashore from thousands of miles away. In 1988 Congress supported efforts to make plastics that decompose by passing a law (PL 100-556) requiring that plastic ring carriers be degradable.

Marine Protection, Research, and Sanctuaries Act

Congress in 1972 passed the Marine Protection, Research, and Sanctuaries Act (PL 92-532) to ban the unregulated dumping of waste materials into the oceans and coastal waters. The law, often referred to as the Ocean Dumping Act, was a major step in curbing the longtime practice of hauling municipal garbage and other types of waste out to sea. It also helped the United States meet its international commitments under the 1972 Convention on the Prevention of Marine Pollution by Dumping of Wastes and Other Matters, which was an ocean dumping treaty hammered out by representatives of ninety-one countries. In addition to restricting dumping, the law is also notable for establishing a system of NATIONAL MARINE SANCTUARIES.

The original version of the Marine Protection, Research, and Sanctuaries Act prohibited the dumping of any radiological, chemical, or biological warfare agent or high-level radioactive waste. It authorized the ENVIRONMENTAL PROTECTION AGENCY to issue permits for the dumping of waste materials that would not unreasonably endanger human health or the environment. Similarly, the U.S. ARMY CORPS OF ENGINEERS could issue permits for the dumping of allowable dredge-and-fill materials. The law also authorized research into the effects of ocean dumping, OVERFISHING, pollution, and other human activities.

In 1988 lawmakers amended the law to end all dumping of U.S. sewage SLUDGE and industrial and medical wastes in the oceans after 1991. This amendment was aimed largely at New York City, which dumped sludge offshore even though New Jersey leaders complained about fouled beaches. In

1992 Congress added provisions to establish a coastal water quality monitoring program. (See also HIGH-LEVEL NUCLEAR WASTE.)

Mass extinction

See EXTINCTION.

Maximum contaminant levels

Under the 1974 SAFE DRINKING WATER ACT, the ENVIRONMENTAL PROTECTION AGENCY (EPA) must set standards for the maximum levels of certain chemicals that are allowable in drinking water systems. The levels that are developed to protect human health are called *primary standards.* Levels that are developed to protect the aesthetics of drinking water—such as taste and odor—are called *secondary standards.*

Setting maximum contaminant levels is a time-consuming process because regulators have little information about the effects of trace amounts of PESTICIDES and other chemicals in drinking water supplies. By 1986 the EPA had set standards for only about two dozen of the more than six hundred contaminants found in drinking water. Frustrated lawmakers directed the agency to set standards for a list of eighty-three contaminants within three years and to come up with twenty-five additional contaminants to regulate every three years thereafter. However, the schedule proved unrealistic. Congress amended the Safe Drinking Water Act again in 1996 to give the EPA the option of issuing regulations for at least five contaminants every five years. The amendments directed the agency to first

establish the maximum safe exposure level, or "maximum contaminant level goal," for a substance. Then the agency must set an actual regulation for the contaminant that is as close to the goal as feasible.

Mercury

A highly toxic heavy metal, mercury is emitted by electric power plants, INCINERATORS, and boilers, as well as by mines and natural sources. People who ingest mercury can develop brain damage and severe kidney and neurological problems. The metal is especially toxic to fetuses and young children. Most human exposure is caused by the consumption of mercury-contaminated fish. (Fish become contaminated because bacteria in waterways transform mercury into methylmercury, which is absorbed by aquatic plants and proceeds up the food chain.) One of the world's worst mercury poisoning episodes occurred in Japan, when mercury discharges into Minameta Bay during the middle of the century contaminated fish, ultimately killing or sickening thousands of residents. The metal also poses a risk to dental workers and others who use mercury measuring devices in the workplace.

In the United States laws such as the CLEAN AIR ACT and the RESOURCE CONSERVATION AND RECOVERY ACT are designed to minimize the amount of mercury that escapes into the environment. Prodded by environmentalists, the ENVIRONMENTAL PROTECTION AGENCY (EPA) took steps in the late 1990s to cut mercury emissions by restricting the incineration of mercury-containing items and analyzing power plant emissions. But some industry officials and members of Congress question whether the EPA regulations are based on overly stringent health standards for the consumption of mercury. Sparking additional controversy, the EPA released a report in 1997 concluding that Americans can generally consume commercial fish without risk. Environmentalists faulted the report, pointing to research indicating that many bodies of water contain high mercury levels, as does some rainfall.

Reducing emissions is an expensive proposition because mercury is more likely than other metals to remain in a gaseous state and pass through such devices as scrubbers. American industry officials contend that much of the pollution is not their fault, but rather can be traced to overseas industrial activities that emit mercury vapor for thousands of miles and to historic mining operations that released mercury that continues to linger in the environment.

Miller, George

Rep. George Miller, D-Calif., served as senior Democrat on the HOUSE RESOURCES COMMITTEE in the 1990s, chairing the panel from 1991 to 1994 and serving as ranking Democrat after Republicans won a majority. He earned a reputation as a bare-knuckled advocate of environmental causes. As chairman in the early 1990s, Miller shepherded through the California Desert Protection Act (PL 103-433), creating new NATIONAL PARKS and wilderness areas in his home state. But he fell short of other goals, such as increasing GRAZING FEES and revamping the GENERAL MINING LAW of 1872, and he infuriated Republicans with partisan tactics. After the 1995 Republican takeover, Miller played a pivotal role in blocking conservative attempts to scale back the ENDANGERED SPECIES ACT

and open up federal lands to oil, gas, and other development. On occasion, he collaborated with the equally combative Republican chairman, DON YOUNG, to strengthen protection for fisheries and increase federal spending for land purchases.

Mining

Mining for coal, gold, and other minerals has caused worldwide environmental damage for centuries, even as it has helped fuel economic growth. Extracting minerals from the earth without causing damage is virtually impossible. However, mining companies sometimes work with environmental groups to minimize the impact of their activities, and conservationists promote RECYCLING and reduced consumption to curtail the demand for new minerals.

Almost every method of mining, if conducted carelessly, has environmental repercussions. Removing metals from the gravel of streambeds can fill the water with suspended solids and smother fish; tunneling can contaminate watersheds; surface mining gouges holes in the earth's surface; and MOUNTAINTOP REMOVAL can bury streams in rubble. Tailings, waste deposits from mining operations, must be stored carefully to avoid toxic runoff. A common problem is acid mine drainage, an acid-producing chemical process that occurs when rock is exposed to air and water.

Certain ores pose particularly high risks. Gold mining can release MERCURY (a major contaminant in the Brazilian Amazon), and tailings from uranium mines may scatter radioactive dust. Even after the minerals are extracted, environmental damage can occur during the processing stage. Smelting (heating the ore to remove the metals) is

Commercial mining fuels economic growth at great cost to the environment. Throughout the nineteenth century and well into the twentieth, air pollution generated by coal mines darkened the skies over industrial centers of the Midwest and Northeast. It also damaged the lungs of miners.
Source: Utah State Historical Society

a significant source of AIR POLLUTION, and more recent techniques can leak toxins such as cyanide into water supplies.

In the United States several laws govern the environmental impacts of mining, including the CLEAN AIR ACT, the CLEAN WATER ACT, and the RESOURCE CONSERVATION AND RECOVERY ACT. In addition, the 1978 SURFACE MINING CONTROL AND RECLAMATION ACT regulates strip mining and mandates the restoration of mined areas. However, surface mining continues to have a significant environmental impact: restoring the land is highly difficult, and about one thousand additional acres are mined each week for coal. Also, more than a century of mining before passage of strict environmental laws has left the United States with a legacy of an estimated half-million or so abandoned mines, a few of which are listed as SUPERFUND sites. The ENVIRONMENTAL PROTECTION AGENCY warns

that cleaning up the mines, which are blamed for contaminating thousands of miles of streams and rivers, will cost tens of billions of dollars.

One of the more contentious mining issues involves the use of PUBLIC LANDS. Policymakers face a tug-of-war between environmentalists and outdoors enthusiasts who treasure the highly scenic lands of the West, and mining companies that want to tap the vast mineral deposits that lie beneath the surface. Under the GENERAL MINING LAW of 1872, federal officials have limited authority to regulate prospecting and hardrock mining on most federal lands. But Congress sharply regulated existing mining operations in NATIONAL PARKS and banned new operations with passage of the 1976 Mining in Parks Act (PL 94-429).

Mining operations adjacent to national parks have also sparked occasional controversy. A proposal by Crown Butte Resources in the early 1990s to develop a gold mine on private land just outside YELLOWSTONE NATIONAL PARK spurred intense environmental protests, and the company withdrew its plan in 1996.

Mobile sources

Significant amounts of AIR POLLUTION can be traced to mobile sources, including cars, trucks, and (to a lesser degree) nonroad equipment such as lawnmowers and boats. Mobile sources contribute significantly to ground-level ozone, nitrogen oxides, carbon monoxide, PARTICULATE MATTER, and other pollutants. Regulators distinguish mobile sources from STATIONARY SOURCES of air pollution, such as factories. Title II of the 1970 CLEAN AIR ACT mandated cleaner running vehicles by calling for a 90 percent reduction in motor vehicle hydrocarbon and carbon monoxide emissions by 1975 and a 90 percent reduction in nitrogen oxide emissions by 1976. These deadlines sparked subsequent debate, and automakers persuaded Congress and the ENVIRONMENTAL PROTECTION AGENCY to grant extensions. However, the requirements did result in substantially cleaner air.

In the 1990 amendments to the Clean Air Act, lawmakers approved more than ninety new emission standards for cars, trucks, and other vehicles. These included a 35 percent reduction in hydrocarbon emissions, and a 60 percent curb on nitrogen oxide emissions, for new cars beginning in 1996; pollution control devices with a ten-year, one-hundred-thousand-mile warranty beginning in 1998; and the gradual introduction of cleaner-burning fuel. Despite the new requirements, cars and trucks are still a major source of pollution—especially because of increased traffic and the growing popular-

ity of SPORT UTILITY VEHICLES. In 1999 the Clinton administration unveiled more stringent clean fuel requirements, known as TIER 2 STANDARDS. It also required sport utility vehicles to meet the same emission standards as those governing automobiles, beginning in 2004.

As cars become more popular worldwide, they are emerging as a leading source of air pollution, especially in developing countries with less stringent emissions requirements. The World Resources Institute, in a 1998–1999 report, estimated that the global fleet is adding about sixteen million motor vehicles per year. This trend is greatly complicating efforts to reverse GLOBAL WARMING because cars emit CARBON DIOXIDE, a GREENHOUSE GAS.

Montreal Protocol on Substances That Deplete the Ozone Layer

Negotiated in 1987 and subsequently amended, the Montreal Protocol on Substances That Deplete the Ozone Layer has been largely successful in phasing out chlorofluorocarbons (CFCs) and other substances blamed for harming the upper atmosphere's ozone layer. The treaty required industrialized nations to end production of CFCs and halons (chemicals that are typically used as fire retardants) in the mid-1990s, and additional ozone-depleting chemicals by 2020. Developing nations, which were allowed to increase production until 1999, must phase out use of CFCs and halons by 2010. The U.S. Senate unanimously ratified the Montreal Protocol in 1988, and it was ultimately signed by more than 160 countries. Subsequent agreements in London and Copenhagen tightened requirements on CFCs and other ozone-depleting chemicals. The chemicals sparked unusual international concern because of research showing they could deplete upper-atmosphere ozone and thereby expose the planet to harmful ultraviolet rays from the sun.

The Montreal Protocol, which greatly expanded a 1985 Vienna agreement on taking steps to protect ozone, has been viewed as a model for international cooperation on the environment. In the late 1980s the United States, Europe, and Japan produced most of the world's CFCs. At the time, the countries estimated that it would cost tens of billions of dollars to phase out the chemicals. Their efforts have helped reduce global consumption of the restricted chemicals by more than 70 percent. However, the restrictions have spurred a massive black market in Freon and other ozone-depleting chemicals in the United States, Europe, and many developing counties. Further clouding the situation, developing countries greatly increased their use of CFCs during the 1990s, making it uncertain whether they will meet the Montreal Protocol's goal of a complete phaseout by 2010. (See also OZONE DEPLETION.)

Opponents of mountaintop removal, a controversial form of coal mining, protest a fundraiser for Sen. Robert C. Byrd, D-W.Va., who in November 1999 sought to overturn a court ruling prohibiting the practice. While coal industry officials say that mountaintop removal is necessary for maintaining jobs, environmentalists charge that it contaminates waterways and destroys fish and wildlife. Source: AP

Mountaintop removal

Mountaintop removal is a controversial form of coal mining in which the top of a mountain or hill is blasted away in order to remove underlying seams of low-sulfur coal. It has become more common since the late 1970s, especially in Kentucky and West Virginia, because of the development of powerful earthmoving equipment and the increased demand for comparatively clean-burning coal. Although mountaintop removal can have devastating aesthetic and environmental effects, it is permitted under the SURFACE MINING CONTROL AND RECLAMATION ACT of 1977. Coal industry officials and labor unions say the practice is critical for maintaining jobs. It also enjoys support among many local political and business officials who can use the flattened land for new shopping centers and housing developments.

But environmentalists condemn mountaintop removal as an especially damaging form of MIN-ING. Workers not only clear away a mountain's trees and blast off its top, but they also dump tons of earth and rocks into adjacent valleys. Since the 1970s this "valley fill" has buried hundreds of miles of streams, destroying fish and wildlife habitat and contaminating a number of Appalachian water-ways. Contending this practice is a violation of the CLEAN WATER ACT, environmentalists have won some preliminary court battles in an effort to re-strict mountaintop removal. In 1999 Sen. Robert C. Byrd, D-W.Va., tried to pass a measure allowing the dumping of mining waste into streams, but the Clinton administration successfully opposed it.

MTBE

MTBE stands for methyl tertiary butyl ethyl, a chemical added to gasoline to cut emissions of car-bon monoxide and other pollutants. The chemical became popular after Congress passed 1990 amendments to the CLEAN AIR ACT requiring the use of reformulated fuel in heavily polluted areas. Such fuel has higher levels of oxygen, emitting few-er pollutants that can cause cancer or other health problems. By early 2000 about 85 percent of the nation's reformulated fuel contained MTBE.

However, MTBE is controversial because it can cause cancer if ingested, making it a threat to water supplies. Scientists in the 1990s warned that the additive, which can leak from UNDERGROUND STORAGE TANKS and move easily through soil, con-taminated as many as nine thousand community wells in thirty-one states. The Clinton administra-tion in 2000 proposed phasing out MTBE. "Ameri-cans deserve both clean air and clean water, and

never one at the expense of the other," ENVIRON-MENTAL PROTECTION AGENCY administrator CAROL BROWNER said. But the administration's solution—using additives such as ethanol that are based on agricultural products—provoked controversy be-cause some scientists believe that such "biofuels" can emit dangerous byproducts. (See also REFOR-MULATED GASOLINE.)

Multiple use

More than half of all federally owned land, in-cluding most of the land administered by the U.S. FOREST SERVICE and the Bureau of Land Manage-ment, is open to multiple uses. This means that the agencies, while providing a measure of protection for the land and its resources, must also balance of-ten conflicting uses that range from such benign activities as hiking and cross-country skiing to more environmentally destructive activities such as MINING, grazing, and logging.

The multiple-use doctrine dates back to the late nineteenth century creation of the national forest system as a source of timber. But Congress has nev-er precisely defined what it means by multiple use. The 1960 Multiple-Use Sustained-Yield Act direct-ed the Forest Service to utilize forests to "best meet the needs of the American people" while providing "sufficient latitude for periodic adjustments in use to conform to changing needs and conditions." As a result, PUBLIC LAND managers have oscillated be-tween allowing wholesale development (encour-aged in the early 1980s by interior secretary JAMES G. WATT) and enforcing tight restrictions that em-phasize conservation (the approach of Forest Serv-ice chief MICHAEL P. DOMBECK in the late 1990s).

Inevitably, multiple use has sparked fierce con-

Timber and Recreation Road Use

Fiscal year	Recreation vehicles (thousands per day)	Timber vehicles (thousands per day)
1953	177	21
1956	263	28
1959	408	33
1962	564	36
1963	613	40
1966	754	49
1969	814	47
1972	920	47
1975	996	37
1978	1,092	40
1981	1,179	32
1984	1,138	42
1987	1,192	51
1990	1,315	42
1993	1,477	21
1996	1,706	15

Source: U.S. Forest Service, "National Forest Road System and Use" (Washington, D.C.: USFS, 1998). Available on the Web at http://www.fs.fed.us/news/roads/roadsummary.pdf.

flicts between environmentalists who warn that logging and mining are destroying important wildlife habitat, and developers who maintain that such activities are vital for rural economies. In the 1990s, however, conflicts escalated as well over recreational uses (see table). Hikers, backpackers, and cross-country skiers objected to the use of mountain bikes and motorized off-road vehicles on fragile hiking trails, and environmentalists denounced motorcycle racing in western deserts as scarring the landscape. The National Park Service has begun to impose restrictions on snowmobiles and other recreational vehicles that can frighten wildlife and cause pollution, but the issue remains contentious on other public lands that are less oriented toward conservation. (See also U.S. DEPARTMENT OF THE INTERIOR.)

Municipal solid waste

Municipal solid waste is the more technical term for what most people refer to as GARBAGE or trash—the everyday items like papers, food scraps, yard clippings, bottles, and boxes that people and businesses regularly throw away. Some of the items, such as BATTERIES and paint, contain hazardous substances. In 1996 every American produced on average about 4.3 pounds of such waste a day, which is far higher than the per capita rate of

U.S. Municipal Solid Waste Trends, 1960–1997

Year	Materials generated[a]	Recovery for recycling	Recovery for composting	Net discards	Combustion	Discards to landfills	Per capita waste generation
1960	88.12	5.61	[b]	82.51	27.00	55.51	2.68
1970	121.06	8.02	[b]	113.04	25.10	87.94	3.25
1980	151.64	14.52	[b]	137.12	13.70	123.42	3.66
1990	205.21	29.00	4.20	171.97	31.90	140.10	4.50
1995	211.36	45.30	9.60	156.45	35.50	120.90	4.40
1997	216.97	48.60	12.10	156.27	36.70	119.60	4.44

Source: U.S. Environmental Protection Agency, Office of Solid Waste and Emergency Response, *Characterization of Municipal Solid Waste in the United States: 1998 Update*, Table ES-1, 5 (Washington, D.C.: EPA, 1999).

Notes: Figures are in millions of tons.

[a]Generation before materials recovery or combustion. Does not include construction and demolition debris, industrial process waste, or certain other waste.

[b]Negligible (fewer than five hundred thousand tons).

any other country and a significant increase over the rate of 2.7 pounds per person per day in 1960 (see table). There are several reasons for the increasing amount of trash: consumption is rising as society becomes richer, smaller households tend to produce more waste per person, and Americans are tending even more toward convenient, disposable items.

With many cities and states running out of space for LANDFILLS, the growing amount of trash is an environmental concern. Although municipal solid waste is primarily a local issue, the 1976 federal RESOURCE CONSERVATION AND RECOVERY ACT (PL 95-510) requires the operators of solid waste disposal facilities to take steps to safeguard the environment. Beginning in the 1980s, the ENVIRONMENTAL PROTECTION AGENCY (EPA) promulgated strict regulations for the placement, construction, and maintenance of landfills. Nevertheless, environmentalists worry that even well-designed landfills may leak, and they also tend to produce methane gas. The major congressional issue regarding municipal solid waste is whether to grant state officials the authority to regulate INTERSTATE SHIPMENTS OF WASTE, an increasingly contentious matter as states running out of landfill space continue to export their garbage to states with such space. Lawmakers have also been deadlocked since 1994 over the question of whether to grant local and state officials authority to direct trash to specific landfills (see also FLOW CONTROL).

The EPA endorses RECYCLING and the reuse of materials as the best strategies for easing solid waste disposal problems. The agency estimates that 27 percent of municipal solid waste is reused, recycled, or composted. Of the rest, 55 percent is disposed in landfills and 17 percent is burned at combustion facilities, also known as INCINERATORS.

Murkowski, Frank H.

After the Republicans swept to power in Congress in the 1994 elections, Sen. Frank H. Murkowski, R-Alaska, took the helm of the SENATE ENERGY AND NATURAL RESOURCES COMMITTEE. Combative by nature and determined to fight for his home state's economic interests, he angered environmentalists by pressing to open the ARCTIC NATIONAL WILDLIFE REFUGE to oil exploration and by seeking more logging in TONGASS NATIONAL FOREST. He also nearly scuttled a popular National Park Service bill in 1996, insisting on a provision granting more flexibility for an Alaskan logging operation. Although he often had to retreat on environmental issues in the face of stiff opposition by the Clinton administration, he won passage of legislation in 1995 allowing the export of oil from Alaska's North Slope. Environmentalists worried that the measure would lead to more oil drilling in Alaska. But Murkowski said it would give the state a needed economic boost. "Our citizens will no longer be discriminated against and kept from selling the state's most valuable resource in the world market," he said.

A major player on the issue of NUCLEAR WASTE, Murkowski favors opening a temporary storage site at YUCCA MOUNTAIN. He is a leading opponent of proposals to ease GLOBAL WARMING by sharply cutting industrial emissions, warning it could set back the nation's economy.

N

National ambient air quality standards

As required by the CLEAN AIR ACT, the ENVIRON-MENTAL PROTECTION AGENCY (EPA) sets standards for the amount of pollution allowed in "ambient air"—the air we breathe. The most common air pollutants covered by the standards are known as CRITERIA AIR POLLUTANTS. They are LEAD, ozone, PARTICULATE MATTER, sulfur dioxide, carbon monoxide, and nitrogen dioxide.

Congress in 1970 approved an ambitious deadline of five years to bring all areas of the country into compliance with the ambient air quality standards. Air quality has improved significantly since then, with the levels of all the criteria air pollutants declining except nitrogen dioxide. However, tens of millions of Americans live in areas that still fail to meet the standards for at least one of the major pollutants. In 1990 Congress passed sweeping amendments to the Clean Air Act that tightened some standards, while adopting a more elaborate system of classifying pollutants to distinguish between areas of marginal and extreme pollution. It granted cities three to twenty years to meet the standards, depending on the severity of their pollution.

In 1997 the EPA issued rules to tighten the standards for ozone and particulates but faced a major court challenge from affected industries.

National Association of Manufacturers

The National Association of Manufacturers (NAM) is one of the most powerful industry lobbying organizations in Washington. D.C., and an implacable opponent of stringent environmental regulations. An umbrella group of 14,000 companies and 350 associations, it positions itself as the nation's largest and oldest multi-industry trade association.

NAM warns that stringent government regulations can undermine the strength of the U.S. economy and set back overseas competitiveness. Instead, it favors curbing pollution through voluntary measures. "Environmental considerations have become an integral part of the way manufacturers design and produce their goods," Jerry J. Jasinowski, president of the association, wrote in a 2000 letter to lawmakers. "While government environmental regulations were the primary drivers thirty years ago, today, international competition and voluntary actions are increasingly pervasive forces for environmental improvement."

Accordingly, NAM has spearheaded legislative and legal campaigns to block implementation of tougher CLEAN AIR ACT regulations and emission limits for GREENHOUSE GASES, as well as limiting CITIZEN LAWSUITS against polluters. The organization works closely on environmental issues with other business groups, including the American Automobile Manufacturers Association, the American Petroleum Institute, the Chemical Manufacturers Association, and the U.S. Chamber of Commerce.

National Environmental Policy Act

The National Environmental Policy Act (NEPA), one of the nation's most venerable environmental laws, requires all federal agencies to formally consider the environmental impacts of major projects or policy decisions. The law affects highway construction, military training, public land management plans, oil and gas development on public lands, and the cleanup of U.S. DEPARTMENT OF ENERGY hazardous waste sites, among other initiatives.

President RICHARD NIXON signed NEPA on January 1, 1970, as his first act of the new decade. The law established environmental protection as a matter of federal policy, setting the goal of creating conditions "in which man and nature can exist in productive harmony." The most far-reaching provision of the law directed federal agencies to create written ENVIRONMENTAL IMPACT STATEMENTS or assessments analyzing the environmental effect of proposed actions and alternatives to those actions. This process does not force the agencies to choose more environmentally friendly options, but it does give time for critics of the projects to marshal their resources in opposition. The law also established a COUNCIL ON ENVIRONMENTAL QUALITY to coordinate government antipollution efforts and oversee implementation of NEPA.

Under the law, agencies prepare three types of environmental analyses: categorical exclusions for minor projects with insignificant environmental impacts, environmental assessments for larger projects with no significant impacts, and environmental impact statements (reviewed by the ENVIRONMENTAL PROTECTION AGENCY) for projects with significant impacts. NEPA encourages public involvement, especially with the first "scooping" stage–meetings or written comments to identify the possible environmental effects of a project. Nevertheless, critics have warned that agencies tend to choose alternative projects that reflect their own interests, rather than options the community would like to consider.

Written much more simply than later environmental laws, NEPA never expires and does not need congressional reauthorization. For that reason, and also because it primarily affects government agencies rather than private businesses, NEPA has generated far less formal debate than later controversial laws governing air and water quality and endangered species. However, some conservative lawmakers fault the law for causing unnecessary litigation and government red tape, costing taxpayers money. Environmentalists have cited NEPA repeatedly in challenges to government actions, including construction of urban and rural highways, the granting of offshore oil leases, and such military actions as low-level Air Force flights.

National Forest Management Act

Congress stepped into the contentious issue of CLEARCUTTING in 1976 with the National Forest Management Act (PL 94-588). The impetus was a 1975 ruling by the U.S. Fourth Circuit Court of Appeals in Richmond, Virginia, that the U.S. FOREST SERVICE was violating its basic charter (the Organic Act of 1897) by allowing the cutting of trees that were not dead, matured, or large-growth and

A 1975 federal court decision restricting clearcutting in the southern Appalachian region drew fire from timber industry executives, who said that the restrictions would reduce lumber yields. A year later, Congress eased the restrictions by passing the National Forest Management Act. Source: Dan Todd, U.S. Forest Service were not individually marked. The court decision was widely interpreted as a ban on clearcutting in the Monongahela National Forest in West Virginia, since the practice usually involved the cutting of young and unmarked trees. A week after the decision, the Forest Service suspended most timber sales from the southern Appalachian region served by the appeals court.

The forest industry, backed by the Forest Service, warned that the restriction could reduce annual softwood yields by 50 percent or more. Instead of appealing to the Supreme Court, it took its case to Congress. Lawmakers sanctioned clearcutting in NATIONAL FORESTS within certain limits. Under the National Forest Management Act, timber harvests could be conducted only when irreversible damage to soil, slope, and watershed would not occur; lands would be restocked within five years; water bodies would remain protected; and the harvesting system used could not be chosen primarily for economic reasons. Lawmakers authorized the Forest Service to use land management plans when deciding whether to permit clearcutting. Congress also authorized $200 million for reforestation efforts and required the Forest Service to protect the diversity of plant and animal communities.

National forests

The country's national forests are the subject of a fierce tug of war between environmentalists, who want to preserve them for wildlife habitat and other ecological benefits, and loggers, who want to cut down trees for timber. As the forests draw more recreational visitors, polls show that most Americans favor preserving them as wilderness, even

though they were originally established largely for timber. Many westerners, however, complain that the growing list of federal restrictions on forest activities is costing them jobs and interfering with hunting and other recreational activities.

The National Forest System encompasses 192 million acres of forests and grasslands, which is more than 8 percent of the nation's land area and more than twice the acreage of all the NATIONAL PARKS (see map). This land comprises some of the wildest landscapes in the United States, including glacier-covered mountains, remote alpine lakes, pristine rivers, and temperate rain forests. The forests provide habitat for endangered species of animals and plants and help maintain the health of watersheds. Originally set aside primarily for logging, MINING, and other types of development, they now are used heavily for outdoor recreation. The U.S. FOREST SERVICE estimated in the late 1990s that the forests were drawing about 800 million recreational visits yearly—triple the visitation at the national parks. The forests are generating about $110 billion in annual revenues from recreation, compared with just $3.5 billion from timber harvesting—a disparity that environmentalists hope will strengthen calls for conservation.

Nineteenth-century Roots

The forest system has its roots in 1891 legislation that authorized the president to set aside public lands as "forest reserves" that would furnish a supply of timber. Although President Theodore Roosevelt and forest service chief Gifford Pinchot acquired large tracts of forest land for conservation in the early twentieth century, the forest service in subsequent decades generally leaned toward the interests of loggers, miners, and cattle ranchers. With the post–World War II housing boom creating demand for lumber, the forest service erected a mas-

The National Forest System

The U.S. Forest Service manages 192 million acres of public forests and grasslands in forty-four states—more than 8 percent of all the land in the United States and more than twice as much land as the National Park Service.

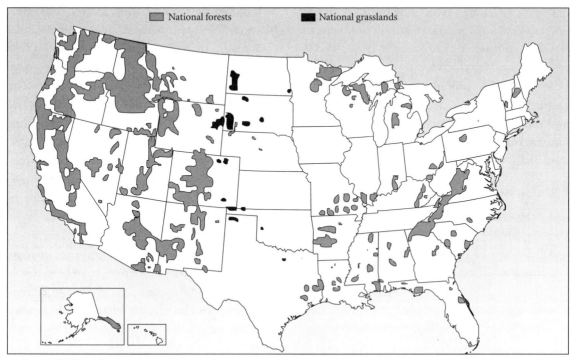

National forests   National grasslands

Source: U.S. Forest Service.

sive road system that ultimately would extend 383,000 miles—more than eight times the length of the interstate highway system. Increasingly powerful equipment and the use of CLEARCUTTING—a controversial but cost-effective technique in which loggers cut down every tree within a certain area—enabled loggers to increase their yield to a 1987 peak of 12.7 billion board feet of timber from federal lands.

Environmental protests initially had little effect. Congress in 1960 passed the Multiple-Use Sustained-Yield Act, which gave the forest service broad leeway to manage the national forests "for outdoor recreation, range, timber, watershed, and wildlife and fish purposes." The law gave considerable discretion—and little exact guidance—to for-

est managers trying to balance MULTIPLE USES that often conflicted. Four years later, however, conservationists gained passage of the WILDERNESS ACT, which authorized Congress to set aside areas that were off-limits to logging and other activities likely to disturb the natural habitat of wilderness areas. Trying to balance demands for more logging with concerns for the long-term health of the forests, Congress in 1974 passed the Resources Planning Act, which reaffirmed the principle that the forests must not be depleted. Two years later lawmakers passed the NATIONAL FOREST MANAGEMENT ACT. This legislation overrode court restrictions by allowing limited clearcutting.

The rather vague directions that the U.S. Forest Service operates under have led to dramatic shifts in policy. In 1981 the conservation-minded administration of President JIMMY CARTER was succeeded by that of RONALD REAGAN, which was intent on managing the forests for the "wise use" of resources instead of conservation. JAMES G. WATT, the controversial interior secretary of the early 1980s, tried to open national forest wilderness lands to mineral exploration, especially along the petroleum-rich Overthrust Belt region in Wyoming, Utah, and Idaho. When lawmakers scrambled to block him, Watt promised that he would not "try to slip things through."

Logging Restrictions

By the end of the 1980s, the informal understanding among timber companies, lawmakers, and forest service officials (sometimes known as the Iron Triangle) that timber harvesting was the top forest priority was coming to an end. The government's listing of the NORTHERN SPOTTED OWL as a threatened species under the ENDANGERED SPECIES ACT touched off intense legal and political battles in the late 1980s and early 1990s. Federal courts ordered restrictions on logging in OLD-GROWTH FORESTS in the Pacific Northwest to preserve the owl's habitat. When Republicans took control of Congress in 1995, they repeatedly tried to scale back the Endangered Species Act so that the habitat of a rare species would not be off-limits to logging and other land uses. But they failed to overcome environmental opposition. Conservatives also pressed to expand road building in the national forests and increase logging limits. One of their few successes came in 1995, when President Clinton signed an appropriations bill that included an environmental rider allowing salvage logging. The measure was intended to remove fallen or diseased trees, but timber companies removed many healthy trees as well.

Perhaps more than any president since THEODORE ROOSEVELT (who established much of the system), BILL CLINTON pegged his environmental legacy to the forests. His last forest service chief, biologist MICHAEL DOMBECK, announced a significant departure from the traditional focus on logging by declaring that the new forest service policy would emphasize ecosystem management. "The health of the land must be our first priority," he said soon after his 1997 appointment. "Failing this, nothing else we do really matters." One year later, Dombeck ordered an eighteen-month moratorium on road building in the forests. Conservative lawmakers assailed the initiative but lacked the votes to override it.

Clinton followed up with a series of acts carving out national monuments from the forests (national monuments have greater protection from development). In 2000 he announced steps to permanently ban road building in more than 40 million acres of national forests. "These areas represent some of the last, best, unprotected wildland anywhere in our nation," the president said. "They are, therefore, our treasured inheritance." Environmentalists generally praised the plan, although they faulted Clinton for leaving out the TONGASS NATIONAL FOREST and allowing logging in the roadless areas. Rural lawmakers, on the other hand, were furious. After hearing Clinton's preliminary plan in 1999, Sen. Judd Gregg, R-N.H., denounced it as an "unprecedented land grab," and Sen. Conrad Burns, R-Mont., angrily accused the administration of waging a war against the West. Loggers warn that such restrictive policies have the potential to hurt the forests: WILDFIRES can be more commonplace if salvage timber is not removed, and deer and elk may no longer be able to graze the grasses and brush that grow in logged areas.

Development aside, the forest service faces a

challenge in managing outdoor recreation. The popularity of the national forests is generating problems that were unforeseen a few decades ago, as hikers, campers, and cross-country skiers complain that all-terrain vehicles and snowmobiles are damaging trails and waterways and destroying the forests' wild character. In 1999 Dombeck called the clash over off-road vehicles "the issue of the next decade."

For many years, the forest service has faced criticism that its BELOW-COST TIMBER SALES program amounts to a subsidy for logging companies. Furthermore, some lawmakers complain about sloppy appraisals when the forest service trades less ecologically fragile lands at the edge of forests for private property in the forest interior. In one notable instance, the forest service in 1994 agreed to trade away land it owned in Colorado near the Telluride ski resort, which it appraised at $640,000. Just eight months after the swap, part of the land was sold for $2.7 million. Sen. Ben Nighthorse Campbell, D-Colo. (he later switched parties) denounced the deal as "a rip-off, pure and simple, of a public resource for private profiteering."

known as the Sustainable Fisheries Act) to put a greater emphasis on fish conservation and habitat protection, the agency has been whipsawed between environmentalists demanding stepped-up protection and commercial and recreational fishermen denouncing strict catch restrictions that they say could put them out of business.

Critics on all sides say the National Marine Fisheries Service has failed to carry out comprehensive surveys of many of the fish stocks it manages, but agency officials respond that they are doing the best they can with limited funding. The agency's broad responsibilities include administering the ENDANGERED SPECIES ACT for marine life, ensuring that coastal development does not damage important marine habitat, and administering assistance programs for the fishing industry.

The agency's roots date back to 1871, when Congress established the U.S. Commission of Fish and Fisheries, which was charged with studying an apparent decline in fish populations off New England. Now part of the NATIONAL OCEANIC AND ATMOSPHERIC ADMINISTRATION, the agency had a budget of $383 million in 1999.

National Marine Fisheries Service

The National Marine Fisheries Service has the difficult task of setting limits on commercial and recreational fishing in order to restore depleted populations of fish and other sea creatures. In the 1980s and early 1990s environmental groups assailed the agency for failing to curb OVERFISHING and ward off a catastrophic decline in commercially valuable species such as Atlantic cod. Since the congressional rewrite of the MAGNUSON FISHERY CONSERVATION AND MANAGEMENT ACT (also

National marine sanctuaries

Under the 1972 MARINE PROTECTION, RESEARCH, AND SANCTUARIES ACT, the United States has a network of marine sanctuaries that are designed to protect fragile ecosystems. Somewhat analogous to NATIONAL FORESTS, the sanctuaries are MULTIPLE-USE areas, where shipping, commercial fishing, and recreational activities are allowed. However, the law restricts such potentially destructive activities as OFFSHORE DRILLING. Some environmentalists contend that the sanctuaries do not live up to their name, and they want portions to be designated off-limits to commercial fishing.

As of 1999 the nation had twelve marine sanctuaries that protected 18,000 square miles of oceans and coasts. The largest sanctuary, in California's Monterey Bay, encompasses 5,300 square miles—one of the largest protected marine areas in the world. The sanctuaries include a range of environmentally important habitats, such as breeding and feeding grounds for whales, turtles, and other rare sea creatures; corals reefs; kelp forests; and historically important objects such as the remains of the U.S.S. *Monitor*, an early Civil War ironclad warship.

National Oceanic and Atmospheric Administration

The largest agency in the U.S. Department of Commerce, the National Oceanic and Atmospheric Administration (NOAA) has emerged as an important environmental agency responsible for monitoring GLOBAL WARMING and conserving marine ecosystems. NOAA plays a key role in protecting estuaries and other coastal ecosystems from pollution and development. It also monitors threats to fragile CORAL REEFS and administers NATIONAL MARINE SANCTUARIES.

In addition to its role as the lead federal agency in researching the oceans, NOAA tracks atmospheric changes and severe weather systems—putting it in the position of releasing data on the politically charged issue of global warming. NOAA also oversees the often embattled NATIONAL MARINE FISHERIES SERVICE, which is trying to balance the often conflicting demands by environmentalists and commercial fishing regarding depleted fish populations.

Created in 1970 as part of a reorganization plan in President RICHARD NIXON's administration, NOAA had a budget in 1999 of $2.2 billion and more than twelve thousand employees.

National Park Service

See U.S. DEPARTMENT OF THE INTERIOR.

National parks

The United States inspired a worldwide national park movement with the establishment of YELLOWSTONE NATIONAL PARK in the territories of Wyoming and Montana in 1872, and Congress continued to designate spectacular scenic areas throughout the twentieth century. In addition to serving as a mecca for outdoors enthusiasts, the parks fulfill an important environmental role by providing habitat for animals and plants, including rain forest species in Olympic National Park, sequoia trees in Sequoia National Park, WOLVES and GRIZZLY BEARS in Yellowstone, and the rare Florida panther in Everglades National Park. However, lawmakers typically designate parks because of outstanding scenery rather than ecological importance. The U.S. DEPARTMENT OF THE INTERIOR's National Park Service manages the lands for human recreation as well as for environmental protection. Park officials are under pressure by Congress to give visitors a satisfying experience—even if that produces conflicts with resident wildlife.

The parks have sparked occasional congressional battles between conservatives who want to restrict the government from setting aside more land and environmentalists who generally—but not always—favor designating new parks (but they have qualms because of the large crowds that tend to congregate in parks, threatening the local ecology). In 1981 President RONALD REAGAN proposed an indefinite moratorium on purchasing land to expand national parks and other PUBLIC LANDS. Administration officials reasoned that the National Park Service should restore existing lands before acquiring new ones. But that was a losing battle politically because of the popularity of the parks. Congress, which acceded to other Reagan requests in the early 1980s, overruled the White House and substantially boosted the administration's request for land acquisition. The following decade, conservatives lost again. President BILL CLINTON's administration eked out a rare environmental victory by winning passage of the 1994 California Desert Protection Act (PL 103-433), which designated Death Valley and Joshua Tree national parks and protected major tracts of land elsewhere in California. However, for the rest of the 1990s the Republican-led Congress demonstrated little interest in setting aside large tracts of scenic land as national parks.

Traffic, Noise, and Other Problems

As a result of their growing popularity, many of the national parks are suffering from significant environmental problems. Poor air quality and traffic jams plague many national parks, such as Grand Canyon in Arizona and Great Smoky Mountain in North Carolina and Tennessee. Rather than enjoying the sounds of nature, visitors often are subjected to the repetitive noise of sightseeing airplanes and other motorized vehicles. Aging park facilities are in such a state of collapse that in 1998 a dilapidated pipe system leaked thousands of gallons of raw sewage in Yellowstone. Wildlife is also suffering, both from past hunting practices that wiped out some larger predators and from more recent

Annual Visits to National Parks (selected years)

Year	Visits (thousands)
1980	47,236
1985	50,035
1990	57,610
1995	64,755
1999	61,250

Source: National Park Service.

introductions of EXOTIC SPECIES that compete with native plants and animals.

When environmentalists refer to national parks, they generally mean "full" national parks, such as Yosemite, Yellowstone, and the Grand Canyon, which were established to protect highly scenic areas. Other lands overseen by the National Park Service, including national monuments and historical sites, have varying degrees of ecological significance. There were fifty-four full national parks at the beginning of 2000, with Congress considering establishing several more. The parks comprised 49 million acres and drew a total of about 65 million visitors yearly by the late 1990s—an increase of more than 15 percent compared with 1990 (see table). Some parks (such as Washington's North Cascades) are suffering little degradation because officials have declined to build many roads or other facilities; others (such as Great Smoky Mountain) are overrun with visitors and are noticeably polluted.

After facing criticism from conservationists for decades because it tried to lure visitors with paved roads and visitor centers, the National Park Service in the 1990s began imposing tougher restrictions. To control traffic jams and parking crushes, it now regulates the number of cars at popular sites. Parks such as Acadia, Denali, and Zion offer shuttle buses, and officials at the Grand Canyon National Park are building a light-rail system that will ferry visitors from a parking lot six miles south of the

Grand Teton National Park, in northwestern Wyoming, represents the ruggedness of the West. But the National Park Service fears tourists may be a bit too rugged on it. Scientists are studying the impact of visitors and pollution on this and several other national parks. Source: National Park Service

canyon. To further reduce noise and pollution, park officials have imposed controversial restrictions on motorized vehicles, such as personal watercraft (better known by trade names such as Jet Skis and WaveRunners) and snowmobiles.

Although traffic restrictions will help with air quality, the National Park Service has limited power to reduce pollution because many of the pollutants in national parks are blown in from coal-burning power plants and other facilities located hundreds of miles away. Prodded by environmental lawsuits, Congress in 1977 amended the CLEAN AIR ACT to impose particularly stringent air quality standards for national parks and other pristine areas. Despite this policy, known as PREVENTION OF SIGNIFICANT DETERIORATION, pollution levels in parks have worsened in recent years. National parks exceeded federal standards for ozone on more than two hundred days in 1999. Vistas at the Grand Canyon have reportedly dropped by as much as 50 percent because of regional HAZE. Much of the pollution is the result of increased

traffic in and near the parks, sprawling development that encroaches near the boundaries of many parks, and emissions by older plants that do not have to meet Clean Air Act standards because of the law's grandfather provisions.

In 1999 the Clinton administration announced a complex regional haze rule for state regulators that was designed to restore national parks and wilderness areas to pristine air quality conditions in sixty-five years. However, affected industries warned that the regulations could cost billions of dollars, and environmentalists chafed over standards that will not take effect for decades.

One of the gravest problems facing national parks is lack of funding. From 1977 to 1998 the number of units in the National Park System (including historical sites and national battlefields) increased from 265 to 376 without an accompanying increase in budget, draining National Park Service resources. As a result, the park service has closed roads and campgrounds, while warning that it lacks enough rangers to stop the theft of such items as petrified wood. The problems continued even as Congress boosted annual funding for the National Park Service during the 1990s from $1.1 billion to $1.9 billion. Environmentalists worry that lawmakers focus on funding construction projects such as visitor centers while shortchanging programs to catalog and ultimately protect natural resources. To give parks more power over their own spending, Congress gave national parks the authority in the late 1990s to keep 80 percent of the money they raised through fees, instead of remitting most of it to the Treasury.

History

The concept of national parks can be traced back to romantic nineteenth-century images of spectacular western scenery, inspired by paintings, novels, and early photographs. As early as 1832 the painter George Catlin mused about the creation of national parks to preserve both nature and the Native American way of life. Congress took a step toward the more modern concept of national parks in 1864, when it transferred control of Yosemite Valley to the state of California on condition that the lands "be held for public use, resort, and recreation . . . inalienable for all time."

Amid publicity about geysers and other geological features of the newly explored Yellowstone area of Wyoming and southern Montana, Congress passed a bill in 1872 to keep more than two million acres in federal control "as a public park or pleasuring ground for the benefit and enjoyment of the people." The bill and subsequent legislation barred "wanton destruction," hunting, and commercial fishing, although the government initially provided little funding to protect the park. In the 1890s Congress designated additional parks, including Sequoia in California and Mt. Rainier in Washington.

In those early years, national parks were administered haphazardly and suffered considerable environmental damage. Park officials introduced nonnative trout and other fish for the enjoyment of fishermen, and they eradicated predators such as wolves and mountain lions to protect grazing animals that were popular with tourists. Overruling environmental objections, Congress in 1913 approved a plan to supply water to San Francisco by flooding the spectacular Hetch Hetchy Valley in Yosemite National Park—a project that may have been the most ecologically destructive in the history of U.S. national parks.

In 1916, with the Interior Department struggling to oversee fourteen national parks and twenty-one national monuments, Congress passed the National Park Service Act. It presented the newly created National Park Service with a difficult mandate: "to conserve the scenery and the natural and historic objects and the wild life therein and to provide for the enjoyment of the same in such manner and by such means as will leave them unimpaired for the enjoyment of future generations."

These arguably conflicting directions spawned decades of controversial policies. The new agency continued to eradicate predators for many years despite the protests of wildlife biologists. To attract tourists and ensure support for the parks, the park service authorized considerable development, including paved roads, lodges, and other facilities that fragmented wildlife habitat. Although the agency at times emphasized biology and conservation, it faced harsh criticism from the likes of writer Edward Abbey for destroying ecosystems and ending the solitude of formerly wild places. The 1964 WILDERNESS ACT, which barred road building and development in designated areas of national parks and other federal lands, signaled the beginning of a greater emphasis on leaving land undisturbed. In recent years, the government has sought to restore the parks to their original condition through such steps as reintroducing predators.

National Priorities List

The National Priorities List is a formal listing of abandoned or uncontrolled HAZARDOUS WASTE sites in the SUPERFUND program. Such sites, typically identified by federal or state officials, are considered a danger to public health because they can leak toxic waste into the air, water, or soil. They are eligible for long-term remedial action.

When people refer to "Superfund sites," they generally mean the sites included on the National Priorities List (as opposed to less contaminated sites that receive Superfund money for relatively quick cleanups). From the inception of Superfund in the early 1980s until the end of 1999, the ENVIRONMENTAL PROTECTION AGENCY (EPA) listed slightly more than 1,400 sites, of which more than 600 had been largely or entirely cleaned up.

National trails system

Congress passed the National Trails System Act of 1968 to provide for access to "open-air, outdoor areas, and historic resources." The system includes national scenic trails, national recreation trails close to urban areas, national historic trails, and connecting or side trails. Although intended for recreation rather than environmental protection, trails such as the Appalachian, Continental Divide, and Pacific Crest are important for conserving habitat and providing wildlife corridors so that animal populations do not become overly isolated.

As of 2000 Congress had designated nearly forty thousand miles of trails, with additional trails designated administratively. The trails are administered by the U.S. FOREST SERVICE, NATIONAL PARK SERVICE, and Bureau of Land Management, as well as state and local agencies. (See also PUBLIC LANDS.)

National Water Quality Inventory

Every two years the ENVIRONMENTAL PROTECTION AGENCY (EPA) submits to Congress a report known as the National Water Quality Inventory. This report, required under the CLEAN WATER ACT, is the primary source for water quality information on U.S. rivers, lakes, ESTUARIES, WETLANDS, coastal waters, and GROUNDWATER. However, because it summarizes water quality studies by states and other jurisdictions that receive federal funding to reduce WATER POLLUTION, the report contains information on only a sampling of water bodies.

In 1998 the inventory concluded that about 40 percent of the nation's rivers, lakes, and estuaries were too polluted for fishing or swimming. Major pollution sources included agricultural activities, municipal sewage treatment plants, air toxins, and abandoned industrial sites. In addition, leaks of chemicals and other hazardous substances from UNDERGROUND STORAGE TANKS threatened to contaminate groundwater.

These pollution findings, although worrisome, represented a considerable improvement over those of the early 1970s, when about two-thirds of the nation's waterways had significant pollution problems. The water quality inventories provided support for more stringent EPA regulations of polluted water runoff in the late 1990s.

National wilderness preservation system

Under the 1964 WILDERNESS ACT, the government has set aside approximately 104 million acres of wilderness, of which 55 percent is in Alaska. Many of the wilderness areas overlay NATIONAL PARKS and NATIONAL FORESTS. They generally are protected more strictly than other PUBLIC LANDS and are among the few places that animals can roam without crossing roads or coming across buildings. Conservationists would like to double the acreage of the wilderness system, but conservative lawmakers worry about the economic impact of setting aside large tracts of land from development.

National wildlife refuge system

The national wildlife refuge system, which has its roots in the establishment of Florida's Pelican Island National Wildlife Refuge in 1903, sparked congressional debate for a number of years over permitted activities. Environmentalists believe the 192-million-acre system should be managed primarily for wildlife habitat, while hunting, fishing, and other sporting enthusiasts want the lands to remain open to recreational pursuits. In 1997 Congress struck a compromise by establishing conservation as the basic mission of the system, though recognizing hunting and other activities as a priority whenever they are compatible with conservation.

Before passage of the 1997 law, Congress had never charted a clear mission for national wildlife refuges. President THEODORE ROOSEVELT established Pelican Island primarily to protect pelicans, egrets, and other birds from being wiped out by plume hunters. Since then, the sprawling and di-

verse wildlife refuge system has grown to encompass more than 500 units that are located in every state, serving a wide variety of uses. The government began opening some of them to hunting in 1924. To the dismay of conservationists, refuge managers at times encouraged hunting to control wildlife populations in the refuges, many of which are located along major bird migratory routes.

With the 1966 National Wildlife Refuge System Administration Act, Congress combined the various wildlife units into one system under the U.S. DEPARTMENT OF THE INTERIOR. Attempts in the 1980s and early 1990s to clarify the system's mission bogged down in disputes between conservationists and recreational users. The differing factions finally struck a compromise in 1997, in part because of negotiations between President BILL CLINTON's administration and congressional Republicans, such as DON YOUNG of Alaska, chairman of the HOUSE RESOURCES COMMITTEE. The resulting National Wildlife Refuge System Improvement Act (PL 105-57) required conservation plans for every refuge and the determination of whether existing recreational uses were compatible with the goal of conservation.

Lawmakers continue to debate allowing certain types of development in the refuges, however. The 19.5-million-acre ARCTIC NATIONAL WILDLIFE REFUGE is the focus of battles between oil and gas proponents who want to conduct limited exploratory drilling and conservationists who want to keep the region pristine.

Such policy disputes aside, the refuges continue to face problems with underfunding and alleged mismanagement. Refuge managers have warned Congress about aging buildings, leaking dikes, and other maintenance problems that could pose a hazard to both wildlife and people. Like other PUBLIC LANDS, the refuges are in danger of being overrun with visitors. They attract about 34 million people yearly.

Natural Resources Conservation Service

The Natural Resources Conservation Service is the lead conservation agency of the U.S. DEPARTMENT OF AGRICULTURE. It oversees farmland programs that are designed to reduce erosion, prevent RUNOFF, preserve wildlife habitat, and protect WETLANDS. One of its most high-profile programs is the CONSERVATION RESERVE PROGRAM, under which farmers receive money for setting aside ecologically sensitive land. Although the agency generally focuses on providing farmers with technical support or funding for conservation practices, it sometimes gets caught in the crossfire between environmentalists and landowners who resent federal restrictions. About 70 percent of land in the United States is privately owned, making the fate of watersheds and forests on that land a critical issue for environmental groups.

The Natural Resources Conservation Service has a budget of nearly $1 billion and 11,000 full-time employees. Originally named the Soil Conservation Service, it was created during the Dust Bowl days of the 1930s to help farmers stop soil erosion and maintain the health of their soil. In recent years, the agency has expanded its focus to protecting farms from being swallowed up by developers and promoting conservation in cities and towns.

Negligible risk

When regulators seek to minimize the health dangers of hazardous chemicals and other pollu-

tants, they often use a negligible-risk standard. This generally means that exposure to a pollutant should pose a lifetime risk of cancer of no more than one in one million (although the risk may be one in one hundred thousand for chemicals that are known carcinogens only in laboratory animals). Such exposure is often referred to as a virtually safe dose, posing a *de minimis* risk.

Regulators contend that this standard ensures that humans have a virtually nonexistent chance of being harmed. But the negligible-risk standard has touched off considerable controversy because there is uncertainty about the effects of PESTICIDES and industrial chemicals. Some environmentalists, who believe that limited testing is failing to uncover the many possible hazards of chemicals, favor a ZERO-RISK standard. Many in industry, however, criticize regulators for limiting exposure to a number of chemicals based on animal testing rather than evidence that the chemicals can cause cancer in humans. (See also RISK ASSESSMENT.)

NIMBY

NIMBY stands for "not in my back yard"—a common cry from citizens when federal, state, or local officials try to build a waste disposal site or clean up a SUPERFUND toxic waste site. "NIMBYism" is the well-organized resistance movement that emerges when members of nearby communities band together and go to court to stop the project. The RESOURCE CONSERVATION AND RECOVERY ACT, SUPERFUND, and many other environmental laws allow these types of CITIZEN LAWSUITS. Increasingly, NIMBYism is taking aim as well at highway projects and other types of development in an effort to stop sprawl. NIMBY actions, it should be noted, are not necessarily limited to citizens' groups. Officials in many states balked over federal directives to build low-level NUCLEAR WASTE sites, and some states have gone to court to restrict INTERSTATE SHIPMENTS OF WASTE.

NIMBY protests aim to protect the environment from dangerous disposal practices. Typically, however, the result is that the controversial waste ends up being disposed of in a neighborhood with less political clout—which often means a minority neighborhood. Drawn-out court battles also greatly add to the costs of Superfund cleanups and the creation of HAZARDOUS WASTE sites. Although environmental organizations that work with local groups contend that greater input from citizens produces better decision making, waste producers and many public officials believe the process often leads to confrontations instead of education. The protesters tend to distrust government officials and reject scientific evidence of the safety of the proposed site. States have tried using financial incentives to get local governments and citizens to agree to hazardous waste sites, but these initiatives have often proved to be ineffective. (See also ENVIRONMENTAL JUSTICE.)

Nixon, Richard M.

Controversial and scarred by scandal, Richard Nixon nevertheless is remembered as perhaps the most accomplished U.S. president on antipollution issues. His first act of the 1970s was to sign on January 1, 1970, the NATIONAL ENVIRONMENTAL POLICY ACT, which established environmental protection as a matter of federal policy. During an age of bipartisan support for the environment, the Republican chief executive also worked with the Democratic Congress on such landmark laws as the 1970 CLEAN AIR ACT and the 1973 ENDANGERED SPECIES ACT, and he used his executive power to create the ENVIRONMENTAL PROTECTION AGENCY (EPA). During its 1969–1974 tenure, the Nixon administration came up with innovative methods to clean up pollution, dusting off an 1899 statute at one point in an attempt to curb industry dumping of waste into waterways.

Nixon's environmental policies, like many other aspects of his troubled political career, resist easy categorization. He listed the environment third among six "great goals" in his 1971 State of the Union address, underscoring his desire "to continue the effort so dramatically begun this year: to restore and enhance our natural environment." Among his many objectives were strengthening pesticide laws, regulating ocean dumping, and imposing restrictions on noise levels. But he vetoed the CLEAN WATER ACT in 1972 because he objected to the bill's multibillion-dollar price tag. Nixon then triggered a constitutional showdown by trying to impound much of the money that the law authorized for new sewage facilities. He also battled against emissions deadlines in the Clean Air Act, tried to give states greater flexibility over antipollution rules, and proposed spending more money on defense and less on pollution reduction. Speaking to business leaders worried about the costs of regulations, he said in 1971, "We are not going to allow the environmental issue … to destroy the industrial system that made this the great country it is."

Nixon, many analysts believe, may have turned to environmental issues for political reasons rather than any deep interest in ecology. He tended toward more moderate positions than many in Congress, often preferring to minimize the costs of regulations and create less stringent goals. However

Many analysts believe that President Richard M. Nixon, who signed the landmark Environmental Policy Act and won passage of major antipollution laws, turned to environmental issues solely for political reasons. He opposed costly regulations and often sought reductions in environmental spending. Source: The White House

politically inspired, these positions had a philosophical basis: avoiding acrimonious conflict with industry. At a time of emerging policy fractures between environmentalists and polluters, Nixon urged Congress in 1972 to "come to grips with the basic factors which underlie our more obvious environmental problems—factors like the use of land and the impact of incentives or disincentives built into our economic system."

But lawmakers, bruised by the failure of more incremental legislation in the 1950s and 1960s, pressed ahead with a "COMMAND-AND-CONTROL" approach that dictated costly antipollution goals. The flurry of legislation that Congress passed, sometimes at Nixon's urging and sometimes over his objections, successfully reversed decades of deteriorating environmental quality. Although these laws still stand today as the bulwark of the nation's environmental protection efforts, they fell short of their ambitious targets and set the stage for continuous conflicts between government regulations and polluters. Ultimately, the legislation of the

Nixon era failed to address the underlying issues the president alluded to in 1972 and has left the country with an uncertain environmental posture.

No net loss

When GEORGE BUSH ran for president in 1988, he endorsed the goal of "no net loss" of the nation's WETLANDS. This meant both minimizing the destruction of existing wetlands and creating new ones. Approximately half the original 220 million acres in the contiguous United States had been destroyed, and scientists belatedly were discovering that wetlands are critical for filtering water and controlling flooding. Despite his campaign pledge, Bush in 1991 sought to relax wetlands regulations to accommodate the needs of farmers, developers, and home builders. He said the new policy would "slow and eventually stop the net loss of wetlands. . . . The plan seeks to balance two important objectives: the protection, restoration, and creation of wetlands, and the need for sustained economic growth and development." The 1991 proposal would have allowed more development by narrowing the definition of wetlands the U.S. ARMY CORPS OF ENGINEERS used when issuing SECTION 404 permits under the CLEAN WATER ACT. It sparked considerable debate but was never adopted.

President BILL CLINTON's administration made no net loss part of official policy in 1993, but the nation continued to lose wetlands at a rate of about 70,000 to 90,000 acres a year. In 1998 the Clinton administration unveiled a new plan to attain a net gain of 100,000 acres of wetlands yearly by 2005. Critics warned that such a goal appeared unrealistic.

"No regrets"

"No regrets" refers to an assortment of U.S. policies that indirectly limit GLOBAL WARMING. The first of the no-regrets plans, unveiled in the final months of President GEORGE BUSH's administration, consisted largely of estimating U.S. emissions of GREENHOUSE GASES and describing environmental and ENERGY EFFICIENCY programs that limit them. It was called "no regrets" because the programs described in the plan were justified for encouraging energy conservation and reducing AIR POLLUTION; any limitation on greenhouse gas emissions was a side benefit. The plan was spurred by the 1992 U.S. ratification of the U.N. Framework Convention on Climate Change, a nonbinding agreement that called on industrialized countries to reduce greenhouse gas emissions to 1990 levels by 2000.

President BILL CLINTON's administration in 1993 issued a revised version of the no-regrets plan that laid out additional programs and explicitly set a goal of meeting the agreement's suggested emissions levels. However, the administration failed to reach this goal because of economic growth, little support from Congress, and the lack of binding regulations in the no-regrets policy.

No surprises

In a bid to make the ENDANGERED SPECIES ACT more user-friendly, President BILL CLINTON's administration in the 1990s began negotiating "no-surprises" provisions with landowners. These are guarantees that once a landowner agrees to conservation measures to protect an endangered species, the government will not impose additional costs or restrictions on the use of the property. In certain cases, the government can undertake additional conservation measures, but only if it pays for them. Congress in the late 1990s debated making such a policy part of the law, rather than an administrative rule, but failed to reach consensus on other Endangered Species Act issues.

Property owners generally have praised the agreements for giving them more certainty over using their property. But environmentalists contend that the agreements disregard the constantly fluctuating state of ecosystems and could lead to inadequate conservation measures. They also warn that related policy measures, known as SAFE HARBOR agreements, which allow a property owner to develop land that may be home to endangered species, can undermine the environment.

Noise pollution

It is almost impossible for Americans to escape unpleasant noise pollution, be it from traffic, radios, airplanes, or lawnmowers. The noise can cause stress and contribute to a wide range of emotional and physical ailments. By some estimates, nearly all Americans suffer from some degree of hearing loss by the time they reach middle age.

When it was created in 1970, the ENVIRONMENTAL PROTECTION AGENCY (EPA) had a mandate to limit noise pollution. Accordingly, it has set standards for noise levels from cars and various types of motors and equipment. Workers are protected from dangerous noise levels by OCCUPATIONAL SAFETY AND HEALTH ADMINISTRATION regulations. In NATIONAL PARKS, officials restrict the use of such vehicles as snowmobiles and personal watercraft,

both to protect animals and to provide a more satisfying experience for people seeking solitude. Amid concerns about aviation noise, Congress in 1990 passed the Airport Noise and Capacity Act (PL 101-71) to enable communities to expedite noise abatement programs.

Nonattainment areas

Nonattainment areas are cities, suburbs, and other regions that fail to meet the NATIONAL AMBIENT AIR QUALITY STANDARDS promulgated under the CLEAN AIR ACT. Even though air quality has improved significantly since 1970, an estimated 133.9 million Americans in 1998 lived in counties that were unable to meet at least one air quality standard, according to the ENVIRONMENTAL PROTECTION AGENCY (EPA). The worst offender, by far, is ozone. The rise in population and increased traffic is making it difficult for many cities to comply with the law, despite more stringent emission standards.

In the 1990 amendments to the Clean Air Act, Congress identified ninety-six cities and counties that had high ozone levels. It classified them on a scale ranging from marginal to severe nonattainment and imposed a series of deadlines for them to meet clean air standards. This approach was more rigorous than the 1970 law, which required only that cities make "reasonable further progress" in combating pollution. The worst offender, Los Angeles, has until 2020 to meet the standards.

In 1997 the EPA attempted to impose more rigorous standards for ozone and PARTICULATE MATTER. The new regulations were challenged in court. If they are enacted, the number of counties failing to meet the ozone standard would more than triple to about 330, and the number of counties failing to meet the particulate matter standard would more than quadruple from 40 to about 170.

Nongovernmental organizations

Nongovernmental organizations (NGOs) are playing an increasingly important role in global environmental protection policies. These private environmental, health, and economic development groups work with both local communities and government agencies. Not as bureaucratic as multilateral agencies, they focus on grassroots efforts to encourage land conservation and sustainable economic practices. They also seek to improve food production and fight diseases. NGOs have proliferated rapidly. It is estimated that there are more than 100,000 worldwide, many based in developing countries.

Non-Indigenous Aquatic Nuisance Act

The Non-Indigenous Aquatic Nuisance Act of 1990 (PL 101-646) was one of the nation's first formal attempts to combat EXOTIC SPECIES, which are nonnative organisms that can damage a habitat. Congress passed the law without dissent to try to curb the spread of ZEBRA MUSSELS, a newly introduced type of freshwater mollusk that was causing havoc in many waterways and drinking water systems. The law requires the Coast Guard to issue binding regulations to prevent ships from accidentally introducing "nuisance species" into the United States. It also established the Aquatic Nuisance Species Task Force, cochaired by the Fish and Wildlife Service and the NATIONAL OCEANIC AND ATMOSPHERIC ADMINISTRATION, which coordinates federal efforts to halt the introduction of foreign species into U.S. water systems.

Nonpoint source pollution

Nonpoint source pollution, sometimes known as runoff, is viewed as the greatest remaining threat to water quality. Efforts to control it have sparked legislative and judicial battles for years. Unlike a discharge from specific factories or sewage plants, nonpoint source pollution cannot be traced to any single outlet. Instead, it typically consists of urban and rural runoff that washes into streams and lakes. The many diffuse sources range from storm drain runoff that contains used motor oil, household chemicals, and lawn PESTICIDES to poor agricultural practices, such as leaking MANURE lagoons or plowing too close to waterways. Mines, construction sites, and other operations contribute to the problem. The ENVIRONMENTAL PROTECTION AGENCY (EPA) reported in 1998 that polluted runoff was the largest cause of WATER POLLUTION, with agricultural runoff in particular degrading many rivers and lakes.

Since 1972 the CLEAN WATER ACT has focused on regulating sewage plants and other POINT SOURCES of pollution by prohibiting them from discharging untreated waste into waterways. Reducing nonpoint source pollution is much more difficult from a technical perspective because the many types of runoff are hard to track. In addition, the pollution is caused by a broad range of politically influential groups that do not want to be regulated. The Democratic-controlled Congress in the early 1990s tried to expand the Clean Water Act to put a greater focus on nonpoint source pollution but was stymied by conservative opposition. When Republicans became the majority in 1995, they mounted an unsuccessful effort to relax many of the law's provisions and allow states to use a voluntary incentive system to ease nonpoint source pollution.

As the congressional deadlock continued, the EPA entered the fray in the late 1990s with a series of plans to reduce nonpoint source runoff. The most controversial and potentially costly proposal, announced by President BILL CLINTON in 1999, was the enforcement of Clean Water Act provisions known as TOTAL MAXIMUM DAILY LOADS. Under these provisions, states would be required to inventory their rivers and lakes, identify the worst cases, and reduce the amount of pollution flowing into them by allocating pollution reductions among various classes of polluters, such as farms, industrial plants, and cities. As Clinton's tenure as president drew to a close, it appeared uncertain whether such a plan could be implemented, both because of the costs and complexities and because of political opposition.

North American Free Trade Agreement

The North American Free Trade Agreement (NAFTA), passed in 1993 after a bitter congressional battle, has provoked criticism from many environmental groups. The pact, which removes trade barriers between the United States, Mexico, and Canada, restricts domestic environmental laws from interfering with trade. Environmentalists worry that this could prevent the United States from trying to protect overseas wildlife by banning certain imports—a tactic that helped promote DOLPHIN-SAFE TUNA techniques in the early 1990s. They also contend that the pact has spurred worsening environmental conditions in Mexico, and it allows U.S. companies to relocate south of the border to take advantage of lax environmental standards.

To assuage such concerns, negotiators in 1993 added the goal of sustainable development in the treaty's preamble. President BILL CLINTON lobbied fiercely for congressional approval, acceding to side agreements to boost North American environmental cooperation. As a result, the trade pact created the Border Environment Cooperation Commission and the North American Development Bank to promote sustainable development and finance environmental infrastructure projects, as well as the Commission for Environmental Cooperation to enforce environmental laws.

Environmentalists split over whether to support NAFTA in 1993, and they remain divided over the trade agreement's impact. On the one hand, NAFTA set a precedent for considering environmental issues in trade arrangements. It also spurred monitoring of environmental conditions across the continent and focused concerns on TRANSBOUNDARY POLLUTION. On the other hand, critics say NAFTA's environmental institutions are underfunded and have limited influence, and they note that the pact has allowed companies to challenge environmental regulations.

North American Precipitation Assessment Program

Congress in 1980 created an interagency body, the North American Precipitation Assessment Program, to study the effects of ACID RAIN. The result was a $500-million, ten-year report on the causes and effects of acid rain as well as strategy control options. The program struck a middle course, challenging the views of extremists on both sides. Although it stated that sulfur dioxide and nitrogen oxides emitted from coal-burning power plants and other sources were increasing the acidity of precipitation, it concluded that forests remained healthy and most lakes and streams were unaffected. Summing up the report's conclusions, program director James R. Mahoney said, "The sky is not falling, but there is a problem that needs addressing."

The report had little impact, since it was released after Congress tackled the acid rain problem through 1990 amendments to the CLEAN AIR ACT. In addition, the North American Precipitation As-

sessment Program faced credibility questions after 1987, when Lawrence Kulp, its director, resigned after reportedly writing an introduction to an interim report that reflected what he thought President RONALD REAGAN's administration wanted to hear.

Northern spotted owl

The formal listing in 1990 of the northern spotted owl as a threatened species set off a fiery battle between timber interests and environmentalists. Environmentalists contended that the ENDAN-GERED SPECIES ACT required that much of the owl's habitat—primarily federally owned OLD-GROWTH

Pitting environmentalists against timber interests, the controversy over the fate of the northern spotted owl tested the limits of the Endangered Species Act. Source: U.S. Fish and Wildlife Service

FORESTS in Washington, Oregon, and northern California—be ruled off-limits to logging regardless of the local economic impact. Lawmakers saw the issue differently. To prevent the loss of tens of thousands of logging jobs, they passed riders on appropriations bills to allow the continuation of limited logging and restrict judicial review of the federal government's logging practices. Environmentalists turned to federal court, which ruled that Congress had overstepped its bounds.

For the next four years, administration officials, lawmakers, and judges weighed in on the issue. It became a key test of the extent to which the government was willing to go to protect a single species. GEORGE BUSH's administration asked Congress to amend the Endangered Species Act to put a greater emphasis on the economic effects of regulatory decisions. When lawmakers could not agree on a bill, the administration proposed setting aside a limited amount of land that could support an estimated 1,340 pairs of owls—fewer than half the number known to exist. In 1992 the ENDANGERED SPECIES COMMITTEE voted to suspend the Endangered Species Act and allow limited logging, but federal court injunctions prevented that from taking place.

After BILL CLINTON was elected president in 1992, he focused on the northern spotted owl controversy in an attempt to demonstrate that it was possible to protect the environment without throwing people out of work. But such optimism was unfounded. The administration's initial forest management plan in 1993, which would have reduced logging to about half the amount cut before the court-ordered ban, drew fire from all sides. The White House then revised the plan, leaning more toward environmental demands by making steeper reductions in logging and establishing reserves of old-growth forest to protect the owl's breeding grounds. That compromise also proved controversial: both environmentalists and the timber industry filed lawsuits against it in 1994. However, a federal judge upheld it.

In the late 1990s, scientists reported that the owl population was continuing to decline slowly but the survival rate of adult females had stabilized—a possible indication that the species would begin to recover.

Nuclear energy

Introduced in the 1950s, nuclear power was billed as the energy of the future, but the technology of safely releasing energy through fission (splitting apart heavy atoms such as uranium) proved far more complicated than initially projected. After an accident in 1978 at the THREE MILE ISLAND facility near Harrisburg, Pennsylvania, public opinion turned sharply against licensing new nuclear plants. In addition to concerns about a reactor meltdown, critics contend there is no safe way to dispose of NUCLEAR WASTE. Some analysts, however, credit the domestic nuclear industry with a remarkably sound safety record and say the risks have been greatly overstated.

In many respects, nuclear energy has been on the wane in recent years. Every unit ordered since 1973 has been canceled because of cost and safety concerns. In 2000 nuclear energy produced about 20 percent of the nation's electricity, down from 22.5 percent in 1995. However, growing concern about GLOBAL WARMING may revive the industry because, unlike power plants that burn FOSSIL FUELS, nuclear power plants do not emit GREENHOUSE GASES. After cutting funding for nuclear energy research and development, President BILL CLINTON's administration in the late 1990s suggested that renewing the licenses of aging nuclear power plants could help the United States curtail greenhouse gas emissions. The NUCLEAR REGULATORY COMMISSION in 2000 agreed to renew the operating license of the Calvert Cliffs nuclear power plant in Maryland, signaling that dozens of other plants also would likely be allowed to continue operations.

The major nuclear energy issue that has embroiled Congress is the disposal of nuclear waste—especially whether to begin depositing waste in Nevada's YUCCA MOUNTAIN. Many environmentalists view nuclear waste as a major problem because radioactive elements can persist for tens of thousands of years, endangering the health of both humans and wildlife. Lawmakers also have waded into other issues. The 1957 Price-Anderson Act (PL 85-256) limited the liability of the nuclear power industry in case of an accident and provided a system for paying some of the damage claims in such an eventuality. In 1988 Congress extended the law but increased the coverage for a single accident from $700 million to $7 billion. Four years later Congress streamlined the process for nuclear plant permits. The nuclear industry had objected for years to provisions in the 1954 Atomic Energy Act (PL 83-703) that required the Atomic Energy Commission (later the Nulear Regulatory Commission) to issue a construction permit to build a plant and then, after the completion of construction, an operating permit to run it. Accordingly, Congress included provisions in the 1992 ENERGY POLICY ACT (PL 102-486) that allowed completed plants to operate without delay if certain construction criteria were met.

Nuclear Regulatory Commission

The Nuclear Regulatory Commission is an independent agency headed by five commissioners appointed by the president of the United States. It regulates nonmilitary uses of nuclear facilities and materials, including the construction, operation, and decommissioning of nuclear reactors, the mining of uranium, and the designation of NUCLEAR WASTE sites—all of which are issues that concern the environmental community. The commission, created in 1976, assumed the regulatory responsibilities that Congress previously had vested in the Atomic Energy Commission.

The commission has won praise from environmentalists for regulating nuclear facilities more strictly and for imposing increasingly rigorous standards on licenses for new facilities. At the same time, however, it has faced criticism because of its close ties to the nuclear industry. Because it proposed less stringent standards than the ENVIRONMENTAL PROTECTION AGENCY (EPA) for the disposal of nuclear waste at Nevada's YUCCA MOUNTAIN, lawmakers have debated which agency should regulate the site. In 2000 the commission began renewing the operating licenses of older nuclear plants, thereby ensuring the continued viability of NUCLEAR ENERGY.

Nuclear waste

Radioactive nuclear waste is the byproduct of producing nuclear weapons, generating nuclear power, and using nuclear materials commercially for medicine, industry, and other purposes. It is generally categorized as high-level or low-level waste. HIGH-LEVEL NUCLEAR WASTE consists of intensely radioactive liquid materials from reprocessing nuclear fuel (separating uranium and plutonium from other elements) and producing materials for nuclear weapons. It often includes transuranic wastes, which are the byproducts of manufactured elements with an atomic number greater than uranium (92). These wastes remain dangerous for extraordinarily long periods, with some elements having half-lives exceeding 200,000 years. Spent fuel, which is used in nuclear reactors until it no longer contributes efficiently to the nuclear chain reaction, is also highly radioactive and is sometimes classified as high-level waste. LOW-LEVEL RADIOACTIVE WASTE consists of such materials as clothing and lab equipment that is contaminated by commercial activities. Low-level waste generally is less radioactive than high-level waste and decays within about 100 years.

Battles over Storage

The disposal of nuclear waste is highly controversial, both because no state wants to be tapped as the repository for dangerously radioactive materials and because some experts maintain that it is impossible to safely dispose of the contaminated waste. The waste emits radiation that, if improperly stored, could sicken or even kill people and cause severe environmental damage. Safe storage is extremely difficult because the waste must be isolated from the environment until the radioactivity decays to safe levels—a process that may take many thousands of years. Although radiation can be a threat in air, soil, or surface water, the most probable pathway for improperly stored waste to reach people is through GROUNDWATER. For that reason, nuclear waste management focuses on preventing groundwater contamination or cleaning up groundwater that has already become contaminated.

Proper storage of nuclear waste received little attention until the mid-1970s—three decades after the detonation of the first atomic bomb. During the cold war, nuclear weapons facilities, including factories, laboratories, and waste disposal sites, were largely closed to public scrutiny and exempt from most regulations. Then came revelations in the 1970s that liquid high-level radioactive waste was leaking from government storage tanks and MINING residues (known as uranium mill tailings) had been dispersed in the environment. Concerns emerged about nuclear power plants running out of space for spent fuel. The nuclear industry had assumed that spent commercial power plant fuel could be reprocessed to yield plutonium, but President JIMMY CARTER was concerned that the recycled plutonium could be diverted to make nuclear bombs. In 1978 Carter vowed that the waste would not be left in temporary storage sites, thus forcing Congress to begin debating the problem instead of leaving it to future generations.

With critics charging that storage methods could not indefinitely safeguard the environment from radioactive contamination, several states passed laws in the 1970s prohibiting the construction of new nuclear power plants or the disposal of radioactive waste. Even low-level waste became controversial, as the three states with low-level disposal facilities (Washington, Nevada, and South Carolina) took steps to restrict imports of out-of-state waste at the end of the 1970s.

Lawmakers have tried to resolve the issue ever since, but they have made limited headway. In 1980 Congress passed the Low-Level Radioactive Waste Policy Act (PL 96-573) to encourage states to enter into regional compacts. However, even though Congress amended the law five years later to impose deadlines, the states had failed to open a new

Nuclear Waste Stored in the United States

State	Metric tons of uranium	State	Metric tons of uranium
Alabama	1,439.4	Montana	0
Alaska	0	Nebraska	353.0
Arizona	464.7	Nevada	0
Arkansas	580.8	New Hampshire	95.3
California	1,318.7	New Jersey	1,186.8
Colorado	15.4	New Mexico	0
Connecticut	1,253.9	New York	1,741.9
Delaware	0	North Carolina	1,575.5
Florida	1,439.8	North Dakota	0
Georgia	1,018.9	Ohio	422.1
Hawaii	0	Oklahoma	0
Idaho	52.0	Oregon	358.9
Illinois	4,292.0	Pennsylvania	2,536.2
Indiana	0	Rhode Island	0
Iowa	235.3	South Carolina	1,789.2
Kansas	226.0	South Dakota	0
Kentucky	0	Tennessee	415.3
Louisiana	389.9	Texas	361.2
Maine	433.0	Utah	0
Maryland	607.8	Vermont	365.9
Massachusetts	428.8	Virginia	1,154.8
Michigan	1,260.4	Washington	218.5
Minnesota	647.7	West Virginia	0
Mississippi	298.5	Wisconsin	809.1
Missouri	240.1	Wyoming	0

Source: U.S. Department of Energy, Energy Information Administration, 1994 Nuclear Fuel Data Survey, http://www.eia.doe.gov/cneaf/nuclear/spt_fuel/sptfl_sum.html.

Note: Figures represent quantities of commercial spent nuclear fuel stored at U.S. nuclear power plants and away-from-reactor facilities.

site by 2000 because of safety concerns about transporting and storing the waste. As a result, low-level radioactive waste was still being stored in temporary facilities across the country (see table).

High-level radioactive waste presents, arguably, even more daunting public policy challenges. By 1980 federal military weapons and research facilities had produced more than 77 million gallons of liquid high-level wastes, most of which were stored in steel tanks in Hanford, Washington; Savannah River, South Carolina; and Idaho Falls, Idaho. In addition, nuclear power plants had accumulated about 25,000 spent fuel assemblies that were stored in pools of water at plant sites. The U.S. DEPARTMENT OF ENERGY warned that reactor sites would run out of storage space in 1986. Throughout the 1970s government officials studied underground formations as possible disposal sites, although it abandoned the first site it examined, in Lyons, Kansas, after experts concluded that water could leak in.

Congress in 1980 debated a temporary solution that would have had the government building aboveground vaults where the waste would have been stored for up to a century. Two years later, however, lawmakers endorsed the concept of an underground site when they passed the Nuclear Waste Policy Act (PL 97-425). Signed into law at the beginning of 1983, the law required the president to make a recommendation by 1987 for a permanent federal repository for storing spent fuel rods and other commercial waste and to recommend a second repository by 1990. The Energy Department also was to provide temporary storage for spent power plant fuel and draft plans for creating vaults to store nuclear waste that could be monitored and eventually removed. Congress exempted radioactive wastes from weapons production from most of the law's regulations. Environmentalists objected to the law, saying the tight deadlines would force the government to make hasty choices and warning that shipping spent fuel around the country would risk theft, accidents, and sabotage.

Focus on Yucca Mountain

By 1987 the Energy Department had narrowed its search to sites in Washington, Texas, and Nevada. Disregarding its 1982 commitment to base the site selection on purely scientific, not political, criteria, Congress amended the Nuclear Waste Policy Act to name YUCCA MOUNTAIN in Nevada as the site where the first exploratory shaft for a permanent repository was to be drilled. If Yucca Mountain were to prove unsuitable, the Energy Department would report to Congress and await further instruction. The amendments also delayed authorization of a temporary waste site and removed the 1982 provision for a second repository, creating a highly politicized situation in which lawmakers from across the country were able to overwhelm the protests of the Nevada delegation. "Congress is behaving like a pack of wolves going in for the kill," said Rep. Barbara F. Vucanovich, R-Nev.

Although the Nuclear Waste Policy Act antici-

pated the opening of the repository by 1998, the Energy Department has run into a series of delays in studying the geology of the site. In 1998 it issued a "viability assessment" that reported no insurmountable problems with Yucca Mountain. However, it is not expected to submit a final recommendation until 2001, and its goal as of 2000 was to open the Yucca Mountain repository by 2010.

After the Energy Department missed its 1998 deadline to begin shipping waste, lawmakers weighed proposals to store waste at an interim facility near Yucca Mountain. This plan drew strong opposition from officials in President BILL CLINTON's administration who contended that a study of Yucca Mountain should be completed first. Lawmakers also are at odds over whether to transfer responsibility for setting safety standards at the repository from the ENVIRONMENTAL PROTECTION AGENCY (EPA) to the NUCLEAR REGULATORY COMMISSION. Some in Congress contend that the EPA standards are overly stringent. Environmentalists, however, say the concept of storing tons of nuclear waste in Yucca Mountain is inherently dangerous, partly because water flowing through rock fractures would pick up radiation and contaminate the water table.

Spent fuel aside, aging U.S. nuclear weapons sites pose a major environmental hazard. The Energy Department projects that cleaning up the sites, which is becoming its biggest activity, will cost approximately $150 billion through 2070. The department unveiled an accelerated program in 1998 that would clean up forty-one sites by 2006, but some environmentalists questioned whether the tight time frame could undercut the quality of the work. Many analysts view the half-century of nuclear weapons development as among the nation's worst environmental disasters, leaving a legacy of sick and endangered workers and more than

100 nuclear weapons and laboratory sites that are severely contaminated and could defy all cleanup efforts.

Nuclear waste has also stirred some concerns overseas. Several countries are planning to open repository sites by 2020 or later. In the 1990s Russia acknowledged using the Sea of Japan and arctic waters near Norway for dumping radioactive wastes, including nuclear reactors. The environmental effects are uncertain.

Nutrients

The nutrients phosphorus and nitrogen are important contributors to water-quality problems. Although both are essential food elements that promote growth, excessive amounts of the nutrients foster ALGAL BLOOMS, which deplete oxygen levels in the water and deprive underwater grasses of sunlight, eventually causing EUTROPHICATION and wiping out much indigenous aquatic life.

State surveys in the late 1990s indicated that overenrichment of water by nutrients was the single biggest source of impaired water quality in rivers, streams, lakes, reservoirs, and ESTUARIES. Excessive nutrient levels have been linked to outbreaks of the deadly microbe PFIESTERIA in the mid-Atlantic states and to a large dead zone in the Gulf of Mexico. AGRICULTURAL RUNOFF is the major source of nutrient problems, followed by municipal sewage plants and nonagricultural runoff.

Since 1972 laws such as the CLEAN WATER ACT have helped dramatically reduce the amount of nutrients in waterways, largely because of improved municipal sewage treatment and restrictions on phosphorus in detergents. However, excessive levels of nutrients remain a primary problem in the Chesapeake Bay, the EVERGLADES, and other ecologically significant waterways. In the late 1990s the ENVIRONMENTAL PROTECTION AGENCY announced a series of plans to reduce agricultural runoff and other types of NONPOINT SOURCE POLLUTION that contribute to nutrient overenrichment and other water-quality problems. But some of its potentially costly plans faced legal challenges and significant congressional opposition. As of 2000 it was unclear when—or if—the regulations would be imposed.

O

Occupational Safety and Health Administration

While the ENVIRONMENTAL PROTECTION AGENCY (EPA) safeguards the general public from hazardous substances, the Labor Department's OCCUPATIONAL SAFETY AND HEALTH ADMINISTRATION (OSHA) is responsible for safeguarding people in the workplace. This is an important issue because workers—whether field hands spraying PESTICIDES or technicians using mercury-measuring devices—often are more exposed than anyone else to toxins. OSHA works with states to develop health, safety, and recordkeeping programs. It also shares RISK-ASSESSMENT responsibilities with the EPA. In 2000 the agency had a budget of about $380 million and twenty-three hundred employees.

Ocean Dumping Act

See MARINE PROTECTION, RESEARCH, AND SANCTUARIES ACT.

Offshore drilling

The outer continental shelf, which extends many miles off the shores of the United States, contains vast reserves of natural gas and oil. In 1998 it was the source of about 25 percent of the nation's natural gas production and nearly 20 percent of its crude oil production, amounting to $18 billion. Most of the active wells are in the Gulf of Mexico, off the coasts of Alabama, Louisiana, and Texas.

The drilling takes place under the aegis of the 1953 OUTER CONTINENTAL SHELF LANDS ACT, which provides for the federal government to lease the lands, obtain fair market value for the lands and any resulting production, and ensure that the environment is protected. The Interior Department's Minerals Management Service administers the program. Since 1954 producers have paid the government about $60 billion for leases and slightly more than that in royalties. Some of that money goes into the LAND AND WATER CONSERVATION FUND.

Offshore drilling has sparked intense environmental concerns since 1969, when a blowout off the coast of Santa Barbara resulted in an oil slick that fouled southern California beaches and killed numerous birds and marine mammals. Throughout the 1980s and 1990s, environmentalists sought to block drilling off the coasts of California and Florida, as well as other states. Congress has included moratoria on new leases in annual Interior Department spending bills since 1982, beginning with California offshore areas and expanding its restrictions to include New England, the mid-Atlantic, the Pacific Northwest, Alaska, and the eastern Gulf of Mexico. The ad-

The subject of environmental concerns since 1969, when an oil spill in Santa Barbara, California, ruined beaches and killed numerous fish and birds, offshore drilling has been restricted by Congress but is still permitted in some ecologically fragile areas. Source: Texaco

undeveloped leases off the coast of California, meaning that oil and gas companies could continue exploratory work in an area thought to contain some one billion barrels of oil. California officials have turned to the courts to try to block the extension.

Oil Pollution Act

In the wake of public outrage over the devastating EXXON VALDEZ oil spill in Alaska, lawmakers broke years of deadlock in 1990 to pass the Oil Pollution Act (PL 101-380). The law is designed both to prevent oil spills and to punish those responsible when spills do occur. It requires spillers to clean up the oil and pay compensation for any economic damages. Although it limits liability depending on the type of vessel or facility involved, those limits are far higher than pre-1990 federal limits and can top $200 million for large tankers. Shippers are required to draft "worst case" oil spill response plans for quick cleanup. The law also beefed up the government's capacity to respond to oil spills by setting up a federal fund for cleanup costs, establishing rapid-response teams, and expanding the president's power to take control of a spiller's cleanup operations.

One of the major differences that had divided lawmakers since the 1970s was whether the federal government should preempt state laws that exposed oil spillers to unlimited liability. The House had long insisted on such preemption but agreed to drop the issue from the 1990 bill because of mounting concern over the environmental and economic costs of oil spills. Lawmakers also divided over provisions to require tankers to have double hulls, which would make them more se-

ministrations of President GEORGE BUSH and BILL CLINTON also imposed restrictions on issuing new leases. Environmentalists would go further, banning drilling off ecologically fragile areas in Florida and California, but congressional supporters of the oil and gas industries want the government to look into whether such offshore areas could be developed without harming the environment.

In recent years the renewal of leases has sparked considerable conflict. The Clinton administration in 1999 agreed to extend thirty-six

Oil Polluting Incidents Reported in and around U.S. Waters, 1970–1997

Year	Number (thousands)	Volume (gallons)
1970	3.711	15,252,992
1971	8.736	8,839,523
1972	9.931	18,805,732
1973	9.014	15,253,580
1974	9.999	15,698,731
1975	9.292	21,520,083
1976	9.422	18,517,949
1977	9.459	8,189,133
1978	10.644	10,864,108
1979	9.834	20,893,558
1980	8.383	12,596,970
1981	7.811	8,920,995
1982	7.484	10,344,797
1983	7.916	8,379,848
1984	8.258	18,005,878
1985	6.169	8,436,248
1986	4.993	4,281,979
1987	4.841	3,608,885
1988	4.998	6,586,004
1989	6.613	13,478,695
1990	8.177	7,915,007
1991	8.569	1,875,953
1992	9.491	1,875,668
1993	8.972	2,067,388
1994	8.960	2,489,273
1995	9.038	2,638,229
1996	9.335	3,117,831
1997	8.624	942,574
1998	8.315	885,303

Source: U.S. Department of Transportation, United States Coast Guard, *Pollution Incidents in and around U.S. Waters: A Spill/Release Compendium: 1969–1998* (Washington, D.C.: DOT, USCG, 1999).

Note: Includes oil spill data for vessels and nonvessels (for example, facilities, pipelines, and other unknown sources).

cure. With President GEORGE BUSH and oil interests opposing a double-hull requirement, Congress worked out a compromise to require almost all tankers to have double hulls by 2010.

Old-growth forests

Some of the most intense environmental disputes in recent years have focused on old-growth forests, especially those in the Pacific Northwest. The preservation of old growth is an environmental priority because such forests are unusually rich in BIODIVERSITY and help maintain healthy watersheds. Loggers, however, often target old-growth stands because they provide particularly valuable timber.

Old growth resists precise definition, but the term generally describes a forest dominated by large, mature tree species that can regenerate in the shade created by the canopy of older trees. Perhaps the most familiar old-growth forests are those in the Pacific Northwest, which are characterized by towering redwood and Douglas-fir trees, a fern-covered forest floor, and large moss-covered trees decaying on the ground. But small tracts of old-growth forests—also known as ancient or late-successional forests—can still be found in other ecosystems across the country, despite more than a century of extensive logging. Although forests have expanded in the United States in recent years, many of them are managed as tree plantations that offer limited ecological benefits. Old-growth forests are rare because they take many centuries to regenerate.

Congress has not passed any legislation directly regulating old-growth forest management. Instead, environmentalists and loggers generally turn to surrogate issues in their debate over old-growth tracts. Environmentalists invoked the ENDANGERED SPECIES ACT in the late 1980s to restrict logging in Pacific Northwest old-growth forests, the habitat of the rare NORTHERN SPOTTED OWL. Since then, rural conservatives have

Environmentalists have invoked the Endangered Species Act to limit logging in old-growth forests. Source: *National Park Service*

scored occasional victories to allow limited old-growth logging in such places as Alaska's TONGASS NATIONAL FOREST but have mostly been on the defensive. In 2000 the Clinton administration took controversial steps to protect groves of ancient sequoia trees in California and impose restrictions on building new roads in national forests.

One of the biggest battles over logging old-growth forests on private lands erupted in the 1990s over plans to cut down one-thousand-year-old redwood trees in California's HEADWATERS FOREST. After a decade of confrontations between environmentalists and loggers, federal and state officials paid $480 million for a package of logging concessions—a sign of the growing value of old-growth forests.

Outer Continental Shelf Lands Act

First passed in 1953, the Outer Continental Shelf Lands Act (PL 83-212) governs offshore oil and gas production. Prior to the 1970s, the law generated little environmental controversy. But when President Richard Nixon's administration advocated the expansion of offshore leasing and exploration beyond the coasts of Louisiana, Texas, and southern California, state officials and environmentalists raised concerns about the effects on beaches and other fragile coastal areas.

After years of debate, lawmakers overhauled the law in 1978 to place a greater emphasis on environmental protection and give states a larger role in leasing decisions. The new legislation (PL 95-372) called for more aggressive management of the outer continental shelf—the underwater margin of the North American continent that extends as far as 150 to 200 miles offshore and contains enormous estimated reserves of natural gas and oil. The law requires the government to develop comprehensive programs for leasing that take into account the environmental sensitivity and marine productivity of different areas. Any plan for production must include a description of environmental safeguards. Lawmakers also set up a more competitive bidding process and enabled people who could be adversely affected by development to file a lawsuit.

Among the most important provisions of the 1978 rewrite were those governing the cleanup of oil spills. Under the revised law, owners and operators of offshore facilities and vessels have unlimited liability for cleanup of oil spills and more limited liability for damages. Congress also established an offshore oil pollution compensation fund, funded by a three-cent-per-barrel fee on oil extracted from the outer continental shelf, which the president can use for cleaning up spills.

Overfishing

Overfishing is a worldwide environmental problem with significant socioeconomic implications. Since the 1950s, huge fleets operated by fishermen from Japan, Russia, the United States, and other countries have gradually depleted fish populations throughout most of the world's oceans. The use of enormous nets and one-thousand-hook longlines, coupled with the effects of WATER POLLUTION and the destruction of coastal WETLANDS, is devastating to fish as well as to the many birds and mammals that feed on them. Subsistence fishermen are having a difficult time supporting themselves as fish populations drop.

The oceans were once thought to have a limitless bounty. But as demand for seafood skyrocketed after World War II because of the population boom, fleets began venturing from their traditional fisheries in the Mediterranean, North Atlantic, and North Pacific to seek fish across the world's oceans. As the boats gradually became more sophisticated, outfitted with depth finders and electronics that could pinpoint a single fish many hundreds of feet below the surface, sea creatures had nowhere to hide. By the late 1990s, fishermen were extracting an estimated 80 million tons of fish and other sea life annually and discarding an additional 20 million tons of BYCATCH, or unwanted

turtles, birds, and other creatures that were inadvertently killed during fishing operations.

Some species have been especially hard hit. The Atlantic bluefin tuna, a powerful warm-blooded fish that can weigh more than one thousand pounds, has been hunted to near-extinction because it is used for Japanese sushi. Shark populations are vanishing, partly as a result of the demand for shark fin soup. In many cases, fishing fleets dispute scientific estimates that fish populations are in peril, and they refuse to stop harvesting prized species. The economic stakes are high. A single bluefin tuna can sell for tens of thousands of dollars.

The United Nations Food and Agriculture Organization warned in 1996 that 60 percent of the world's important fish stocks were "in urgent need of management" because they were declining or being fished to their biological limit. The international organization also warned that the situation is worsening because demand for seafood is likely to increase to 110 to 120 million tons in 2010. Analysts predict that meeting such a demand will require doubling the use of fish farms, or AQUACULTURE (which can also damage the environment), while simultaneously promoting more sustainable fishing techniques so the oceans will produce more fish. But environmentalists believe instead that there will be a widening gap between supply and demand because it is likely that aquaculture will grow only moderately and the ocean catch will level off or even decline. Under such a scenario, fish prices will increase beyond the reach of low-income families, especially in developing countries where fish is an important source of protein.

The outlook is bleak because of the relentless pressure of POPULATION GROWTH and the lack of coordination among nations to rein in their fleets

Stock Levels of U.S. Fisheries, 1995–1997

Fishery	Stock level relative to long-term potential yield (number of species)				
	Below	Near	Above	Unknown	Total
Northeast demersal	21	2	0	2	25
Northeast pelagic	1	0	3	0	4
Atlantic anadromous	4	0	1	0	5
Northeast invertebrate	1	4	1	2	8
Atlantic highly migratory pelagic	7	2	0	1	10
Atlantic shark	1	0	1	1	3
Atlantic coastal migratory pelagic	1	3	0	3	7
Atlantic/Gulf/Caribbean reef fish	9	3	0	16	28
Southeast drum and croaker	3	0	0	4	7
Southeast menhaden	0	2	0	0	2
Southeast/Caribbean invertebrate	2	7	0	5	14
Pacific Coast salmon	2	3	0	0	5
Alaska salmon	1	1	3	0	5
Pacific Coast and Alaska pelagic	0	6	1	0	7
Pacific Coast groundfish	8	4	2	5	19
Western Pacific invertebrate	1	0	0	0	1
Western Pacific bottomfish*	2	4	0	0	6
Pacific highly migratory pelagic	1	11	2	1	15
Alaska groundfish	5	10	8	4	27
Alaska shellfish	3	0	1	1	5
Subtotal	73	62	23	45	203
Nearshore species	14	26	0	40	80
Total assessed species	87	88	23	85	283

Source: U.S. Department of Commerce, National Oceanic and Atmospheric Administration, and National Marine Fisheries Service, *Our Living Oceans, Report on the Status of U.S. Living Marine Resources* (Washington, D.C.: DOC, NOAA, NMFS, 1999).

Notes: Long-term potential yield (LTPY) is the maximum long-term average catch that can be achieved from the resource. This term is analogous to the concept of maximum sustainable yield. Stock level relative to LTPY is a measure of stock status. The present abundance level of the stock is compared with the level of abundance that on average would support the LTPY harvest. This level is expressed as below, near, above, or unknown relative to the abundance level that would produce LTPY. *Demersal* = bottom-dwelling fish such as flounders, skates, and dogfish. *Pelagic* = mid-water fish such as bluefish, anchovies, sardines, and squid. *Anadromous* = fish that ascend rivers to spawn, such as salmon, shad, and striped bass. *Invertebrate* = lobsters, clams, scallops, shrimp, and so on. *Highly migratory* = high-seas (oceanic) fish such as tuna, swordfish, and billfish. *Coastal migratory* = fish that range from the shore to the outer edge of the U.S. continental shelf, such as king and Spanish mackerel, dolphin fish, and cobia. *Reef fish* = fish that prefer coral reefs, artificial structures, and other hard-bottom areas, such as snappers, groupers, and amberjacks. The reef-fish fishery also includes tilefish that prefer sand-bottom areas.

* = also includes armorhead.

and allow fish populations to recover. However, individual countries have taken some steps toward a more sustainable approach that limits commercial fish catches and minimizes harm to other species. Cyprus and the Philippines, for example, produced higher yields after imposing improved management programs, New Zealand cut subsidies for shipbuilders, and many Western nations have adopted tougher fishing controls.

In the United States, Congress passed the MAG-NUSON FISHERY CONSERVATION AND MANAGE-MENT ACT in 1976 to try to regulate fishing practices. Nevertheless, several fisheries became depleted because of lax restrictions. Lawmakers in 1996 revamped the Magnuson Act (also called the Sustainable Fisheries Act) to put a greater emphasis on conservation and reducing BYCATCH. But environmentalists want tighter restrictions. They warn that popular species, such as eastern blue crabs and Alaska pollock, otherwise may not be able to maintain their numbers. Under pressure from environmentalists, the United States has also taken steps to improve international fishing techniques by imposing boycotts on countries that do not use TURTLE EXCLUDER DEVICES or otherwise try to minimize bycatch. Such boycotts, however, sometimes violate international trade rules (see also GLOBAL ECONOMY).

Ozone

Ground-level ozone, unlike ozone in the stratosphere, is a dangerous pollutant (see SMOG).

Ozone depletion

Ozone is a gas that forms a thin protective layer around the earth, filtering out most of the sun's ultraviolet (UV) radiation. Unlike ground-level ozone (a dangerous pollutant that causes SMOG), stratospheric ozone is regarded as important for the maintenance of life on earth. A 1 percent loss of ozone can result in a 2 percent increase in the amount of UV radiation that reaches the earth—which could cause about one million cases of human skin cancer.

In the early 1970s researchers began to warn that chlorofluorocarbons (CFCs), chemicals used for refrigeration and air conditioning, could release chlorine into the upper atmosphere and destroy ozone. More than most environmental threats, ozone depletion sparked a quick reaction. Research into the issue persuaded the United States to ban CFCs from domestic aerosol products in 1978. In 1985 twenty-two nations signed the Vienna Convention for the Protection of the Ozone Layer, pledging to take steps to stop ozone depletion. After scientists found an "ozone hole" over the Antarctic, the United States and other nations went much further, agreeing to phase out CFCs under the 1987 MONTREAL PROTOCOL ON SUBSTANCES THAT DEPLETE THE OZONE LAYER. Subsequently, the nations agreed to additional restrictions on chemicals blamed for ozone depletion. As a result, global consumption of CFCs and other ozone-destroying substances has dropped by more than 70 percent. This progress is threatened, however, because many countries have a booming black market in CFCs and halons, which are firefighting chemicals that also contribute to ozone depletion.

Because CFCs remain in the atmosphere for some time, the ozone layer is expected to thin further before it begins to recover. Scientists hope that stratospheric ozone levels will gradually rebound in the mid- to late twenty-first century.

P

Particulate matter

Particulate matter, which has spurred a series of legal and regulatory battles, is a type of AIR POLLUTION that is composed of solid particles or liquid droplets. The particles can be emitted directly into the air or formed when gaseous pollutants react in the air. They can cause serious health problems, including lung damage and bronchitis, as well as such environmental effects as reduced visibility.

Regulators distinguish between fine particles that are smaller than 2.5 microns in diameter (referred to as PM-2.5) and coarse particles up to 10 microns in diameter (PM-10). Fine particles, which are emitted by motor vehicles and industrial plants, cause particularly severe health problems because they are drawn deeply into the lungs and trigger inflammatory reactions. Coarser particles, released into the air by materials handling, crushing and grinding operations, agricultural plowing, and vehicles traveling on unpaved roads, generally are expelled by the body's protective mechanisms.

The ENVIRONMENTAL PROTECTION AGENCY (EPA) regulates particulate matter under the CLEAN AIR ACT. Initially, the agency focused on coarse particles, or soot. It set a single standard in 1987 for particles up to 10 microns in diameter. The American Lung Association filed a lawsuit in 1993 to force the agency to set a separate standard for fine particles because of health concerns. After losing the lawsuit, the EPA in 1997 announced PM 2.5 standards that could require new controls on vehicle exhaust and power plant and factory emissions. However, business groups went to court and won a 1999 appellate court decision blocking both the new particulate matter standards and new ozone standards. The U.S. Supreme Court is expected to issue a ruling in the case (*American Trucking Associations v. EPA*) in 2001.

Like most other elements of air pollution, levels of particulate matter have declined in recent years because of federal regulations. Since the EPA began monitoring particulate matter in 1988, PM-10 concentrations have fallen by more than 25 percent. However, about forty counties exceeded allowable levels of particulate matter before the 1997 EPA standards, and about 120 additional counties faced the prospect of exceeding the proposed tighter standards. Particulate matter is an especially big problem in the arid western states, where suspended particles tend to linger in the air.

Passenger pigeon

The demise of the passenger pigeon is often cited as the classic example of EXTINCTION of a species in the twentieth century. The pigeons were so numerous—they were the most plentiful bird in the nineteenth century and perhaps ever—that the naturalist John James Audubon reported seeing a single flock that appeared to contain more than one billion birds. But the nation's growing population meant a death sentence for the species, which were hunted relentlessly as food. A single shotgun blast could bring down more than one hundred birds on the wing, and a skillfully laid net could trap as many as three thousand roosting pigeons.

Even though it became clear in the 1880s that the species faced annihilation, the government failed to take protective steps. By the early 1900s, the few remaining wild specimens had disappeared. The Cincinnati Zoological Gardens, foreseeing the fate of the passenger pigeon, acquired a few pairs in 1879 and tried to breed them. But the birds fared poorly in captivity. The last remaining passenger pigeon, Martha, who hatched in 1885, died in 1914.

Lawmakers in the 1960s often cited the case of the passenger pigeon when debating the need to save species from extinction. Their efforts eventually led to the 1973 ENDANGERED SPECIES ACT.

PCBs

PCBs is the common term for polychlorinated biphenyls—a class of more than two hundred thick, viscous chemical compounds that can have highly toxic effects on people and wildlife. First manufactured in the United States in 1929, PCBs came to be widely used in industrial processes, especially electronics and printing, because of the capacity of the chemicals to conduct heat without conducting electricity. But their toxicity was vividly demonstrated in 1968, when PCB contamination of rice-bran oil killed about 20 people in Japan and sickened about 1,700 others. In 1976 the U.S. Congress passed the TOXIC SUBSTANCES CONTROL ACT (PL 94-469), which called for a ban on the manufacture and distribution of PCBs by 1979.

By the time Congress took action, an estimated several hundred million pounds of PCBs had been released into the environment through accidental spills and poorly constructed waste sites. Slow to degrade, the chemicals have caused some of the nation's worst toxic pollution problems, including heavily contaminated sediment in the Hudson River and the GREAT LAKES. PCBs are blamed for causing intelligence deficits and other problems in the children of women who, while pregnant, ate contaminated freshwater fish.

Since the government ban, levels of PCBs have plummeted. The number of people with high levels of PCBs in their tissues dropped from 12 percent of the population in the late 1970s to near 0 percent in the late 1980s. PCB contamination in fish in the Great Lakes has declined by as much as 90 percent since the 1970s.

Many countries, however, continue to use PCBs, and the chemicals remain a major worldwide environmental problem. Long-lived animals high on the food chain are particularly vulnerable to PCBs because they accumulate large amounts of the compound by eating contaminated prey. In marine mammals such as seals and whales, PCBs have been linked to weakened immune systems, tumors, and reproductive problems. Researchers speculate that the chemicals act as ENDOCRINE DISRUPTORS by mimicking the effects of hormones.

Persistent organic pollutants

Scientists use the term *persistent organic pollutants* to refer to a number of industrial chemicals, PESTICIDES, and other chemical substances that do not quickly break down in the environment and may cause adverse health effects in people and wildlife. Examples of such hazardous substances include PCBS, DIOXIN, and DDT. The chemicals become increasingly concentrated as they move up the food chain to people in a process known as bioaccumulation. Persistent organic pollutants can be carried in the air thousands of miles from their release, and they have been found in otherwise pristine regions such as the Arctic.

Efforts in the United States to regulate persistent organic pollutants have been complicated because of conflicting scientific data about the toxicity of many of the substances. Nevertheless, the ENVIRONMENTAL PROTECTION AGENCY banned most use of DDT in 1972 and subsequently imposed stringent regulations for dioxin. Congress in 1976 passed the TOXIC SUBSTANCES CONTROL ACT, which prohibited the manufacture and distribution of PCBs. However, scientists continue to report significant concentrations of persistent organic chemicals in the GREAT LAKES. Many developing countries continue to use the chemicals, putting worldwide cleanup efforts at risk.

Since the mid-1990s, more than one hundred nations have negotiated ways to largely eliminate the use of twelve "priority" persistent organic pollutants, including aldrin, chlordane, PCBs, dioxin, and DDT. The negotiators, working with the U.N. ENVIRONMENT PROGRAMME, hope to reach an agreement by the end of 2000.

Pesticides

Pesticides are widely used chemicals that destroy insects, weeds, fungi, and other organisms that may be harmful. Since the development of new classes of highly toxic synthetic pesticides in the 1940s, farmers in the United States and worldwide have applied millions of tons of the chemicals to boost food production and reduce the populations of disease-spreading insects. But the devastating side effects on the health of both people and wildlife have spurred repeated calls for tighter restrictions.

As early as the 1960s, the issue of pesticide contamination of air, water, and even food became so heated that it helped give birth to the powerful ENVIRONMENTAL MOVEMENT. The issue has continued to provoke legislative battles and lawsuits. Congress has passed and amended a series of laws since 1947 to govern pesticide use, but it has been unable to quell concerns over whether traces of toxic chemicals in food pose a threat to consumers—especially to infants and young children.

Information on worldwide pesticide use tends to be spotty, but the chemicals are increasingly common. Global use, which appeared to increase by about tenfold between 1955 and 1985, reached more than 2.5 million tons in 1995.

Developing countries usually apply pesticides less intensively than the United States and other industrialized countries, but many of them allow the use of older, highly toxic insecticides that are cheaper—and far more dangerous—than new products. In 1998 the World Resources Institute reported that tens of millions of people worldwide could be exposed to intensive pesticide levels and hundreds of millions to lower levels. People who work with pesticides or live near farms in developing countries are at greatest risk of suffering acute poisoning, which can cause temporary nausea and flu-like symptoms or more severe responses like paralysis or even death.

In the United States, more than twenty thousand pesticide products are on the market. Some pesticides, such as insecticidal soaps, pose no known risks to humans. Others have the potential

Although essential to agriculture, pesticides in high doses can cause human health disorders and destroy plants and wildlife. Source: U.S. Department of Agriculture

to sicken or kill. U.S. consumers buy about $11 billion of pesticides yearly. Farmers are the heaviest users, but pesticides are also commonly applied in houses, offices, schools, and offices. The chemicals are used to kill household bugs and germs, disinfect operating rooms, maintain golf courses, and hold down populations of lice, mosquitoes, and rats.

Common classes of pesticides include:

CHLORINATED HYDROCARBONS. These synthetic organic insecticides block nerve signal transmission. They include highly toxic chemicals, such as DDT, aldrin, and dieldrin, that can kill organisms at concentrations of just a few parts per billion.

ORGANOPHOSPHATES AND CARBAMATES. These two classes of chemicals, which also affect the neurological system, can be even more toxic than chlorinated hydrocarbons. But they degrade in the environment within a few hours or days.

NATURAL ORGANIC PESTICIDES. These include nicotine, pyrethrum, and other substances that are derived from plants. They are most toxic to insects but can sometimes be used to kill other animals.

Synthetic forms are more stable and toxic than natural forms.

INORGANIC PESTICIDES. These are highly toxic substances such as arsenic and LEAD that do not break down in the environment.

Synthetic Chemicals and Public Debate

Farmers have used natural pesticides such as arsenic and sulfur since the days of ancient civilizations in China and Greece. Europeans gradually developed more sophisticated compounds. But the real turning point came in the late 1930s, when chemists began creating synthetic pesticides, such as DDT, by substituting elements in naturally occurring carbon molecules. These highly toxic agents, some of which were derived from military nerve gas experiments during World War II, enabled farmers after the war to dramatically increase their yields and produce a "Green Revolution." They also helped safeguard the public health by depleting populations of malaria-carrying mosquitoes and other dangerous insects.

As useful, even essential, as pesticides are, they can cause both acute and chronic human health disorders. Although scientists are divided over the effects of pesticides, research studies have provided evidence that high levels of pesticides on food and in the environment can cause effects ranging from breast and prostate cancer to aggressiveness and reduced motor skill ability. Infants and children are considered especially vulnerable to the effects of such chemicals. The chemicals may act as EN-DOCRINE DISRUPTORS, affecting the reproductive systems of both humans and wildlife.

Farmworkers who apply the chemicals or work in fields are the most dangerously exposed segment of the U.S. population. They suffer from thousands of acute illnesses each year brought on by exposure to pesticides, according to government statistics, and they also have high rates of cancer and birth defects. Pesticides take a devastating toll on wildlife as well. In 1991 a train carrying thirteen thousand gallons of the pesticide metam sodium derailed in California, dumping its lethal cargo into the Sacramento River and destroying all animal and plant life in the river for forty miles. Even when used routinely, the chemicals can enter the food chain and be passed along from plants to animals, causing acute illnesses and possibly genetic disorders. The controversial pesticide DDT, now banned in the United States, is blamed for nearly wiping out the BALD EAGLE, peregrine falcon, and many other species of birds. Since the 1972 ban on DDT, the birds have made a dramatic comeback.

Many in the chemical and agricultural industries contend that pesticide hazards are overstated. They point to the development of new classes of biochemical pesticides that are designed to affect only targeted species and break down more quickly in the environment, thereby causing less damage. Farmers are also making an effort to use the chem-

icals less intensively by turning to INTEGRATED PEST MANAGEMENT techniques (such as releasing beneficial insects to combat pests) or even growing their crops organically. However, maintaining yields without the chemicals can be difficult. Without synthetic pesticides, farmers warn that they would likely have to dedicate much of their working hours to pulling weeds and figuring out how to avoid devastating losses like the fungal infection of the nineteenth century that wiped out Ireland's potato crop and caused famine.

Much of the public debate over pesticides has focused on the possible effects of chemicals on consumers. The Environmental Working Group and other environmental organizations have issued reports showing that traces of toxic chemicals can be detected in drinking water and many types of food, including baby food. Whether low amounts of such residues are harmful is a matter of heated debate. Researchers lack comprehensive data on the issue. Medical experts and environmental advocates alike urge people to continue eating fresh fruits and vegetables, saying the benefits of such food outweigh the possible hazards of ingesting small amounts of chemicals. But they also say that consumers should thoroughly wash fruits and vegetables and peel them when possible.

Political Battles

The sharp divisions over pesticide dangers have impeded congressional action. In response to early reports of the toxicities of the new wonder chemicals, lawmakers first waded into the issue of pesticide regulation with the FEDERAL INSECTICIDE, FUNGICIDE, AND RODENTICIDE ACT of 1947. The act established a process, now administered by the ENVIRONMENTAL PROTECTION AGENCY (EPA), to register every pesticide for every intended use. The law attempted to satisfy all sides by stating that a

Pesticide Residues on Food Samples (selected years)

	Samples without residues (percent)						
Year	Grains and grain products	Milk, dairy products, and eggs	Fish, shellfish, and meats	Fruits	Vegetables	Other	Total
1980	48	64	29	47	60	64	54
1985	48	78	35	64	66	78	65
1990	54	91	32	51	62	79	60
1995	33	100	80	48	48	80	54
1998	63	97	79	42	71	87	65

Source: U.S. Department of Health and Human Services, Food and Drug Administration, *Pesticide Program Residues Monitoring: 1998* (Washington, D.C.: HHS, FDA, 1999); and earlier annual reports.

Notes: Domestic food samples are collected as close as possible to the point of production. Fresh produce is analyzed as the unwashed, whole, raw commodity. Although a percentage of samples contain pesticide residues, the percentage of samples with over-tolerance residues (as set by the Environmental Protection Agency) is low. Between 1973 and 1986, 3 percent of samples were classed as violative; between 1987 and 1996, less than 1 percent were violative; in 1997, 1.2 percent were violative; and in 1998, 0.8 percent were violative.

pesticide must not cause "unreasonable adverse effects on the environment" while also urging regulators to consider the "potential benefits" of the product.

Seven years later, Congress passed the FOOD, DRUG, AND COSMETIC ACT, requiring the appropriate federal agency (eventually the EPA) to establish maximum levels of pesticide residues that could be allowed on raw foods and some processed foods. In 1958 lawmakers amended the law with the so-called DELANEY CLAUSE that barred the use of all cancer-causing chemicals on commodities used in processed foods. This law was to become controversial over the next three decades because scientific advances enabled regulators to detect increasingly minute traces of chemical residues in foods (see table).

Concerns about pesticides crystallized in 1962 with the publication of Rachel Carson's landmark bestseller, SILENT SPRING. Carson, a marine biologist, warned that DDT and other chemicals were contaminating the food chain and endangering virtually all life on Earth, including humans. Despite heated criticism of the book by chemical

manufacturers, the public's concern about the toxicity of DDT helped spur sweeping environmental protection laws and a 1972 ban on DDT.

Throughout the 1980s and early 1990s, lawmakers faced growing pressure from all sides to amend pesticide laws. Manufacturers and farmers grew increasingly concerned over the restrictive Delaney clause, which applied a much tougher health standard to processed food than to fresh produce. Since it was impossible to determine which fruits and vegetables would end up in a can and which in the fresh-produce section, regulators started permitting pesticide residues on both types of food as long as the residues posed no more than a "NEGLIGIBLE RISK" of causing cancer. At the same time, the EPA was running hopelessly behind in meeting pesticide registration deadlines, raising concerns that older chemicals were not being properly regulated.

Congress was finally jolted into action by federal court decisions in the 1990s requiring the EPA to apply the Delaney clause standard to all food—and potentially to revoke the use of dozens of common pesticides. "If the matter is not dealt with, the country is looking at something on the order of a fairly major calamity," warned Rep. John D. Dingell, D-Mich.

To head off such an eventuality, lawmakers in both chambers unanimously passed the FOOD QUALITY PROTECTION ACT in July 1996. The new law replaced the Delaney clause with a single health standard that requires the EPA to make sure that the chemicals in both raw and processed food pose a "reasonable certainty" of no harm from all combined sources of exposure. This is a strict standard commonly interpreted to mean that the residues could not result in a more than a one in one million chance of causing cancer. It also requires the agency to consider the cumulative effects of different pesticides on human health and to take into account the greater vulnerability of infants and children, assuming an additional tenfold safety factor in cases where the science is incomplete.

The EPA review has generated enormous controversy. The agency, which has until 2006 to make sure that pesticide products conform to the new law, is focusing particularly on carbamates and organophosphates—two classes of highly toxic chemicals that are widely used to protect produce from insects. Seven environmental and consumer groups quit an EPA advisory panel in 1999 amid charges that the agency was coming under the influence of advocates of pesticides. The same year, the AMERICAN FARM BUREAU FEDERATION and its allies sued the EPA for allegedly basing important decisions about pesticides and food safety on questionable assumptions and incomplete science. When the EPA took action later to ban one pesticide altogether and restrict the use of a second, it came under fire from farmers who warned of economic losses and environmentalists who denounced the continued use of controversial chemicals. Some rural lawmakers proposed amending

the Food Quality Protection Act to make it more difficult for the EPA to restrict pesticide use.

Pfiesteria

Dubbed "the cell from hell," pfiesteria is a microscopic organism found in water that produces a toxin deadly to fish and harmful to people. Pfiesteria outbreaks in Maryland and North Carolina in the 1990s were blamed for killing more than one billion fish and sickening some residents. Although the cause of pfiesteria is disputed, some scientists blame the organism on MANURE and other farm byproducts that get swept into waterways. The outbreaks have raised concerns about new threats to water quality and have spurred proposals by some lawmakers and ENVIRONMENTAL PROTECTION AGENCY officials to tighten regulations on farm operations. (See also AGRICULTURAL RUNOFF; AMERICAN FARM BUREAU FEDERATION.)

Pittman-Robertson

The common name for the Federal Aid in Wildlife Restoration Act of 1937, Pittman-Robertson was one of the first laws to try to restore wildlife habitat and research wildlife management issues. The law, named after its major sponsors, Sen. Key Pittman, D-Nev., and Rep. A. Willis Robertson, D-Va., imposes taxes on hunting equipment (including sporting guns, handguns, ammunition, and archery equipment) and distributes the money to states based on a formula that weighs land area and the number of licensed hunters. Congress amended the law in 1970 to provide funding for hunter education programs and develop target ranges.

The law, spurred by concerns about diminishing game bird populations, is credited with protecting bird habitats and helping to restore wild turkeys, which were rare in the 1930s. Pittman-Robertson has sparked little controversy, although some outdoors advocates want officials to put a greater emphasis on restoring habitat for wildlife that can be hunted.

Point sources

Point sources of WATER POLLUTION are facilities that dump waste directly into water supplies. In 1972 the CLEAN WATER ACT required industries, utilities, and sewage-treatment plants to curb the discharge of toxic wastes and end the once-common practice of dumping raw sewage into lakes and rivers. Although controversial at the time because of the high cost of treating waste, the law has greatly reduced point source pollution. Regulators are now putting a greater focus on NONPOINT SOURCE POLLUTION, which is runoff that comes from diverse sources and is harder to control.

However, point source pollution remains a significant fiscal and regulatory issue. Federal and state governments make more than $2 billion of new loans each year for the construction of sewage treatment and other facilities designed to control water pollution, but local officials say they need more money. Aging municipal sewers overflow repeatedly, dumping dangerous pathogens into waterways. In 1995 congressional conservatives tried to amend the Clean Water Act to allow federal, state, and local officials to waive regulatory requirements for point sources, provided that such actions did not harm the environment. They retreated in the face of opposition by President BILL CLINTON and environmentalists who claimed the bill would harm the nation's water quality. In the late 1990s the ENVIRONMENTAL PROTECTION AGENCY imposed tighter regulations on point sources that discharge polluted runoff from urban areas and large agricultural facilities.

Polluter pays

A controversial provision of the 1980 SUPERFUND hazardous waste law, "polluter pays" requires any organization that contributed to a hazardous waste site to fund the cleanup costs. The provision is blamed for slowing down the cleanup process because it inadvertently encourages lawsuits among dozens or even hundreds of polluters (known as potentially responsible parties, or PRPs) battling to shift cleanup costs onto other polluters. Critics also regard it as unfair because it sometimes targets individuals or companies that contributed only small amounts of waste and did not violate any laws. Environmentalists contend that the costs of Superfund and other types of cleanups should, in principle, be borne by polluters rather than taxpayers. Legislators have debated changing or even repealing the polluter pays provision, but they have not been able to figure out how else to pay for billions of dollars of cleanups.

Polluter pays is part of a broader legal doctrine generally holding polluters responsible for environmental damage. However, Congress has often set liability limits to protect nuclear power plants, oil tankers, and other industrial facilities from facing highly costly lawsuits. (See also RETROACTIVE LIABILITY.)

Pollution standards index

See AIR QUALITY INDEX.

Population growth

The dramatic increase in the number of people, both in the United States and throughout the world, is one of the root causes of environmental degradation. By clearing forests for development and consuming natural resources, the world's six billion-plus people are causing HABITAT LOSS, DEFORESTATION, OVERFISHING, AIR POLLUTION, and WATER POLLUTION. The environmental toll aside, burgeoning numbers of people in developing countries face constant hunger and lack access to clean water and adequate health care. Some biologists warn that the earth cannot simultaneously support billions of people and healthy populations of many animals and plants that need large, pristine habitats to survive. Other analysts, however, say that population growth by itself does not inevitably cause environmental problems. Instead, they blame CONSUMPTION (especially in wealthy countries) and a lack of pollution controls.

The world's population increased exponentially during the twentieth century. After rising gradually to about 1 billion by 1700 and 1.6 billion in 1900, it skyrocketed to 6 billion in 1999, largely because of advances in food production, sanitation, and medicine (see figure). The growth rate peaked in the 1970s at 2 percent a year. It then began to decline because of the availability of family planning information and contraceptives, as well as expanded work opportunities for women in developing countries. Controlling population growth, howev-

er, is difficult for a number of reasons, among them opposition to contraception on religious grounds and the desire of many couples to have more than two children.

Despite the decreasing fertility rate (the number of babies born per woman), the United Nations projects that the world's population will continue to increase for at least the next few decades, reaching between 7.3 billion and 10.7 billion people by 2050. Population growth is an especially troublesome problem in developing countries—often the same countries with TROPICAL RAIN FORESTS and other ecologically important habitats. Women in many African countries have as many as six or seven children, compared with a fertility rate of fewer than 1.5 in some western European countries (see table).

Signs of environmental strains have been apparent for decades. To overcome regional food shortages, China and many nations in Africa and Latin America adopted more intensive agricultural

World Population Growth, 1700–2050

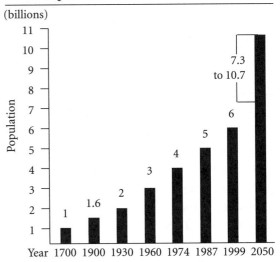

Source: Population Reference Bureau.

Highest and Lowest Fertility Rates, 2000

The fertility rate—the average number of children that women in a country have—is generally higher in Africa and Western Asia and lower in North America, Europe, and Eastern Asia. In the future, according to United Nations projections, small differences in childbearing levels will result in large differences in global population. If women average a moderate two children, population would rise to 11 billion in the twenty-first century and level off. If women average 2.5 children, population would pass 27 billion by 2150. But if the fertility rate fell to 1.6 children, population would peak at 7.7 billion in 2050 and drop to 3.6 billion by 2150.

Countries with the highest fertility rates		*Countries with the lowest fertility rates*	
Niger	7.5	China, Hong Kong SAR[a]	1.0
Democratic Republic of the Congo	7.2	Bulgaria	1.1
Somalia	7.0	Czech Republic	1.1
Uganda	6.9	Andorra	1.2
Angola	6.8	China, Macao SAR[a]	1.2
Burkina Faso	6.8	Estonia	1.2
Western Sahara	6.8	Georgia	1.2
Ethiopia	6.7	Italy	1.2
Mali	6.7	Latvia	1.2
Chad	6.6	Russia	1.2[b]

Sources: *CQ Researcher,* July 17, 1998, 604; Population Reference Bureau, "2000 World Population Data Sheet," http://www.prb.org/ pubs/wpds2000/wpds2000_Infant_Mortality-Life_Expectancy_ At_Birth.html.

[a]SAR = special administrative region.

[b]Other countries with fertility rates of 1.2 were San Marino, Slovenia, and Spain.

methods in the 1960s and 1970s, leading to water shortages and soil problems, such as the buildup of salt and other minerals. (In some cases, catastrophic famine resulted.) Countless millions of farmers, displaced by large ranching operations, are clearing previously unspoiled hillsides to grow crops. The demand for food has led to overfishing in many parts of the world, causing a decline in fish even in relatively pristine waters near Antarctica.

International efforts to rein in population growth are spearheaded by the United Nations Population Fund, which has promoted family-planning techniques since 1969. In 1994 delegates at the International Conference on Population and Development called for stabilizing the world's population by emphasizing improve-

ments in women's health and job opportunities, as well as family planning. Government-subsidized contraception has helped countries such as Mexico cut its fertility rate. Other population control efforts, however, have fueled a backlash. In the 1970s, for example, in India the government of Indira Gandhi was driven out of office after forcing millions of men to undergo vasectomies. China gave up its "one child" policy after widespread resistance to forced abortions. On the other hand, countries in southern Europe are offering economic incentives to couples who have children because the low domestic birthrate has caused a decline in population.

The United States has balked at contributing to worldwide family planning efforts because of the politically charged issue of abortion. In 1984 President RONALD REAGAN initiated the so-called Mexico City policy (named for a population conference held there) that prohibited federal funding of any nongovernmental organization involved in abortion activities. President BILL CLINTON overturned that policy shortly after taking office in 1993. But congressional conservatives throughout the 1990s pressed to cut off funding for any population control activities related to abortion.

Even though it is less densely populated than other industrialized countries, the United States also faces the pressures of population growth. The Census Bureau projects that, largely because of immigration, the number of people living in the United States will double during the twenty-first century to about 570 million people. This increase may help the economy by guaranteeing a supply of workers, but it is spurring environmentally harmful development in previously isolated regions, especially in the mountainous western states. New highways and subdivisions are paving over the habitats of such familiar species as mountain lions and prairie dogs. Environmentalists worry that growing demand in the arid Southwest may deplete water resources and increase pollution. Nevertheless, policymakers generally favor allowing more immigrants because of the need for skilled workers.

Port and Tanker Safety Act

Congress passed the Port and Tanker Safety Act (PL 95-474) in 1978 in reaction to a series of calamities in which oil tankers broke apart, blew up, or ran aground, spilling millions of gallons of oil in valuable fishing waters. The bill imposed stricter safety standards on oil tankers, mandating better control of ship traffic and requiring tankers to install electronic navigation and communications equipment. It also restricted the discharge of oil during routine tanker operations. The provisions generally followed an international accord reached that year by the Intergovernmental Maritime Consultative Organization, which includes sixty-two nations. Oil spills had been a major concern of environmentalists since an accident off Santa Barbara in 1969 fouled southern California beaches.

The 1978 legislation beefed up the 1972 PORTS AND WATERWAYS SAFETY ACT, which gave the U.S. Coast Guard authority to prevent intentional and accidental oil discharges. Lawmakers failed to add provisions to increase the liability of oil spillers, but they returned to the issue in 1990 with the OIL POLLUTION ACT. (See also EXXON VALDEZ).

Ports and Waterways Safety Act

One of the first laws that tried to prevent oil spills, the 1972 Ports and Waterways Safety Act (PL 92-340) gave authority to the Coast Guard to supervise marine traffic in congested areas in U.S. waters. It was passed at a time of growing concern about both the marine environment and the increased congestion in ports. The legislation authorized the Transportation Department to protect the environment by establishing comprehensive regulations for the design, maintenance, and operation of vessels carrying hazardous liquid bulk cargoes, including oil and inflammable liquids. (See also PORT AND TANKER SAFETY ACT.)

Precautionary principle

The precautionary principle holds that certain activities should be restricted even before there is evidence of danger to human health or the environment. Environmentalists who support this principle contend that new chemicals and industrial processes can pose such a threat that policymakers cannot afford to wait for years of scientific data before restricting them. The precautionary principle is, in many respects, the opposite of the "SOUND SCIENCE" philosophy favored by many conservatives. Proponents of the sound science view argue that regulators should not impose restrictions unless the scientific evidence of possible harm is overwhelming.

The precautionary principle can be traced back to laws in the 1970s. The NATIONAL ENVIRONMENTAL POLICY ACT requires government agencies to assess possible environmental harm before undertaking major actions, the CLEAN AIR ACT directs regulators to apply an ample margin of safety when imposing emission standards, and the CLEAN WATER ACT originally called for the elimination of all polluted discharges into waterways by the 1980s. More often, however, regulators have adopted a RISK ASSESSMENT approach in which they weigh scientific studies before imposing restrictions.

Some treaties, such as the 1987 MONTREAL PROTOCOL ON SUBSTANCES THAT DEPLETE THE OZONE LAYER, have adopted a precautionary approach. Environmentalists contend that the precautionary principle must be used to limit the emissions of GREENHOUSE GASES, warning that severe ecological damage will result if nations take too long to act.

Predator and pest control

The U.S. DEPARTMENT OF AGRICULTURE administers a controversial program to poison, shoot, relocate, or otherwise control mammals and birds that threaten livestock and crops. The program stems from the Animal Damage Control Act of 1931, although federal efforts to control predators date back to the late nineteenth century.

The Agriculture Department's Wildlife Services program protects crops and livestock by controlling predators. Although environmentalists call the program cruel and ineffective, government officials say it prevents millions of dollars of agricultural losses. Source: Corbis

Environmentalists generally view such policies as a cruel and largely ineffective way of killing coyotes, bobcats, prairie dogs, and other animals. But Agriculture Department officials, who changed the name of the Animal Damage Control program to Wildlife Services in 1997, say it is a cost-effective way of preventing millions of dollars of agricultural losses. Rather than killing destructive animals, government agents sometimes try to scare them with noisemakers or (in the case of large predators like mountain lions) release them far away from ranches. The Agriculture Department spent an estimated $28 million on the program in 2000. Rep. Peter DeFazio, D-Ore., tried unsuccessfully to scale back the program several times in the late 1990s by proposing to cut some of its funding.

Prescribed burns

See WILDFIRES.

Prevention of significant deterioration

Spurred by a 1972 federal court decision *(Sierra Club v. Ruckelshaus)* to prevent the buildup of HAZE and other AIR POLLUTION in pristine areas, Congress in 1977 amended the CLEAN AIR ACT to create the prevention of significant deterioration policy. This policy directs regulators to impose particularly strict standards for air pollution in relatively pristine areas such as NATIONAL PARKS.

The 1977 legislation established three categories for areas having cleaner air than national ambient standards. The cleanest, Class I, included most national parks and wilderness areas. Class II included most other areas exceeding clean air standards. Ad-

ditional areas, known as Class III, could be designated after hearings and studies. The amendments directed the ENVIRONMENTAL PROTECTION AGENCY to set standards for nitrogen oxides, hydrocarbons, and other pollutants. States have had to adjust their clean air implementation plans accordingly.

Prevention of significant deterioration is an important policy because it restricts industries from setting up operations in less-developed areas and forces policymakers to focus on protecting an entire region. It has helped to encourage attempts in recent years to regulate power plants and other industrial facilities that emit pollutants that drift hundreds of miles into pristine areas, contributing to pollution in national parks. (See also NATIONAL AMBIENT AIR QUALITY STANDARDS.)

Private property rights

Concern over the rights of private property owners has fueled a backlash against environmental regulations, especially in the western United States. Political conservatives, landowners, developers, and major agricultural and industrial groups argue that if the government wants to impose restrictions on the use of private land to protect the environment, it should compensate landowners for the resulting loss in property value. Since the government can scarcely afford such compensation, a successful property rights movement could greatly scale back restrictions on developing private land. This is a significant issue because private lands contain most of the nation's WETLANDS and other biologically diverse habitats. Environmentalists warn that if farmers are allowed to drain marshes to grow crops or if developers are allowed to plow under the habitat of rare animals to build a shopping center, the effects on the nation's BIODIVERSITY could be devastating.

The gist of the property rights argument is that the government, by restricting landowners from developing their land, is reducing the land's potential economic value and therefore taking money from the owner. Advocates of property rights say their land is protected by the Fifth Amendment to the Constitution, which reads in part, "nor shall private property be taken for public use, without just compensation." This amendment initially aimed to prevent the government from seizing land for such purposes as building a highway without paying the landowner. Beginning in 1922, however, the U.S. Supreme Court has held that, in exceptional cases, the government must compensate landowners for regulations that prevent them from fully utilizing their property. In a 1922 case (*Pennsylvania Coal Co. v. Mahon*), Oliver Wendell Holmes wrote that the government had to compensate a coal company for restrictions on underground mining. He reasoned that "If regulation goes too far it will be recognized as a taking."

Throughout much of the twentieth century, property rights faded as a legal issue. The Supreme Court ruled against landowners in cases involving such issues as local zoning laws and restrictions on industrial operations. But, beginning in the 1980s, advocates of private property rights reacted to the flurry of environmental laws by reopening the debate over government compensation. They launched a series of lawsuits challenging government restrictions on wetlands development, MINING operations, SUPERFUND hazardous waste cleanups, the "rails to trails" program (which converts abandoned railroad beds to pedestrian and biking paths), and, to a lesser degree, the ENDANGERED SPECIES ACT.

Property owners have won some legal victories,

including a 1992 Supreme Court ruling that ordinances forbidding development in a floodplain amounted to a taking of private property. But the Supreme Court is deeply divided on the question of property rights, and many of the legal issues remain unsettled. In general, the courts have indicated that the government must pay compensation only when its regulations virtually eliminate any economic use of a parcel of land. Even in those exceptional cases, the courts may consider whether the regulations, by improving the area, actually help to increase the value of the undeveloped parcel.

Elected officials also have given property owners relatively little to cheer about. In his last year of office, President RONALD REAGAN signed off on a top goal of the property rights movement by requiring federal agencies to conduct a "takings" analysis before issuing new regulations. Critics said the executive order went beyond constitutional takings principles, and subsequent administrations generally ignored it.

When the Republicans won control of Congress in the 1994 midterm elections, they vowed to put a greater emphasis on private property rights. They steered legislation through the House of Representatives that would have compensated landowners for property value losses stemming from federal wetlands or endangered species laws or to changes in federally granted water rights. Conservatives said the legislation amounted to simple justice for property owners. "If someone thinks protection of the BALD EAGLE or the NORTHERN SPOTTED OWL is important, they ought to be willing to pay for it," said Rep. Lamar Smith, R-Texas. But the legislation died in the Senate in the face of opposition from President BILL CLINTON and concerns by many lawmakers that such a bill could cost the government billions of dollars and undermine environmental regulations.

The issue has continued to simmer. The House passed a largely symbolic measure in 2000 that would have given developers increased power to sue over losses in property values. Conservative lawmakers have also introduced bills requiring agencies to conduct analyses before imposing land use restrictions; some favor compensating private landowners and businesses for the cost of complying with environmental regulation.

Property rights advocates also have had mixed success on the state level. Some state legislatures have passed takings legislation, but the laws generally require only that agencies conduct a takings impact analysis before issuing new regulations. Environmental groups and local government officials have fended off proposed legislative action and voter referendums in many states by arguing that compensation requirements would benefit only a few property owners, while requiring takings impact analyses would merely produce more bureaucratic red tape.

Public lands

Federal ownership of lands has sparked considerable controversy in recent years. Many developers and advocates of PRIVATE PROPERTY RIGHTS, especially in the western United States, say the federal government is infringing on state and individual rights by imposing restrictions on the use of vast tracts of land. But environmentalists want the government to designate more land as wilderness, therefore forestalling any development. A complicating factor is the growing popularity of NATIONAL PARKS, NATIONAL FORESTS, and other public lands, some of which are suffering from overcrowding and pollution. These conflicting pressures have led to repeated legislative debates over a variety of public land issues, including setting restrictions on logging, grazing, and other uses; balancing competing recreational uses; and appropriating money to purchase more land.

The federal government owns 657 million acres of land, or about 29 percent of the nation's land area, according to the Congressional Research Service. Four agencies have primary responsibility for overseeing the land: the National Park Service, the Fish and Wildlife Service, and the Bureau of Land Management, which are in the U.S. DEPARTMENT OF THE INTERIOR, and the Forest Service, in the U.S. DEPARTMENT OF AGRICULTURE. More than 90 percent of federally owned land is in the West (for data on federally owned land, see table).

Public lands have varying degrees of environmental protection. National parks have comparatively strict environmental regulations that generally preclude hunting and MINING. In contrast, national forests, national preserves, and public lands under the Bureau of Land Management generally are operated under MULTIPLE-USE policies that allow mining, grazing, logging, and hunting so long as the environment is not severely degraded. No development—not even road building—is allowed in wilderness areas.

Conflicts in public land policy can be traced back to the nineteenth century. The federal government pursued a variety of sometimes conflicting policies: selling land in western territories cheaply to encourage development; retaining control of vast expanses of forests to ensure a supply of timber for logging companies; and setting aside tracts of land such as Yosemite Valley as early as the 1860s to give the public access to especially beautiful or unique areas. By the first third of the twentieth century, the government also focused on preserving wildlife habitat for hunting and fishing.

Federally Owned Land by State, 1997

State	Total (1,000 acres)	Owned by federal government* Acres (1,000)	Percent	State	Total (1,000 acres)	Owned by federal government* Acres (1,000)	Percent
Alabama	32,678	1,080	3.8	Montana	93,271	25,485	27.3
Alaska	365,432	171,788	47.0	Nebraska	49,032	515	1.1
Arizona	72,688	31,337	43.1	Nevada	70,264	56,082	79.8
Arkansas	33,599	2,740	8.2	New Hampshire	5,769	734	12.7
California	100,207	44,757	44.7	New Jersey	4,813	102	2.1
Colorado	66,486	24,129	36.3	New Mexico	77,766	26,218	33.7
Connecticut	3,135	7	0.2	New York	30,681	197	0.6
Delaware	1,266	2	0.2	North Carolina	31,403	2,028	6.5
District of Columbia	39	9	23.5	North Dakota	44,452	1,413	3.2
Florida	34,721	2,645	7.6	Ohio	26,222	280	1.1
Georgia	37,295	1,458	3.9	Oklahoma	44,088	678	1.5
Hawaii	4,106	350	8.5	Oregon	61,599	31,809	51.6
Idaho	52,933	32,992	62.3	Pennsylvania	28,804	623	2.2
Illinois	35,795	405	1.1	Rhode Island	677	3	0.5
Indiana	23,158	394	1.7	South Carolina	19,374	935	4.8
Iowa	35,860	30	0.1	South Dakota	48,882	2,577	5.3
Kansas	52,511	350	0.7	Tennessee	26,728	1,576	5.9
Kentucky	25,512	1,083	4.2	Texas	168,218	2,008	1.2
Louisiana	28,868	745	2.6	Utah	52,697	33,898	64.3
Maine	19,848	145	0.7	Vermont	5,937	377	6.3
Maryland	6,319	157	2.5	Virginia	25,496	2,279	8.9
Massachusetts	5,035	52	1.0	Washington	42,694	11,939	28.0
Michigan	36,492	3,980	10.9	West Virginia	15,411	1,077	7.0
Minnesota	51,206	4,069	7.9	Wisconsin	35,011	1,733	5.0
Mississippi	30,223	1,276	4.2	Wyoming	62,343	30,878	49.5
Missouri	44,248	1,658	3.7				

Source: U.S. Census Bureau, *Statistical Abstract of the United States: 1999,* Table 394 (Washington, D.C.: U.S. Government Printing Office, 1999), 240.

*Excludes trust properties.

With the stirrings of a greater environmental consciousness in the 1960s, Congress began taking steps to focus on preserving the ecology of public lands. The 1964 WILDERNESS ACT authorized the creation of wilderness areas that would remain untouched by any type of development. In the 1970s lawmakers authorized CLEAR CUTTING in national forests but also set limits on the practice. Congress passed the Federal Land Policy and Management Act in 1976 to direct the Bureau of Land Management to administer its lands for the purposes of sustained yield and multiple uses.

Greater interest in land protection crystallized with the 1980 ALASKA NATIONAL INTEREST LANDS CONSERVATION ACT, which set aside more than one hundred million acres, much of it as wilderness. In the following decade, lawmakers preserved millions of acres in California through the 1994 California Desert Protection Act (PL 103-433). Environmentalists scored additional victories in the 1990s by persuading President BILL CLINTON to designate large tracts of land as national monuments and stop the building of national forest roads. The National Park Service, formerly criticized by environmentalists for building roads and visitor centers in pristine areas, has begun taking steps to limit traffic and restrict the use of snowmobiles and personal watercraft.

However, many in Congress favor allowing more development on public lands to help rural economies and to decrease the nation's dependence on imported oil. Alaskan lawmakers repeatedly introduce bills that would allow exploratory drilling in a portion of the ARCTIC NATIONAL WILDLIFE REFUGE. Other proposals would increase logging limits in national forests, pare back grazing restrictions on RANGELANDS, create more facilities at popular national parks, and build roads through protected areas. As the population in the West continues to grow, the pressures to allow more development on public land appear certain to intensify.

Congress also is at odds over increased funding for the LAND AND WATER CONSERVATION FUND, which pays for the purchase of new public lands. Some conservatives contend that the federal government already owns too much land in the United States; others argue that Washington needs to set aside more areas to check the impact of urban sprawl.

There are eight major types of public land units:

NATIONAL PARKS. Supervised by the National Park Service, so-called full national parks are the "crown jewels" of the American landscape. At the beginning of 2000, the nation had fifty-four such national parks, including popular destinations like Great Smoky Mountain, Grand Canyon, Yellowstone, and Yosemite.

OTHER NATIONAL PARK SERVICE UNITS. The National Park Service also oversees national monuments and national preserves, which provide varying degrees of protection for areas with significant natural resource or historical value. Other park service units include national seashores, national recreation areas, and national battlefields and historic sites. Overall, the park service manages a total of 378 units on 77 million acres.

National Forests. The National Forest System comprises 192 million acres of forests and grasslands, with significant amounts of acreage in the southern Appalachians as well as the West. Originally managed primarily for logging, the forests have become a major focus of environmentalists who want to stop new road construction and leave large tracts of land undisturbed.

NATIONAL WILDLIFE REFUGE SYSTEM. Managed by the Fish and Wildlife Service, the system encompasses 93 million acres, including 512 national wildlife refuges, 198 waterfowl production areas, 50 wildlife coordination areas, and 114 other sites. More than 80 percent of the system is in Alaska. The 1997 National Wildlife Refuge System Improvement Act stressed conservation as the overriding goal of the refuges. However, most refuges also allow hunting and fishing, as well as limited mining and grazing activities.

BUREAU OF LAND MANAGEMENT PUBLIC LANDS. The Bureau of Land Management supervises activities on about 265 million acres, mostly in eleven western states. Under the 1934 TAYLOR GRAZING ACT and the 1976 FEDERAL LAND POLICY AND MANAGEMENT ACT, the lands are managed for multiple uses, including grazing, mining, outdoor recreation, water supply, and wilderness. This broad mandate has spurred particularly heated battles between environmentalists and developers.

WILDERNESS AREAS. Under the 1964 Wilderness Act, Congress has set aside more than 100 million acres of land that are largely protected from commercial activities and motorized vehicles, although hunting, mineral prospecting, and continued livestock grazing may be allowed. Much of the land is in national parks and national forests.

NATIONAL TRAILS. Under the 1968 NATIONAL TRAILS SYSTEM ACT, Congress has designated twenty national scenic and historic trails that total nearly 40,000 miles. Additional trails have been designated administratively. Although the trails are primarily for recreation or education, they can provide protected corridors for wildlife.

NATIONAL WILD AND SCENIC RIVERS. The 1968 NATIONAL WILD AND SCENIC RIVERS ACT authorized the designation of three types of rivers: wild, recreational, and scenic, with varying degrees of environmental protection. The National Wild and Scenic Rivers System, managed by a variety of federal agencies, comprises 155 rivers totaling 10,896 miles.

Public notification

Public notification refers to requirements in several laws that the public be kept informed of potential environmental threats. In the EMERGENCY PLANNING AND COMMUNITY RIGHT-TO-KNOW ACT of 1986, Congress directed companies to disclose hazardous chemical emissions, including those that are within lawful limits. Ten years later, lawmakers added public notification provisions to the SAFE DRINKING WATER ACT requiring public water systems to alert their customers about levels of contaminants that exceed safe levels.

R

Radon

Radon is a colorless, odorless radioactive gas that is formed by the natural breakdown of uranium in rock and soil. It occurs widely at low levels outdoors but averages much higher levels indoors because it tends to seep into buildings. A major contributor of INDOOR AIR POLLUTION, radon is one of the leading causes of lung cancer (behind smoking). However, scientists are sharply divided over whether low exposures are harmful.

In 1988 Congress passed the $45-million IN-DOOR RADON ABATEMENT ACT to set up programs to study and mitigate radon contamination in homes, schools, and federal buildings. The law included a provision directing the ENVIRONMENTAL PROTECTION AGENCY (EPA) to drop any suggestion in its consumer literature of a minimum acceptable level of radon indoors. However, support for radon abatement programs gradually diminished. When the EPA in 1993 proposed voluntary guidelines for builders to take protective measures against the gas, critics said the costs of such a program were excessive for the relatively small risk posed by radon. The House passed legislation in 1994 that would have required real estate agents and homeowners to supply prospective buyers or renters with EPA pamphlets on radon hazards. But the Senate failed to take action.

Rain forests

See TROPICAL RAIN FORESTS.

Rangelands

Federal rangelands, managed by the Bureau of Land Management, are the subject of an ongoing policy tug-of-war between environmental and western interests in Congress. Environmentalists are concerned that overgrazing is damaging much of the approximately 169 million acres of federal land in the West open to livestock. But western conservatives want to ensure continuing low-cost access to ranchers, who say they are careful stewards of the land. The issue has its roots in the nineteenth century practice of western ranchers and cattle operators using federal land for grazing. To prevent rangeland degradation, the U.S. FOREST SERVICE in the early twentieth century established a leasing policy and GRAZING FEES. Congress tightened oversight with the 1934 Taylor Grazing Act.

Grazing fees have sparked some of the most contentious rangelands debates in recent years. Environmentalists argue that the fees amount to a subsidy because they are only about one-fifth of the fees on private lands. But Clinton administration attempts to more than double the fees in 1993 ran into unyielding Senate opposition.

Officials also have clashed over the thorny issue of how to balance commercial and recreational uses on the land while preserving native ecosystems. In 1995 interior secretary BRUCE BABBITT announced a series of regulations that generally favored the environmental position. He established resource advisory councils, made up of commodity users, conservation interests, and other stakeholders, to make recommendations on PUBLIC LANDS management. He also gave members of the "interested public" a chance to weigh in on specific grazing decisions, even though westerners contended this would give residents in far-flung states leverage over western grazing policy. In addition, Babbitt said title to range improvements and water developments made by ranchers would remain with the federal government.

Western conservatives repeatedly have tried to override or amend the rules. In 1997 they proposed a 36 percent increase in grazing fees in exchange for giving ranchers a greater voice in land policy. But they failed to win Senate passage. Similarly, livestock producers have failed to block most of the new rules in court.

Reagan, Ronald

Few presidents have been as successful in scaling back environmental initiatives as Ronald Reagan. In his 1980 campaign for the White House, the staunchly conservative Californian pledged to cut the costs that environmental regulations imposed on businesses and communities. Once in office, he consistently took the side of industry, cutting spending on environmental programs, opening up PUBLIC LANDS to development, and vetoing measures passed by a more environmentally minded Congress. Although environmentalists conceded that some regulations were overly inflexible, they regarded Reagan's initiatives as highly destructive and marshaled their resources into a desperate defense of the landmark environmental laws of the 1970s. The resulting clashes produced something of a stalemate. The environmental community proved its political mettle by checkmating many of Reagan's proposals, driving a few new laws through Congress, and forcing the most controversial administration officials out of office. But Reagan succeeded in drastically scaling back the federal regulatory apparatus, focusing the environmental debate on the costs of regulations, and stalling the momentum of the ENVIRONMENTAL MOVEMENT.

One of Reagan's first actions after taking office in 1981 was to issue Executive Order 12291. This directive required federal agencies to prepare a REGULATORY IMPACT ANALYSIS for new regulations and to demonstrate that the benefits of the proposed regulation would exceed the costs. The president also cut environmental spending so drastically that the ENVIRONMENTAL PROTECTION AGENCY's budget dropped by about one-third between 1980 and 1983, and the agency lost one-fifth of its personnel. Even as it focused on larger tax and spending issues, the administration tried repeatedly to scale back the CLEAN AIR ACT (parts of which were criticized by White House budget director David Stockman as "staggering excess built upon dubious scientific and economic premises") and cut CLEAN WATER ACT sewer grants. Many of its initiatives died in Congress. Nevertheless, the administration undercut the environmental movement so completely that, at the end of Reagan's first term, ten major environmental laws had expired or were up for renewal

Reagan's early environmental appointees provoked a storm of criticism, even from many mod-

During his two terms, President Ronald Reagan consistently sided with industry in debates over environmental policy. He opposed environmental regulations, dismantled environmental programs, and encouraged development of public lands.
Source: *Jack Kightlinger, The White House*

erates. The combative interior secretary JAMES G. WATT repeatedly battled Congress and his own subordinates as he attempted to open up wilderness areas and the outer continental shelf to oil and gas drilling, and sell small, hard-to-manage federal tracts to private owners. EPA administrator Anne M. Burford faced numerous allegations about "sweetheart deals" with polluters and lax enforcement of HAZARDOUS WASTE laws. Both Burford

and Watt resigned under fire in 1983. But environmentalists complained about other, less-controversial administration officials, such as John B. Croswell Jr., a former timber company counsel who oversaw the U.S. FOREST SERVICE and pressed for increased logging in OLD-GROWTH Northwest forests.

With Democrats gaining strength in Congress, the Reagan White House stressed pragmatism over ideology in its second term. The president signed a bill in October 1986 that significantly expanded the SUPERFUND hazardous waste program after Republican lawmakers warned him that a veto would hurt their election-day prospects. Reagan also signed the landmark MONTREAL PROTOCOL ON SUBSTANCES THAT DEPLETE THE OZONE LAYER, as well as expansions of the SAFE DRINKING WATER ACT and the ENDANGERED SPECIES ACT. He continued, however, to stress budget priorities over environmental protection, pocket-vetoing a 1986 reauthorization of the Clean Water Act because "this bill so far exceeds acceptable levels of intended budgetary commitments that I must withhold my approval." Congress overrode the veto.

The Reagan presidency stands as something of a divide in the modern environmental movement. Before 1981, environmentalists could count on bipartisan sympathy for many of their initiatives. But during the Reagan years and after, businesses and private property advocates succeeded in drawing attention to the economic costs of environmental protection, as well as to the lack of SOUND SCIENCE underpinning many regulatory decisions. The environmental movement, which once appeared irresistible, has yet to recover.

Reasonable certainty of no harm

A health-based standard, "reasonable certainty of no harm" governs the amount of pesticides that are allowable in food. In the 1996 FOOD QUALITY PROTECTION ACT, lawmakers used the phrase to strike a compromise between environmentalists, who favored a "ZERO RISK" standard to ban human carcinogens in food, and the agricultural industry, which preferred a "NEGLIGIBLE RISK" standard that considered the risk of exposure to a single PESTI-

CIDE. Although not precisely defined by Congress, the reasonable certainty of no harm standard is commonly interpreted as meaning that people would have no more than a one-in-one-million chance of developing cancer from aggregate exposure to pesticide residues.

Recycling

Far from being a recent phenomenon, recycling used to be a common way for households and businesses to cut their costs. In the nineteenth century, for example, scraps of cloth were used to make paper. Since the 1960s, environmentalists have revived recycling to reduce both the demand for raw materials and the amount of garbage going into LANDFILLS. As of 1996, 27 percent of all MUNICIPAL SOLID WASTE was being recycled or composted, compared with 7 percent in 1960, according to the ENVIRONMENTAL PROTECTION AGENCY (EPA). Certain materials, such as old cars and other steel products, aluminum cans, and newspapers are relatively easy to recycle, but many types of plastic are more difficult (see table).

Although recycling primarily falls under the jurisdiction of state and local governments, Congress

Recycling Rates of Selected Materials (percent)

Auto batteries	93.8
Steel cans	58.2
Aluminum packaging	52.0
Paper and paperboard	40.8
Yard waste	38.6
Glass containers	28.7
Plastic containers	22.9
Tires	18.7

Source: U.S. Environmental Protection Agency, "Basic Facts," http://epa.gov/epaoswer/non-hw/muncpl/facts.htm, July 2000.

Although supported by environmentalists and mandated by federal and state laws, recycling has been criticized as economically unworkable. A saturation of the market for recyclable materials has prompted officials to reevaluate curbside programs, which have greatly increased the size of recycling collections. Source: PhotoDisc

EPA in 1988 set a recycling goal for the United States of 25 percent. At the same time, many communities introduced curbside pickup of recyclables, greatly increasing the amount of newspapers, bottles, cans, and other items sent to recycling plants. To further spur recycling, President BILL CLINTON in 1993 issued an executive order requiring all federal agencies to eventually buy printing and writing paper with at least 30 percent recycled content.

But as recycling has become more popular, the economics of the industry are becoming highly volatile. In the mid-1990s, for example, an oversupply of paper forced some paper-processing facilities out of business, causing some recycling operators to dump papers at local landfills. Critics question whether state and local government mandates are hurting the recycling market by saturating it with materials. Environmentalists, however, continue to support such programs, contending that recycling can be made more cost-efficient. They point to more densely populated countries such as Germany that have higher recycling rates than that of the United States, partly because a lack of landfill space has placed a greater emphasis on reducing solid waste.

has passed several laws to encourage recycling efforts. The 1970 Resource Recovery Act authorized grants and research into recovering useful materials from solid waste. Six years later, the sweeping RESOURCE CONSERVATION AND RECOVERY ACT authorized funding for research and demonstration projects on converting waste to energy and recovering such materials as glass and plastic. Amid concerns about diminishing space in the landfills, the

Reformulated gasoline

Adding oxygen to gasoline can result in cleaner burning motor vehicle fuel. Such reformulated gasoline combusts more completely, reducing emissions of carbon monoxide. The most commonly used oxygenates are MTBE and ethanol.

The 1990 amendments to the CLEAN AIR ACT required the nine smoggiest cities to begin using reformulated gasoline by 1995, although such fuel is more expensive. In addition, cities that had not attained carbon monoxide emission standards had to use gasoline containing 2.7 percent oxygen in 1992. In 2000 the Clinton administration announced a plan to phase out MTBE because the chemical had apparently contaminated water supplies. Instead, it called for the increased use of ethanol and other "biofuels" derived from agricultural products such as corn. The use of such additives can boost the farm economy, but many environmentalists regard them as potentially highly polluting.

Regional fishery management councils

The establishment of eight regional fishery management councils under the 1976 MAGNUSON FISHERY CONSERVATION AND MANAGEMENT ACT inadvertently set the stage for an environmental disaster in the 1980s. The councils, composed of members appointed by the commerce secretary from lists of nominees submitted by governors, had the responsibility for managing fishing in the U.S. exclusive economic zone that extends two hundred miles out to sea. But they appeared to bungle their mission by failing to balance the biological realities of fish management with the economic demand of fishermen to sell more fish. Swayed by the demands of commercial fishermen, several of the councils permitted almost unrestricted fishing. As a result, many commercially valuable species were severely depleted.

Congress directed the councils to put a greater emphasis on conservation when it amended the Magnuson act in 1996.

Regional haze

See HAZE.

Regulatory impact analysis

In 1981 President RONALD REAGAN directed agencies to conduct a detailed regulatory impact analysis before proposing a major new regulation. Agencies had to demonstrate that the benefits of a regulation would exceed its likely costs, although environmentalists contended this was really a backdoor attempt to undercut environmental laws. In 1993 President BILL CLINTON significantly relaxed the requirements for the analyses. Regulatory impact analyses have not had a clear impact on federal rulemaking. Agencies have not conducted them consistently, sometimes failing to consider several alternatives to the proposed regulation. (See also REGULATORY RELIEF.)

Regulatory relief

Regulatory relief is the generic term for scaling back regulations and providing state governments, businesses, and individuals with more flexibility. From the time that President RICHARD NIXON vetoed the 1972 CLEAN WATER ACT because of its costly regulations, the demand for regulatory relief has been the primary political obstacle to tougher environmental protection. Even though polls show that most Americans support a cleaner environment, they also indicate uneasiness over government mandates and regulatory costs.

At times, conservatives have blunted environmental initiatives by pressing for SOUND SCIENCE (requiring environmental agencies to amass clear-cut scientific evidence before imposing a new rule) and COST-BENEFIT ANALYSIS (requiring the government to balance the benefits of a regulation with the costs to both business and society). Twice in recent decades, regulatory relief came to the political forefront—first with the 1980 election of President RONALD REAGAN, then with the 1994 election of a Republican majority in Congress. In both cases, the antiregulatory forces failed to dismantle environmental laws, although they successfully cut funding to administer them.

The Regulatory System

Under the U.S. government system, agency officials—not lawmakers—write regulations. When Congress passes a law, it falls to the agency responsible for enforcement to interpret the law's provisions and write the regulations needed to implement it. This process gives considerable discretion to Washington bureaucrats, who (as critics point out) never have to face the voters. Although most agencies engage at one time or another in controversial rulemaking, the ENVIRONMENTAL PROTECTION AGENCY (EPA) has been especially embattled. It has a difficult task in applying conflicting scientific and health research to such complex matters as determining safe levels of PESTICIDES in food or judging the degree to which airborne particulates trigger asthma. The EPA routinely faces lawsuits and congressional hearings for imposing new regulations, just as it faces lawsuits and hearings for failing to act. A key question is whether the EPA should impose restrictions before amassing data on the potential dangers of a chemical (an approach known as the PRECAUTIONARY PRINCIPLE) or wait until it has irrefutable scientific evidence.

The vast network of environmental regulations, steadily proliferating since the early 1970s, has spurred misgivings even among some environmentalists. The regulations are so complex that a single congressional act—the 1990 amendments to the CLEAN AIR ACT—generated more than ten thousand pages of regulations within a few years. Intent on preventing further harm to the nation's degraded environment, the government has imposed countless mandates for industrial emissions, discharges into waterways, toxic waste disposal, and construction in ecologically sensitive areas, as well as for such seemingly mundane activities as obtaining soil samples or fishing for cod.

Many of the regulations have sparked legislative and legal battles. Critics say the government overreached with regulations forcing local authorities to spend billions of dollars to remove ASBESTOS from school buildings, banning the use of the pesticide ALAR on apples, and establishing stringent standards for DIOXIN based on a few experiments with animals. In many respects, the modern ENVIRONMENTAL MOVEMENT, which took shape in the 1960s with relatively simple and idealistic concepts such as preventing companies from continuing to pollute waterways, has deteriorated into a series of trench battles over regulatory details.

Whether the regulations are worth the costs is a central question in the ongoing debate over environmental policy. Business groups have claimed that government regulations of all types, including those designed to protect the environment, cost Americans more than a half-trillion dollars a year and suffocate commercial innovation. They also say that new regulations in the 1990s failed to substantially improve environmental quality. On the other hand, environmentalists say that government spending on the environment amounts to no more than about 2 percent of gross domestic product and is far less than spending on defense and health care. Environmentalists also bristle at the notion of reducing ecological protection to a bottom-line activity, contending that the benefits of a clean and healthy environment that can be passed down to future generations cannot be quantified.

At the same time, many environmentalists concede that some regulations are too costly and inflexible. For example, SAFE DRINKING WATER ACT requirements for years forced many municipal water systems to divert resources into testing for contaminants that posed virtually no threat to local water supplies. In 1996 Congress made the law more flexible. Similarly, many environmentalists and developers alike want to overhaul the ENDANGERED SPECIES ACT and the SUPERFUND hazardous waste program to put a greater focus on habitat protection and environmental cleanup rather than sweeping mandates that trigger conflicts and lawsuits. Some would also like to place a higher priority on such pervasive threats as INDOOR AIR POLLUTION, rather than a continued emphasis on POINT SOURCES of pollution such as factories.

History

The battle over regulatory relief stems from the 1970s, when Congress adopted a COMMAND-AND-CONTROL system of pollution prevention. The resulting laws used federal mandates and specific benchmarks to force compliance. The rationale for this rather hardline approach was that earlier environmental laws, which gave states more leeway, failed to curb pollution. As a result of the command-and-control system, laws such as the Clean Water Act and the Clean Air Act succeeded in curbing pollution. But they fell well short of the goal of largely eliminating pollution by the 1980s.

When Reagan took office in 1981, he pledged to cut regulatory costs. One of his first actions was to issue Executive Order 12291, requiring any agency considering a major new regulatory proposal to prepare a REGULATORY IMPACT ANALYSIS and demonstrate that the regulation's benefits would likely exceed its costs. The policy provoked a bitter debate between conservatives who defended it as a sensible strategy for curbing excessive regulations and critics who viewed it as an assault on environmental laws. Despite the controversy, the executive order was poorly implemented, partly because of the difficulty in quantifying the values of environmental regulations. It also failed to spur systematic analyses of the costs of regulations.

The Reagan administration failed in other ways to appreciably scale back regulations. Lawmakers rejected proposals to scale back provisions of the Clean Air Act and the Clean Water Act. They assailed policies by administration officials such as Interior Secretary JAMES G. WATT and EPA Administrator Anne M. Burford that opened up more PUBLIC LANDS for mineral extraction and emphasized negotiations over enforcement as an antipollution strategy. Both officials were forced out of office in 1983. On the other hand, Reagan won congressional approval for deep budget cuts to the EPA and other environmental offices. These cuts effectively advanced the cause of regulatory relief for several years by weakening the government's ability to promulgate new regulations and enforce existing ones.

Republican lawmakers who swept to power in the 1994 elections made regulatory relief one of their top priorities. The House in 1995 passed a wide-ranging bill that would have required agencies to conduct detailed cost-benefit studies and to analyze the risks that new regulations sought to address. The proposal also would have forced the government to compensate landowners who lost

10 percent or more of their property because of a regulation. But the legislation died in the Senate when Majority Leader Bob Dole, R-Kan., failed to overcome Democratic resistance.

The Republicans had no better success with a controversial attempt to pare back major environmental laws governing WATER POLLUTION, HAZARDOUS WASTE, and endangered species. In 1995 the House passed a rewrite of the Clean Water Act that would have allowed federal, state, and local officials to ease or waive certain requirements, and it would have opened the door for a more voluntary approach to pollution standards. But environmentalists blocked the bill in the Senate. Similarly, most efforts to insert provisions in spending bills to block the EPA from enforcing certain antipollution laws failed in the face of opposition by Democrats and the Clinton administration. House Speaker Newt Gingrich, R-Ga., conceded in late 1995 that his party had "mishandled the environment all spring and summer." Although Republicans and Democrats worked together in 1996 to add more flexibility to regulations governing safe drinking water and pesticide residues in food, efforts to pass other types of regulatory relief generally failed in the 1990s.

Renewable energy

For several decades, environmentalists have supported the development of renewable types of energy to reduce consumption of highly polluting FOSSIL FUELS. Such energy can be produced from renewable natural sources, including the sun, wind, vegetation, moving water, and the warmth of the earth (see table). In addition, new technologies offer the promise of other sources of energy, such

as methane gas from LANDFILLS. However, scientists differ over whether renewable energy (also known as alternative energy) can be harnessed without harming the environment or whether it can significantly reduce traditional fuel consumption.

Government analysts have suggested that renewable energy could supply more than half the nation's energy needs by 2030—if the government aggressively develops it. In 1998 renewable energy sources supplied about 7.5 percent of the nation's energy needs, a slight increase above the 7.3 percent level in 1990, according to the government's Energy Information Administration. Most renewable energy came from hydropower and biomass (described below).

Federal support of alternative energy sources dates back to the oil shocks of the 1970s. To reduce dependence on imported oil, President JIMMY CARTER in 1977 unveiled an energy policy he called "the moral equivalent of war." The policy called for numerous conservation measures, the creation of the U.S. DEPARTMENT OF ENERGY, and substantial funding increases for solar energy and other renewable energy sources. One year later, Congress passed the Public Utilities Regulatory Policies Act (PL 95-617), which encouraged the development of small-scale electric power plants fueled by renewable sources. The Reagan administration, however, sharply cut funding for renewable energy programs and allowed tax credits to expire in 1995. The administration even removed the White House's solar panels, which had been installed during the Carter days.

Congress returned to the issue with the 1992 ENERGY POLICY ACT. The law provided tax incentives for renewable fuels and required the government to use vehicles powered by alternative fuels, such as methanol, ethanol, compressed natural gas,

U.S. Renewable Energy Production by Source (selected years)

| Year | Renewable energy source (quadrillion Btu) | | | | | Total renewable energy (quadrillion Btu) | Total U.S. energy production (percent) |
	Conventional hydroelectric	Geothermal	Biomass	Solar	Wind		
1960	1.608	0.001	1.320	0.000	0.000	2.929	6.84
1970	2.634	0.011	1.431	0.000	0.000	4.076	6.42
1980	2.900	0.110	2.485	0.000	0.000	5.495	8.17
1990	3.033	0.344	2.632	0.063	0.023	6.095	8.61
1998	3.391	0.314	3.052	0.074	0.036	6.867	9.42

Source: U.S. Department of Energy, Energy Information Administration, *Annual Energy Review 1998*, Table 1.2 (Washington, D.C.: Government Printing Office, 1999), 7.

Notes: Renewable energy comes from the following sources: conventional hydroelectric power, geothermal power, biomass (biofuels), solar energy, and wind energy. Hydroelectricity generated by pumped storage is not included in renewable energy estimates. *Conventional hydroelectric* includes electricity net imports from Canada that are derived from hydroelectric energy; it excludes pumped storage production. Geothermal power comprises electricity imports from Mexico that are derived from *geothermal* energy, which includes grid-connected electricity and excludes shaft power and remote electrical power. *Biomass* is organic material, such as wood, wood waste, peat, wood sludge, municipal solid waste, agricultural waste, straw, tires, landfill gases, fish oil, and ethanol blended into motor gasoline. *Solar* includes photovoltaic energy. *Wind* includes grid-connected electricity and excludes direct heat applications.

or hydrogen. Lawmakers continued funding some renewable energy programs in the 1990s but generally rejected Clinton administration proposals to provide billions of dollars in tax incentives. Despite protests from some fiscal conservatives, rural lawmakers backed the continuation of a tax credit for ethanol, which is derived from corn and other products.

Promoting the use of alternative-fuel motor vehicles has become a major environmental goal because of concerns about SMOG and GLOBAL WARMING. Electric cars are often classified as zero-emissions vehicles because they do not emit any tailpipe exhaust. However, producing electricity to power them often involves burning FOSSIL FUELS, which produces CARBON DIOXIDE and contributes to global warming. Some manufacturers are instead using fuel cells that combine hydrogen and oxygen to produce electricity, or building hybrid cars, which use both gasoline and an electric motor.

Major types of renewable energy include:

SOLAR. Energy from the sun has been harnessed for decades, primarily to warm buildings and water. Recently developed photovoltaic conversion systems transform sunlight directly into electricity. Although it is nonpolluting, the technology remains costly and relies on consistent sunshine.

WIND. Wind turbines can generate electricity relatively inexpensively. Clusters of wind turbines, sometimes called wind farms, have been developed in California and some other states, as well as parts of northern Europe and Asia. The turbines are nonpolluting, but they can block coastal and mountain views. Environmentalists have raised concerns about endangered birds flying into the turbine blades.

GEOTHERMAL. The internal heat of the earth can provide hot water or steam for heating buildings or generating electricity. Such energy is only usable when it is concentrated in a "thermal reservoir," such as a geyser or dry rock formation. Environmentalists warn that geothermal energy has the potential to cause water contamination, interfere with water supplies, and release harmful pollutants into the air.

HYDROPOWER. Fast-flowing water that rushes out of reservoirs and moves turbine blades can reliably generate large amounts of electricity without causing pollution. However, hydropower requires the construction of DAMS, which can devastate freshwater ecosystems. Scientists are exploring other ways of using water to create energy, such as harnessing the movement of waves or tides, or taking advantage of the temperature difference between warm ocean surface water and colder water below.

BIOMASS. Organic material, including plant and animal waste, wood, and GARBAGE, can be converted into fuels or used directly for heat or electricity. The material can be burned to produce energy (wood burning is a common example) or converted by bacteria or other microorganisms into liquid or gaseous fuels. Two of the best known biomass products are ethanol and methanol. Farmers support expanded use of ethanol, derived from corncobs and other plant products, but environmentalists worry that it can be highly polluting. Methanol is a key ingredient in a gasoline additive, MTBE, which is blamed for contaminating GROUNDWATER supplies. (See also REFORMULATED GASOLINE.)

Resource Conservation and Recovery Act

One of the nation's most important environmental laws, the Resource Conservation and Recovery Act (PL 94-580) is designed to safeguard the public health by regulating the disposal of both hazardous and nonhazardous solid waste. Potentially hazardous substances that come under the law's scope include waste solids, sludges, liquids, and certain gases, regardless of whether they are generated by industrial operations or municipally operated waste facilities. The 1976 law (abbreviated as RCRA and pronounced "rik-rah") also seeks to reduce consumption by promoting programs to recycle and recover used products. Although less controversial than such sweeping environmental laws as the CLEAN AIR ACT and CLEAN WATER ACT, RCRA has generated debate over whether its standards are adequately enforced or overly stringent.

Congress passed RCRA in 1976 with little dissent, spurred by concerns that many states would shortly run out of GARBAGE disposal sites. The new law amended the 1965 SOLID WASTE DISPOSAL ACT and the 1970 Resource Recovery Act, reflecting the evolution of solid waste management concerns from more efficient disposal to RECYCLING and finally to reducing the amount of waste generated. The legislation also sought to address growing concerns about the public health impacts of HAZARDOUS WASTE. It banned the once-common practice of open dumping and required waste disposal facilities to take steps to prevent hazardous substances from entering the environment. In many ways, it paved the way for passage of the more controversial SUPERFUND law in 1980 that was designed to clean up the nation's most toxic waste sites.

RCRA provides for comprehensive cradle-to-grave regulation of hazardous waste. It requires the ENVIRONMENTAL PROTECTION AGENCY (EPA) to develop criteria for identifying hazardous waste, considering such factors as toxicity, flammability, corrosiveness, or other hazardous characteristics. The agency uses a "manifest system" that tracks hazardous wastes from their origin to their disposal sites. Owners and operators of hazardous waste treatment, storage, or disposal facilities (often abbreviated as TSD) have to obtain permits and meet certain performance standards. Under RCRA the EPA has the authority to require businesses to clean up hazardous waste that they have released into the environment. RCRA also establishes safety standards for waste disposal facilities, such as requiring LANDFILLS to install liners to prevent waste from leaking into GROUNDWATER.

The law allows states to administer their own hazardous waste programs as long as they meet federal standards. States are allowed to impose more stringent requirements than those of the federal program, although they cannot impose less stringent requirements. States also have to maintain an inventory of all sites where hazardous waste has been stored. RCRA authorizes grants to state and local governments to develop solid waste management programs.

One of RCRA's principal goals is to divert materials from the solid waste stream so they can be recycled. To that end, it requires the Commerce Department to promote waste recovery technologies and encourage markets for recovered waste.

In the years following the 1976 passage of RCRA, the EPA had trouble implementing a regulatory program that covered thousands of types of business wastes throughout the nation. It did not finish issuing the main regulations for the hazardous waste program until 1982, provoking criticism by environmentalists for the slow pace—especially after revelations of significant DIOXIN contamination in the community of Times Beach, Missouri. Congress responded in 1984 by tightening federal controls over how business and industry handled hazardous waste. To address apparent loopholes that had enabled as much as half of the

nation's hazardous waste to avoid regulation, lawmakers took the controversial step of regulating small businesses that produced hazardous waste, such as dry cleaners and service stations. They also broadened the law to regulate UNDERGROUND STORAGE TANKS that contained petroleum and other hazardous substances. At a time of considerable tension between Congress and the Reagan administration, lawmakers spelled out requirements in extensive detail and imposed tight deadlines.

In the late 1990s lawmakers considered several proposals to reduce the costs of hazardous waste treatment and give the law more flexibility. The proposals included exempting hazardous waste from most regulation if it was treated so thoroughly that it no longer exhibited hazardous characteristics. Congress also weighed exempting certain landfills in arid areas from groundwater monitoring requirements. Such proposals were broadly supported by industries and environmentalists, but foundered due to differences over technical issues like setting treatment standards.

Retroactive liability

The most contentious portion of the SUPERFUND hazardous waste law is its broad liability scheme, which holds any organization that generated, transported, or stored waste at a HAZARDOUS WASTE site potentially liable for millions of dollars of cleanup costs. Critics say this provision is unfair because it punishes polluters—also known as potentially responsible parties, or PRPs—for decades-old actions that did not violate any laws at the time. The provision also has spurred time-consuming and expensive lawsuits among polluters seeking to avoid liability. Environmentalists, however, generally endorse the principle that polluters should pay for their actions.

Lawmakers have repeatedly debated paring back retroactive liability so it would cover only waste disposal after 1980, when SUPERFUND was passed, or after 1987, when a new insurance policy was adopted. This approach would speed the cleanups and reduce the amount of both private and public money spent on legal actions. But it also would shift the cleanup costs to taxpayers or force the government to scale back the Superfund program—neither of which is politically desirable. (See also POLLUTER PAYS.)

Rio conference

See EARTH SUMMIT.

Risk assessment

Before writing environmental rules, federal agencies generally conduct an assessment of the risks that the regulated substances pose to human health and the environment. Since the 1970s, for example, the ENVIRONMENTAL PROTECTION AGENCY has used science-based techniques, submitting many of its significant regulatory proposals to peer review panels. Nevertheless, the government is constantly buffeted by critics on the right and the left who charge that it fails to conduct proper risk assessments when making decisions. Industry officials contend that federal agencies bias their research to justify the need for regulation; en-

vironmentalists say agencies fail to adequately consider the cumulative impact of exposure to numerous hazardous substances. Such disputes frequently wind up in court.

Part of the problem with risk assessment is that it is a highly inexact science. Officials must contend with the potential side effects of thousands of hazardous chemicals, many of which have existed for no more than a few decades. It will take many years to determine their long-term effects. Determining whether PESTICIDE residues in food, for example, pose a danger to young children could involve decades of study of people who were exposed to such pesticides. Lacking data on the direct impact of a substance, regulators often fill in the gaps with laboratory animal tests, computer simulations, and other extrapolative techniques. Even when scientists have spent years studying potentially dangerous substances, they frequently disagree over the risks posed by those substances (ASBESTOS and DIOXIN sparked particularly fierce disputes). For that reason, policymakers repeatedly have to make judgment calls about risks, leaving them vulnerable to the charge that they are failing to follow SOUND SCIENCE.

Government leaders have had limited success in imposing more discipline on risk assessment. In 1993 President BILL CLINTON required all regulatory agencies to consider "to the extent reasonable" the risks posed by substances within their jurisdictions and to explain how their actions would reduce those risks. Two years later Congress debated—and ultimately rejected—controversial REGULATORY RELIEF legislation that would have directed agencies to conduct detailed risk assessments before imposing major regulations. In addition, Congress has failed to produce a definition for an ACCEPTABLE RISK. As a result, it falls to regulators to determine the degree to which substances that pose a public risk must be restricted.

Roadless areas

Roadless areas comprise large swaths of land in NATIONAL FORESTS and Bureau of Land Management PUBLIC LANDS. Such areas typically are located in rugged terrain, are not easily accessible from major roads, or are ecologically sensitive. In the 1970s the U.S. FOREST SERVICE conducted two roadless area reviews, known as RARE I and RARE II, to inventory roadless areas of five thousand acres or more for their wilderness value. Since that time, the Forest Service has built roads in some of the areas, and Congress has designated others as wilderness, meaning they are to be left untouched. But about sixty million acres of national forest lands outside wilderness areas remain roadless.

The issue of whether to build roads in these areas has sparked intense debate since the 1970s. Environmentalists worry that new roads damage watersheds and wildlife habitat, and open up more wild areas to logging. Timber companies and their congressional allies counter that the roads help to reduce rural unemployment, open up more forests for recreation, and fulfill the Forest Service's mandate of ensuring a supply of timber. Although timber companies can use helicopters to log in roadless areas, the debate over roadbuilding is part of a larger debate over how much logging should be allowed in national forests.

In 1998 Forest Service chief MICHAEL P. DOMBECK announced a controversial plan to halt all road construction in roadless areas for eighteen months. The moratorium was designed to allow the agency to catch up on repairing its 373,000-

Roadless areas have been a battleground of environmentalists and timber companies since the 1970s. In 2000 President Bill Clinton proposed a controversial moratorium on roadbuilding in national forests. Source: Harold E. Malde, The Nature Conservancy

mile road network and crafting a new road construction policy. Two years later, President BILL CLINTON announced steps to permanently prevent roadbuilding in about forty million acres of the forests. Many lawmakers assailed the landmark plan as an indirect scheme to create wilderness areas—which only Congress has the power to create. But environmentalists applauded the initiative. (See also WATERSHED MANAGEMENT.)

Roosevelt, Theodore

An avid outdoorsman, Theodore Roosevelt is arguably the most important figure in the history of American land preservation. After assuming the presidency in 1901 upon the assassination of William McKinley, Roosevelt used his authority aggressively to proclaim more than 100 million acres of NATIONAL FORESTS. His ally in government, Gifford Pinchot, ran the U.S. FOREST SERVICE with an eye to SUSTAINABLE USE, limiting logging and other disruptive activities. Despite questionable legal authority, Roosevelt designated Florida's tiny Pelican Island as a national wildlife refuge in 1903—the first such refuge in the country. Later in his administration, Roosevelt used the ANTIQUITIES ACT to protect the Grand Canyon, even though that law had been designed originally to protect archaeological sites and other historical objects. In all, Roosevelt is credited with establishing more than 150 million acres of forests, parks, and other preserves. He eloquently summed up the conservation ideal when he said of the Grand Canyon: "Leave it as it is. You cannot improve on it. The ages have been at work on it and man can only mar it. What you can do is keep it for your children, your children's children, and for all who come after all."

By modern standards, Roosevelt was not a stalwart environmentalist. He believed in "utilitarian conservation," which emphasized preserving forests to provide future timber and jobs, rather than to shelter wild animals and rare plants. Nevertheless, Roosevelt's aggressive conservation policies fueled a backlash from commercial developers. In 1907 Congress curbed the president's power to create new national forests. But Roosevelt's legacy endures. The national forest and NATIONAL WILDLIFE REFUGE SYSTEMS that he helped to create are regarded as vital habitat for rare plant and animal species. They are still managed in part on the Roosevelt principles of MULTIPLE USE and sustained yield. Roosevelt's land conservation methods, although controversial, continue to influence policy: both JIMMY CARTER and Bill Clinton used the Antiquities Act to preserve large tracts of land in Alaska, Utah, and other states.

Ruckelshaus, William

The first administrator of the ENVIRONMENTAL PROTECTION AGENCY (EPA), William D. Ruckelshaus was a political moderate who sought bipartisan consensus on environmental issues. He became involved in environmental issues as a deputy state attorney general in Indiana, helping to draft the Indiana Air Pollution Act of 1963. President RICHARD NIXON nominated him to head the newly created EPA in 1970. In his confirmation hearings, Ruckelshaus pledged to strictly enforce antipollution measures. "Obviously, if we are to make progress in pollution abatement, we must have a firm enforcement policy at the federal level," he told the Senate Public Works Committee.

Easily confirmed by the Senate, Ruckelshaus earned a reputation for aggressively protecting the environment. He announced a wide-ranging ban in 1972 on the controversial pesticide DDT, despite protests from the chemical industry. After leaving the EPA in 1973 for the position of deputy attorney general, he refused Nixon's request to fire special prosecutor Archibald Cox—a decision that won Ruckelshaus national praise for political integrity but cost him his job.

In 1975 Ruckelshaus took a job with the timber products company Weyerhaeuser. For a time, he pressed for changes in environmental laws to reduce excessive costs and paperwork requirements on industry. President RONALD REAGAN tapped him in 1983 to serve again as EPA administrator and help repair an agency battered by scandal. During his eighteen-month tenure, Ruckelshaus persuaded the administration to increase EPA budgets, improved staff morale, and tightened regulations on LEAD in gasoline and PESTICIDE use. But he had limited influence in the conservative administration. When he pressed for curbs on coal-fired power plant emissions that caused ACID RAIN, Reagan called for further study of the issue instead. Ruckelshaus resigned shortly after Reagan won reelection in 1984.

Runoff

See NONPOINT SOURCE POLLUTION.

S

Safe Drinking Water Act

The Safe Drinking Water Act (PL 93-523) is the primary federal law governing the purity of the nation's drinking water supply. Congress, spurred by reports of possible carcinogens in drinking water, passed the measure in 1974 to authorize the ENVIRONMENTAL PROTECTION AGENCY (EPA) to set national standards for drinking water. Lawmakers amended the act in 1986 to tighten the EPA's oversight of drinking water, then amended it again in 1996 to focus on the most dangerous contaminants.

The law directs the EPA to set MAXIMUM CONTAMINANT LEVEL goals for more than eighty chemical and bacteriological pollutants, and to require specific treatment techniques for each contaminant. The EPA uses a RISK ASSESSMENT process to ensure that an average person who drinks two liters of water a day does not develop cancer or other severe health problems because of contaminants in the water. The agency also establishes secondary standards governing the taste, appearance, and odor of drinking water, and regulations for the protection of underground water sources. Bottled water must meet the same standards that the EPA sets for tap water. Under the 1996 amendments, the EPA is to issue regulations for at least five contaminants in 2001, then another five in 2006 and every five years thereafter.

Unlike other major environmental laws passed in the early 1970s, such as the CLEAN WATER ACT and the ENDANGERED SPECIES ACT, the Safe Drinking Water Act has sparked relatively few ideological battles. That is because it primarily affects publicly administered water systems and state governments rather than private industries, and it provides grants to state and local governments for research about drinking water and for the upgrade of water systems. The 1996 reauthorization won widespread bipartisan support. Even such a stalwart critic of environmental regulations as Rep. Charlie Norwood, R-Ga., said at the time: "Everybody in my district is for clean water, including me."

The Safe Drinking Water Act is credited for ensuring that the United States has one of the safest water supplies in the world. Nevertheless, reports of seriously contaminated water persist. A Centers for Disease Control study in 1994 estimated that nine hundred thousand people become ill annually, and nine hundred die, because of dangerous organisms in drinking water. One of the most high-profile and deadly incidents was the 1993 outbreak of CRYPTOSPORIDIUM in Milwaukee's drinking water supply, which left four thousand people hospitalized and may have resulted in fifty or more deaths. At the time that Congress amended the law in 1996, 8.6 percent of the nation's fifty-five thousand community water systems reported a violation of one or more drinking water health standards. Safeguarding water purity is increasingly expensive. That is because the nation's growing population and sprawling development is encroaching on WATERSHEDS, and polluted runoff from farms and city streets threatens many drinking water sources. Traces of hazardous chemicals such as PESTICIDES have been detected in tap water.

Much of the discussion over the law since the 1996 reauthorization has focused on two issues: the EPA's ability to issue new regulations on schedule and the amount of money needed to improve drinking water safety. In 1999, the General Accounting Office warned that the EPA may fail to meet the 2006 deadline to issue additional regulations because public health studies can take four years or more to complete. Some environmentalists and public health advocates want to improve procedures for screening contaminants. They also would like to tighten the standards to make the water supply safe for vulnerable groups such as infants, the elderly, and people with AIDS. But water system officials worry that the costs for tighter standards could be prohibitive. As it is, drinking water systems are spending an estimated $25 billion yearly to operate and maintain their systems.

In contrast to the situation in the United States and other industrialized nations, contaminated water remains a major problem in developing countries. An estimated 1.4 billion people have no access to safe drinking water, and contaminated water supplies are blamed for contributing to the high infectious disease death rate. As the world's population increases, some regions also face the prospect of severe WATER SCARCITY.

History

Throughout the nineteenth century, contaminated water in the United States and Europe caused widespread outbreaks of diarrheal diseases such as cholera and typhoid. Such diseases were the third leading cause of death in the United States at the beginning of the twentieth century. As researchers found out that these diseases could be spread

through drinking water, cities began developing purification methods, such as filtering water through sand and, eventually, treating water with chlorine. Congress gave a boost to clean water advocates in 1899 when it passed the Rivers and Harbors Act, which prohibited the dumping of waste into navigable waters.

By World War II, stringent government bacteriological standards ensured a safe supply of drinking water. However, the use of new classes of synthetic chemicals caused concerns about widespread contamination. States were responsible for the quality of drinking water, but their standards varied dramatically. In 1974, the EPA found possible carcinogens in the drinking water of New Orleans, and a widely publicized report by the Environmental Defense Fund warned of a "significant relationship" between cancer deaths and drinking water in the New Orleans area. Amid suggestions that the situation in New Orleans was not unique, Congress in 1974 passed the Safe Drinking Water Act—believed at the time to be the most comprehensive law in history to protect water supplies. The act directed the EPA to set national standards for water safety and empowered the agency to bring suit against states that failed to comply. It also directed the EPA to establish regulations for state programs protecting underground water sources. Under the law, states were allowed to grant certain variances and exemptions to water systems (for example, water systems could get seven-to-nine-year exemptions if they lacked the economic means to meet the standards).

Revising the Law

In 1986, amid criticism that the EPA was regulating only a few of the many dozens of contaminants in drinking water, Congress significantly strengthened the law, increasing penalties, tightening compliance deadlines, and making it more difficult for states to grant variances. Over the objections of President RONALD REAGAN, lawmakers required states to develop GROUNDWATER protection programs. They gave the EPA more authority to control the underground injection of wastes that could contaminate groundwater.

If some worried that the original law was too lax, others criticized the 1986 amendments for being far too inflexible. The EPA could not meet the ambitious requirement of establishing standards for twenty-five additional contaminants every three years. Furthermore, water systems found themselves in the troubling situation of having to test for substances unlikely to be found in their water, which diverted their resources from other problems. After taking office in 1993, EPA Administrator CAROL BROWNER warned that the revised act denied the agency flexibility, requiring it to focus on a long list of contaminants instead of targeting those that posed the greatest health risk. In 1996, Congress reauthorized the Safe Drinking Water Act—an impressive feat at a time when lawmakers found themselves deadlocked over most other major environmental policies. Key elements of the rewrite included:

• A $7.6 billion grant program for states that set up revolving loan funds. States use the funds to provide low-cost financing to water systems for infrastructure and other activities to improve water purity.

• Giving the EPA the option of issuing regulations for at least five new contaminants every five years, instead of setting standards for twenty-five new contaminants every three years. The EPA must consider a COST-BENEFIT ANALYSIS when setting the new standards.

• Requiring the EPA to set drinking water standards for arsenic and radon, and to study the health effects of sulfate.

• Requiring water systems to notify customers within twenty-four hours of failing to comply with any drinking water standard, and to publish annual reports with details on contaminant levels.

• Allowing small systems to use the best available, affordable technology to treat their water systems.

• Permitting water systems to reduce their monitoring of a contaminant that was not detected or was found at very low levels.

Safe harbor

A safe harbor agreement is a voluntary arrangement between a landowner and the government under the ENDANGERED SPECIES ACT. The landowner agrees to careful stewardship of the land for a given number of years in order to try to increase the population of an endangered plant or animal. At the end of the specified period, the owner can develop the property even if the elevated numbers of the endangered species will be reduced. The owner, however, is responsible for notifying the government so officials can remove as many of the plants or animals as possible and take other steps to retain the advantages of the agreement.

The Clinton administration made use of safe harbor agreements, as well as NO-SURPRISES provisions, to ease criticism that the Endangered Species Act sets back development and land values. But safe harbor agreements receive mixed reviews. Environmentalists say they fail to commit a landowner to supporting the recovery of a species; PRIVATE PROPERTY RIGHTS advocates say they provide little incentive to offset property use restrictions.

Salmon

This economically important fish started to roil political waters in the 1990s. Due to the depletion of salmon stocks, the federal government in 1998 listed nine West Coast salmon populations as threatened or endangered under the ENDANGERED SPECIES ACT. This marked the first time the act was used to protect a species whose habitat was in a metropolitan area, and the listing threatened to restrict growth in the fast-growing cities of Seattle and Portland, Oregon. One year later, the government began taking steps for a similar listing for Atlantic salmon in Maine, provoking protests from state officials who worried about the impact to the state's blueberry and aquaculture industries.

To bring back wild salmon to the Northwest, the government weighed a controversial plan to remove four DAMS on the Snake River in Washington. Other strategies considered by the NATIONAL MARINE FISHERIES SERVICE, all of which generated local opposition, included restoring habitat on federal lands, cutting back on fishing, and changing hatchery operations to emphasize restoring wild fish. The salmon controversy spurred a flurry of activity in Congress, with western lawmakers pressing federal agencies to come up with ways of protecting the fish other than breaching dams. Salmon fishing disputes also strained relations in the late 1990s between the United States and Canada, but the two countries reached an accord over managing the fish in 1999.

Salvage logging

Salvage logging is the practice of removing fallen or diseased trees from otherwise healthy forests.

To protect forests from wildfires and limit the spread of disease, the U.S. Forest Service encourages salvage logging, the removal of fallen or diseased trees from otherwise healthy forests. Source: Hank Lebo, Jeroboam Inc.

Also known as timber salvage, it is intended to protect publicly owned forests from WILDFIRES or the spread of diseases. However, the practice is controversial because it can enable timber companies to skirt logging restrictions and remove healthy trees for lumber, while leaving behind dead trees that have no commercial value.

In 1995, Congress passed a fiscal rescissions bill (PL 104-19) that angered environmentalists because it contained an ENVIRONMENTAL RIDER allowing companies to expedite salvage logging in OLD-GROWTH FORESTS. President BILL CLINTON, who signed the bill, later tried to repeal the logging provision but was unable to work out a compromise with lawmakers. However, he helped block efforts by rural conservatives who wanted to expand salvage logging by speeding up the U.S. FOREST SERVICE review process of such operations.

In 1999, the Forest Service announced it would consider tightening the definition of salvage logging to reduce or even eliminate the cutting of live trees as part of a larger program to preserve forest ecology.

Secondary treatment

Required under the CLEAN WATER ACT, secondary treatment refers to advanced methods in waste treatment systems. Whereas primary treatment removes solid material from wastewater, secondary treatment uses natural organisms and aeration (similar to bubbling in streams) to remove toxins. This process removes metals as well as organic chemicals such as detergents and PESTICIDES.

The widespread use of secondary treatment is credited as one of the biggest reasons that the quality of the nation's waterways has improved since the early 1970s. However, secondary treatment is expensive, and Congress occasionally considers bills to exempt particular municipal waste facilities from the secondary treatment requirement. In 1995, for example, Rep. Brian P. Bilbray, R-Calif., won passage of a provision exempting San Diego from applying secondary treatment to sewage before discharging it in the ocean.

Section 404

Section 404 of the 1972 FEDERAL WATER POLLUTION CONTROL ACT (commonly referred to as the CLEAN WATER ACT) is the keystone of federal protection of WETLANDS. It is so important that policymakers and many in the private sector frequently mention "section 404 requirements" and "section 404 permits" when discussing wetlands regulations. The section requires anybody wishing to engage in dredge and fill operations that would affect wetlands to get a permit. Activities affected by this program include residential and commercial development, water resource projects such as DAMS and levees, infrastructure projects such as roads and airports, and the conversion of wetlands for farming and forestry. However, section 404 permits are not required for the draining or flooding of wetlands or for many farming and ranching activities. The program also exempts wetlands that are not linked to a tributary water system. The U.S. ARMY CORPS OF ENGINEERS is responsible for issuing the permits, and the ENVIRONMENTAL PROTECTION AGENCY (EPA) has veto authority over them.

To obtain a section 404 permit, an applicant must demonstrate that the project does everything practicable to minimize environmental damage. The applicant also must take steps to restore damaged wetlands or create new ones to offset wetland destruction.

As with other wetlands programs, section 404 has spawned decades of conflicts. Developers regard the permitting process as overly burdensome, but environmentalists say it should be expanded to include smaller wetlands and more types of activities. Environmentalists also have misgivings about the Corps' administration of the program. In fact, Sen. Edmund S. Muskie, D-Maine, a principal author of the Clean Water Act, said in 1976 that he wished the EPA oversaw the program instead. These concerns stem from the implementation of section 404, when the Corps initially interpreted it as applying to navigable waters only. Environmentalists won a 1975 court ruling that Congress intended the program to apply to all waters. In 1976, lawmakers considered nullifying the court decision, but they retreated in the face of environmental protests. Subsequently, however, construction and logging companies persuaded lawmakers to exempt federal projects specifically authorized by Congress from section 404 requirements.

Since 1996, the Corps has adopted increasingly strict criteria, including requiring permits for the filling in of wetlands that are as small as one-third of an acre. However, developers won several federal court decisions in the late 1990s that ruled the Corps had exceeded its authority by regulating certain landscaping and excavation activities and claiming jurisdiction over isolated wetlands.

Sediment pollution

Sediments are loose particles of sand, soil, silt, and other substances that are washed from the land into water, usually after heavy precipitation. When they collect in waterways due to careless construction, farming, logging, and MINING activities, they can cloud the water, blocking sunlight from reaching aquatic plants and destroying fish and wildlife habitat. More dangerously, many sediments have become contaminated with toxic substances such as DDT and polychlorinated biphenyls (PCBS). These contaminated sediments present a serious health and economic problem across much of the country, especially in the GREAT LAKES, coastal areas, and heavily trafficked inland waterways.

The contaminated sediments most directly affect worms, larvae, and other tiny creatures at the bottom of the water. They are then ingested by animals higher up in the food chain in a process known as bioaccumulation, resulting in higher concentrations of toxins in fish, birds, and other animals. As a result, officials frequently have to issue fish consumption advisories to protect people from eating toxic substances.

The ENVIRONMENTAL PROTECTION AGENCY estimates that about 1 to 4 percent of all the sediment dredged each year to deepen harbors and clear shipping lanes is so contaminated that it requires special, and sometimes costly, handling.

Several federal and state agencies are responsible for minimizing the impact of contaminated sediments. More than ten federal laws, including SUPERFUND, the CLEAN WATER ACT, and the NATIONAL ENVIRONMENTAL POLICY ACT, seek to reduce sediment problems by identifying and cleaning up the most contaminated sites, and by restricting additional discharges into waterways.

Senate Energy and Natural Resources Committee

The Senate Energy and Natural Resources Committee has primary jurisdiction over energy issues that are of key environmental concern, including MINING, oil and gas drilling on ecologically sensitive land, and the disposal of NUCLEAR WASTE. The committee also oversees contentious PUBLIC LANDS issues. Its jurisdiction includes logging in NATIONAL FORESTS and preserving the ecology of increasingly crowded NATIONAL PARKS.

The committee tends to be dominated by members who come from energy-producing states and are sympathetic to the needs of the oil, coal, and

Sens. J. Bennett Johnston (left), D-La., and Malcolm Wallop, R-Wyo., confer in September 1994 on legislation before the Senate Energy and Natural Resources Committee. Johnston, who chaired the committee from 1987 to 1995, often broke with party ranks to support energy producers in his homestate. Source: Kathleen Beall, Congressional Quarterly

natural gas industries. For years, it was chaired by Sen. J. Bennett Johnston of Louisiana, a conservative Democrat who did not hesitate to break with party ranks in order to support his homestate energy producers. In 1995, Sen. FRANK H. MURKOWSKI, R-Alaska, took over the gavel and pressed to open up more of Alaska's North Slope to oil exploration. He also backed the interests of loggers and PRIVATE PROPERTY RIGHTS advocates who wanted to pare back land use restrictions.

Senate Environment and Public Works Committee

The Senate Environment and Public Works Committee has the broadest jurisdiction over environmental regulatory issues of any committee in the Senate. Major environmental laws that come under its purview include SUPERFUND, the CLEAN WATER ACT, and the ENDANGERED SPECIES ACT. It also handles flood control and transportation bills, some of which—such as omnibus surface transportation legislation—have considerable bearing on the environment. The committee's broad jurisdiction includes waste disposal, ocean protection, and various coastal issues. However, issues involving PUBLIC LANDS typically are handled by the SENATE ENERGY AND NATURAL RESOURCES COMMITTEE.

Partisan differences on the Environment and Public Works Committee were muted during most of the 1990s because senior Republican JOHN H. CHAFEE of Rhode Island tended to side with environmentalists. As chairman, he refused to take up legislation written by House Republicans that would have pared back the Clean Water Act. After his death in 1999, he was succeeded by the more conservative ROBERT SMITH, R-N.H.

Sierra Club

One of the nation's oldest and most influential environmental groups, the Sierra Club was founded in 1892 under the leadership of legendary conservationist John Muir. Prior to the emergence of the modern ENVIRONMENTAL MOVEMENT in the 1960s and 1970s, the Sierra Club lobbied the government to set aside land in NATIONAL PARKS and other preserves. It also fought against such environmentally harmful proposals as the damming of Hetch Hetchy Valley in Yosemite National Park and other types of development.

Since the 1970s, the Sierra Club has been at the forefront of numerous legal battles. It forced Congress to broaden the CLEAN AIR ACT with a successful 1972 federal lawsuit, *Sierra Club v. Ruckelshaus,* and it launched politically potent television ads in the 1990s. No longer regarded as a radical organization, it has about a half-million members and belongs to the so-called GROUP OF 10, environmental organizations that engage in mainstream political efforts (although it is less compromising than some

others). The Sierra Club has chapters in almost every state as well as several Canadian provinces.

Sikes Act

The 1960 Sikes Act (PL 86-797) directs the Interior Department and Defense Department to work together to maintain fish and wildlife resources on military lands. This is a significant environmental issue because the Defense Department administers twenty-five million acres of land, much of it isolated and ecologically important. The military has the difficult task of considering environmental protection while conducting weapons testing and battle training. Congress amended the law in the 1970s and 1980s to authorize wildlife conservation and rehabilitation programs, and to direct the military to work with trained environmental professionals. In 1997, lawmakers passed provisions that called for integrated plans to protect entire ecosystems on military reservations.

Silent Spring

Silent Spring is the 1962 landmark book by marine biologist Rachel Carson that helped galvanize the ENVIRONMENTAL MOVEMENT. Hugely controversial, the bestseller contended that the use of PESTICIDES had caused widespread contamination of the food chain and posed global health and environmental hazards. The title alluded to the effect of insecticides, weedkillers, and other common chemicals on songbird populations, but Carson warned that people, too, were at risk from exposure to chemicals that persisted in the environment. "Along with the possibility of the extinction of mankind by nuclear war, the central problem of our age has therefore become the contamination of man's total environment," Carson wrote.

Silent Spring sparked an immediate outcry. The chemical industry criticized it as misleading and exaggerated, but President John F. Kennedy appointed a special panel to look into its findings, and Congress held hearings on the issues it raised. The book helped spur the creation of grassroots environmental organizations, laying the groundwork for the U.S. ban of the toxic insecticide DDT in 1972.

Sludge

Sludge typically refers to the semisolid materials (or "biosolids") that settle out of wastewater at a sewage treatment plant. It can also consist of semisolid wastes produced by controls on WATER POLLUTION and AIR POLLUTION. Although a byproduct of antipollution measures, sludge itself often contains HAZARDOUS WASTE that must be handled carefully to prevent environmental contamination. Some sludge can be used as fertilizer, but often it is burned or disposed in a LANDFILL.

Smith, Robert

Sen. Robert Smith, R-N.H., took over the chairmanship of the SENATE ENVIRONMENT AND PUBLIC WORKS COMMITTEE in 1999 after the death of Sen. JOHN H. CHAFEE, R-R.I. Unlike his conservation-minded predecessor, Smith tended to side with industry in efforts to scale back ENVIRONMENTAL PROTECTION AGENCY regulations. He clashed with environmentalists by repeatedly seeking to overhaul the SUPERFUND hazardous waste program and

do away with provisions that hold polluters liable. However, Smith has drawn praise from environmentalists on occasion by opposing funding for western irrigation projects and supporting efforts to increase GRAZING FEES and fees associated with MINING activities. He has also backed efforts to protect northeastern forests by reducing ACID RAIN. Criticizing some GOP leaders for compromising on abortion and other issues, Smith briefly bolted the Republican Party in 1999 during a longshot run for the White House. But he rejoined the party after Chafee's death in order to chair the committee.

Smog

Although smog sometimes refers to sulfurous emissions (which caused four thousand deaths during a particularly severe AIR POLLUTION episode in London in 1952), regulators use the term to describe a photochemical reaction resulting in ground-level ozone. Also known as "photochemical smog," it is the most widespread pollutant in the United States. In 1998, 131 million people lived in counties with unhealthy levels of ozone, according to the ENVIRONMENTAL PROTECTION AGENCY. Using its authority under the CLEAN AIR ACT, the agency proposed more stringent ozone standards in 1997. This would have tripled the number of out-of-compliance counties to about three hundred, but in 1999, business groups won a federal appeals court decision that blocked the plan from taking effect, at least temporarily.

Smog is created when sunlight acts on nitrogen oxides and volatile organic compounds in the air to produce ozone. (Ground-level ozone should not be confused with stratospheric ozone, which shields the earth from ultraviolet radiation). Smog is difficult to regulate because the emissions that lead to its formation come from many sources, including automobiles, electric power plants, fuel combustion, gasoline vapors, paints, and chemical solvents. The pollutant causes significant health problems, aggravating asthma and weakening resistance to colds and other infections. In the environment, smog is blamed for damaging trees and other plants, costing as much as several billion dollars a year in lost crop yields and reducing visibility. It can also damage rubber, fabric, and other materials.

Snail darter

A rare, three-inch fish, the snail darter came to national prominence in the 1970s, when its endangered status was used to try to stop a $131 million Tennessee Valley Authority DAM project. The battle over whether to save it embroiled both Congress and the Supreme Court, eventually causing even environmentally minded lawmakers to warn that the ENDANGERED SPECIES ACT had gone too far.

The saga began when landowners along the Little Tennessee River, trying to halt construction of the nearby Tellico Dam and save their condemned property, filed a lawsuit in 1976 charging that the dam would violate the Endangered Species Act because it would destroy the habitat of the rare fish. Even though the dam was nearly completed, the Supreme Court ruled in 1978 that construction must be stopped unless Congress exempted the project from the law. The decision set off a furor, with some in Congress charging that efforts at federal protection of wildlife were running amok. "There is not a district in this country that will be immune from the kind of problem we are facing unless the law is changed," warned Rep. John Buchanan, R-Ala. Lawmakers amended the Endangered Species Act in 1978 to set up a cabinet-level

Seeking to halt construction of the Tellico Dam in 1976, landowners along the Little Tennessee River charged that the dam would destroy the habitat of the snail darter, a rare fish protected by the Endangered Species Act. Congress in 1979 permitted construction to proceed by exempting the dam from the restrictions of the act. Source: Tennessee Valley Authority

board called the ENDANGERED SPECIES COMMIT-TEE, which had the power to exempt a project from the law. In its first decision, the board voted in January 1979 against an exemption for the Tellico Dam. But Congress later that year voted to exempt the dam, and President JIMMY CARTER reluctantly signed the measure into law.

The dispute marked a turning point in regulatory battles, with developers successfully tagging an environmental law as overreaching and inflexible. It also ushered in an era of numerous lawsuits and legislative battles over the Endangered Species Act.

Solid Waste Disposal Act

Congress passed the Solid Waste Disposal Act (PL 89-272) in 1965 as part of a clean air measure. The legislation set up a cost-sharing program with states to survey waste disposal issues and develop waste management plans. Lawmakers greatly amended the bill in 1970 to focus on reclaiming materials from solid waste. Six years later, they rewrote the law so extensively to govern all aspects of solid waste disposal that it is now known by the title of its 1976 version: the RESOURCE CONSERVATION AND RECOVERY ACT.

Sound science

Although sound science generally refers to objective and carefully conducted scientific research, the term is sometimes used in policy circles as a criticism of environmental regulations. Industry representatives say the ENVIRONMENTAL PROTECTION AGENCY should be forced to rely on sound science when promulgating regulations, rather than using conflicting data that may be extrapolated from a few animal experiments. Agency officials, however, contend that they are using the best science available. Many environmentalists suspect that the demand for sound science is merely a tactic to delay regulations since it may take decades for scientists to analyze fully the long-term effects of new chemicals. They often prefer to apply the PRECAUTIONARY PRINCIPLE, which holds that hazardous materials pose such a grave public health danger that the government should impose regulations even before all the scientific evidence is in.

The battle over sound science is played out repeatedly in congressional and court battles over issues ranging from GLOBAL WARMING to the effects of MANURE on waterways. In some cases, such as 1970s restrictions on LEAD in gasoline, officials have an overwhelming amount of scientific data to back their decisions. More often, however, researchers produce mixed data about a pollutant, forcing regulators to make a judgment call. This means regulators have great discretion.

In 1995, the House passed REGULATORY RELIEF legislation that would have required agencies to present detailed scientific evidence on the health risk of a substance before issuing a major regulation. However, the Clinton administration sharply objected on the grounds that such a requirement would make it almost impossible for agencies to safeguard public health. The proposal died in the Senate.

Species recovery plans

When a plant or animal species is listed as threatened or endangered under the ENDANGERED SPECIES ACT, the Fish and Wildlife Service prepares a species recovery plan that outlines steps to restore the population. Recovery efforts include protecting or restoring habitat, captive breeding, reintroducing the species into parts of its former range, and providing technical assistance to landowners. As with other aspects of the Endangered Species Act, species recovery plans can be controversial. They often take years to prepare and may lead to strict land use restrictions. The recovery of a single species may cost the government millions of dollars.

thermore, sport utility vehicles and other vehicles in the light truck category emit more pollutants because they are exempt from some government emission standards.

In 1999, the Clinton administration announced new TIER 2 rules to require that vehicles weighing up to 8,500 pounds, including sport utility vehicles, would have to meet the same emissions standards as passenger cars by 2004. The White House estimated that the new requirements would add about $250 to the cost of a sport utility vehicle.

Sport utility vehicles

The popularity of sport utility vehicles and other larger motor vehicles is complicating efforts to clean up AIR POLLUTION and reduce GLOBAL WARMING. In 2000, sport utility vehicles, pick-up trucks, and vans accounted for about half the sales of new motor vehicles bought for personal and small business use. These larger vehicles use far more gasoline than compact cars, contributing to rising U.S. emissions of GREENHOUSE GASES. Fur-

State implementation plans

The CLEAN AIR ACT divides responsibility for antipollution efforts between the federal and state governments. While the ENVIRONMENTAL PROTECTION AGENCY (EPA) promulgates regulations, state officials have to create implementation plans indicating how they will meet the federal standards. States are responsible for enforcing special air quality standards in pristine areas under the PREVENTION

Exempt from some government emission standards, sport utility vehicles (SUVs) use more gasoline and produce more pollutants than do compact cars. The Clinton administration in 1999 unveiled its so-called tier 2 emission standards, which required SUVs to meet the same standards as passenger cars by 2004. Source: Douglas Graham, Congressional Quarterly

OF SIGNIFICANT DETERIORATION program and for devising strategies to reduce pollution in NONATTAINMENT AREAS that exceed federal standards.

This approach has succeeded in significantly reducing air pollution. But it also has fueled conflicts between federal and state officials, as well as between industries and environmentalists. Each state is required to calculate emissions in its area and then determine how much of the total pollution "load" is the responsibility of each polluter—a difficult and technical process that sparks battles over the extent to which each polluter may face emission restrictions. Environmentalists warn that states often are unduly influenced by polluters, and therefore fail to enforce their own plans. State and federal officials have often been at odds over EPA attempts to restrict roadbuilding and commuting patterns. For their part, some state officials say they are doing everything possible to crack down on polluters within their borders. They point out that a failure to meet national standards is often the result of air pollutants that blow in from power plants and other emission sources hundreds of miles beyond their jurisdiction.

Stationary sources

Factories and other immobile facilities that emit AIR POLLUTION are regulated as stationary sources under the CLEAN AIR ACT. They are significant sources of such pollutants as PARTICULATE MATTER (soot), nitrogen oxides, sulfur dioxide, and LEAD. When Congress passed the Clean Air Act in 1970, it directed the ENVIRONMENTAL PROTECTION AGENCY to set maximum emission standards for new stationary sources, which states would enforce. However, it exempted many existing facilities from such

expensive requirements as installing scrubbers. Although the law succeeded in improving air quality, neither stationary sources nor MOBILE SOURCES (mostly cars and trucks) met the law's original stringent goals.

In 1990, lawmakers amended the Clean Air Act and imposed a new set of requirements on stationary sources. These included emission limits on HAZARDOUS AIR POLLUTANTS and an EMISSIONS TRADING program intended to reduce sulfur dioxide emissions. The revisions have succeeded in greatly reducing emission of sulfur dioxide and other pollutants that cause ACID RAIN. But environmentalists warn that lax enforcement is allowing many older industrial facilities to continue emitting harmful levels of pollutants.

Stormwater

See NONPOINT SOURCE POLLUTION.

Sugar price supports

The U.S. DEPARTMENT OF AGRICULTURE supports growers and processors of sugar cane and sugar beets through a program of loans and import restrictions. This price-support program has drawn fire from environmentalists because the phosphorus that growers use to fertilize their fields in south Florida may seep into local waterways and degrade portions of the EVERGLADES, the nation's largest WETLAND and the habitat of many rare species. Environmentalists also contend that the import quotas have undermined sugar growers in places such as the Caribbean and the Philippines, displacing small farmers and ultimately contributing to DEFORESTATION and other ecological problems. (Free-market conservatives and manufacturers who use sugar also criticize the program for economic reasons, arguing that it costs U.S. consumers almost $2 billion yearly in the form of higher sugar prices.)

Congress last revised the program in 1996 as part of an omnibus farm bill, freezing the loan price and slightly altering the loans in a way that could make domestic prices more volatile. However, it retained the basic structure of the program.

Superfund

In 1980 Congress passed the Comprehensive Environmental Response, Compensation, and Liability Act (CERCLA), better known as Superfund. The law (PL 96-510) is designed to clean up hundreds of the most toxic waste dumps and make polluters liable for the costs. For those cases in which the responsible party is unknown or cannot pay, the cleanup is financed by the program's multibillion-dollar "Superfund." Congress extensively amended the law in 1986 with the Superfund Amendments and Reauthorization Act, or SARA. But it has failed to reauthorize it since, and it allowed the taxes that support the fund to expire in 1996. As a result, the program is operating on dwindling amounts of funding.

Although the concept of Superfund may seem straightforward, the program is highly controversial. To some critics, it is even something of a poster child of environmental regulations run amok. That is because Congress originally authorized Superfund as a $1.6-billion, five-year program that was supposed to solve the problem of HAZARDOUS WASTE dumps. Instead, Superfund has cost taxpayers and companies many times that amount and

U.S. Superfund Sites, 1980–2000

Year	National Priorities List (NPL) sites	Non-NPL Superfund sites
1980	0	8,689
1981	0	13,893
1982	160	14,697
1983	551	16,023
1984	547	18,378
1985	864	22,238
1986	906	24,940
1987	967	27,274
1988	1,195	29,809
1989	1,254	31,650
1990	1,236	33,371
1991	1,245	35,108
1992	1,275	36,869
1993	1,321	38,169
1994	1,360	39,099
1995	1,374	15,622
1996	1,210	12,781
1997	1,194	9,245
1998	1,192	9,404
1999	1,217	9,237
2000	1,226	9,297

Source: U.S. Environmental Protection Agency (EPA), Office of Emergency and Remedial Response, Superfund Hazardous Waste Site Query (Internet database), April 25, 2000.

Notes: Data are cumulative. The 1995 data reflect the removal of more than twenty-four thousand sites from the Superfund inventory as part of EPA's brownfields initiative to help promote economic redevelopment of these properties.

has spurred so much legal battling over who should take responsibility that the average cleanup lasts twelve years. Despite the myriad problems, lawmakers could not find a way to reform the program in the 1990s. As of 2000, they faced the prospect of many additional years of wrangling over how to keep financing it. Critics, including many small business owners who have been dragged into years of lawsuits, say the program is a waste of money that has inadvertently delayed cleanups because of unreasonable cleanup requirements and time-consuming litigation, thereby

The controversial Superfund program is administered by the Environmental Protection Agency (EPA), which maintains a national priorities list of the most toxic hazardous waste sites. Residents of this African-American neighborhood built on top of the Agriculture Street Landfill in New Orleans petitioned the EPA to relocate them from the area, now a Superfund site. Source: Environmental Justice Resource Center

jeopardizing public health. Even advocates concede that the program is overly slow and costly. But they credit it with cleaning up hundreds of the nation's most contaminated sites and preventing new releases of toxic waste throughout the country.

The ENVIRONMENTAL PROTECTION AGENCY (EPA) administers Superfund. The program itself consists of both emergency short-term "removals" to clean up relatively limited amounts of toxic waste within a year and long-term "remedial actions" to clean up more extensive and highly contaminated sites. After assessing a site, EPA officials decide whether to place it on the NATIONAL PRIORITIES LIST of the nation's most toxic waste sites (see table). When people refer to a "Superfund site," they generally mean one that is on the national priorities list.

A Costly Program

From the program's inception through the beginning of 2000, the EPA placed slightly more than 1,400 sites on the list. Of those sites, about 190 were cleaned up and deleted from the list by the end of 1999; an additional 400 were in the final stages of cleanup. Through 1998, the program cost polluters more than $15 billion and the government more than $14 billion, according to a General Accounting Office report. The report estimated that cleaning up most of the remaining sites would require an additional $8.2 billion to $11.7 billion, but EPA officials warned that these costs would likely be even higher.

Why is the program so costly to administer? The primary reason involves disputes over who should pay for the cleanups. The law assigns liability to anyone who once contributed to the site—even if the contribution was minimal and the polluter broke no law at the time. This "joint and several liability" approach means that it makes no difference who is negligent or who is more responsible for a spill or a leak. Once the victims or the government is reimbursed, the companies involved can sue each other, thus forcing the courts to sort out the relative degrees of negligence. Since the average site costs about $20 million to clean up, it makes sense for polluters to go to court instead of paying the bill. As a result, primary polluters often sue others who contributed to the site, who in turn sue still others in order to spread out the costs of cleanup.

This unwieldy process has ensnared school districts, restaurants, dry cleaners, banks, and many other Main Street businesses and organizations that did nothing more than haul their waste to the local LANDFILL. Lawmakers fume that the process makes little sense. "Reforming Superfund is not a luxury; it is a necessity," Rep. Blanche Lambert-Lincoln, D-Ark., testified at a 1996 congressional hearing. "Small businesses and charitable organizations such as the Girl Scouts have been hauled into court; large corporations who have contributed only a small amount of hazardous waste have been liable for the lion's share of the cleanup because of their deep pockets; banks have been held liable only because they have mortgages on the land."

Accordingly, the biggest debate on Capitol Hill over reauthorizing Superfund is about whether to continue holding polluters responsible for the cleanups. Businesses argue that the law's "POLLUTER-PAYS" provision is unfair because it punishes companies for decades-old actions that did not violate any law at the time (hazardous waste dumping used to be largely unregulated). But environmentalists support the provision, contending that businesses profited from the cheap dumping. Even lawmakers who oppose the polluter-pays provision cannot agree on how to finance the cleanups otherwise. They do not want to charge taxpayers for the cost of cleaning up a careless company's dumping.

Lawmakers also are at odds over whether to reauthorize taxes for the Superfund trust fund. The fund pays for cleanups when financially viable polluters cannot be found, and it also supports EPA enforcement and management activities. Superfund taxes, which had raised about $1.5 billion a year until expiring in 1996, included excise taxes on petroleum and certain chemicals as well as a corporate environmental income tax.

Another issue that has provoked legislative debate for years involves the law's cleanup standards. Conservatives say the standards are overly strict and expensive. They tend to favor sealing up the site and minimizing the risk that any toxic substances would leak into the environment, rather than actually removing the waste. Many environmental groups, however, say it is essential to treat or remove the waste. In fact, some worry that the current standards are not stringent enough.

Superfund has sparked battles over other issues as well. Lawmakers are under pressure to give more cleanup authority to states and to pass a BROWNFIELDS program that would restore low-level contaminated sites, which could then be used for economic development.

With lawmakers deadlocked, EPA officials have taken it upon themselves to try to streamline the program and speed up the process. The CLINTON administration moved to take many small businesses and municipalities off the list of responsible parties. It also set up interest-bearing accounts whose earnings will help cover cleanup costs, and it appointed an ombudsman to each of the ten EPA regions. Unveiling a set of initiatives in 1996, EPA administrator CAROL BROWNER said: "With these reforms, we are following through on our efforts to fundamentally improve the Superfund program by limiting the costly role of lawyers and increasing community participation." But congressional critics say the program is getting even more inefficient. A 1998 General Accounting Office report concluded that it took almost twice as long to list a site in the 1990s than it had in the late 1980s, and that cleanup time tripled.

History

Hazardous waste did not top the environmental agenda until the late 1970s, when officials discovered that toxic waste from a nearby dump was leaking into houses in an upstate New York subdivision known as LOVE CANAL. The crisis and ensuing evacuation of Love Canal served as a wake-up call to Americans that industrial dumping could pose as great a threat to their health as the more publicized threats to clean air and clean water. Government investigators in the late 1970s found thousands of chemical dump sites—some beneath tennis courts, church parking lots, a yacht club, a cemetery, and other heavily trafficked areas. Overall, EPA officials estimated that there could be up to fifty thousand hazardous sites nationwide, of which as many as two thousand could be extremely dangerous. At the time, existing laws offered only minimal protection. The 1976 RESOURCE CONSERVATION AND RECOVERY ACT authorized cleanup but did not provide any funding, and the CLEAN WATER ACT provided limited funding for cleaning up spills in water but not on land.

Even as lawmakers began debating the issue of toxic waste cleanup in 1980, an abandoned chemical dump in Elizabeth, New Jersey, exploded on April 21, sending toxic fumes into the air just five miles from downtown Manhattan. Months later, lawmakers responded to the nationwide crisis by passing CERCLA and establishing a $1.6 billion Hazardous Substance Response Trust Fund to help finance it. Although the compromise legislation did not cover oil spills or contain the tough liability provisions requested by President JIMMY CARTER, it nevertheless gave the federal government the authority and money to clean up spilled or dumped chemicals in emergencies, as well as the power to sue those responsible. The law broadly defined hazardous waste as any toxic substance, with the exception of most petroleum products, natural gas, and synthetic fuels, which were covered under other environmental laws. It applied to dumps in any location that could affect the air, land, surface water, GROUNDWATER, or public water supplies, as well as to most types of toxic releases in the environment that posed a real or potential threat to the public.

Congress set up the trust fund for five years. Most of the fund's revenues came from chemical and oil companies. It was designed to pay 90 percent of the cleanup costs of abandoned mines and other sites where no responsible party could be found. The remaining 10 percent would be paid by the states in which the sites were located. Lawmakers considered a plan to compensate the victims of hazardous waste dumping, but rejected it because of the high costs. On the issue of liability, which was controversial even during the bill's passage, CERCLA exempted companies that could prove they were careful with packaging, labeling and handling, and had tried to ensure that the transporter would properly dispose of the waste.

The program ran into trouble from the beginning, in part because of the changing of the guard after the 1980 elections. The newly installed administration of President RONALD REAGAN seemed ambivalent about Superfund. In 1983, congressional investigators charged that the administration tended to settle for inadequate cleanups, negotiating with dumpers instead of going to court to recover full costs. The high-profile charges led to the firing of Rita M. Lavelle, the Superfund director, and the resignation of EPA Administrator Anne M. Burford. At the same time, officials warned that the cleanups would cost billions of dollars more than had been originally anticipated. The initial list of several hundred sites expanded to more than a thousand. Annual appropriations for the program rose accordingly, from about $320 million a year in the early 1980s to $1.5 billion yearly in the 1990s.

Sweeping Amendments

Under pressure from the environmental community, President Reagan in 1986 reluctantly expanded the program by signing the Superfund Amendments and Reauthorization Act. The amendments increased program funding by five-fold, to $8.5 billion, partly by imposing an environmental income tax on businesses. The measure also laid down timelines for EPA actions and stressed more stringent cleanup standards to ensure the detoxification of sites whenever possible instead of the burial of waste in landfills. To speed the process, it offered incentives to polluters to settle quickly with the government on cleanup costs. The law allowed the EPA to release from liability so-called de minimis parties—polluters that had contributed only small amounts of toxic waste to a site.

The amendments broadened the program in other ways as well. Perhaps most significant was Title III of the legislation, which created a new law— the EMERGENCY PLANNING AND COMMUNITY RIGHT-TO-KNOW ACT. This required industries to provide local communities with information about the chemicals they handled and dumped. The amendments also gave victims of toxic dumping a longer opportunity to sue. Finally, lawmakers attached a $500 million measure to clean up leaking UNDERGROUND STORAGE TANKS, a major source of groundwater contamination.

Despite the amendments, the program continued to face criticism from all sides. A study in 1992 showed that the government was paying more than half the cost of cleanups, and a study in 1994 found that more than a third of the program's money had gone toward legal fees. Fearing that the program would not be reauthorized when the 1986 amendments were due to expire in 1991, lawmakers added a provision extending Superfund's taxing and funding authority until the end of 1995.

When BILL CLINTON took office in 1993, he placed a major emphasis on overhauling the troubled program as a centerpiece of his environmental regulatory agenda. He called for creating an arbitration process to replace the time-consuming lawsuits, a fairer liability scheme, and a $300 million annual fund to pay for "orphan" sites where no responsible polluters could be found. The new administration also proposed a more flexible set of cleanup standards, contending that a Superfund site targeted for road construction should not have to meet the same standards as a site zoned for future housing. Despite this framework, partisan differences and a late-session dispute over Superfund taxes doomed a reauthorization proposal in 1994.

When Republicans took over Congress one year later, they proposed to scale back or even repeal the law's RETROACTIVE LIABILITY provision by excusing at least some polluters from paying for the cleanups. Instead, the government trust fund would provide much of the funding. Republicans also wanted to relax cleanup standards by requiring the EPA to consider costs. But the plan foundered when conservatives, who were trying to cut government spending at the same time, could not come up with another funding source. "I don't think it's practical to find the money in the budget or to raise taxes by any means," said Rep. W. J. Billy Tauzin of Louisiana. With lawmakers at an impasse, budget negotiators simply extended Superfund taxes into 1996.

Surface Mining Control and Reclamation Act

In 1977 Congress ended years of debate over regulating strip mining by passing the Surface Mining Control and Reclamation Act (PL 95-87). This landmark bill aimed to reduce the destructive impact of coal mining by imposing environmental standards and requiring mine operators to return mined lands to their approximate original contours. However, the law has drawn criticism because of inconsistent enforcement and scientific doubts about the effectiveness of reclamation.

Regulating strip mining became a major environmental issue in the 1970s, especially after the international oil embargo spurred a greater emphasis on coal production. About half of all coal is extracted by strip mining operations, which cause severe environmental damage by stripping off vegetation, soil, and rock layers to expose underlying minerals. By the late 1970s, strip mining for coal and other minerals had damaged an estimated four million acres across the country and had polluted thousands of miles of streams. In West Virginia and other Appalachian states, the landscape was scarred with thousands of bare and sterile acres, decapitated hills, acidified streams, and abandoned mine headwalls. In western prairies and grasslands, surface mining had left a legacy of furrowed lands that were so bare and scarred as to resemble moonscapes.

Under the law, programs administered by states and monitored by the U.S. DEPARTMENT OF THE INTERIOR require MINING operators generally to keep waste materials off steep slopes, preserve topsoil for reclamation, prevent damage to water systems, stabilize and revegetate waste piles, and notify the public about blasting schedules. Miners must meet special performance and reclamation standards for mining on alluvial valley floors in arid and semi-arid areas, as well as on prime farmland and steep slopes. The law also established a permitting system that requires mine operators to submit descriptions of their mining goals and reclamation plans. Operators have to obtain performance bonds to cover the full cost of reclamation.

To reclaim abandoned mines, including the processes of sealing off the shafts and using the land for farming and other purposes, the law set up the ABANDONED MINE RECLAMATION FUND. It also established the Office of Surface Mining Reclamation and Enforcement in the U.S. DEPARTMENT OF THE INTERIOR to enforce mining regulations and oversee reclamation activities. However, reclamation is very expensive and difficult because topsoil is dispersed during mining operations, and it may take centuries or even longer for mined land to regain its former fertility. Fragile western sites with scarce rainfall and limited original vegetation are particularly difficult to restore.

To overcome industry opposition to the legislation, environmentalists made several key concessions. Congress agreed to focus the bill on strip mining for coal, rather than adding restrictions on mining operations for copper and other minerals. The law also contains several exemptions and it permits mining operators to engage in MOUNTAINTOP REMOVAL without having subsequently to return the land to its original contours—an issue that erupted as a major controversy in the late 1990s because of the devastating environmental effects of blasting the tops off mountains.

In the early 1980s, Interior Secretary JAMES G. WATT rewrote many of the law's regulations to provide REGULATORY RELIEF. But his efforts to give states more discretion foundered. With the federal Office of Surface Mining Reclamation and Enforcement facing steep budget cuts and with state regulators working with limited funding, states lacked the resources to enforce the law. General Accounting Office reports in the 1980s warned that fines often were not levied for mining violations. Since the mid-1980s, funding for federal surface mining programs has increased. However, surface mining remains a significant environmental concern, with about one thousand additional acres disturbed each week in coal mining operations (see also MINING).

Sustainable Fisheries Act

Passed by Congress in 1996 as a rewrite of the MAGNUSON FISHERY MANAGEMENT AND CONSERVATION ACT, the Sustainable Fisheries Act was a significant victory for conservationists seeking to end OVERFISHING. The law requires the NATIONAL MARINE FISHERIES SERVICE to place a greater emphasis on restoring fish populations and protecting habitat from being damaged by development, pollution, and other threats. It was spurred by concerns that the Magnuson Fishery Management and Conservation Act had failed to stabilize populations of commercially valuable fish.

Sustainable use

When natural resources can be harvested for year after year without becoming depleted, this is referred to as sustainable use. U.S. laws promote sustainable use in several ways. The 1960 Multiple-Use Sustained-Yield Act and other laws seek to limit logging in NATIONAL FORESTS to sustainable levels; the 1992 ENERGY POLICY ACT encourages the development of renewable energy sources; the 1996 SUSTAINABLE FISHERIES ACT guards against the depletion of fish populations; and agricultural laws administered by the NATURAL RESOURCES CONSERVATION SERVICE attempt to help farmers increase yields without depleting the soil. Despite such policies, U.S. consumption of food, energy, consumer products, and other goods severely strains the environment.

International policymakers promote "sustainable development"—the concept that countries can build their economies without depleting their natural resources. The 1992 EARTH SUMMIT produced a blueprint for achieving sustainable development in the twenty-first century.

Swampbuster

Under 1985 omnibus farm legislation, farmers who plow under WETLANDS generally lose federal subsidies. Known as swampbuster, this provision is highly controversial, with many growers and PRIVATE PROPERTY RIGHTS advocates contending it is an overzealous government intrusion into farming. Environmentalists, however, worry that the program has been enforced haphazardly, especially because more than one million tracts of agricultural land that may contain wetlands have yet to receive formal wetlands determinations from the government. In 1996, lawmakers made the program somewhat more flexible by exempting penalties under certain conditions and allowing farmers to mitigate wetlands losses.

T

Three-Mile Island

The worst nuclear power accident in U.S. history occurred on March 28, 1979, at the nuclear power plant on Three-Mile Island, near Harrisburg, Pennsylvania. As the result of a number of factors—including the shutting down of auxiliary cooling pumps for maintenance—water flooded the reactor building and the core overheated. Technicians warned of the possibility of a catastrophic explosion or a nuclear fuel meltdown.

On March 30 Gov. Richard L. Thornburgh asked pregnant women and young children living within five miles of the plant to evacuate. However, conflicting information about the dangers and the lack of any prior evacuation plans caused considerable confusion. By April 3 officials said they had the situation under control.

Although catastrophe was averted, the accident crystallized the public's fears about nuclear power. President JIMMY CARTER convened a commission—named after its chairman, Dartmouth University president John Kemeny—that concluded in 1979 that "fundamental changes are necessary if those [nuclear power] risks are to be kept within tolerable limits."

Seven years later, an explosion at the Soviet Union's poorly designed Chernobyl nuclear power

Support for nuclear energy plummeted after a radiation leak at the Three-Mile Island plant in Pennsylvania in 1979. Today, nuclear energy generates about 20 percent of U.S. electricity. Source: Tim Shaffer, Reuters

plant complex killed dozens of people and released dangerous amounts of radiation that may ultimately cause thousands of cancer deaths. The disaster whipped up further political resistance in the United States to building new nuclear plants, leaving the domestic nuclear power industry all but moribund. (See also NUCLEAR ENERGY.)

Tier 2 standards

The 1990 amendments to the CLEAN AIR ACT required the ENVIRONMENTAL PROTECTION AGENCY to impose tighter emission, or "tier 1," standards on automobiles and light trucks beginning with the 1994–1996 model years. The law also directed the agency to study the need for further reductions, known as "tier 2." After notifying Congress that more stringent pollution measures were necessary, the Clinton administration in 1999 unveiled tier 2 standards requiring cars and light trucks to significantly reduce emissions of carbon monoxide, formaldehyde, nitrogen oxides, nonmethane organic gases, and PARTICULATE MATTER. The proposed standards will be phased in during a six-year period beginning in 2004. For the first time, new SPORT UTILITY VEHICLES, vans, and light trucks that weigh up to eighty-five hundred pounds will have to meet the same standards as cars.

To help automakers comply, the tier 2 standards also require that the sulfur content in gasoline be cut from an average of about 340 parts per million to 30 parts per million by 2004. This requirement is important because sulfur can limit the ability of catalysts in vehicle emission control systems to convert pollutants to less harmful gases. Not surprisingly, officials of the petroleum industry objected to the new standards (although their protests were comparatively muted); environmentalists hailed them.

Timber subsidies

See BELOW-COST TIMBER SALES.

Tongass National Forest

The seventeen-million-acre Tongass National Forest in southeastern Alaska is the largest of the nation's NATIONAL FORESTS and perhaps the most environmentally significant temperate rain forest in the world. The rugged land, designated as a national forest by President THEODORE ROOSEVELT in 1907, contains lush coastal tracts of spruce, hemlock, and cedar trees that provide habitat for numerous rare plant and animal species—and wood for lumber mills.

The question of whether to protect this vast region or use part of it for logging has embroiled policymakers for decades. President JIMMY CARTER designated large portions of the Tongass as wilderness in 1978, despite protests by local timber companies such as the Ketchikan Pulp Co. and the Alaska Pulp Corp. Officials in the administrations of Presidents RONALD REAGAN and GEORGE BUSH, however, permitted annual logging of about 450 million board feet, even though environmentalists objected.(A board foot is one square foot of lumber one inch thick. About forty acres of the Tongass forest could produce one million board feet.)

Trying to strike a compromise, the U.S. FOREST SERVICE announced a plan in 1997 to reduce annual logging to 267 million board feet or less and protect 1.1 million acres considered critical for wildlife. Predictably, the plan made nobody happy. Loggers objected to the reduced harvesting, which they feared would further depress the already weak local economy. Environmentalists warned that the plan would expose OLD-GROWTH forests to logging.

Efforts to protect the forest in recent years have been complicated by the fact that both of Alaska's Republican senators chair powerful committees, and they favor increased logging. Accordingly, when President BILL CLINTON in 2000 announced a policy to protect much of the national forest system from road building, he left out the Tongass—even though that exemption drew fire from the environmental community.

Total maximum daily loads

Total maximum daily loads (TMDLs) are the maximum amounts of pollutants that may be discharged into highly polluted bodies of water. Under a controversial provision of the CLEAN WATER ACT, state officials are supposed to establish TMDLs for bodies of water that remain degraded even after the use of standard pollution controls.

To do this, officials should analyze all sources of pollution and come up with a plan to reduce the total amount of pollutants entering the water. Then they must take the politically difficult step of assigning discharge limits to the different classes of polluters, such as farmers, municipal facilities, and factory operators. In other words, all polluters of a waterway would have to operate under a common cap.

Officials have been understandably reluctant to enforce this provision, contained in section 303 of the Clean Water Act. Instead, they have focused on easily identifiable POINT SOURCES of pollution that discharge waste directly into waterways. But after

environmental groups filed more than twenty lawsuits, the ENVIRONMENTAL PROTECTION AGENCY (EPA) announced in 1999 that it would begin requiring states to implement the TMDLs.

If the regulations are widely implemented, they could help clean up many of the estimated 40 percent of the nation's waterways that remain significantly polluted. The regulations could also spur a market in WATER POLLUTION, with polluters that are able to reduce discharges more than the law requires selling their excess ability to others that are continuing to pollute. Such a scheme would be similar to the EMISSIONS TRADING program of the CLEAN AIR ACT.

However, the EPA proposal is sparking major legislative and legal battles. Affected industries, such as farming and forestry, worry that the regulations could force them out of business. State officials, who want the program to be implemented more flexibly, contend that tracking down the many diffuse sources of pollution would be so complex and expensive that they could not effectively implement the regulations.

Because of such objections, rural lawmakers of both parties are lining up against imposing TMDLs. They argue that the law does not explicitly mention regulating NONPOINT SOURCE POLLUTION, such as motor oil and other contaminants that wash off streets into streams. "I don't believe the EPA has the statutory authority to implement these proposed rules," Rep. Joe Skeen, R-N.M., said in 1999.

Toxic Substances Control Act

Passed by Congress in 1976 after five years of debate, the Toxic Substances Control Act (PL 94-

469) established a national policy that adequate data be developed on the health and environmental effects of chemicals. The measure was the first to require premarket testing for potentially dangerous chemicals, and it made data collection the responsibility of manufacturers and processors. The law singled out a highly toxic class of industrial chemicals known as polychlorinated biphenyls (PCBS), calling for a complete ban on the manufacturing and distribution of them by 1979.

Environmentalists regarded passage of the law as a major victory. Although it did not impose as strict a regulatory structure as they would have liked, they hoped to strengthen it over the years. Since 1976 Congress has added provisions to reduce exposure to ASBESTOS, RADON, and LEAD.

Toxics Release Inventory

The Toxics Release Inventory is a publicly available, online database maintained by the ENVIRONMENTAL PROTECTION AGENCY that reports the releases of hundreds of designated toxic substances into the air, water, and land. Created under the 1986 EMERGENCY PLANNING AND COMMUNITY

U.S. Toxic Releases by Industry, 1988, 1995, and 1997

| Industry | Pounds of toxic substances released | | | Percentage change, 1988–1997 |
	1988	1995	1997	
Apparel	1,048,961	1,260,746	817,329	−22.1
Chemicals	1,055,611,740	546,643,304	519,129,158	−50.8
Electrical equipment	134,042,669	31,872,667	26,158,202	−80.5
Fabricated metals	163,833,118	94,584,794	81,172,054	−50.5
Food	8,414,635	5,224,392	5,213,000	−38.0
Furniture	62,412,288	42,164,977	24,892,695	−60.1
Leather	13,699,921	4,407,246	4,208,084	−69.3
Lumber	33,056,013	31,542,259	25,091,620	−24.1
Machinery	70,744,411	23,610,134	19,121,806	−73.0
Paper	207,840,633	179,640,320	181,559,981	−12.6
Petroleum	73,096,751	42,990,233	42,850,660	−41.4
Plastics	158,575,935	113,412,580	95,304,534	−39.9
Primary metals	649,920,076	495,602,763	616,157,848	−5.2
Printing	61,234,598	30,967,327	24,484,493	−60.0
Stone/clay/glass	38,754,943	21,956,660	27,586,607	−28.8
Textiles	36,875,477	16,021,698	16,941,074	−54.1
Tobacco	251,946	95,226	196,961	−21.8
Transportation equipment	215,000,245	116,336,180	96,806,810	−55.0
Miscellaneous	32,750,257	13,354,606	9,804,514	−70.1
Other	322,909,461	140,376,830	116,386,106	−64.0
Total	3,395,866,689	1,964,926,244	1,941,870,147	−42.8
Federal facilities	NA	6,730,862	3,707,932	N/A

Source: U.S. Environmental Protection Agency, Office of Pollution Prevention and Toxics, *1997 Toxics Release Inventory: Public Data Release* (Washington, D.C.: EPA, 1999).

Notes: Figures include onsite and offsite releases. Federal facilities were not required to report before 1994. NA = not available. N/A = not applicable.

RIGHT-TO-KNOW ACT, the inventory has proven to be a useful indicator of toxic emissions, even though it excludes many types of releases.

The 1998 inventory showed that 7.3 billion pounds of toxic materials had been released during the year. That total dwarfed earlier reports because, under a 1997 executive order by President BILL CLINTON, it included releases from hardrock MINING and electric power plants for the first time. But the volume of releases among manufacturing industries that had been tracked regularly fell by about 45 percent since the first report in 1988 (for toxic releases by industry, see table). Texas, Tennessee, and Louisiana have been among the worst offenders on the inventories, although the report's broader scope in 1998 meant that four mining states led the list: Nevada, Arizona, Utah, and Alaska.

The reports do not provide a comprehensive picture of toxic contamination. They lack information on human exposure or the specific toxicity of chemicals. In some ways they underreport the situation by excluding nonindustrial companies such as dry cleaners and facilities that employ fewer than ten people. In other ways they overreport by including chemicals that are released within plant or mining site boundaries (although environmentalists contend that such releases often make their way eventually into the air, soil, or water). Nevertheless, the Toxics Release Inventory provides environmentalists with a powerful weapon by illustrating the nature and sources of toxic substances near homes and businesses across the country.

Trans-Alaskan Pipeline Authorization Act

The passage of the Trans-Alaskan Pipeline Authorization Act of 1973 (PL 93-153) represented a major victory by the oil industry over the powerful environmental movement of the early 1970s. The act resulted from the first of a series of significant battles that have erupted in the United States and other countries over permitting energy development in fragile arctic areas. It could portend trouble for environmentalists trying to prevent development in such places as the ARCTIC NATIONAL WILDLIFE REFUGE.

The pipeline battle had its roots in 1968, when an Atlantic Richfield Company well struck oil on Alaska's North Slope. Amid estimates that the North Slope could contain more than one hundred billion barrels of oil—more than all other known U.S. oil reserves combined—eight companies set up the Trans-Alaska Pipeline System (later the Alyeska Pipeline Service Company) as a joint enterprise to build an access road and four-foot pipeline from the wells to the port city of Valdez in southern Alaska. There, the oil would be shipped to the continental United States. Much of the pipeline route crossed federal lands, sparking concerns that it would block caribou migrations and damage the delicate arctic environment. Opponents also warned that the tanker traffic between Valdez and Washington's Puget Sound could imperil biologically rich coastal waters.

Environmentalists successfully fought the plan in courts. They forced the government to issue detailed ENVIRONMENTAL IMPACT STATEMENTS under the NATIONAL ENVIRONMENTAL POLICY ACT and won a ruling that the proposed right-of-way for the pipeline across public lands would far exceed the twenty-five feet on either side permitted under the Mineral Leasing Act of 1920. But at the height of the 1973 energy crisis, Congress overwhelmingly passed the Trans-Alaskan Pipeline Authorization Act, which directed the U.S. DEPARTMENT OF THE INTERIOR immediately to authorize construction of the 789-mile pipeline. The bill removed the 25-foot limit and barred future challenges to the pipeline based on the National Environmental Policy Act. It also expedited procedures for consideration of other court challenges.

Although the carefully constructed pipeline has not suffered major accidents, environmentalists' fears were realized when the EXXON VALDEZ spilled an estimated eleven million gallons of North Slope oil in Prince William Sound, devastating the biologically diverse coastal waters.

Transboundary pollution

Pollutants regularly cross national boundaries, often affecting neighboring countries or even the entire earth. Such transboundary pollution occurs because wind and ocean currents transport emissions thousands of miles. This means that even those nations that undertake antipollution measures may suffer environmental degradation because of industrial activities far beyond their borders. For example, some contaminants in the GREAT LAKES can be traced to Mexico; Swedish forests are in decline because of industrial emissions in Germany and England; and remote regions in Greenland and Antarctica suffer from contamination from PESTICIDES and heavy metals. Some pollutants, such as chlorofluorocarbons, or CFCS, affect the entire world by causing changes to the atmosphere. Environmentalists sometimes use the term "global commons" to describe the interconnectedness of the world environment.

Transboundary pollution problems have forced an unprecedented amount of international cooperation on environmental issues. The first major conference to focus on transboundary pollution was the 1972 Conference on the Human Environment, in Stockholm, Sweden. Although the 113-nation conference was important mostly as a symbol of growing environmental concerns, it led to the creation of the U.N. ENVIRONMENT PROGRAMME to help coordinate international environmental efforts. Twenty years later, the Conference on Environment and Development, known as the EARTH SUMMIT, drew representatives from more than 170 countries and encouraged international efforts to tackle such environmental threats as GLOBAL WARMING and DEFORESTATION.

International environmental talks have largely focused on three issues: ACID RAIN, OZONE DEPLETION, and global warming. Of the initiatives undertaken to address these issues, efforts to phase out use of ozone-destroying chemicals have been the most successful. In 1987 forty-seven nations agreed to reduce such chemical use under the MONTREAL PROTOCOL ON SUBSTANCES THAT DEPLETE THE OZONE LAYER. Acid rain, however, remains a significant problem throughout much of the world, especially because of the burgeoning use of coal-burning power plants in developing countries such as China. Global warming also has resisted easy solutions, largely because of disputes over how to apportion restrictions on emissions of GREENHOUSE GASES. AIR POLLUTION issues aside, nations also have taken steps to protect the marine environment with the LAW OF THE SEA treaty and preserve the pristine nature of Antarctica by banning MINING under the ANTARCTICA TREATY.

In many ways, tackling transboundary pollution is more difficult than solving domestic environmental problems. One reason is that the polluting nations frequently are not interested in costly antipollution measures unless their own environment is affected. In the 1970s, for example, Scandinavian countries suffering forest damage from acid rain had little success in persuading Germany and England to curb their emissions until those countries also began to suffer from the effects of the emissions.

Second, nations are fiercely independent, and they tend to regard international economic agreements as potentially undermining their sovereignty. Some conservatives in the U.S. Congress, for example, are so resistant to international interference that they object to funding for a United Nations program that designates U.S. parks as WORLD HERITAGE SITES.

Third (and perhaps most important), nations have profoundly conflicting economic interests. These interests often pit northern industrial countries against less developed countries in the south. President GEORGE BUSH, for example, refused to sign the 1992 CONVENTION ON BIOLOGICAL DIVERSITY because he was concerned that it would have committed the United States to share environmentally benign technological innovations with poorer nations, potentially costing U.S. companies their competitive advantage. More recently, many members of Congress have criticized the KYOTO PROTOCOL, a treaty designed to minimize global warming, on the grounds that it could set back domestic industries and undermine American supremacy. Conversely, developing nations balk at strict curbs on deforestation, which contributes to global warming, because developing the forested lands will reap short-term economic benefits. These countries want more money and other forms of aid from wealthy countries in exchange for setting aside biologically diverse land.

Nevertheless, the severity of the environmental problems is spurring an unprecedented amount of cooperation on environmental and economic matters. Some U.S. policymakers believe that their efforts to curb air pollution may be of little avail if Brazil destroys most of its rain forests or if China builds hundreds of coal-burning power plants. To foster international cooperation, tens of thousands of NONGOVERNMENTAL ORGANIZATIONS in the United States and other nations are working together to promote sustainable development. The U.S. Agency for International Development plays a leading role in working with such private organizations, as well as with government officials in developing countries, to advance economic strategies that do not harm the environment. (See also SUSTAINABLE USE.)

Tropical rain forests

Tropical rain forests are a prime focus of international conservation efforts because they are believed to be the most diverse ecosystems on Earth. The largest surviving areas are in South America's Amazon basin, central Africa, and Indonesia. Biologists estimate that tropical rain forests harbor roughly one-half of the world's species, and they worry that intense DEFORESTATION could impoverish the earth's "genetic library" and impair research efforts into the treatment of diseases. The forests' dense vegetation, which stores carbon, helps offset the effects of GLOBAL WARMING. By affecting local weather patterns and regulating water runoff, the forests also minimize soil erosion, flooding, and desertification.

The tropical rain forests cover about three million square miles, which is perhaps half their original land area. They are under siege from a multitude of interests: slash-and-burn farmers, logging companies, miners, developers, and others. Wide swaths of forests were destroyed in 1997 and 1998 because of catastrophic fires. At the current rate of

A prime focus of international conservation efforts, tropical rain forests are prized for their biodiversity. Visitors to Panama's Gamboa Rain Forest Resort, a popular destination with "ecotourists," may explore the forest's dense vegetation and natural beauty by riding an aerial tram.
Source: Alberto Lowe, Reuters

destruction, scientists believe that only remnants of rain forests will remain by the middle of the twenty-first century.

Although saving the tropical rain forests is a top priority of environmentalists, it is a relatively minor issue in Washington, D.C. Lawmakers have focused more on whether to allow expanded logging in temperate rain forests in the United States, such as Alaska's TONGASS NATIONAL FOREST. Nevertheless, Congress in 1998 passed a DEBT-FOR-NATURE bill to slow tropical rain forest destruction. The legislation seeks to reward developing countries that take steps to preserve forested areas by forgiving debts that those countries owe to the United States. In addition, the Clinton administration joined more than thirty other nations in pledging a total of $2.75 billion to the GLOBAL ENVIRONMENT FACILITY to promote environmental initiatives worldwide. It also worked with other Group of Seven (or G7) industrialized nations in pledging funding to save the Brazilian Amazon.

Turtle excluder devices

Turtle excluder devices, or TEDs, are designed to prevent endangered sea turtles from drowning in shrimp nets. The devices consist of panels of large mesh webbing or metal grids that are inserted into the nets in such a way that shrimp are funneled through and trapped, while turtles and other larger marine creatures are deflected out. Shrimpers, who say the devices cause them to lose as much as 30 percent of their catch, sometimes deride them as "trawler eliminator devices." Government tests, however, have indicated that no more than 10 percent of the catch is lost.

The devices have sparked heated battles in the United States and in other countries. With U.S. shrimp boats killing at least eleven thousand rare sea turtles yearly (and possibly several times that number, according to the National Academy of Sciences), the NATIONAL MARINE FISHERIES SERVICE issued a rule in 1987 requiring all shrimpers to use TEDs by the spring of 1988. When shrimp fishers protested, lawmakers agreed to add language to a 1988 ENDANGERED SPECIES ACT reauthorization bill (PL 100-478) that delayed the TED mandate until May 1989 for offshore shrimpers and until spring 1990 for shrimpers in inland bays and sounds. The devices became mandatory after repeated court battles.

To protect domestic fishers, Congress in 1989 passed legislation (PL 101-162) that amended the Endangered Species Act to prohibit shrimp imports from nations whose fishing practices harmed turtles. The administration of President GEORGE BUSH in 1991 accordingly banned shrimp imports from several Caribbean nations. But environmentalists wanted a broader ban. In 1992 the Earth Island Institute went to court to force sanctions against all nations whose shrimpers had failed to reduce sea turtle deaths by 97 percent—the rate credited to the U.S. shrimp industry's use of TEDs.

After a series of legal battles, the International Court of Trade in 1995 ruled that countries that export shrimp to the United States must adopt turtle conservation measures. Shrimp-exporting nations, led by India, Malaysia, Pakistan, and Thailand, struck back by filing a complaint with the WORLD TRADE ORGANIZATION, alleging that the U.S. requirement violated free trade. In 1998 the World Trade Organization ruled against the United States, leaving the future of international TED requirements uncertain. (See also BYCATCH.)

U

Underground injection wells

Companies sometimes dispose of liquid HAZ-ARDOUS WASTE by injecting it into geologic formations that may be as deep as several thousand feet beneath the earth's surface. This "deep well injection" technique has been used since the 1950s, at first with little regulation. Careless injection techniques can contaminate underground drinking water supplies. In 1975, for example, injection wells in Texas and Louisiana leaked hazardous waste into aquifers.

Several laws, including the 1974 SAFE DRINKING WATER ACT and the 1976 RESOURCE CONSERVATION AND RECOVERY ACT, direct the ENVIRONMENTAL PROTECTION AGENCY to regulate underground injection. The agency has banned the injection of wastes near underground sources of drinking water and imposed other standards to minimize the possibility of leaks. In 1999 it issued rules for an estimated six hundred thousand shallow underground wells, prohibiting the construction of new large-capacity cesspools and motor vehicle waste disposal wells.

Underground storage tanks

The ENVIRONMENTAL PROTECTION AGENCY (EPA) estimates that there are at least 370,000 leaks of gasoline and other substances from under-ground storage tanks in the United States, threatening GROUNDWATER and creating other environmental hazards. Many of the nation's several million chemical storage tanks are at abandoned gasoline or industrial sites, and their contents and exact locations frequently are unknown.

Congress first addressed this problem through 1984 amendments to the RESOURCE CONSERVATION AND RECOVERY ACT. The amendments directed the EPA to set standards for installing the tanks, such as requiring that they have double walls or be placed in concrete vaults. Small-business owners have criticized the requirements as costly and unnecessary, and about 40 percent of active tanks failed to meet a 1998 requirement that all tanks be upgraded, replaced, or shut down.

In 1986 lawmakers rewriting SUPERFUND law created the Leaking Underground Storage Tank Trust Fund to pay for cleanups in those cases in which the owner or operator of the tank fails to clean up a spill. The money is raised through a 0.1-cent-per-gallon motor fuels tax, which generates about $150 million yearly. The 1986 law also requires most tank owners and operators to demonstrate that they have the financial means to pay for cleanups and property damage compensation. Most states have established assurance funds to help reimburse the costs of cleanups and save tank owners and operators the cost of purchasing private insurance.

To speed the cleanup of leaking tanks, the House of Representatives passed legislation in 1997 that would have required the EPA to transfer at least 85 percent of the money in the trust fund every year to states and would have given the states more flexibility over spending it. However, the measure died in the Senate.

U.N. Environment Programme

The U.N. Environment Programme was created in 1972 at the Conference on the Human Environment in Stockholm, Sweden, to "monitor, coordinate, and catalyze" international environmental activities. It plays an important role in reporting on global environmental trends and directing the attention of world policymakers to such problems as international shipments of HAZARDOUS WASTE, OVERFISHING, and HABITAT LOSS. It has also encouraged such global agreements as the 1987 MONTREAL PROTOCOL ON SUBSTANCES THAT DEPLETE THE OZONE LAYER.

Although most international organizations are based in industrialized nations, the U.N. Environment Programme is in Nairobi, Kenya. It aggressively advocates strong measures to protect the environment. "Our knowledge of ecosystems has increased dramatically, but it has simply not kept pace with our ability to alter them," Klaus Toepfer, the executive director, said in 2000. "We can continue blindly altering Earth's ecosystems, or we can learn to use them more sustainably."

Other United Nations agencies complement the work of the Environment Programme. They include the U.N. Development Programme, which distributes funding for environmental programs, and the U.N. Commission on Sustainable Development, which monitors the implementation of programs initiated at the 1992 EARTH SUMMIT.

Unfunded mandates

An unfunded mandate is a costly requirement that the U.S. Congress imposes on state or local governments without providing money to pay for it. Conservatives have long pressed for restrictions on unfunded mandates, although many environmentalists suspect that their efforts are really backdoor attempts to undermine federal regulations. In 1995 Congress passed legislation (PL 104-4) making it more difficult to impose an unfunded mandate. The law specifies that any legislative proposal that would impose unfunded costs of more than $50 million on state and local governments is subject to a formal objection or "point of order"—although a majority of lawmakers can simply vote to override the point of order. The law also requires agencies to conduct cost-benefit analyses of many new regulations. (See also REGULATORY RELIEF.)

Uranium Mill Tailings Radiation Control Act

Congress in 1978 passed the Uranium Mill Tailings Radiation Control Act (PL 96-604) to clean up an estimated twenty-five million tons of potentially hazardous uranium wastes. The wastes, known as tailings, had been generated in eight western states and Pennsylvania, where twenty-four mills had produced uranium for nuclear weapons for the U.S. government. At one time, the wastes were considered so harmless that they often were used in building construction. However, scientists and environmentalists began warning that the tailings posed a cancer risk because they contained low levels of the radioactive element radium, which decays to produce RADON.

Destruction of wetlands is one of the environmental problems caused by urban sprawl. This residential development abuts tidal wetlands near Maryland's Chesapeake Bay. Source: Scott J. Ferrell, Congressional Quarterly

Under the law, the U.S. DEPARTMENT OF ENERGY is responsible for cleaning up the sites under the guidance of the NUCLEAR REGULATORY COMMISSION and the ENVIRONMENTAL PROTECTION AGENCY. The federal government pays 90 percent of the cleanup costs, with the affected states paying the remaining 10 percent. The law also provides for stricter controls on the handling and disposal of wastes resulting from uranium processing. Prior to the legislation, the federal government had no explicit authority to regulate the wastes. (See also NUCLEAR WASTE.)

Urban sprawl

Since the post–World War II housing boom, the United States has become suburbanized—so much so that by 1990 the country had become the first in history to have more suburbanites than rural and city residents combined. Bulldozing land for housing developments and malls causes a host of environmental problems, including the destruction of WETLANDS and other ecologically important habitat, increased AIR POLLUTION from traffic congestion, and polluted RUNOFF from suburban streets.

Sprawl also is contributing to the destruction of an estimated three million acres of farmland annually and sparking concerns that new subdivisions are scarring the dramatic western landscape. Despite environmental concerns, the American dream of owning a house with a yard is making it difficult to restrain growth.

Urban sprawl is mainly a local and state issue. States such as Maryland and Vermont have mounted especially aggressive efforts to designate areas for green space. But the issue has also attracted the attention of federal officials, who in the 1990s began to support efforts to restrain growth. Congress approved funding to protect farms from being swallowed up by developers as part of 1996 farm legislation (PL 104-127). After voters in thirty-one states in 1998 approved more than 150 ballot initiatives encouraging growth management and inner-city revitalization, the Clinton administration unveiled a LANDS LEGACY INITIATIVE to try to help state and local governments preserve open space and enhance parks.

Some federal transportation programs also encourage more compact development. For years, environmentalists complained that building new roads spurred new development instead of relieving congestion. The 1991 INTERMODAL SURFACE TRANSPORTATION EFFICIENCY ACT tried to take aim at that problem by setting aside money for bike and pedestrian paths, boosting mass transit funding, and directing local officials in heavily polluted areas to focus on alternative modes of transportation instead of building more roads. In 1999 environmentalists won a landmark court battle that forced the sprawling city of Atlanta to pare back its highway construction program or face the loss of federal transportation money.

The United States is hardly alone in facing problems with urban sprawl. Cities are growing worldwide at four times the rate of rural areas, and the number of people living in urban areas is projected to double between 1990 and 2025. This growth is causing severe environmental and health prob-lems, with millions of people living in slums that lack adequate water, sanitation, or garbage collection services. Some countries, such as Indonesia, are attempting to restrict development in environmentally sensitive areas while boosting basic services in crowded communities.

U.S. Army Corps of Engineers

A civilian-run agency of the Pentagon, the Army Corps of Engineers has the responsibility of taming the nation's waterways. The agency constructs DAMS and flood-control projects, dredges navigable channels, and operates hydropower plants. The corps, which began overseeing civil engineering projects in the early nineteenth century, has traditionally emphasized economic development over conservation. As a result, its projects have devastated the environment by interfering with the natural ebb and flow of thousands of miles of rivers and filling in ecologically sensitive backwaters and WETLANDS. In many cases, its attempts to reroute rivers appeared to exacerbate flooding while spurring little barge traffic or other economic growth. Costly attempts by the corps to replenish ocean beaches are also controversial, because they can change the ecosystems of BARRIER ISLANDS while failing to provide much long-term protection for coastal buildings.

In recent years agency officials have attempted to repair environmental damage by restoring rivers and streams to their natural channels. But such projects often run into local opposition, since cities and farms have developed along the artificially constructed waterways.

Few government agencies have drawn as much environmental criticism as the Army Corps of Engineers. Even as the corps puts an increased emphasis on preserving natural resources, private environmental groups (and sometimes the ENVIRONMENTAL PROTECTION AGENCY) assail dredging plans that would worsen water pollution by slowing down river flow, while burying riverbanks and nearby areas in dredged debris. Fiscal conservatives pile on as well, contending that dozens of corps projects that cost billions of dollars are a waste of taxpayers' money.

Congress deserves some of the blame for authorizing questionable projects that are popular with voters back home. On the other hand, the corps may be supplying lawmakers with unreliable information. In 2000 a SENATE ENVIRONMENT AND PUBLIC WORKS subcommittee held hearings into whether the corps inflated the economic benefits of some proposed projects to win increased government funding.

The corps is responsible for approving SECTION 404 permits, which govern the dredging and filling of wetlands under the CLEAN WATER ACT. Environmentalists contend that the corps rarely rejects permit applications. But corps officials at times have proposed expanding the program to require developers to obtain permits before disturbing smaller and more isolated wetlands. The purpose would be to give better protection to all types of wetlands.

In 2000 the Army Corps of Engineers had about thirty-six thousand employees and an annual budget of more than $11 billion.

U.S. Department of Agriculture

The Agriculture Department is not as identified with environmental issues as is the ENVIRONMEN-

TAL PROTECTION AGENCY (EPA) or the U.S. DEPARTMENT OF THE INTERIOR. However, its conservation programs are designed to help protect nearly 75 percent of the nation's land area, much of which is in private hands. The department's NATURAL RESOURCES CONSERVATION SERVICE works with farmers and other landowners to protect WETLANDS and other wildlife habitat, reduce soil erosion, and prevent farm byproducts such as MANURE from contaminating waterways. The U.S. FOREST SERVICE oversees the 192-million-acre system of NATIONAL FORESTS and RANGELANDS, comprising an area larger than Texas.

The department's agricultural offices generally stay out of environmental battles. Farmers tend to view Agriculture Department officials as sympathetic to their needs, more interested in providing information about PESTICIDES or aiding them with environmentally friendly cropping activities than in mandating certain procedures. Even though environmentalists wish the department would try to wean farmers off ecologically destructive practices, they generally focus their energies on the EPA, which regulates pesticides and tracks AGRICULTURAL RUNOFF. But one Agriculture Department agency is regularly embroiled in environmental battles: the U.S. FOREST SERVICE. For decades, environmentalists and loggers have whipsawed the agency over the issue of regulating timber activities and building roads for logging trucks.

Founded in 1862, the department's initial mission was to assist farmers rather than to protect the environment. But during the dust bowl days of the 1930s, it began to focus on preventing soil erosion. Congress greatly expanded its environmental mandate with 1985 legislation that stressed wetlands protection and created the CONSERVATION RESERVE PROGRAM to pay farmers to set aside environmentally fragile land. The Agriculture Department, which also oversees food stamps and other nutrition programs, has an annual budget of about $50 billion.

U.S. Department of Energy

The often-criticized Energy Department is important to environmentalists because it oversees the cleanup of NUCLEAR WASTE and funds alternative energy and ENERGY EFFICIENCY programs. Created by Congress in 1976, the department frequently has been mired in controversy as a result of poor administration—especially regarding the security of its nuclear weapons program. It has the difficult mandate of trying to promote new uses of energy while encouraging energy conservation.

In the 1980s the department tended to side with advocates of FOSSIL FUELS and NUCLEAR ENERGY, but the Clinton administration placed a greater emphasis on conservation and alternative energy sources such as biofuels. The agency has survived several attempts to dismantle or greatly overhaul it. In 1999 it had a budget of $16.6 billion and about eighteen thousand employees.

Perhaps the department's greatest environmental challenge is cleaning up the nation's nuclear weapons facilities. In the early 1990s it became apparent that a half-century of poor management of the weapons sites had left a legacy of sick and endangered workers, as well as one of the worst contamination problems in the nation. The Clinton administration promised to confront the problem aggressively. It initially estimated that cleanup at the seventeen major military weapons facilities in twelve states would cost $28 billion to $50 billion over five years. Those estimates have since been discarded as overly optimistic. In the late 1990s the

Energy Department concluded that cleaning up more than one hundred nuclear weapons and laboratory sites across the country will cost about $150 billion through 2070. But environmentalists have questioned the quality of the cleanups, and some have warned that the total bill could exceed $250 billion. The enormous cleanup program could turn the Energy Department into the largest environmental agency.

U.S. Department of the Interior

Created in 1849 to take care of the nation's domestic affairs, the U.S. Interior Department has acquired responsibilities that touch on virtually every aspect of resource conservation. The sixty-five-thousand-employee department administers NATIONAL PARKS, wildlife refuges, and other PUBLIC LANDS; enforces the ENDANGERED SPECIES ACT and other fish and wildlife laws; conserves WETLANDS and estuarine areas; regulates MINING activities; and oversees dam construction. It also administers Native American lands and programs, which is an important environmental function because western tribal lands contain a high proportion of the nation's mineral wealth. However, it does not focus on antipollution regulations (that is the responsibility of the ENVIRONMENTAL PROTECTION AGENCY).

For the better part of a century, the Interior Department has been a battleground between those wishing to conserve the nation's natural resources and those wishing to use them for profit. Its mandate—to ensure "balanced use" of natural resources—places it in the center of conflicts between environmentalists, recreational users, ranchers, miners, energy companies, and others. The Interior Department also perches precariously on a regional divide: most public lands are in the West, where there is simmering resentment of federal intrusion. As a result, interior officials have been unreliable advocates for conservation. Tensions between the department and the environmental community erupted into open warfare when President RONALD REAGAN's controversial interior secretary, JAMES G. WATT, moved to open the public domain to MINING and oil and gas exploration. Subsequent secretaries under Reagan and President GEORGE BUSH were only slightly more sympathetic to environmentalists. Bush's interior secretary, Manuel Lujan Jr., resisted efforts to protect the endangered Graham red squirrel. "Do we have to save every subspecies?" he asked. President BILL CLINTON's interior secretary, BRUCE BABBITT, was far more supportive of environmental protection, and he imposed some restrictions on mining and grazing. But many of his conservation initiatives were thwarted by fierce western resistance.

Each of the Interior Department's agencies has a significant impact on the environment:

The *Bureau of Indian Affairs* oversees more than 55 million acres of tribal lands. Part of the agency's mandate is to help tribes with environmental issues, such as cleaning up HAZARDOUS WASTE sites, managing water supplies, and restoring bison herds. The bureau also focuses on badly needed economic development and education programs. Created in 1834 and often mismanaged, the bureau was placed in the Interior Department in 1973.

The *Bureau of Land Management* is one of the government's most important land agencies, overseeing more acreage than the combined total of the NATIONAL FOREST and NATIONAL PARK systems. Its jurisdiction includes more than 250 million acres of mostly western grasslands, prime timber and mining lands, and wilderness areas. The agency

also is responsible for arranging leases for mineral exploration of the outer continental shelf. Created in 1946 from the Interior Department's Grazing Service and General Land Office, the Bureau of Land Management has suffered from chronic underfunding and a poor management structure. Although it operates under MULTIPLE-USE and sustained yield principles that are similar to those of the U.S. FOREST SERVICE, environmentalists fault it for being far more sympathetic to the demands of developers and ranchers than to their own. However, the bureau also draws fire from the other side by restricting use of its lands.

The *Bureau of Reclamation* was established in 1902 to provide water to the West. During much of the twentieth century, it constructed DAMS and reservoirs that spurred economic development but drowned scenic canyons and devastated aquatic ecosystems. With WATER SCARCITY becoming a growing concern in the West, the Bureau of Reclamation is focusing on balancing water needs while placing a greater emphasis on environmental protection.

The *Minerals Management Service* oversees OFFSHORE DRILLING and other mineral extraction activities on the outer continental shelf. It also oversees mining royalty programs.

The *National Park Service,* established in 1916 to promote both conservation and outdoor recreation, oversees 77 million acres, of which about 65 percent is in Alaska. The 378 units overseen by the park service include "full" national parks such as YELLOWSTONE and Yosemite, as well as national monuments, national seashores and lakeshores, national recreation areas, national battlefields, and historic sites. In recent decades lawmakers have designated dozens of additional historic sites and museums, diverting National Park Service resources from ecologically sensitive parks. Among its environmental activities, the park service catalogs plant and animal species, seeks to restore ecosystems by reintroducing rare species such as WOLVES, and strives to remove EXOTIC SPECIES, which may threaten the environment. However, only about 8 percent of the park service's $1.9 billion budget in 2000 was devoted to natural resource protection.

The *Office of Surface Mining,* created by the 1977 SURFACE MINING CONTROL AND RECLAMATION ACT, is a small agency (its annual budget is less than $300 million) that regulates surface mining activities on federal lands and Indian reservations, as well as in a few states that do not have their own surface mining programs. In addition, the agency restores lands damaged by abandoned mines.

The *U.S. Fish and Wildlife Service* administers the Endangered Species Act. As a result, it often finds itself buffeted by developers who want to clear land or retain economically important dams and by environmentalists who insist on stringent conservation measures. The agency oversees the 93-million-acre NATIONAL WILDLIFE REFUGE SYSTEM, monitors hunting and fishing activities, and operates fish hatcheries. It has come under criticism from environmentalists for emphasizing hunting and fishing over conservation.

The *U.S. Geological Survey,* created in 1879 to classify public lands and explore mineral resources, has broadened its mission to track environmental threats such as exotic species and to develop recovery programs for endangered species (such as those for breeding and rearing whooping cranes). The agency assesses worldwide energy and mineral resources, including oil and gas reserves in such ecologically sensitive areas as the ARCTIC NATIONAL WILDLIFE REFUGE. Since 1996 the agency has also administered the National Biological Service,

which provides information on protecting ecosystems.

U.S. Forest Service

The U.S. Forest Service, a traditional ally of logging and MINING interests, is in the center of a fierce debate over PUBLIC LANDS policy. It oversees the 192-million-acre NATIONAL FOREST system, which includes ecologically sensitive grasslands as well as forested areas. The largest agency in the Agriculture Department, it has an annual budget of $3 billion and employs about thirty thousand people. The Forest Service is charged with the difficult task of balancing MULTIPLE USES on its lands. These include logging and mining activities and outdoor recreation, as well as the protection of watersheds and other environmentally significant features. It charges low or BELOW-COST prices to timber companies to encourage logging (spurring charges that the government is subsidizing the timber industry) but also welcomes hundreds of millions of recreational users every year. Among the Forest Service's responsibilities are maintaining a 373,000-mile road network in the forests, suppressing wildfires, and conducting research on forestry issues.

The United States set up a Bureau of Forestry in 1880 to provide information on timber harvesting and other forest management techniques to private woodlot owners. Congress began setting aside public lands as "forest reserves" in 1891, opening them to commercial logging in 1897 under the Organic Administration Act. At the beginning of the twentieth century, President THEODORE ROOSEVELT and Forest Service chief Gifford Pinchot purchased more than one hundred million acres of land. For many subsequent decades, the Forest Service emphasized logging and mineral extraction to help fuel the nation's economic growth. Congress in 1960 passed the Multiple-Use Sustained-Yield Act, which directed the agency to manage forests for "outdoor recreation, range, timber, watershed, and wildlife and fish purposes." But lawmakers have never given the Forest Service enough guidance on balancing such conflicting uses. As a result, the agency has veered from encouraging more development (especially during the Reagan administration) to sharply restricting logging and other commercial activities (especially during the Clinton administration).

W

Water pollution

Water pollution is a devastating health and environmental problem in much of the world. Numerous pollutants can kill fish and other creatures, render water unsafe for swimming and fishing, contaminate drinking water supplies, and exacerbate water shortages. Wealthy countries such as the United States, Canada, Japan, and many western European nations have improved water quality through sewage treatment and strict environmental regulations. As a result, most of their lakes and rivers are safe for fishing and swimming, and drinking water causes few health problems.

Many developing countries, however, suffer from catastrophic pollution problems because they lack sewage treatment or environmental controls on industrial facilities. In the late 1990s some 1.4 billion people did not have access to safe drinking water, and 2.9 billion lacked adequate sanitation, according to estimates reported by the World Resources Institute—a situation that may be worsening because of WATER SCARCITY. Epidemiologists blame dirty water for causing 80 percent of the diseases in developing countries, including diarrhea, hepatitis, and cholera. Throughout the 1990s, developing countries invested more money in water and sewage treatment plants, thanks in part to international funding. But they are facing mounting problems with industrial discharges that can contaminate both surface and GROUNDWATER.

There are many types of pollutants that threaten water, including microorganisms such as typhoid and cholera that cause infectious diseases, oxygen-demanding wastes such as sewage that deplete oxygen needed by fish, nutrients that spur ALGAL BLOOMS and kill fish, inorganic toxins such as heavy metals and acids that can poison both people and wildlife, and organic chemicals such as PESTICIDES that have highly toxic effects. The pollutants come from numerous point and nonpoint sources (see tables showing major sources of water pollution). POINT SOURCES, such as factories, sewage treatment plants, and MINING operations discharge pollutants from specific locations. NONPOINT SOURCES, which are harder to regulate because they are scattered and diffuse, include farms, construction sites, logging areas, and city streets and lawns. A major nonpoint source of pollution is the atmosphere, because air pollutants frequently settle into water bodies.

Aquatic environments can also be disrupted by DAMS, GARBAGE, and industrial processes that produce heat. Another environmental threat is the overpumping of groundwater, which is used for drinking water and agriculture. When the groundwater level drops, salt water can begin to intrude into the aquifer. In addition, surface water bodies that rely on the aquifer may begin to diminish, and the land itself can sink.

Even the oceans are showing the strains of pollution. Although the United States and other countries have enacted laws against the dumping of waste at sea, AGRICULTURAL RUNOFF and other types of pollution appear to be depleting local

Leading Sources of Pollution in Rivers and Streams

	Assessed river miles (percent)	Impaired river miles (percent)
Agriculture	20.27	58.62
Hydromodification	6.86	19.83
Urban runoff/storm sewers	3.84	11.09
Municipal point sources	3.45	9.99
Resource extraction	2.99	8.66
Forestry	2.38	6.87
Land disposal	2.37	6.84
Habitat modification	2.19	6.33

Source: U.S. Environmental Protection Agency, Office of Water, *The Quality of Our Nation's Waters: A Summary of the National Water Quality Inventory: 1998 Report to Congress,* Figure 4 (Washington, D.C.: EPA, 2000), 7.

Notes: The United States has 3,662,255 miles of rivers and streams. In 1998 states and other jurisdictions assessed 23 percent (842,319) of those miles, focusing primarily on perennial streams (those that flow year round). Of the assessed miles, 65 percent fully support designated uses and 35 percent are impaired.

Leading Sources of Pollution in Lakes, Reservoirs, and Ponds

	Assessed lake acres (percent)	Impaired lake acres (percent)
Agriculture	13.84	30.61
Hydromodification	6.75	14.93
Urban runoff/storm sewers	5.33	11.79
Municipal point sources	4.96	10.96
Atmospheric deposition	3.53	7.81
Industrial point sources	2.88	6.36
Habitat modification	2.39	5.29
Land disposal	2.18	4.82

Source: U.S. Environmental Protection Agency, Office of Water, *The Quality of Our Nation's Waters: A Summary of the National Water Quality Inventory: 1998 Report to Congress,* Figure 7 (Washington, D.C.: EPA, 2000), 9.

Notes: The United States has 41,593,748 acres of lakes, reservoirs, and ponds. In 1998 states and other jurisdictions assessed 42 percent (about 17.4 million) of those acres. Of the assessed acres, 55 percent fully support designated uses and 45 percent are impaired.

populations of fish and other marine organisms. Researchers have identified about fifty "dead zones" in coastal areas. One of the largest, in the Gulf of Mexico, is caused by excessive fertilizers and other substances that flow down the Mississippi River. The marine environment is also degraded by plastic substances that can entangle, choke, or poison marine life, and by garbage that has become so ubiquitous that even remote beaches are littered with debris from thousands of miles away.

The United States relies on a web of complex federal laws to ensure water quality. Foremost among these are the 1972 CLEAN WATER ACT, which requires that waste be treated before it is discharged into waterways, and the 1974 SAFE DRINKING WATER ACT, which mandates treatment techniques for dozens of contaminants. Other laws, such as the 1976 RESOURCE CONSERVATION AND RECOVERY ACT, seek to prevent HAZARDOUS WASTE from leaking into waterways.

The laws have produced mixed results. Thanks to strict water purification standards, the nation claims one of the purest drinking water supplies in the world, although occasional contamination still persists. Surface water pollution, however, remains so endemic that as much as 40 percent of the nation's waterways are too polluted for basic recreational purposes such as fishing and swimming, according to estimates by the ENVIRONMENTAL PROTECTION AGENCY (EPA). Although that percentage represents an advance compared with the early 1970s, when approximately two-thirds of waterways were degraded, it falls far short of government goals. Furthermore, environmentalists question the EPA monitoring reports because they focus on only a handful of indicators and exclude such pollutants as heavy metals.

The nation's growing population—especially in coastal areas—sprawling development, and more concentrated agricultural operations threaten to

Flooding caused by Hurricane Floyd in September 1999 devastated North Carolina's water supply, contaminating public water systems with debris, water-borne disease, and untreated wastewater. In the aftermath of what officials called the worst environmental, agricultural, and human disaster in the state's history, a workman removed from a flooded road some of the one hundred thousand hogs killed by the disaster. Source: Alan Marler, AP overwhelm further antipollution efforts. Environmentalists want to put a greater focus on regulating nonpoint sources of pollution, especially large farms. But lawmakers have deadlocked over such proposals. Prodded by environmental lawsuits, the Clinton administration proposed a series of more stringent regulations in the late 1990s that could impose sweeping restrictions on commercial and agricultural discharges, but ran into ferocious criticism in Congress.

Beginning in the 1980s, the government placed a stepped-up focus on protecting groundwater, which supplies about half the nation's drinking water. In 1999 the EPA reported that groundwater appeared to be less polluted than surface water, but the agency had limited information about its condition. Groundwater is threatened both by overpumping and by many of the same contaminants that affect surface water. (See also FEDERAL WATER POLLUTION CONTROL ACT; GREAT LAKES; MERCURY; PCBS; PFIESTERIA; TOTAL MAXIMUM DAILY LOADS.)

Water projects

See DAMS.

Water scarcity

Lack of freshwater, already a significant problem for the world's growing population, is expected to emerge as one of the most pressing natural resource issues of the twenty-first century. Increased water demand, unequal distribution of water supplies, and widespread WATER POLLUTION is starting to undermine agricultural production and cause widespread human health problems in de-

veloping countries. Water scarcity is also threatening ecological damage by wiping out many populations of freshwater fish, contaminating soil, and spurring the construction of environmentally destructive DAMS. More than most other environmental pressures, the lack of freshwater has the potential to spark major international conflicts.

From 1900 to 1995, global water consumption rose at more than twice the rate of POPULATION GROWTH, largely because of increasing agricultural and industrial use. Although worldwide water supplies remain plentiful, clean water is so unevenly distributed that close to three billion people may lack safe drinking water, adequate sanitation, or both. The United Nations warns that the situation is likely to get worse: Two-thirds of the world's population will likely live in countries where consumption significantly exceeds supply by 2025. The most severe shortages are in the tension-ridden Middle East and other arid sections of Africa and Asia. In much of the world, governments are weighing the politically unpopular step of increasing the price of water to encourage conservation.

The United States is blessed with relatively plentiful water resources. The U.S. Geological Survey has estimated that the total renewable supply of water in the contiguous forty-eight states is about fourteen hundred billion gallons per day, which is many times the nation's water consumption. However, the water is unequally distributed, and some areas with the greatest need are running short of supply—particularly because of the population boom in the West. This is spurring heavy use of both GROUNDWATER and surface water supplies, raising the prospect of serious environmental consequences.

In much of the country, enormous groundwater aquifers are slowly being depleted. The vast Ogallala Aquifer, which underlies eight states in the arid

Projected Water Vulnerability in 2025, Taking into Account National Economic Status

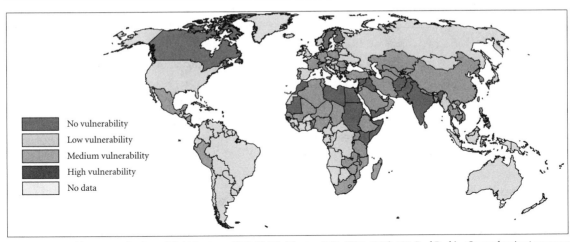

Sources: World Resources Institute, *World Resources 1998–99* (Washington, D.C.: WRI, 1999), 190; Paul Raskin, *Comprehensive Assessment of the Freshwater Resources of the World* (Stockholm Environment Institute, Stockholm, 1997), 66–67.

Note: Data for map taken from mid-range projections, Water Resources Vulnerability Index I, Conventional Development Scenario for 2025.

high plains, is so overused that wells have dried up in many places. Texas farmers and ranchers have depleted the Edwards Aquifer to the point that springs feeding the San Pedro River have dried up. The consequences may haunt the United States for some time, because aquifers take centuries or even longer to recharge (much of the groundwater in the Midwest likely was left by Ice Age glaciers). The loss of groundwater can lead to the depletion of surface water features such as WETLANDS and lakes. It can even cause the earth itself to sink in a process known as subsidence. California's San Joaquin Valley is believed to have sunk more than thirty feet in the last fifty years because of groundwater pumping.

Growing population pressures are also sparking water fights over diversions from rivers and other surface water bodies. Although easterners have engaged in some skirmishes—including a tug-of-war between Georgia, Alabama, and Florida over withdrawing water from the Apalachicola River—the biggest water crises are in the arid West. Booming cities such as Las Vegas are putting intense pressure on limited water supplies. Perhaps the most contentious debate is over the use of the Colorado River, which supplies water for millions of residents and farmers in seven states. The seventeen-hundred-mile-river, a formerly potent force that carved the Grand Canyon, is interrupted by seventeen dams and is laced with salt and PESTICIDE residues by the time it trickles into the Gulf of Mexico. In California water diversions by Los Angeles have destroyed habitat for fish and birds, and drastically shrunk the surface area of Mono Lake, east of Yosemite National Park.

Water use has sparked numerous lawsuits in the United States for many decades, reflecting regional rivalries as well as environmental concerns. Eastern states generally adhere to a form of the "riparian principle," allowing landowners to claim a large portion of the water running through their properties as long as they take into account other consumers' needs. Western states, however, tend to operate under a concept known as the "right to capture" or "prior appropriation." In principle, this water use approach permits the owners of lake and river frontage to consume as much water as they want at little or no cost and without considering the impact on other water users, although they may have to demonstrate that they are not taking more water than they can reasonably use.

Water scarcity, unlike such environmental issues as AIR POLLUTION and water pollution, has generally spurred little debate in Congress. Throughout much of the twentieth century, lawmakers overwhelmingly approved vast water projects. These projects boosted western development and benefited agriculture—an especially big water user in the West—but at the expense of flooded canyons and the destruction of downstream habitat. The political tide began turning against dams and other water projects in 1977. President JIMMY CARTER tried (with mixed success) to eliminate funding for western water projects, which he criticized as being overly costly and environmentally destructive. In recent years, environmentalists have won several battles to tear down dams, restoring free-flowing rivers to their natural state. The battle over dams is especially contentious in the Northwest, where environmentalists who want to tear down dams to restore endangered SALMON populations are encountering intense resistance among local residents.

Solving the problem of water scarcity in the United States, as well as globally, may necessitate both conservation and increased supply. Congress spurred conservation measures with the 1992 ENERGY POLICY ACT, which established federal minimum efficiency standards for showerheads and other plumbing equipment, and mandated the use of LOW-FLOW TOILETS. Environmentalists say far more water can be conserved through the use of more efficient consumer appliances, a farming emphasis on "drip" irrigation systems that deliver measured amounts of water directly to plants, and

industrial adoption of dry cooling systems. They also point to the use of recycled water in California, where treated wastewater is used for irrigation and other nondrinking uses. On the supply side, engineers are focusing on the desalination of ocean water. The process is three to four times more expensive than other freshwater supplies, but offers the potential of almost unlimited water.

Watershed management

A watershed is an area that drains into a body of water, such as a stream, lake, or bay. The U.S. Geological Survey has divided the United States and its territories into more than twenty-one hundred basic watershed units, of which the smallest is about seven hundred square miles.

Much as wildlife conservation has developed from protecting individual species to protecting ecosystems, clean water regulations have developed from protecting individual rivers and lakes to protecting the rivulets, ditches, and other geological features that drain into them. Using its authority under the CLEAN WATER ACT and other laws, the ENVIRONMENTAL PROTECTION AGENCY requires states to monitor pollution throughout their watersheds, both to preserve wildlife and to safeguard drinking water supplies. Watersheds receiving the most attention include the Everglades, the Chesapeake Bay, and the San Francisco Bay and delta.

In 1997 the EPA released its first Index of Watershed Indicators to report on the status of the nation's watersheds. It concluded that 16 percent of the watersheds in the continental United States have good water quality, 36 percent have moderate water quality problems, and 21 percent have serious problems. The agency lacked the necessary information to evaluate the remaining 27 percent.

Part of the impetus for protecting watersheds comes from the 1996 reauthorization of the SAFE DRINKING WATER ACT. The law requires states to map watersheds that supply tap water and to identify regulated contaminants in the area. These Source Water Assessment and Protection programs also seek to protect GROUNDWATER, which supplies most drinking water in rural areas.

The focus on watershed protection is not without controversy. Protecting an entire area means reducing all types of NONPOINT SOURCE POLLUTION, such as fertilizers and motor oils that wash off fields and streets into streams. It can also lead to restrictions on timber activities that could damage streams. As a result, farmers and loggers in particular are concerned that the emphasis on protecting even isolated rivulets threatens their livelihood. (See also TOTAL MAXIMUM DAILY LOADS.)

Watt, James G.

James Watt, the most controversial secretary of the U.S. DEPARTMENT OF THE INTERIOR in recent memory, served from 1981 to 1983. The Wyoming native, who won Senate confirmation by an 83-12 margin despite environmentalists' misgivings, moved forcefully to open NATIONAL FORESTS and other PUBLIC LANDS to development of coal, oil, gas, and other natural riches. He emphasized the "wise use" of natural resources rather than ecology. "The key to conservation is management," he said in 1981. "Conservation is not the blind locking away of huge areas and their resources because of emotional appeals." Unperturbed by environmental objections, President RONALD REAGAN named Watt chairman of the President's Cabinet Council on Natural Resources and the Environment, putting the interior secretary in a position to influence conservation policies throughout the executive branch.

Watt's combative style and conservative politics initially won the support of many westerners. But environmental groups began demanding his ouster within months. When Watt leased vast coal and oil to private companies at a time when world energy markets were slack, environmentalists and economists both warned that the secretary was violating his obligation as trustee of public lands to obtain fair market value for them. Watt's inflammatory speeches also began alienating conservatives who feared he would become a political liability. In 1983 the embattled secretary publicly joked that he had appointed "a black, . . . a woman, two Jews, and a cripple" to an Interior Department commission. Under fire, Watt submitted his resignation to Reagan on October 9, 1983. He was replaced by William P. Clark, an administration troubleshooter who softened some of Watt's policies and worked to mend fences with Congress and the environmental community.

Wetlands

The protection of wetlands has sparked considerable debate since the early 1970s. Conservationists regard wetlands as a top priority because they help control flooding, filter out impurities, and harbor rare plants and animals. But developers and property rights advocates worry that government agencies use an expansive definition of wetlands, thereby banning construction on land that is actually dry for much of the year. Sen. Pat Roberts, R-Kan., an ally of farmers, sometimes scoffs at protecting places that "no self-respecting duck" would land in—even though such places may have ecological value.

Scientists use the term *wetland* to refer to a broad category of landforms that are wet for at least part of the year, and as a result have particular types of vegetation and soil. They include swamps, saltwater and freshwater marshes, bogs, and prairie potholes. Wetlands can be found in every state, even in arid sections of the West. The Florida EVERGLADES is the nation's best-known wetland and a perennial battleground between environmentalists and developers.

Prior to heightened environmental awareness in the 1960s and 1970s, the government generally encouraged the destruction of wetlands because it viewed them as undesirable breeding grounds for mosquitoes and diseases. As a result, barely more than 100 million acres remain of the estimated 220 million acres of wetlands that once existed in the continental United States. (Alaska, however, has more wetlands than do all other states combined, most of it tundra.) The destruction of wetlands is continuing, albeit at a much slower rate. The ENVIRONMENTAL PROTECTION AGENCY estimated in the 1990s that the nation lost wetlands at a net rate of about 70,000 to 90,000 acres per year, mostly to development and agriculture. Environmental groups contend the rate of loss may be closer to 120,000 acres a year (for losses by state, see table).

The primary federal law protecting privately owned wetlands is the 1972 CLEAN WATER ACT. It generally requires anyone engaging in dredge-and-fill operations on wetlands to obtain a SECTION 404 permit from the U.S. ARMY CORPS OF ENGINEERS. Environmentalists want to tighten the permitting requirements because farmers and ranchers often do not have to obtain permits and certain activities destructive to wetlands are exempt, such as drainage. Developers, however, want to streamline permitting requirements that they regard as overly cumbersome. In the late 1990s the Army Corps of Engineers gradually tried to impose stricter permitting procedures and began requiring permits for wetlands as small as one-third of an acre. But it faced a series of court challenges.

Even before the Clean Water Act, lawmakers moved to protect wetlands with the 1961 Wetlands Loan Act (PL 87-383). It set up a system that used "duck stamp" receipts paid by hunters to purchase wetlands that provided habitat for migrating waterfowl. Since the 1980s lawmakers have created several agricultural programs, such as SWAMPBUSTER and the WETLANDS RESERVE PROGRAM, to encourage farmers to leave wetlands undisturbed. Another government tactic to protect wetlands is to place them in such land programs as the NATIONAL WILDLIFE REFUGE SYSTEM. In recent years officials have turned increasingly to the strategy of wetlands mitigation. This strategy may take the form of requiring a developer to restore a filled wetland or create a new one to compensate for destroying wetland acres. States have widely differing wetlands rules, sometimes requiring mitigation sites in the same watershed as the destroyed wetland, and sometimes taking a more lax position that allows mitigation many miles away. Restoring wetlands is a difficult task that relies on rain and GROUNDWATER. Scientists disagree over whether restored or artificially created wetlands fill the same niche as natural, undisturbed wetlands.

One of the biggest questions confronting policymakers is how to define a wetland. Federal agencies rely on a 1987 Army Corps of Engineers manual that uses criteria relating to specific vegetation, soil, and hydrology. In 1991 the Bush administration proposed narrowing the definition to include only areas that have saturated soil for twenty-one

Wetlands Losses by State, 1780s–1980s

State	Total area (millions of acres)	Wetlands area (millions of acres) 1780s	Wetlands area (millions of acres) 1980s	Wetlands losses (percent)	State	Total area (millions of acres)	Wetlands area (millions of acres) 1780s	Wetlands area (millions of acres) 1980s	Wetlands losses (percent)
Alabama	33.03	7.57	3.78	50	Montana	94.17	1.15	0.84	27
Alaska	375.30	170.20	170.00	<1	Nebraska	49.43	2.91	1.91	35
Arizona	72.90	0.93	0.60	36	Nevada	70.75	0.49	0.24	52
Arkansas	33.99	9.85	2.76	72	New Hampshire	5.95	0.22	0.20	9
California	101.56	5.00	0.45	91	New Jersey	5.02	1.50	0.92	39
Colorado	66.72	2.00	1.00	50	New Mexico	77.87	0.72	0.48	33
Connecticut	3.21	0.67	0.17	74	New York	31.73	2.56	1.03	60
Delaware	1.32	0.48	0.22	54	North Carolina	33.66	11.09	5.69	49
Florida	37.48	20.33	11.04	46	North Dakota	45.23	4.93	2.49	49
Georgia	37.68	6.84	5.30	23	Ohio	26.38	5.00	0.48	90
Hawaii	4.12	0.06	0.05	12	Oklahoma	44.75	2.84	0.95	67
Idaho	53.47	0.88	0.39	56	Oregon	62.07	2.26	1.39	38
Illinois	36.10	8.21	1.25	85	Pennsylvania	29.01	1.13	0.50	56
Indiana	23.23	5.60	0.75	87	Rhode Island	0.78	0.10	0.07	37
Iowa	36.03	4.00	0.42	89	South Carolina	19.88	6.41	4.66	27
Kansas	52.65	0.84	0.44	48	South Dakota	49.31	2.74	1.78	35
Kentucky	25.85	1.57	0.30	81	Tennessee	27.04	1.94	0.79	59
Louisiana	31.05	16.19	8.78	46	Texas	171.10	16.00	7.61	52
Maine	21.26	6.46	5.20	20	Utah	54.35	0.80	0.56	30
Maryland	6.77	1.65	0.44	73	Vermont	6.15	0.34	0.22	35
Massachusetts	5.28	0.82	0.59	28	Virginia	26.12	1.85	1.07	42
Michigan	37.26	11.20	5.58	50	Washington	43.64	1.35	0.94	31
Minnesota	53.80	15.07	8.70	42	West Virginia	15.48	0.13	0.10	24
Mississippi	30.54	9.87	4.07	59	Wisconsin	35.94	9.80	5.33	46
Missouri	44.60	4.84	0.64	87	Wyoming	62.66	2.00	1.25	38

Source: T. E. Dahl, *Wetlands Losses in the United States: 1780s to 1980s* (Washington, D.C.: U.S. Department of the Interior, Fish and Wildlife Service, 1991).

days during the growing season, or standing water for fifteen consecutive days at other times during the year. Under fire, the administration never implemented the plan. In 1995 a report by the National Academy of Sciences highlighted the need to recognize regional differences in wetlands, as well as the need for more research on wetlands and better training on wetlands delineation.

Recent administrations have pledged wetlands preservation, albeit with mixed results. In 1988 GEORGE BUSH backed a policy of NO NET LOSS of wetlands during his presidential campaign. Five years later, the Clinton administration unveiled a plan that sought to end the loss of wetlands while ensuring regulatory flexibility. In 1998 the administration announced a goal of increasing wetlands by 100,000 acres a year by 2005, partly by encouraging the creation or restoration of wetlands to offset the loss of existing wetlands. Increasingly, efforts to clean up the GREAT LAKES, Chesapeake Bay, and other degraded bodies of water are focusing on the creation of more wetlands, which act as natural sponges and filters.

Congress has debated wetlands protection

many times since the 1972 passage of the Clean Water Act. In 1976 environmentalists turned back an amendment that would have limited the law's wetlands provisions to areas near navigable waterways. Wetlands issues came to the fore again in 1995, when conservatives attempted to rewrite the Clean Water Act. Their proposal—which passed the House but stalled in the Senate—would have required the government to classify wetlands based on their ecological importance and ease regulations on less essential wetlands. The only substantial wetlands action that lawmakers took in the 1990s was to reauthorize farm policy in 1996, extending the Wetlands Reserve Program to 2002 and capping enrollment at 975,000 acres. It also created the ENVIRONMENTAL QUALITY INCENTIVES PROGRAM to provide stepped-up assistance to farmers who want to preserve wetlands and other natural features.

Wetlands Reserve Program

Created by 1990 farm legislation (PL 101-624), the Wetlands Reserve Program is a voluntary program that seeks to restore WETLANDS on agricultural lands. The program, administered by the U.S. DEPARTMENT OF AGRICULTURE, pays farmers who convert lands to wetlands instead of continuing to use them for planting. The size of the program is capped at 975,000 acres, but there have been proposals to increase it by as many as 250,000 acres annually. In 1996 farm legislation (PL 104-127), Congress extended the program through 2002.

Whaling

The international campaign to end whaling, represented by the ubiquitous "Save the Whales" bumper stickers of the 1970s, has come to symbolize the dramatic turnaround in environmental attitudes that took place in the last decades of the twentieth century. After being hunted relentlessly for hundreds of years, the dozen or so species of great whales are now admired for their size and grace by millions of people who flock to whale-watching cruises. Like California's sequoia trees and Brazil's vast rain forests, the large and intelligent ocean mammals provoke a reflexive support of environmental protection in many Americans—sometimes to the exasperation of whalers in Japan, Norway, and other countries who want to return to the hunt.

The United States largely banned the hunting of whales and other ocean mammals in its waters in 1972, with the passage of the MARINE MAMMAL PROTECTION ACT. During the next twenty-five years, the United States led international efforts to protect dolphins from being killed by commercial fishermen, insisting on imposing standards for DOLPHIN-SAFE TUNA despite vigorous protests by trading partners. (Dolphins are part of the whale family, but they are not classified as great whales.) Although whaling has stirred occasional clashes in the United States—especially over the rights of indigenous people to conduct traditional hunting of gray whales and other whales—members of both political parties generally strongly oppose commercial whaling.

Internationally, the situation is more complicated. The INTERNATIONAL WHALING COMMISSION imposed a moratorium on whaling beginning in 1985–1986 because of concerns that rare species

Despite an international moratorium on commercial whaling, Japanese and Norwegian crews kill hundreds of whales yearly. A Norwegian vessel hunted minke whales in the North Sea in July 1999, provoking protests by Greenpeace. Source: Cunningham-Greenpeace, Reuters

such as blue whales and right whales were in danger of EXTINCTION. As a result, some whale populations are recovering. However, Japanese and Norwegian whalers continue to kill hundreds of the animals yearly—especially minke whales—because the commission has limited authority.

Besides battling over the commission's moratorium, nations also are at odds over a more binding regulation by the CONVENTION ON INTERNATIONAL TRADE IN ENDANGERED SPECIES OF WILD FAUNA AND FLORA that prohibits the buying and selling of whale products. Whaling advocates claim there is no need to protect such species as the minke whale, which has a worldwide population of about one million. But environmentalists worry that opening the doors to limited trade in whale products will spur widespread hunting that could devastate whale populations. Because whales are slow to reproduce and are susceptible to the effects of pollution, many whale species remain very rare even with the international restrictions in place. Some types of whales—such as the northern right whale—appear to be headed toward extinction.

Wild and Scenic Rivers Act

Spurred by concerns about the loss of free-flowing rivers to DAMS and pollution, Congress in 1968 passed the Wild and Scenic Rivers Act. The law established a National Wild and Scenic Rivers System—a complement of sorts to the National Park System—to protect rivers with important scenic, recreational, fish and wildlife, and other values. Waterways are divided into three categories. *Wild river areas* are rivers or sections of rivers that are unpolluted and free of impoundments, have undeveloped shorelines, and are generally inaccessible except by trail. *Scenic river areas* are free of impoundments, and have largely undeveloped shorelines, but are accessible in places by roads. *Recreational river areas* are readily accessible by road or railroad, may have some shoreline development, and may have undergone past impoundment or diversion. The U.S. DEPARTMENT OF THE INTERIOR has primary jurisdiction over the system, in conjunction with the U.S. DEPARTMENT OF AGRICULTURE.

The law takes a rather moderate approach toward conservation. It allows recreational activities on the rivers, including fishing and boating. Although it bars the construction of DAMS or other major projects that would greatly affect the rivers' flow or water quality, it permits limited development along the banks, as well as development upstream and downstream of the designated section. The government can acquire land along the banks to protect the area but does not typically seek to protect the surrounding watershed. The goal of the law is to preserve the character of a river, rather than to lock it away as a wilderness. Officials sometimes use the term "living landscape" to describe wild and scenic rivers. More than 150 rivers have been designated, mostly in the Northwest.

The Wild and Scenic Rivers Act has stirred occasional controversy. Government agencies such as the U.S. FOREST SERVICE, members of Congress, or state or local officials can propose rivers for the designation. Conservationists contend that this political process tends to exclude sections of wild rivers that businesses want to develop, while PRIVATE PROPERTY RIGHTS advocates worry that the law gives government control over development decisions.

Wilderness Act

The 1964 Wilderness Act is the nation's strictest land conservation law. It authorizes Congress to set aside relatively untouched federal areas to protect the environment and enable people to pursue solitude and primitive recreation. The law defines a wilderness as "an area where the earth and its community of life are untrammeled by man, where man himself is a visitor who does not remain . . . which is protected and managed so as to preserve its natural conditions." Accordingly, wilderness areas generally have no roads or buildings and are off-limits to motorized vehicles. Logging and other commercial activities are typically banned. The act was the culmination of years of lobbying by conservation groups. But environmentalists had to make several concessions, including allowing the continuation of ongoing activities such as livestock grazing and mineral prospecting. The law also permits fire, insect, and disease control and—subject to presidential approval—water project developments.

The Wilderness Act required the Interior and Agriculture departments to review ROADLESS AREAS of 5,000 acres or more in the federal lands system to determine whether such areas should be designated as wilderness. Under the 1976 Land Policy Management Act, the Bureau of Land Management must also identify potential wilderness areas. However, only Congress can designate a wilderness area. The original act set aside more than 9 million acres of wilderness in thirteen states. By the beginning of 2000, the NATIONAL WILDERNESS PRESERVATION SYSTEM comprised 624 wilderness areas totaling about 104 million acres, or about 4.5 percent of the U.S. landmass. Wilderness areas, most of which are in the West, generally overlay NATIONAL PARKS and NATIONAL FORESTS. Depending on where the lands are located, they are managed by the National Park Service, the Forest Service, the U.S. FISH AND WILDLIFE SERVICE, and the Bureau of Land Management.

Lawmakers engaged in a series of battles throughout the 1970s and early 1980s over how much of the land in national forests should be designated as wilderness. After several environmental lawsuits and two surveys of national forest roadless areas, Congress passed twenty separate bills in 1983–1984 to designate 8.3 million acres of forests as wilderness, while allowing commercial uses in another 13.5 million acres of previously undeveloped land. Lawmakers also squared off in the early 1980s over a Reagan administration proposal to allow oil and gas exploration in wilderness areas—especially in the Rocky Mountain Overthrust Belt formation in Wyoming, Utah, and Idaho. Company officials contended they could extract oil and gas without damaging the environment by using slant drilling techniques that would enable them to drill wells from outside a wilderness area's boundaries. This drilling was allowed under the original Wilderness Act, which permitted the interior secretary to lease oil, gas, coal, and other resources in wilderness areas for a twenty-year period, expiring at the end of 1983. But Congress blocked the administration's plan.

The ultimate size of the National Wilderness Preservation System continues to provoke controversy. Environmentalists want to eventually expand wilderness areas to about 200 million acres. But developers and many rural advocates are concerned about losing land for both commercial use and motorized recreation. Two areas that have received considerable scrutiny are the ARCTIC NATIONAL WILDLIFE REFUGE, where environmentalists want to designate the coastal plain to prevent oil drilling, and Utah's red rock canyon country, where environmentalists and Utah officials have clashed over whether to set aside about 1 million acres or as many as 9 million acres. After taking control of Congress in 1994, Republicans came under fire for failing to designate any new wilderness areas for the rest of the decade. However, they supported efforts in 2000 to designate new wilderness in Colorado.

The political debates aside, some conservationists worry that the wilderness areas are being reshaped by EXOTIC SPECIES and overrun with visitors. Since 1970 recreational use of wilderness areas has increased by about sevenfold, according to government estimates.

Wildfires

Wildfires are an important environmental concern in the West, where dry conditions can easily cause large swaths of forests to go up in smoke. Beginning in the late nineteenth century, when U.S. troops used buckets to battle fires in YELLOWSTONE NATIONAL PARK, the government sought to suppress fires in NATIONAL FORESTS and other preserves. Public fears of forest fires increased after a wind-driven inferno known as the "Big Blowup" claimed the lives of dozens of people, most of them firefighters.

However, a century of fire suppression greatly changed the ecology of western forests. As dry brush and small trees began to dominate the landscape, the risk of catastrophic fires increased. When huge sections of Yellowstone National Park were destroyed by fire in 1988, it became apparent that wildfires could not be entirely suppressed.

Beginning in the 1970s, the U.S. FOREST SERVICE tried to restore the natural landscape through prescribed burns, or limited blazes meant to clear out dead wood. However, prescribed burns are highly controversial because they sometimes blaze out of control. In 2000 firefighters lost control of such a burn in New Mexico's Bendelier National Monument. The resulting fire forced evacuations in Los Alamos and threatened the nation's largest nuclear weapons research laboratory. Nevertheless, Forest Service officials, who want more funding for fire fighting efforts, continue to support prescribed burns as an essential tactic for controlling wildfires.

The issue of wildfires has also roiled the debate over building additional roads in NATIONAL FORESTS. Timber companies say the roads would help contain fires by allowing limited logging and helping firefighters gain access to remote areas, but environmentalists say the roads would interfere with the forest ecology and aggravate fire conditions.

Windblown pollution

Windblown pollution refers to air pollutants that are blown for hundreds or even thousands of miles before returning to earth. As a result, undeveloped areas such as NATIONAL PARKS are recording high levels of SMOG and HAZE because of industrial activity hundreds of miles away. The Northeast is sometimes referred to as the "tailpipe" of the nation because of the pollutants that come from the industrial Midwest.

This type of movement makes it highly difficult to control AIR POLLUTION. The motor vehicles and industrial plants that emit pollutants are often located beyond the regulatory reach of the affected area. Federal and state officials have repeatedly clashed over whether the costs to reduce windblown pollution should be borne by polluters or the states affected by the pollution. In 1990 Congress struck a compromise, amending the CLEAN AIR ACT to set up an EMISSIONS TRADING program to control midwestern power plant emissions that were drifting over eastern states. But officials in affected states continue to complain about older power plants that are not regulated under the Clean Air Act.

Such movement of pollutants also crosses national borders, creating widespread ACID RAIN problems and degrading undeveloped areas that are thousands of miles away from any industrial activity. It is sometimes described as "long-range transport of pollution." (See also TRANSBOUNDARY POLLUTION.)

Wolves

The reintroduction of wolves to their former hunting grounds represents one of the federal government's boldest and most controversial initiatives to restore endangered species. In 1995 the U.S. FISH AND WILDLIFE SERVICE transplanted fourteen gray wolves from Canada to YELLOWSTONE NATIONAL PARK, where the predators had been wiped out seventy years ago by federal hunters and trappers. Within five years, those wolves and an additional fifty-two that the government subsequently transplanted to Yellowstone and parts of Idaho had multiplied to more than three hundred. Buoyed by this success, officials began weighing plans for further wolf reintroductions from Maine to Colorado, as well as reintroducing other predators such as GRIZZLY BEARS and Canadian lynx to remote western regions.

Wolves were a dominant predator in the nineteenth century. But early settlers, fearing for both themselves and their livestock, generally shot them on sight, and a bounty program by the federal government nearly drove the wolf to extinction early in the twentieth century. Amid greatly changing environmental values, the government eventually protected the gray wolf under the 1973 ENDANGERED SPECIES ACT.

Wolves are important ecologically because they hold down populations of large prey like elk, thereby protecting vegetation from being overgrazed and providing food for scavengers like ravens and grizzly bears. But ranchers and farmers say the predators threaten livestock. In a concession to western lawmakers, the government designated the wolf population as experimental, meaning that wolves could be shot if caught in the act of attacking sheep or cattle on rangeland. The AMERICAN FARM BUREAU FEDERATION nevertheless went to court to try to stop the reintroduction program, but the 10th Circuit Court of Appeals in Denver ruled against it in 2000.

Unlike the Yellowstone reintroduction, Fish and Wildlife Service attempts to reintroduce the endangered Mexican gray wolf to the Southwest have been stymied by poachers. However, the government successfully reintroduced the red wolf to North Carolina.

World Bank

Created after World War II to promote economic development, the World Bank is a long-term lending institution that is overseen by its member nations. Environmentalists have criticized it for funding DAMS, pipelines, and other large-scale industrial projects for decades without regard to the environmental consequences. Some of the projects took a toll on indigenous peoples by wiping out native animals and plants. In the 1990s the World Bank began putting a much greater focus on such issues as SUSTAINABLE USE of natural resources, and it set aside loans for smaller, community-oriented projects. It also helped foster efforts to coordinate global environmental programs. However, it continues to get mixed reviews from environmentalists who contend it sometimes disregards its own rules on limiting environmental damage. In recent years the World Bank has faced mounting challenges from opponents of global trade. The bank employed more than eleven thousand people at the beginning of 2000 and had a total of $200 billion in loans on its books. (See also GLOBAL ECONOMY.)

World Heritage sites

The United Nations Educational, Scientific, and Cultural Organization designates World Heritage sites to draw attention to the world's most valued natural and cultural places. This program, created under a 1972 treaty that was initiated largely by the United States, had designated 630 sites in 118 countries as of 2000. The United States is home to 20 of the sites, including YELLOWSTONE and Grand Canyon national parks and the Statue of Liberty. The World Heritage program provides funding to nations that request help with protecting their sites. It also seeks to coordinate scientific research.

Although the program had sparked little controversy over the years, congressional conservatives in the late 1990s began pressing for legislation requiring congressional approval for any new Heritage site. They said this approval was necessary to ensure that domestic land-use decisions would not face international interference. Democrats ridiculed such proposals, pointing out that the United Nations has no authority over the sites. In actuality, the debate appeared to be about whether Congress would get to play a role in the designations or continue to leave all authority with the executive branch. Conservatives won a small victory when they inserted a provision in a 1999 omnibus spending bill (PL 106-113) restricting U.S. funding for the program.

World Trade Organization

The World Trade Organization (WTO) is an international organization of more than 130 countries, including the United States, whose rules govern most world trade. Formed in 1995 to imple-ment the General Agreement on Tariffs and Trade, the WTO has sparked heated controversy—culminating in riots in Seattle in 1999—because critics believe that its efforts to reduce trade barriers are damaging the U.S. economy and undermining environmental and worker protection standards throughout much of the world. U.S. policymakers generally back its free trade approach because domestic businesses want improved access to overseas markets. However, some lawmakers on both the left and the right worry that the WTO is spurring global trade in a way that hurts U.S. workers and forces the nation to cede its sovereignty to unelected foreign bureaucrats.

Environmentalists are especially concerned because they do not want hard-won antipollution standards in the United States and other Western countries to be watered down in the name of free trade. The WTO ruled several times in the late 1990s that U.S. environmental laws amounted to unlawful trade barriers. For example, it determined that the United States could not reject imported gasoline from Venezuela and other countries that failed to meet CLEAN AIR ACT standards. Similarly, it threw out U.S. restrictions on the imports of shrimp that were caught without the use of TURTLE EXCLUDER DEVICES.

Despite such rulings, WTO officials say their efforts will ultimately help the environment by creating greater prosperity and international cooperation. In a 2000 speech, WTO's director-general Mike Moore said: "We all realize that no nation can now enjoy clean water, air, manage an airline, even organize a tax system, or hope to contain or cure AIDS or cancer without the cooperation of others. Thus we must seek democratic internationalism and cooperation if we are to prosper and enjoy balanced development on our crowded planet." (See also GLOBAL ECONOMY.)

Y

Yellowstone National Park

The decision of the federal government in 1872 to establish Yellowstone National Park in the territories of Wyoming and Montana was a landmark conservation event, spurring a worldwide movement to set aside land into NATIONAL PARKS and other preserves. President Ulysses Grant and Congress were motivated by reports of geysers and other geological wonders in the Yellowstone region, as well as by the lobbying of the Northern Pacific Railroad Company, which wanted a major tourist attraction near its main line in Montana. Legislatively, it was an easy matter to establish the park. After all, the land was already in federal hands and Congress merely had to stipulate that it would remain in federal custody "as a public park or pleasuring ground for the benefit and enjoyment of the people."

For better or worse, the 2.2-million-acre park has set the tone for the national park system. It is an important sanctuary for large mammals, including GRIZZLY BEARS and bison, as well as for people seeking natural beauty. But the developed sections have been battered in recent years by the same problems that are afflicting dozens of newer national parks: overcrowding, pollution, and poor maintenance. Some three million people flock to Yellowstone yearly, causing traffic jams and overwhelming visitor facilities. The sewage system is so old that it leaked thousands of gallons of raw sewage in the late 1990s, and officials in 1998 temporarily closed the popular Dunraven Road, which they deemed unsafe because it had not been resurfaced since 1942. Concerns are also mounting that the park's rare animals could face problems with inbreeding as they become increasingly isolated because of development beyond the park's boundaries.

To help restore Yellowstone's wild character, the National Park Service took several controversial steps in the 1990s. It reintroduced gray WOLVES over the vehement protests of nearby ranchers and weighed a ban on snowmobile use despite objections by many local residents. In the appropriations bill for the Interior Department in 1998, Congress agreed to allow national parks to keep at least 80 percent of the money they collected from park fees instead of remitting it to the Treasury. This agreement should help Yellowstone officials begin to meet a backlog of tens of millions of dollars of maintenance projects.

Young, Don

As the chairman of the HOUSE RESOURCES COMMITTEE in the last half of the 1990s, Rep. Don Young, R-Alaska, aggressively battled environmentalists in an effort to reduce regulations and open up public lands to oil, gas, and other types of development. He succeeded in lifting a ban on

As chairman of the House Resources Committee, Rep. Don Young, R-Alaska, sought to reduce environmental regulations and clear the way for development on public lands. He also worked with environmentalists on legislation aiding fisheries and national parks. Source: Scott J. Ferrell, Congressional Quarterly

the export of oil from Alaska's North Slope, but he failed to pass measures that would have allowed oil exploration in the ARCTIC NATIONAL WILDLIFE REFUGE, increased logging in TONGASS NATIONAL FOREST, and pared back provisions in the ENDANGERED SPECIES ACT. Combative by nature, Young clashed repeatedly with the committee's ranking Democrat, GEORGE MILLER of California, and outraged environmentalists in 1998 when he demanded the names of Clinton administration officials who were members of, or contributed money to, environmental organizations. But he also worked with environmentalists on significant measures, including bills to protect fisheries, create new NATIONAL PARKS, and boost funding for land purchases through the LAND

AND WATER CONSERVATION FUND. First elected in 1973, Young became the committee's senior Republican in 1985.

Yucca Mountain

In 1987 Congress designated Yucca Mountain, in Nevada, as the best potential site for an underground repository to store highly radioactive waste from the nation's nuclear power plants. The legislation, which directed the U.S. DEPARTMENT OF ENERGY to study the feasibility of the site, has drawn strenuous opposition from Nevada's small congressional delegation, as well as from environmentalists who fear the consequences of trucking tons of NUCLEAR WASTE across the country every year and storing it in a potentially unsafe place. The nuclear power industry, however, contends it can be handled safely.

Yucca Mountain is a six-thousand-foot ridge about one hundred miles northwest of Las Vegas. It sits above the water table and is composed of tuff, a compacted volcanic ash. Scientific studies have focused on whether nuclear waste at the site would be safely contained for ten thousand years without risks of it leaking into groundwater or through faults in the rock, or being dangerously disturbed by earthquakes or volcanic activity. Critics contend that future fractures in the rock could allow rain and melted snow to flow through the repository, picking up radioactive material and carrying it to the water table. In 1998 a coalition of more than two hundred environmental groups cited this risk as one of the chief reasons that the site should be disqualified.

The Energy Department, which is expected to issue a final report on the site's suitability in 2001, has spent about $6 billion intensely surveying the site. (The money, appropriated annually by Congress, comes from a nuclear energy fund that is collected from nuclear power users.) In 1998 it issued an interim analysis, or "viability assessment," that reported no insurmountable problems with the site. The government plan is to open the repository in 2010 and continue receiving waste until 2033, but it is highly uncertain that the project will remain on schedule.

The battle over Yucca Mountain dates back to the 1970s, when the federal government began exploring the possibility of using an underground repository for tons of nuclear waste. In 1982 Congress passed the Nuclear Waste Policy Act (PL 97-425), directing the president to recommend a repository by 1987. The Energy Department narrowed its search to Texas, Washington, and Nevada, but lawmakers in 1987 amended the law to name Yucca Mountain as the sole site to be surveyed. The 1987 vote was highly politicized, and it has sparked acrimonious legislative battles ever since.

With nuclear power plants running out of temporary storage space, lawmakers in the late 1990s began weighing proposals to temporarily store waste near Yucca Mountain as early as 2003. They stepped up their efforts after the Energy Department failed to meet a 1998 deadline to accept waste from commercial reactors, but they could not muster the two-thirds majority to override a threatened veto by President BILL CLINTON. The White House insisted that the government focus its resources on a permanent repository, rather than an aboveground one. Lawmakers also clashed over a plan to give authority for setting safety standards to the NUCLEAR REGULATORY COMMISSION instead of the ENVIRONMENTAL PROTECTION AGENCY (EPA). Advocates of using Yucca Mountain for the waste contended that EPA standards would be overly stringent, making it virtually impossible to open the repository.

Z

Zebra mussels

A small freshwater mollusk about the size of a fingernail, the zebra mussel is one of the most destructive EXOTIC SPECIES in the United States. Government officials believe it was inadvertently transported from Europe to North America in the ballast water of a ship in the late 1980s. First discovered in North America in 1988, the zebra mussel spread rapidly throughout the GREAT LAKES and the Mississippi River region, establishing colonies throughout much of the East and Midwest. The mollusk is notorious for proliferating in the pipes of drinking water systems, hydroelectric plants, and industrial facilities, constricting water flow and affecting heating and cooling systems.

In 1990 Congress passed the NON-INDIGENOUS AQUATIC NUISANCE SPECIES PREVENTION AND CONTROL ACT, coordinating federal efforts to prevent the spread of zebra mussels and other exotic species. A variety of methods may be used to wipe out zebra mussel colonies, including chemical agents, hot water or steam, and biological predators. But the mollusk has spread because of its penchant to attach itself to the bottoms of boats that move from one waterway to another.

Zero risk

Zero risk is the strictest possible health standard. It is designed to protect people from even a minute chance of being harmed by a pollutant. Congress has rarely tried to impose this standard because it usually involves severe economic costs. For example, the 1958 DELANEY CLAUSE, which barred any trace of a cancer-causing chemical in processed foods, was replaced in 1996 when farmers warned they could not continue growing food without using certain PESTICIDES that can cause cancer. Rather than insisting on zero risk, regulators may seek to minimize chemical exposure by applying a NEGLIGIBLE RISK health standard or requiring polluters to use the BEST AVAILABLE CONTROL TECHNOLOGY to reduce pollution discharges.

On occasion, Congress has indirectly used a zero risk standard by banning discharges of dangerous chemicals. In the 1972 CLEAN WATER ACT, lawmakers approved a "zero discharge" goal that would have entirely eliminated many types of WATER POLLUTION by 1985. But industry could not meet that goal without greatly reducing the use of toxic chemicals. A more successful use of zero discharge is the 1987 MONTREAL PROTOCOL ON SUBSTANCES THAT DEPLETE THE OZONE LAYER, in which the United States and other countries agreed to phase out all use of chlorofluorocarbons (CFCS).

Reference Material

Environmental Organizations

The following organizations can provide extensive information on the topics covered in this book. All maintain highly useful Web sites. This is not intended to be an exhaustive list of environmental policy sources; rather; it provides a starting point for those wishing to delve more deeply into the subject.

American Farm Bureau Federation, Washington Office, 600 Maryland Ave. S.W., #800, Washington, DC 20024; (202) 484-3600. Fax, (202) 484-3604. Web, www.fb.com.

Federation of state farm bureaus in fifty states and Puerto Rico. Promotes agricultural research. Interests include commodity programs, domestic production, financial assistance to the farmer, foreign assistance programs, rural development, the world food shortage, and inspection and certification of food.

American Forest and Paper Assn., Regulatory Affairs, 1111 19th St. N.W., #800, Washington, DC 20036; (202) 463-2700. Fax, (202) 463-2785. Web, www.afandpa.org.

Membership: manufacturers of wood and specialty products and related associations. Interests include tax, housing, environmental, international trade, natural resources, and land-use issues that affect the wood products industry.

Conservation International, 2501 M St. N.W., #200, Washington, DC 20037; (202) 429-5660. Fax, (202) 887-5188. Web, www.conservation.org.

Works to conserve tropical rain forests through economic development; promotes exchange of debt relief for conservation programs that involve local people and organizations. Provides private groups and governments with information and technical advice on conservation efforts; supports conservation data gathering in Latin America, Africa, Asia, and the Caribbean.

Environmental Defense Fund, 257 Park Ave. South, New York, NY 10010; (212) 505-2100. Fax, (212) 505-0892. Washington Office, 1875 Connecticut Ave. N.W., #1016, Washington, DC 20009-5728; (202) 387-3500. Fax, (202) 234-6049. Web, www.edf.org.

Citizens' interest group staffed by lawyers, economists, and scientists. Conducts research and provides information on pollution prevention, environmental health, water resources, water marketing, litigation of water pollution standards, wetlands, toxic substances, acid rain, tropical rain forests, and protection of the Amazon rain forest and the ozone layer. Takes legal action on environmental issues.

Environmental Law Institute, 1616 P St. N.W., #200, Washington, DC 20036; (202) 939-3800. Fax, (202) 939-3868. Web, www.eli.org.

Research and education organization with an interdisciplinary staff of lawyers, economists, scientists, and journalists. Publishes materials on environmental issues, sponsors education and training courses, issues policy recommendations, and cosponsors conferences on environmental law.

Friends of the Earth, 1025 Vermont Ave. N.W., #300, Washington, DC 20005-6303; (202) 783-7400. Fax, (202) 783-0444. Web, www.foe.org.

Environmental advocacy group concerned with environmental, public health, and energy-related issues, including clean air, water, and groundwater; energy conservation; international water projects; transportation of hazardous wastes; global warming; and toxic substances and pesticides. Specializes in federal budget and tax issues related to the environment; ozone layer and ground water protection; and World Bank and International Monetary Fund reform.

Global Environmental Facility, 1818 H St. N.W., #G-6005, Washington, DC 20433; (202) 473-8324. Fax, (202) 522-3240. Web, www.gefweb.org.

Provides grants and concessional funding to developing countries for projects that protect the global environment and promote sustainable economic growth. Focuses on climate change, biological diversity, international waters, and stratospheric ozone; interests include deforestation and desertification. Projects are managed through the World Bank, U.N. Development Programme, and U.N. Environment Programme.

Greenpeace USA, Washington Office, 1436 U St. N.W., Washington, DC 20009; (202) 462-1177. Fax, (202) 462-4507. Web, www.greenpeaceusa.org.

Seeks to protect the environment through research, education, and grassroots organizing. Interests include chemical and nuclear waste dumping, solid and hazardous waste disposal, and protection of marine mammals and endangered species. Supports the establishment of Antarctica as a world park, free of industry, military presence, and nuclear power and weaponry. (Headquarters in Amsterdam, Netherlands.)

League of Conservation Voters, 1920 L St. N.W., #800, Washington, DC 20036; (202) 785-8683. Fax, (202) 835-0491. Web, www.lcv.org.

Works to support the environmental movement by helping elect environmentally concerned candidates to public office.

National Association of Manufacturers, 1331 Pennsylvania Ave. N.W., #600, Washington, DC 20004-1790; (202) 637-3000. Fax, (202) 637-3182. Web, www.nam.org.

Represents industry views (mainly of manufacturers) to government on national and international issues. Reviews legislation, administrative rulings, and judicial decisions affecting industry. Conducts programs on environmental trade and other business issues.

National Audubon Society, 700 Broadway, New York, NY 10003; (212) 979-3000. Fax, (212) 353-0377. Public Policy, Washington Office, 1901 Pennsylvania Ave. N.W., #1100, Washington, DC 20006; (202) 861-2242. Fax, (202) 861-4290. Web, www.audubon.org.

Citizens' interest group that promotes environmental preservation. Provides information on water resources, public lands, rangelands, forests, parks, wildlife and marine conservation, and the national wildlife refuge system.

National Parks and Conservation Assn., 1300 19th St. N.W., #300, Washington, DC 20036-6404; (202) 223-6722. Fax, (202) 659-0650. Information, (800) 628-7275. Web, www.npca.org.

Citizens' interest group that seeks to protect national parks and other park system areas.

National Wildlife Federation, 8925 Leesburg Pike, Vienna, VA 22184; (703) 790-4000. Fax, (703) 790-4040. Web, www.nwf.org.

Promotes conservation of natural resources; provides information on wildlife, the environment, and resource

management; takes legal action on environmental issues; promotes preservation of natural resources.

Natural Resources Defense Council, 40 W. 20th St., New York, NY 10011; (212) 727-2700. Fax, (212) 727-1773. Washington Office, 1200 New York Ave. N.W., #400, Washington, DC 20005-4709; (202) 289-6868. Fax, (202) 289-1060. Web, www.nrdc.org.

Environmental organization staffed by lawyers and scientists who undertake litigation and research. Interests include air, water, land use, forests, toxic materials, natural resources management and conservation, preservation of endangered plant species, and ozone pollution.

Resources for the Future, 1616 P St. N.W., Washington, DC 20036; (202) 328-5000. Fax, (202) 939-3460. Web, www.rff.org.

Engages in research and education on environmental and natural resource issues, including forestry, multiple use of public lands, costs and benefits of pollution control, endangered species, environmental risk management, energy and national security, and climate resources. Interests include hazardous waste, the Superfund, and biodiversity.

Sierra Club, 85 2nd St., 2nd Floor, San Francisco, CA 94105; (415) 977-5500. Fax, (415) 977-5799. Washington Office, 408 C St. N.E., Washington, DC 20002; (202) 547-1141. Fax, (202) 547-6009. Web, www.sierraclub.org.

Citizens' interest group that promotes protection of natural resources. Interests include the Clean Air Act; the Arctic National Wildlife Refuge; protection of national forests, parks, and wilderness; toxins; global warming; promotion of responsible international trade; and international development lending reform.

U.N. Environment Programme (UNEP), P.O. Box 30552, Nairobi, Kenya, (254) (2) (62) 1234. Fax, (254) (2) (62) 3927. Web, www.unep.org.

Promotes international cooperation on all environment matters.

U.S. Chamber of Commerce, Environmental and Regulatory Affairs, 1615 H St. N.W., Washington, DC 20062-2000; (202) 659-6000. Fax, (202) 463-5327. Web, www.uschamber.org.

Monitors operations of federal departments and

agencies responsible for environmental programs, policies, regulatory issues, and food safety. Develops policy on all issues affecting the production, use, and conservation of natural resources, including fuel and nonfuel minerals, timber, water, public lands, on- and offshore energy, wetlands, and endangered species.

U.S. Public Interest Research Group, 218 D St. S.E., Washington, DC 20003; (202) 546-9707. Fax, (202) 546-2461. Web, www.pirg.org.

Coordinates grassroots efforts to advance environmental and consumer protection laws; conducts research on environmental issues, including toxic and solid waste, air and water pollution, pesticides, endangered species, forest and wildlife preservation, alternative energy sources, and energy conservation.

Wilderness Society, 900 17th St. N.W., Washington, DC 20006-2506; (202) 833-2300. Fax, (202) 429-3958. Web, www.wilderness.org.

Promotes preservation of wilderness and the responsible management of all federal lands, including national parks and forests, wilderness areas, wildlife refuges, and land administered by the Interior Dept.'s Bureau of Land Management.

World Conservation Union, 28 Rue Mauverney, CH-1196 Gland, Switzerland, (41) (22) 999-00-01. Fax, (41) (22) 999-00-02. U.S. Office, Washington Office, 1630 Connecticut Ave. N.W., 3rd Floor, Washington, DC 20009; (202) 387-4826. Fax, (202) 387-4823. Web, www.iucn.org.

Membership: world governments, their environmental agencies, and nongovernmental organizations. Studies conservation issues from local to global levels; interests include protected areas, forests, oceans, polar regions, biodiversity, species survival, environmental law, sustainable use of resources, and the impact of trade on the environment.

World Resources Institute, 10 G St. N.E., #800, Washington, DC 20002; (202) 729-7600. Fax, (202) 729-7610. Press, (202) 729-7745. Web, www.wri.org.

International organization that conducts research on environmental problems and studies the inter-relationships of natural resources, economic growth, and human needs. Interests include forestry and land use, renewable energy, fisheries, and sustainable agriculture. Assesses environmental policies of aid agencies.

Worldwatch Institute, 1776 Massachusetts Ave. N.W., 8th Floor, Washington, DC 20036; (202) 452-1999. Fax, (202) 296-7365. Web, www.worldwatch.org.

Research organization that focuses on interdisciplinary approach to solving global environmental problems. Interests include natural resources and human needs, environmental threats to food production, and quality of life.

World Wildlife Fund, 1250 24th St. N.W., #400, Washington, DC 20037; (202) 293-4800. Fax, (202) 293-9211. Web, www.wwf.org.

Conducts scientific research and analyzes policy on environmental and conservation issues, including pollution reduction, land use, forestry and wetlands management, parks, soil conservation, and sustainable development. Supports projects to promote biological diversity and to save endangered species and their habitats, including tropical forests in Latin America, Asia, and Africa.

Congressional Committees Responsible for Environmental Policy

Following are the congressional committees with jurisdiction over environmental issues. In addition to the committees listed here, several other committees touch on environmental matters, including the House Agriculture Committee, House Transportation and Infrastructure Committee, Senate Agriculture, Nutrition, and Forestry Committee, and Senate Commerce, Science, and Transportation Committee.

House Committees

Appropriations Committee, Subcommittee on Interior

Staff director: Deborah A. Weatherly
Minority staff assistant: Del Davis
Address: B-308 Rayburn Bldg., Washington, D.C. 20515
Phone: (202) 225-3481

Jurisdiction: Appropriation of the revenue for the support of the following agencies, programs, and activities: Department of the Interior, except the Bureau of Reclamation; Economic Regulatory Administration; Energy Information Administration; Energy Department emergency preparedness; Energy Department Office of Hearings and Appeals; Strategic Petroleum Reserve; naval petroleum and oil shale reserves; fossil energy research and development; clean coal technology; energy conservation; alternative fuels production and related matters; Alaska Gas Pipeline Authorities; Advisory Council on Historic Preservation; Commission of Fine Arts; Energy Security Reserve; Forest Service; Franklin Delano Roosevelt Memorial Commission; Holocaust Memorial Council; Indian education; Indian health services and facilities; Institute of American Indian and Alaska Native Culture and Arts Development; Institute

of Museum Services; National Capital Planning Commission; National Foundation on the Arts and the Humanities; National Gallery of Art; National Indian Gaming Commission; Navajo and Hopi Indian Relocation Commission; Pennsylvania Avenue Development Corporation; Simon Wiesenthal Center; Smithsonian Institution; Woodrow Wilson International Center for Scholars.

Appropriations Committee, Subcommittee on Veterans Affairs, Housing and Urban Development, and Independent Agencies

Staff director: Frank Cushing
Minority staff director: Del Davis
Address: H-143 Capitol Bldg., Washington, D.C. 20510
Phone: (202) 225-3481

Jurisdiction: Appropriation of the revenue for the support of the Department of Veterans Affairs; Department of Housing and Urban Development; American Battle Monuments Commission; Army cemeterial expenses; Chemical Safety and Hazard Investigation Board; Corporation for National and Community Service; community development financial institutions; Consumer Information Center; Consumer Product Safety Commission; Council on Environmental Quality; Office of Environmental Quality; Court of Veterans Appeals; Environmental Protection Agency; Federal Deposit Insurance Fund; Affordable Housing Program; Bank Enterprise Program; FSLIC Resolution Fund; Federal Emergency Management Agency; Interagency Council on the Homeless; National Aeronautics and Space Administration; National Commission on American Indian, Alaska Native, and Native Hawaiian Housing; National Commission on Financial Institution Reform, Recovery, and Enforcement; National Credit Union Administration; National Science Foundation; National Space Council; Neighborhood Reinvestment Corporation; Department of Health and Human Services Office of Consumer Affairs; Office of Science and Technology Policy; Points of Light Foundation; Resolution Trust

Corporation; Office of the Inspector General; Selective Service System.

Commerce Committee

Minority staff director and chief counsel: Reid Stuntz
Staff director: James E. Derderian
Address: 2125 Rayburn Bldg., Washington, D.C. 20515
Phone: (202) 225-2927

Jurisdiction: Interstate and foreign commerce generally, including commerce as it affects the environment. Environment-related aspects of its jurisdiction include interstate energy compacts; measures relating to the exploration, production, storage, supply, marketing, pricing, and regulation of energy resources, including all fossil fuels, solar energy, and other unconventional or renewable energy resources; measures relating to the conservation of energy resources; measures relating to energy information generally; measures relating to (A) the generation and marketing of power (except by federally chartered or federal regional power marketing authorities), (B) the reliability and interstate transmission of, and ratemaking for, all power, and (C) the siting of generation facilities, except the installation of interconnections between government water power projects; measures relating to general management of the Department of Energy, and the management and all functions of the Federal Energy Regulatory Commission; national energy policy generally; regulation of the domestic nuclear energy industry, including regulation of research and development reactors and nuclear regulatory research; nuclear and other energy, and nonmilitary nuclear energy and research and development, including the disposal of nuclear waste.

Resources Committee

Majority staff director: Lloyd Jones
Minority staff director: John A. Lawrence
Address: 1324 Longworth Bldg., Washington, D.C. 20515
Phone: (202) 225-6065

Jurisdiction: Public lands generally, including entry, easements, and grazing; mining interests generally; fisheries and wildlife, including research, restoration, refuges, and conservation; forest reserves and national parks created from the public domain; forfeiture of land grants and alien ownership, including alien ownership of mineral lands; Geological Survey; international fishing agreements; interstate compacts relating to apportionment of waters for irrigation purposes; irrigation and reclamation, including water supply for reclamation projects, and easements of public lands for irrigation projects, and acquisition of private lands when necessary to complete irrigation projects; measures relating to the care and management of Indians, including the care and allotment of Indian lands and general and special measures relating to claims that are paid out of Indian funds; measures relating generally to the insular possessions of the United States, except those affecting the revenue and appropriations; military parks and battlefields, national cemeteries administered by the secretary of the Interior, parks within the District of Columbia, and the erection of monuments to the memory of individuals; mineral land laws and claims and entries thereunder; mineral resources of the public lands; mining schools and experimental stations; marine affairs (including coastal zone management), except for measures relating to oil and other pollution of navigable waters; oceanography; petroleum conservation on the public lands and conservation of the radium supply in the United States; preservation of prehistoric ruins and objects of interest on the public domain; relations of the United States with the Indians and the Indian tribes; Trans-Alaska Oil Pipeline (except ratemaking).

Senate Committees

Appropriations Committee, Subcommittee on Interior

Minority clerk: Peter Kiefhaber
Clerk: Bruce Evans
Address: 131 Dirksen Bldg., Washington, D.C. 20510
Phone: (202) 224-7233

Jurisdiction: Appropriation of revenue for the support of the following agencies, programs, and activities: Bureau of Indian Affairs; Bureau of Land Management; Bureau of Mines; clean coal technology; Commission of Fine Arts; Economic Regulatory Administration; Emergency Preparedness; Department of Energy: fossil energy, naval petroleum and oil shale reserves, energy conservation, Strategic Petroleum Reserve, Energy Information Administration, Office of Hearings and Appeals; Federal Inspector for the Alaska Gas Pipeline; Forest Service; Franklin Delano Roosevelt Memorial Commission; Historic Preservation Fund; Holocaust Memorial Council; Indian education; Indian Health Service; Institute of American Indian and Alaska Native Culture and Arts Department; Institute of Museum Services; Department of the Interior (except for Bureau of Reclamation); John F. Kennedy Center for the Performing Arts; Land and Water Conservation Fund; Minerals Management Service; National Capital Arts and Cultural Affairs; National Capital Planning Commission; National Endowment for the Arts; National Endowment for the Humanities; National Foundation on the Arts and Humanities; National Gallery of Art; National Indian Gaming Commission; National Park Service; National Portrait Gallery; National Zoological Park; Office of Construction and Management; Office of Inspector General, Department of the Interior; Office of Navajo and Hopi Indian Relocation; Office of Surface Mining Reclamation and Enforcement; Office of the Secretary, Department of the Interior; Office of the Solicitor, Department of the Interior; Outer Continental Shelf; Pennsylvania Avenue Development Corporation; Smithsonian Institution; territorial and international affairs; U.S. Fish and Wildlife Service; Woodrow Wilson International Center for Scholars; Advisory Council on Historic Preservation.

Appropriatons Committee, Subcommittee on VA, HUD, and Independent Agencies

Minority clerk: Paul Carliner
Clerk: Jon Kamarck
Address: 130 Dirksen Bldg., Washington, D.C. 20510
Phone: (202) 224-7211

Jurisdiction: Appropriation of revenue for the support of the following agencies, programs, and activities: American Battle Monuments Commission, Commission on National Community Service, Consumer Information Center, Consumer Product Safety Commission, Council on Environmental Quality and Office of Environmental Quality, Department of Army cemeterial expenses, Department of Housing and Urban Development, Environmental Protection Agency, Federal Emergency Management Agency, Federal Housing Administration, Federal Insurance Administration, Government National Mortgage Association, Interagency on the Homeless, NASA, National Credit Union Administration Central Liquidation Facility, National Fire Academy, National Institute of Building Science, National Science Foundation, National Space Council, Neighborhood Reinvestment Corporation, Office of Consumer Affairs, Office of Science and Technology Policy, Points of Light Initiative Foundation, Resolution Trust Corporation (inspector general only), Selective Service System, U.S. Fire Administration, Department of Veterans Affairs.

Energy and Natural Resources Committee

Staff director: Andrew Lundquist
Minority staff director: Robert "Bob" Simon
Address: 364 Dirksen Bldg., Washington, D.C. 20510
Phone: (202) 224-4103

Jurisdiction: Energy policy, regulation, conservation, research, and development; coal; energy-related aspects of deep-water ports; hydroelectric power, irrigation, and reclamation; mines, mining, and minerals generally; national parks, recreation areas, wilderness areas, wild and scenic rivers, historic sites, military parks, and battlefields; naval petroleum reserves in Alaska; nonmilitary development of nuclear energy; oil and gas production and distribution; public lands and forests; solar energy systems; territorial possessions of the United States.

Environment and Public Works Committee

Majority staff director: David Conover
Minority staff contact: J. Thomas Sliter
Address: 410 Dirksen Bldg., Washington, D.C. 20510
Phone: (202) 224-7854

Jurisdiction: Environmental policy, research, and development; air, water, and noise pollution; construction and maintenance of highways; environmental aspects of outer continental shelf lands; environmental effects of toxic substances other than pesticides; fisheries and wildlife; flood control and improvements of rivers and harbors; nonmilitary environmental regulation and control of nuclear energy; ocean dumping; public buildings and grounds; public works, bridges, and dams; regional economic development; solid waste disposal and recycling; water resources.

Bibliography

Air Pollution

Bryner, Gary C. *Blue Skies, Green Politics: The Clean Air Act of 1990 and Its Implementation.* 2d ed. Washington, D.C.: CQ Press, 1995.

Hill, Marquita K. *Understanding Environmental Pollution.* New York: Cambridge University Press, 1997.

Rajan, Sudhir Chella. *The Enigma of Automobility: Democratic Politics and Pollution Control.* Pittsburgh: University of Pittsburgh Press, 1996.

Coastal Development

Hinrichsen, Don. *Coastal Waters of the World: Trends, Threats and Strategies.* Washington, D.C.: Island Press, 1998.

Lencek, Lena, and Gideon Bosker. *The Beach: The History of Paradise on Earth.* New York: Viking Penguin, 1998.

Millemann, Beth. *And Two If By Sea.* Coast Alliance Inc., 1988.

Pilkey, Orrin, and Katharine Dixon. *The Corps and the Shore.* Washington, D.C.: Island Press, 1996.

Safina, Carl. *Song for the Blue Ocean.* New York: Henry Holt, 1997.

Endangered Species

Mann, Charles C., and Mark L. Plummer. *Noah's Choice: The Future of Endangered Species.* New York: Knopf, 1995.

Quammen, David. *The Song of the Dodo: Island Biogeography in an Age of Extinctions.* New York: Touchstone Books, 1997.

Shogren, Jason F., and William D. Ruckelshaus. *Private Property and the Endangered Species Act: Saving Habitats, Protecting Homes.* Austin: University of Texas Press, 1999.

Stalcup, Brenda. *Endangered Species: Opposing Viewpoints.* San Diego, Calif.: Greenhaven Press, 1996.

Wilson, Edward O. *The Diversity of Life.* Cambridge: Harvard University Press, 1992.

Energy and the Environment

Easterbrook, Gregg. *A Moment on the Earth: The Coming Age of Environmental Optimism.* New York: Penguin Books, 1995.

Gelbspan, Ross. *The Heat Is On: The High Stakes Battle over Earth's Threatened Climate.* Reading, Mass.: Addison-Wesley, 1997.

Environmental Issues

Council on Environmental Quality. *Environmental Quality: The 1997 Report of the Council on Environmental Quality.* Washington, D.C.: Government Printing Office, 1998. Updates are available at http://ceq.eh.doe.gov/nepa/reports/reports.htm.

Cunningham, William P., and Barbara Woodworth Saigo, eds. *Environmental Science.* Burr Ridge, Ill.: WCB/McGraw-Hill, 1999.

World Resources Institute, U.N. Environment Programme, U.N. Development Programme, and World Bank. *World Resources: A Guide to the Global Environment.* New York and Oxford: Oxford University Press, 1998.

Environmental Justice

Bullard, Robert D. *Dumping in Dixie: Race, Class and Environmental Quality.* New York: Harper Collins, 1996.

Bullard, Robert D., ed. *Unequal Protection: Environmental Justice and Communities of Color.* San Francisco: Sierra Club Books, 1994.

Szasz, Andrew. *EcoPopulism: Toxic Waste and the Movement for Environmental Justice.* Minneapolis: University of Minnesota Press, 1994.

Environmental Movement

Bast, Joseph L., Peter J. Hill, and Richard C. Rue. *EcoSanity: A Common-Sense Guide to Environmentalism.* Lanham, Md.: Madison Books, 1994.

Howard, Philip K. *The Death of Common Sense: How Law Is Suffocating America.* New York: Random House, 1994.

Mann, Charles C., and Mark L. Plummer. *Noah's Choice: The Future of Endangered Species.* New York: Alfred A. Knopf, 1995.

Mowrey, Marc, and Tim Redmond. *Not In Our Backyard: The People and Events That Shaped America's Modern Environmental Movement.* New York: William Morrow, 1993.

Rosenbaum, Walter A. *Environmental Politics and Policy.* 4th ed. Washington, D.C.: CQ Press, 1998.

Environmental Priorities

Brower, Michael, and Warren Leon. *The Consumer's Guide to Effective Environmental Choices: Practical Advice from the Union of Concerned Scientists.* Pittsburgh: Three Rivers Press, 1999.

Easterbrook, Gregg. *A Moment on the Earth: The Coming of Age of Environmental Optimism.* New York: Penguin Books, 1995.

Gelbspan, Ross. *The Heat Is On: The High Stakes Battle over Earth's Threatened Climate.* Reading, Mass.: Addison-Wesley, 1997.

Hertsgaard, Mark. *Earth Odyssey: Around the World in Search of Our Environmental Future.* New York: Broadway, 1999.

Rosenbaum, Walter A. *Environmental Politics and Policy,* 4th ed. Washington, D.C.: CQ Press, 1998.

Food Safety

Rissler, Jane, and Margaret Mellon. *The Ecological Risks of Engineered Crops.* Cambridge: MIT Press, 1996.

Global Warming

Gore, Sen. Al. *Earth in the Balance: Ecology and the Human Spirit.* Boston: Houghton Mifflin, 1992.

Intergovernmental Panel on Climate Change. *Climate Change 1995: The Science of Climate Change.* New York: Cambridge University Press, 1996.

Singer, S. Fred, ed. *Global Climate Change: Human and Natural Influences.* New York: Paragon House, 1989.

Hazardous Waste

Hill, Marquita K. *Understanding Environmental Pollution.* New York: Cambridge University Press, 1997.

Indoor Air Pollution

Baechler, M. C., et al. *Sick Building Syndrome: Sources, Health Effects, Mitigation.* Park Ridge, N.J.: Noyes Data Corp., 1991.

Cole, Leonard A. *Element of Risk: The Politics of Radon.* AAAS Press, 1993.

Hines, Anthony L., et al. *Indoor Air: Quality & Control.* New York: PTR Prentice Hall, 1993.

Samet, Jonathan M., and John D. Spengler, eds. *Indoor Air Pollution: A Health Perspective.* Baltimore: Johns Hopkins University Press, 1991.

Tate, Nicholas. *The Sick Building Syndrome.* Far Hills, N.J.: New Horizon Press, 1994.

National Forests

Devall, Bill, ed. *Clearcut: The Tragedy of Industrial Forestry.* San Francisco: Sierra Club Books/Earth Island Press, 1993.

Miller, Char. *American Forests: Nature, Culture, and Politics.* Lawrence: University Press of Kansas, 1997.

O'Toole, Randal. *Reforming the Forest Service.* Washington, D.C.: Island Press, 1988.

Pinchot, Gifford. *Breaking New Ground.* Washington, D.C.: Island Press, 1947 (commemorative ed., 1998).

Pesticides

Carson, Rachel. *Silent Spring.* Boston: Houghton Mifflin, 1962.

Colborn, Theo, Dianne Dumanoski, and John Peterson Myers. *Our Stolen Future.* New York: Dutton, 1996.

Population and the Environment

Appleman, Philip, ed. *An Essay on the Principle of Population: Thomas Robert Malthus.* New York: W. W. Norton, 1976.

Brown, Lester R., Michael Renner, and Christopher Flavin. *Vital Signs 1998: The Environmental Trends That Are Shaping Our Future.* New York: W. W. Norton, 1998.

Rohe, John F. *A Bicentennial Malthusian Essay: Conservation, Population and the Indifference to Limits.* Rhodes & Easton, 1997.

Property Rights

Coyle, Dennis J. *Property Rights and the Constitution: Shaping Society Through Land Use Regulation.* Albany: State University of New York Press, 1993.

Ely, James W., Jr. *The Guardian of Every Other Right: A Constitutional History of Property Rights.* New York: Oxford University Press, 1992.

Epstein, Richard A. *Takings: Private Property and the Power of Eminent Domain.* Cambridge: Harvard University Press, 1985.

Helvarg, David. *The War Against the Greens: The 'Wise Use' Movement, the New Right, and Anti-Environmental Violence.* San Francisco: Sierra Club Books, 1994.

Nedelsky, Jennifer. *Private Property and the Limits of Constitutionalism: The Madisonian Framework and Its Legacy.* Chicago: University of Chicago Press, 1991.

Rain Forests

Collins, Mark, ed. *The Last Rain Forests.* New York: Oxford University Press, 1990.

Kramer, Randall, Carel van Schaik, and Julie Johnson, eds. *Last Stand.* New York: Oxford University Press, 1992.

Southgate, Douglas. *Tropical Forest Conservation.* New York: Oxford University Press, 1998.

Tangley, Laura. *The Rainforest.* New York: Chelsea House, 1992.

Recycling

Ackerman, Frank. *Why Do We Recycle? Markets, Values, and Public Policy.* Washington, D.C.: Island Press, 1997.

Urban Sprawl

Fulton, William. *The Reluctant Metropolis: The Politics of Urban Growth in Los Angeles.* Point Arena, Calif.: Solano Press, 1997.

Langdon, Philip. *A Better Place to Live: Reshaping the American Suburb.* Amherst: University of Massachusetts, 1994.

Orfield, Myron. *Metropolitics: A Regional Agenda for Community and Stability.* Washington, D.C.: Brookings Institution Press and Lincoln Institute of Land Policy, 1997.

Rusk, David. *Cities Without Suburbs.* Washington, D.C.: Woodrow Wilson Center Press, 1995.

Rybczynski, Witold. *City Life.* New York: Simon & Schuster, 1995.

Water Scarcity

Cayne, Bernard S. *Food and Water: Threats, Shortages and Solutions.* Woodbridge, Conn.: Blackbirch Graphics, 1992.

Gottlieb, Robert. *A Life of Its Own.* New York: Harcourt Brace Jovanovich, 1988.

Starr, Joyce Shira. *Covenant over Middle Eastern Waters: Key to World Survival.* New York: Henry Holt, 1995.

Worster, Donald. *Rivers of Empire: Water, Aridity, and the Growth of the American West.* New York: Pantheon, 1985.

Summaries of Major Environmental Laws: Clean Air Act, Clean Water Act, Endangered Species Act, and Superfund Hazardous Waste Law

Clean Air Act

On December 18, 1970, Congress completed action on the most comprehensive air pollution control bill up to that time in U.S. history. The $1.1-billion, three-year program, which set specific deadlines for the reduction of certain hazardous automobile emissions, was signed into law by President Richard M. Nixon December 31.

Final Provisions

As signed by the President Dec. 31, HR 17255 (PL 91-604) contained the following major provisions:

Air Quality Standards

- Required the administrator of the Environmental Protection Agency (EPA) to publish a list of air pollution agents for which air quality criteria would be issued; the first such list must be published within 30 days of enactment of the bill. Specific criteria must be issued within 12 months after the pollutants were designated.
- Required the administrator to publish national primary and secondary ambient (average) air quality standards for each agent which was already cited as a pollutant when the bill went into effect. For other pollution agents, the administrator must publish national standards at the same time pollutants are designated. (Primary standards specify the minimum air quality needed to protect public health, and secondary standards promote public welfare.) The administrator must promulgate primary air quality standards; states must devise plans for secondary standards.

- Authorized the administrator to specify and set emission standards for hazardous air pollutants—those having a proven relationship to increased human death rates or serious illness. The administrator could grant waivers of up to two years for compliance with the standards. The President also was authorized to grant such waivers if he found technology did not exist or if national security required such action. States had the primary task to enforce the regulations.
- Required the administrator to publish periodically, starting within 90 days of enactment of the bill, lists of the categories of new stationary (non-mobile) pollution sources and set emission standards. The administrator could formulate or enforce plans where states failed to act.
- Required the administrator to emphasize research on the effects of air pollution agents, singly and in combinations, on public health and welfare.

State Implementation Plans

- Required each state, after public hearings, to adopt plans for implementing, maintaining and enforcing the standards and goals promulgated for each air control region, or portion of a region, within that state. Such plans must be submitted to the federal government within nine months after the standards and goals were promulgated and were to be approved or disapproved within four months. The administrator could approve the plan if it provided for attainment of primary air quality standards in three years; included emission requirements and schedules of compliance; included provisions for monitoring devices; included effective procedures to control new pollution sources; provided for intergovernmental cooperation; provided that each state would have adequate personnel, funding and authority to enforce the plan, and provided for periodic inspection and testing of motor vehicles. The administrator could grant extensions of up to 18 months for submission of plans, and up to three years for implementation of plans.
- Authorized the administrator to formulate plans for states which did not submit plans or which submit-

ted plans that were not approved; the administrator could also provide for hearings if the states made no such provision, or he could require the revision of already approved plans if he later found them to be inadequate.

- Required each state to be responsible for air quality within its boundaries. Existing interstate and intrastate air quality control regions were maintained; the administrator was directed to designate other control regions within 90 days.

- Authorized the EPA to provide up to two-thirds of the planning costs and up to half of the operating costs of establishing or improving air quality control programs serving a single municipality, or up to 75 per cent of planning costs and 60 per cent of operating costs for programs serving two or more municipalities. Part of these grants could be in the form of technical aid provided by federal personnel.

- Authorized the EPA to provide 100 per cent of costs for two years, and 75 per cent of costs thereafter, for implementation plans for interstate air quality control regions.

Automobile and Fuel Regulations

- Authorized the administrator to set emission standards for all potentially dangerous pollutants from new motor vehicles and engines.

- Required that engines of automobiles and other light duty vehicles, beginning with model year 1975, must comply with standards lowering emissions of carbon monoxide and hydrocarbons by 90 per cent compared with the model year 1970 levels; and by model year 1976 with standards lowering emissions of nitrogen oxides by 90 per cent compared with the model year 1971 level. The administrator must report annually to Congress on matters relevant to control systems.

- Permitted manufacturers to apply for one-year extensions of the carbon monoxide and hydrocarbon deadlines after Jan. 1, 1972, and for the nitrogen oxide deadline after Jan. 1, 1973. The administrator must act on the requests within 60 days; if he granted the requests, he was required to establish interim

standards at the same time. The National Academy of Sciences was authorized to study the technological feasibility of meeting the standards.

- Required passenger car pollution control standards to be effective for five years or 50,000 miles, whichever was less, according to regulations set by the administrator. He could also set standards for other types of vehicles and engines.

- Prohibited the sale of new cars or engines not in compliance with standards; prohibited the removal of pollution control devices. Violations would be subject to a civil penalty of up to $10,000.

- Required the administrator to conduct tests on new vehicles or engines submitted by manufacturers or new pollution abatement devices and to issue one-year certifications of conformity. The administrator could also perform assembly line tests and suspend or revoke certification of non-conforming vehicles manufactured after that date or produced prior to that date and still in the manufacturer's possession. The suspension would continue until conformity was again achieved. EPA employees could inspect plants and records.

- Required warranties, under standards set by the administrator, which would cover all purchasers and would require the manufacturer to bear costs of repairs to achieve compliance. After a vehicle had been sold, an inspection of its pollution abatement devices could be made only with the owner's permission.

- Authorized the administrator to control or prohibit sale of any fuel or fuel additive if he found that emissions from it would endanger public health or interfere with passenger cars' pollution control devices. The administrator must take into account technical and cost factors. No state could implement regulations regarding fuels which were stricter than federal levels unless such regulations were part of its air quality plan. Civil penalties were set at $10,000 per day.

- Authorized the administrator to grant states up to two-thirds of the cost of developing and maintaining effective vehicle inspection programs and emission testing and control programs.

- Established a federal low-emission vehicle procurement program in the federal government. The government was authorized to purchase any vehicles certified to be low-polluting at a premium price of up to 150 per cent of the lowest cost of conventional car models which they were replacing. The premium could be raised to 200 per cent for especially innovative cars. The bill authorized $5-million for fiscal 1971 and $25-million annually for fiscal 1972 and 1973.
- Authorized the administrator to encourage research on air pollution in relation to fuels and low-emission alternatives to the existing internal combustion engine with authorizations of $75-million for fiscal 1971; $125-million for fiscal 1972, and $150-million for fiscal 1973.

Enforcement

- Authorized the administrator to seek injunctions to stop pollution sources which endangered public health, if local or state authorities had not acted to seek abatement.
- Authorized citizens or groups to bring suits in federal courts against either the administrator—for failure to perform specified duties—or alleged violators, including government agencies.
- Authorized the attorney general to go to court to require that the owner of any patent relating to emission limitations make the information available to any person who needed it in order to comply with standards set by the bill. The court would determine payments to the patent owner.
- Set punishments for violations of implementation plans. The administrator was required to give prior notification to both the person violating the plans and the state in which the violation occurred. If corrective action was not taken, he could issue an order requiring compliance or bring civil suits against the violator. A person who knowingly violated an implementation plan or an abatement order could be punished by a fine of up to $25,000 for each day of violation and a year in prison, or up to $50,000 per day and two years in prison for persons with previous vi-

olations. Anyone convicted of falsifying information or tampering with monitoring devices was subject to a fine of up to $10,000 and six months in prison.

Aircraft

- Required the administrator, following a study and hearings, to formulate standards for aircraft emissions. The secretary of transportation was to help formulate the standards and enforce them. States could not implement standards more stringent than those set by the federal government. The administrator of the Federal Aviation Administration must set aviation fuel standards, following consultation with the EPA administrator.

Noise Pollution

- Established within the EPA a new Office of Noise Abatement and Control to study noise pollution and its effect on the public health and welfare. The office would be authorized to look into problems associated with all types of noise, including sonic booms. One year after enactment of the bill, the administrator would be required to report on the study to the President and Congress, and to request new legislation. The bill authorized $30-million for the noise program.

Funds

- Authorized for carrying out provisions of the act other than those specified above: fiscal 1971, $125-million; fiscal 1972, $225-million, and fiscal 1973, $300-million.

Clean Water Act

On October 18, 1972, Congress overrode President Richard M. Nixon's veto of the Federal Water Pollution Control Act Amendments of 1972, which was at the time the most comprehensive and expensive environmental legislation in the nation's history. The amendments, known as the Clean Water Act, initiated a major change in the basic federal approach to water pollution by adding strict limits on what could be discharged into waterways to existing standards for water quality. Nixon had withheld approval of the controversial measure awaiting the outcome of an executive-legislative tussle over the extensive powers to curb federal spending he had requested. When the Senate Oct. 17 balked at granting such broad authority, Nixon vetoed the water bill. The bill was strongly opposed by major industries and by some state and local officials, but was endorsed by most environmental organizations.

Final Provisions

As cleared by Congress over the President's veto, S 2770 contained major provisions which:

Title I—Research

- Declared it the act's objective to restore and maintain the chemical, physical and biological integrity of the nation's waters.
- Established as a national goal elimination of pollutant discharges into U.S. waters by 1985 and as an interim goal achievement of water quality safe for fish, shellfish, wildlife and recreation by July 1, 1983.
- Established as a national goal elimination of discharges of toxic pollutants in toxic amounts, providing federal financial aid to build public waste treatment works, developing areawide waste treatment management plans and making a major research effort to develop technology to eliminate pollutant discharges.
- Directed the administrator of the Environmental Protection Agency (EPA) to administer the act and provide for public participation in development of regulations.
- Authorized the administrator to make a maximum of 50 per cent federal grants to states for administrative expenses of planning agencies (for a maximum of three years) developing comprehensive water quality control plans for river basins, bays or lakes.
- Directed the administrator to study the special water pollution problems of oil spills, marine sewage equip-

ment (especially on small boats), pesticides, waste oil, estuary pollution, total sewage, agricultural and other rural pollution, fresh water aquatic ecosystems, river systems and thermal discharges.
- Authorized the administrator to make a maximum of 75 per cent research and development grants (for demonstration purposes only) for storm sewers, joint municipal-industrial treatment systems, water recycling methods and agricultural pollution.
- Directed the administrator to set up special demonstration projects (with a maximum of 75 per cent federal participation) to eliminate pollution of the Great Lakes, with particular attention to the rehabilitation and environmental repair of Lake Erie.
- Authorized a one-year study of Lake Tahoe and the Tahoe Basin ecosystem and the need for federal oversight.
- Directed the administrator to identify and eliminate stationary toxic pollution sources in ports and harbors.

Title II—Construction Grants

- Declared the purpose of the title to require waste treatment management plans and practices which applied the best practicable technology, were on an areawide basis, encouraged recycling and reclamation and integrated facilities.
- Authorized the administrator to make grants to state or local agencies for the construction of publicly owned treatment works, with a maximum 75 per cent federal share.
- Authorized grants to be allotted to the states on the basis of need, as determined by the EPA.
- Authorized some reimbursement of states and municipalities for treatment work construction begun between 1966 and 1972 (not more than 80 per cent) and between 1956 and 1966 (not more than 30 per cent).
- Directed the President to prepare a water resources plan for all U.S. basins; plans must be completed by Jan. 1, 1980, with annual progress reports to Congress required.

Title III—Standards and Enforcement

- Made the discharge of any pollutant by any person unlawful except as authorized by a discharge permit (Title IV).
- Provided that existing interstate and intrastate water quality standards remain in effect subject to EPA approval and revision.
- Directed the administrator to develop and publish detailed water quality information and guidelines for effluent limitations.
- Required industrial dischargers by July 1, 1977, to meet effluent limitations based on use of the "best practicable control technology currently available," as defined by the EPA administrator. Required publicly owned treatment works to meet effluent limitations based on secondary treatment (the second step in waste treatment in which bacteria consume the organic parts of the wastes) by the same date.
- Required industrial discharges by July 1, 1983, to meet effluent limitations based on use of the "best available technology economically achievable" as determined by the administrator: limits would be based on categories or classes of industries, and would be aimed at elimination of discharges if technologically and economically achievable. Industries could seek relief based on economic capability. Public treatment works must use best practicable technology over the life of the works by the same date.
- Directed the administrator to list categories of industrial pollution sources and set national performance standards—including zero-discharge, if practicable—for each new source. States could take over enforcement if laws were as strict as federal standards. If new factories complied with provisions of the bill, they would not be subject to more stringent standards for at least 10 years.
- Directed the administrator to submit a water quality inventory report to Congress by Jan. 1, 1974, and required states to submit such reports by Jan. 1, 1975.
- Directed the administrator to list toxic (seriously harmful to human or other life) pollutants and to set

effluent limitations—including prohibition of discharge, if needed—to provide "an ample margin of safety."
- Prohibited discharge of radiological, chemical or biological warfare agents or high-level radioactive waste.
- Required the administrator to set effluent limitations for thermal discharges (discharge of water at different temperature from receiving waters) that would ensure a balanced population of fish, shellfish and wildlife.
- Provided criminal penalties of between $2,500 and $25,000 per day or one year in prison or both; $50,000 per day or two years or both for second offenses; and civil penalties of up to $10,000 per day.
- Declared it to be U.S. policy that there should be no discharges of oil or hazardous substances into U.S. waters, adjoining shorelines or contiguous zone waters.
- Set civil penalties for oil or hazardous substance discharges of up to $50,000 (per discharge), with no limit for willful discharges.
- Directed the states to prepare plans to restore fresh water lakes and authorized federal grants for clean lakes projects.
- Established a 15-member national commission to investigate the technological aspects of achieving the 1983 economic, social and environmental goals in the act.

Title IV—Permits and Licenses

- Required applicants for federal discharge licenses or permits to first obtain state, interstate agency or EPA certification that the discharge would comply with effluent limits set under the act.
- Authorized the EPA administrator, after opportunity for public hearings, to issue permits for pollutant discharges, including previously exempt municipal discharges, under certain conditions and if they met other requirements of the act.
- Authorized states to conduct their own discharge permit programs if approved by the EPA.
- Declared existing permits issued under the 1899 Refuse Act to be valid, but provided that no new permits could be issued after the bill's enactment.

- Authorized the administrator to suspend state programs which did not meet federal guidelines; but the administrator could veto individual state permits only during the interim period before the guidelines were issued.

Title V—General Provisions

- Established a 10-member water pollution control advisory board.
- Gave the administrator emergency powers to bring suit in district court to stop pollution presenting an imminent health or welfare hazard.
- Authorized citizen suits against the U.S. government, other federal agencies or the EPA administrator. Defined citizens as persons having an interest adversely affected.
- Forbade the firing of or discrimination against the employees who filed proceedings or testified under provisions of the act, with procedures for review by the secretary of labor.
- Provided for judicial review of the administrator's actions in circuit courts of appeals.
- Provided that nothing in the act would deny the right of states or interstate agencies to set pollution control standards at least as stringent as federal standards.
- Directed the President to study the feasibility of a separate environmental court system and to report to Congress within one year.
- Directed the President to study the national policies and goals in the bill and to report within two years.
- Established an Environmental Financing Authority to help finance the non-federal share of the costs of any waste treatment construction project.
- Exempted EPA actions under the act from the requirements for filing a statement detailing the impact on the environment of major federal projects as mandated by the National Environmental Policy Act of 1969 (PL 91-190), except for federal grants for construction of publicly owned sewage treatment plants and permits issued for pollutant discharges from new sources.

Endangered Species Act

Enactment of the Endangered Species Act of 1973 added muscle to the federal program protecting fish and wildlife, and for the first time authorized protective measures for plants as well. The bill, signed by President Richard M. Nixon in December, extended federal authority to species "threatened" with extinction as well as those in immediate danger of becoming extinct ("endangered" species). A threatened species list was added to the endangered species list that had been kept by the Interior Department's U.S. Fish and Wildlife Service since 1967.

Provisions

As signed into law, major provisions of S 1983 (PL 93-205):

- Authorized the Interior Secretary to list and issue regulations to protect species of wildlife, fish and plants threatened with extinction as well as those considered endangered (in immediate danger of becoming extinct).
- Made it a federal offense to take (hunt, trap, capture, etc.); buy, sell or transport in interstate commerce; and import or export endangered or threatened species or products made from them. Taking of plants was not prohibited. Alaskans engaged in activities necessary for subsistence were exempted from the prohibitions, and special permits to engage in prohibited acts could be issued, in cases of economic hardship or for scientific research, and for projects aimed at enhancing the propagation or survival of a species.
- Established fines of $10,000 for violations of the act committed knowingly or by commercial operators, $5,000 for violations of regulations and $1,000 for violations committed unknowingly.
- Permitted states to impose protective regulations tighter than those required by the federal government.
- Required the Interior Secretary to consider citizen petitions seeking to change species listings or have species added or removed from lists if such petitions were backed by substantial evidence.

- Authorized $10-million, available through fiscal 1977, for federal grants paying up to two-thirds of the costs of state programs for conservation and management of endangered and threatened species. The Interior Secretary was to enter into cooperative agreements with states that came up with satisfactory program plans.
- Authorized the Secretaries of Interior and Commerce to acquire lands and waters for the purpose of protecting, restoring or propagating endangered and threatened species. The existing $15-million ceiling on the use of funds from the Land and Water Conservation Fund for this purpose was repealed.
- Authorized the Commerce Department to manage endangered and threatened species affected by sport and commercial fishing in the ocean, in accordance with the jurisdictional change made by Reorganization Plan No. 4 of 1970.
- Authorized appropriations of $27.5 million for fiscal 1974-76 to administer the act.
- Implemented the Convention on International Trade in Endangered Species of Wild Fauna and Flora.
- Directed all federal agencies and departments to ensure that their programs or programs they funded did not "jeopardize the continued existence" of endangered and threatened species, or "result in the destruction or modification of habitat" considered by the Interior Secretary to be critical to an endangered or threatened species.
- Authorized citizens to bring civil suits seeking enforcement of the prohibition on taking of endangered species, or to remedy alleged violations of the act.

Superfund Hazardous Waste Law

In the waning days of the 1980 session, the 96th Congress resurrected and cleared a drastically scaled-down version of President Jimmy Carter's 1979 proposal to establish a $1.6-billion emergency "Superfund" to clean up toxic contaminants spilled or dumped into the environment. Neither environmentalists nor the chemical in-

dustry were entirely happy with the final bill. But the administration gave it reluctant support. The final bill contained weaker liability provisions than the president had sought. It also did not cover oil spills, as Carter had proposed. Carter signed the bill Dec. 11, after noting that congressional leaders had promised to deal with oil spills in the 97th Congress.

Provisions

As signed into law Dec. 11, HR 7020 (PL 96-510) contained the following major provisions:

The Fund

- Established a $1.6-billion Hazardous Substance Response Trust Fund covering fiscal 1981-85, with $1.38 billion (86 per cent) coming from fees on the chemical and oil industries and $220 million (14 per cent) coming from general revenues appropriated by Congress.
- Provided that the fees would be collected on 45 specified substances, based initially on the quantity of such substances produced by an individual company and adjusted later to reflect the number of incidents in which the fund had to clean up each of the particular substances.
- Provided that the fund could pay for the following losses resulting from spills of hazardous chemicals: 90 per cent of the operation and maintenance costs of any remedial action taken at the site of the spill (states would pay the other 10 per cent); loss of natural resources and costs of restoring lost resources up to $50 million; and costs of health studies and diagnostic examinations for persons injured by chemical spills, but not other medical expenses.

Liability

- Imposed liability equivalent to that in the Clean Water Act (PL 92-500) for government cleanup costs and damage to natural resources of up to $50 million on anyone releasing hazardous substances into the environment.
- Provided that the only defenses to liability were an act of God, an act of war or the act of a third party.

- Exempted from the bill's liability spills and dumps that were in compliance with permits issued under the Clean Water Act, Solid Waste Disposal Act (PL 94-580), 1972 Marine Protection, Research, and Sanctuaries Act (PL 92-532), Safe Drinking Water Act (PL 93-523), the Clean Air Act (PL 95-95) and Atomic Energy Act of 1954 (PL 84-141).

Emergency Response

- Authorized the president to order a company to remove or control hazardous substances threatening the public health, welfare or environment.
- Authorized the president to order whatever emergency cleanup action he deemed necessary—by either the government or the responsible party—to protect the public whenever a pollutant was released or there was "the substantial threat" of such a release.
- Provided that government measures could include cleanup and temporary or permanent provision of alternative water supplies and housing.

Scope

- Defined hazardous substances as any toxic substance identified under certain sections of the Clean Water Act, the Clean Air Act, the Solid Waste Disposal Act and the Toxic Substances Control Act (PL 94-469).
- Exempted spills or releases of petroleum, natural gas and synthetic fuels and their derivatives, unless identified in another act as hazardous.
- Authorized the president to designate as hazardous other substances that could present substantial danger to public health, welfare and the environment.
- Provided that the law applied to release of hazardous substances into the air, land, navigable waters, ground water or public water supplies, at disposal sites, facilities and vessels.

- Defined "release" as "any spilling, leaking, pumping, pouring, emitting, emptying, discharging, injecting, escaping, leaching or dumping" into the environment, or any other release "which presents or may present" a substantial danger to the public.
- Exempted releases in the workplace and releases of nuclear materials or byproducts, normal field applications of fertilizers and engine exhausts.

Legislative Veto

- Provided that if within 60 days of promulgation of any agency regulation written to carry out the act either the House or the Senate passed a resolution disapproving the regulation, or if both houses adopted such a resolution within 90 days, the regulation would not become effective.

Penalties

- Required anyone in charge of a facility found to have released a hazardous substance to notify immediately the appropriate federal agency or face up to $10,000 in fines.
- Required owners or operators of facilities where hazardous substances were stored or disposed of to notify the administrator of the appropriate government agency of the existence of the facility or site, and to specify the amount and type of hazardous substances there and any likely discharges from that facility. Provided that failure to comply could result in a fine of up to $10,000 and/or imprisonment for up to one year.
- Required deeds for hazardous waste disposal sites to disclose the location of toxic chemicals on the site. Provided that violators would be subject to a $10,000 fine and/or up to a year in prison and would be liable for any damage resulting from chemical releases.

Index

DATE DUE

APR 2 2 2004			
GAYLORD			PRINTED IN U.S.A.